Also by Joan Nathan

Joan Nathan's Jewish Holiday Cookbook

The Foods of Israel Today

Jewish Cooking in America, Expanded Edition

The Jewish Holiday Baker

Jewish Cooking in America

The Jewish Holiday Kitchen

The Children's Jewish Holiday Kitchen

An American Folklife Cookbook

The Flavor of Jerusalem (with Judy Stacey Goldman)

The New
American
Cooking

Joan Nathan

Alfred A. Knopf New York 2005

THIS IS A BORZOI BOOK
PUBLISHED BY ALFRED A. KNOPF

www.aaknopf.com

Library of Congress Cataloging-in-Publication Data

Nathan, Joan.
    The new American cooking / by Joan Nathan.— 1st ed.
        p. cm.
    Includes bibliographical references and index.
    ISBN 1-4000-4034-5
    1. Cookery, American.   I. Title.
TX715.N275 2005
641.5973—dc22   2004042328

Printed in Singapore

First Edition

In memory of chef Jean-Louis Palladin,

who, through his unbounded enthusiasm for American foods and flavors,

inspired us to look at our own cooking in a new light.

Born in southwest France, May 7, 1946

Died in Washington, D.C., November 25, 2001

Contents

The New
American
Cooking

Introduction

I n the summer of 2001, the Smithsonian National Museum of American History added Julia Child's kitchen to its permanent collection, placing her in the company of American icons like Thomas Edison and Muhammad Ali. At the opening reception, guests were served a stunning menu of American food, including seared bison filet with pepper relish and *pappadam*, a purple Cherokee tomato tartlet with goat cheese and herbs, and a local organic sweet tomato tartlet with basil and ricotta gelato. These were not the kind of classic French dishes that Julia introduced to the American public, I thought to myself. Instead, the meal was a wonderful mosaic of healthy, natural, spicy foods from a vast variety of cultures, the kind of food that Americans have been embracing more and more heartily in recent years.

I think that experience really set the course for this new book, *The New American Cooking*. I felt compelled to discover how and why the transformation in American food came about, to seek out the people, both known and unknown, who were responsible for the new openness in our tastes. Indeed, that's the best definition I have of American food today—a new receptivity to exploring the old and the new and melding the two. Until now I have written mostly about Jewish food, a tale of amazing evolution and adaptation both in this country and in Israel. But I have always been interested in the larger picture of how other ethnicities have affected America and the way we eat. With myriad immigrant groups, we are living now in one of the most exciting periods in the history of American food. For those who cook at home, there is an almost endless array of ingredients and spices from which to choose. Those who eat out in ethnic and upscale restaurants have a wide variety of delicious dishes that were unavailable a decade ago.

According to the Library of Congress, in the past thirty years there have been more than three thousand American cookbooks published, more than the number published in the previous two centuries combined. The world's food is now literally at our fingertips.

When I told my children what I had in mind, they said a new American book had to include Cheez Whiz and McDonald's. No, I insisted. We all know about the growing power of fast-food chains and agribusiness, of people not eating together as a family, of processed microwave meals and the couch-potato syndrome. During a recent visit to the Missouri countryside, I stopped at a mega supermarket in a small town surrounded by farmland. In the midst of strawberry fields and streams overflowing with trout, I found myself in a market where everything was plastic and processed. I often think about the author Barbara Kingsolver's comment: "Many adults, I'm convinced, believe that food comes from grocery stores."

But that's the downside. What I wanted to explore is the positive aspect of American food today. Over the past few years, I have crisscrossed this country, from California to Alaska, from Washington, D.C., to Puerto Rico. I watched a young man handcraft cheese in the Northeast Kingdom of Vermont. At dawn I accompanied chef Alan Wong and his students to the Honolulu fish auction. I gathered wild rice with Ojibwe Indians in northern Minnesota, I ate a Japanese-inspired omelet with a musician in the heart of the Ozarks, and I ate Sunday dinner with a family of Cambodian farmers in Lowell, Massachusetts. I have explored home kitchens, farms, processing plants, and restaurants, seeking out people who have helped to make American food what it is today. It is these people, with their stories and their recipes, who fill the pages of this book.

The year 1965, when I graduated from the University of Michigan, was a time of momentous change both for me personally and for the country. After my junior year studying abroad in Paris, where my taste buds were opened, I was ready for Julia Child's *Mastering the Art of French Cooking* and Craig Claiborne's *New York Times Cookbook*, both of which had been published in 1961. Other graduates of that same period would take cooking to the next level—chefs like California's Alice Waters, who used local organic crops, artisanal cheeses, free-range chicken, and grass-fed beef in her Berkeley haunt, Chez Panisse.

When in college, none of us would have guessed that the March on Washington or the antiwar movement would affect the way we eat. But they did. The Voting Rights Act of 1965, which gave African Americans the right to vote, also enhanced the dignity of black culture and cuisine in the eyes of white Americans. Meanwhile, the antiwar movement influenced a new generation of eaters, who began to demand what the sociologist Warren Belasco has called "counter cuisine"—an attempt to return to a natural, more simple way of life. In those years, health food consciousness was growing among fringe groups, who started eating new and "weird" foods in their vegetarian diet such as soy milk, brown rice, and yogurt. All these, and many others like them, are considered staples today.

Until 1965, immigrants to the United States came mainly from European countries like France, Germany, Hungary, Italy, Poland, and the Soviet Union. But the Johnson administration, widening its response to the civil rights movement and the Vietnam War, passed the 1965 Immigration Act, eliminating the rigid immigration quota system of the 1952 McCarran-Walter Act. As a result, there was a large influx of new immigrants, many of them from Latin America and others from countries like Vietnam, Thailand, Afghanistan, and Lebanon—countries not even mentioned in the 1970 census. All brought with them new foods and new flavors. As *The New Yorker* writer Calvin Trillin aptly put it, "I have to say that some serious eaters think of the Immigration Act of 1965 as their very own Emancipation Proclamation."

In the Iron District of Newark, New Jersey, once primarily home to Portuguese immigrants, the demographics are changing—when I visited the seventy-five-year-old Popular Fish Market there, lines of Portuguese and now also Spanish and Brazilian immigrants had their pick of eel, clams, corvine, frozen sardines, lobsters, and baccalhau (dried cod). In New York City, a subway ride takes you to a Chinatown that now includes a varied Asian population with their different foodways. Pedestrians in Manhattan nosh on vegetarian soul food, Chinese-Mexican food, and Vietnamese or Puerto Rican bagels. Cross the Hudson River, and you enter a Japanese neighborhood with a mega supermarket devoted to Japanese food. Cross the East River, and just whiff the pungent Indian spices as you emerge from the subway in Jackson Heights.

On the West Coast, students at the University of California at San Diego choose among Peking duck, barbecue pork, and Mexican wraps; nearby, La Jolla Mexican workers eat

Chinese food while making Japanese furniture. And throughout the country, new American farmers—Hmong, West African, and Brazilian, to name a few—are harvesting their native crops and selling them at farmers' markets.

While new immigrants were leaving India, Thailand, Afghanistan, and Lebanon, the Peace Corps and other international programs gave young Americans a chance to experience the cultures of faraway lands. In 1965 Pan Am launched their "fly now, pay later" program, encouraging Americans to travel abroad using their new credit cards and giving them a chance to experience foods they had never tasted before.

In 1976, the American Culinary Federation changed the category "Chef" in the U.S. Department of Labor's Dictionary of Occupational Titles from "domestic" to "professional." This new status represented years of lobbying by the late chef Louis Szathmery of the Bakery in Chicago and others, who felt that chefs were not getting their due.

Although the late Julia Child was not herself a "professional" chef, she was the first to demystify cooking for most Americans, through her cookbooks and television shows. In the early 1980s, as I toured the country while working on my *American Folklife Cookbook*, I visited firemen in Chicago who wouldn't have missed Julia's show for anything (except maybe a fire). Today, my children and their friends watch the Food Network as entertainment instead of MTV. The Food Network, public television, and satellite stations instruct us in Chinese, Indian, African, and regional Italian cooking. Now people everywhere in the United States can easily explore new cooking cultures and techniques.

Many of the cuisines we've embraced, especially Asian, have also given us a taste for healthier cooking. "Health food" is not something new in America; it goes back to the Shakers and Sylvester Graham in the nineteenth century. But then the emphasis was on what was bad for us, using extreme diets to cure us of our ills rather than stressing what was good for us—and what tasted good, too. Today we can look to such delicious dishes as fish with shiitake mushrooms, ginger, and cilantro (page 287), tofu-portobello burgers (page 243), and pomegranate chicken (page 316) for tasty and healthful eating.

Although health food stores sprang up around the country in the 1960s, they did not have access to the abundance of carefully grown fresh organic produce that we have today. Much of the credit for bringing health food to the masses goes to John Mackey, who had the canniness and spunk to capitalize on what he saw as a growing trend. In 1974, the twenty-five-year-old hippie and six-time college dropout opened Safer Way, then one of twenty-five health food stores in Austin, Texas. While most of the other twenty-four stores are now defunct, Safer Way has grown into Whole Foods, the largest chain of natural foods supermarkets with an organic slant in the country, with 165 stores coast to coast and growing. Whole Foods has also spurred other supermarkets to stock their shelves with a growing number of organic products.

Meanwhile, talented cooks like Deborah Madison were helping to propel vegetarian food into restaurants and homes with dishes and recipes that people actually wanted to eat. In the 1970s Deborah lived in the San Francisco Zen Center, where she cooked brown rice and plain miso. "When I went to Chez Panisse and tasted real food," she told me, "I thought I had died and gone to heaven." Madison cooked there for a while, and then in 1979 was the chef at Greens, in San Francisco, when it opened, catapulting vegetarian cooking into the mainstream of good American food.

Today, organizations like Slow Food USA and the Southern Foodways Alliance, which promote artisanal and traditional foodways and sustainable agriculture, are growing in reaction to the fast-food culture. Happily, these movements are spreading around the world. With them, organizations like American Livestock Breeds Conservancy and Seed Savers Exchange work to ensure that American native animal breeds and plants will continue to thrive in twenty-first-century kitchens.

As more and more mothers joined the workforce in the 1960s and 1970s, more families resorted to eating out or relying on prepared, packaged, and takeout foods. But there has also been a welcome increase in the number of dads in the kitchen. Michael and Ariane Batterberry, now the editors of *Food Arts* magazine, noticed this early on. When they did a pilot for a new magazine they were launching called *Food & Wine* in the 1970s, they found that their readership was 49 percent male, and the average age of these men was twenty-seven or twenty-eight. "We noticed a new generation of American men expressing interest and even a love of food and wine," said Michael. It turns out they were right.

When both parents work, children are often left with caregivers, some of whom may now come from Latin America, Africa, and Asia. They prepare the majority of homemade foods, giving home cooking an ethnic twist. When my children were little, I depended on a number of women who cooked Haitian, Gambian, and Salvadorean dishes, and soon my children preferred this food to peanut butter and jelly or fast foods. Occasionally, they would cook their food for me and my friends, which is how I learned how to make Marcel Auguste's Haitian vegetable stew (page 227) and Maria Gudiel's yuca fritters (page 101). I know other families whose children have come to relish spicy chicken *yasa* from Gambia (page 310), squash from Mauritius (page 254), and *pancit*, a Chinese noodle dish made for special occasions in the Philippines (page 196). I like to think that all these caregivers are creating a generation of more sophisticated palates.

Jean-Louis Palladin was one of the first chefs in America to champion fresh, locally grown products. Now the Jean-Louis Palladin Foundation is promoting the close connection between farmers and chefs.

Americans have always loved kitchen gadgets—apple corers, sifters, eggbeaters. The electric blender was a great boon for puréeing, and the food processor has really revolutionized home cooking as a time-saving device, enabling us to chop pounds of onions, knead dough, crumble stale bread, and reduce veggies to a fine purée, all at the push of a button. And we are constantly coming up with new devices, discovering that a carpenter's rasp makes the best cheese grater ever and that lining a baking sheet with a silicone mat eliminates endless pan scrubbing. And these gadgets are not just for the professionals. Just look at any home kitchen catalog. What will be next?

There is also concern today about where our food comes from, and it is often chefs who have led the way. There is no better example than the late Jean-Louis Palladin, a French chef who came to the United States and sought out growers of good native products so he could use in his cooking the kind of local produce he'd grown up on in France. Rooted in the classic French tradition, he was not bound by it, but instead felt liberated by our many ethnic strands. Having grown up with the sense of *terroir*, in the unique character and flavor imparted by local geography that Americans are only now discovering, he found grass-fed lamb raised on a farm in Pennsylvania, lobsters from Maine, local corn, and corn muffins made by black cooks at a church supper in Washington. He incorporated these American foods into his own unique style of cooking. And he set an example for others.

Today, were he alive, I'm sure he would be inspired by the number of good cheeses being handmade all over America—gouda, soft cheeses, blue cheeses, goat cheeses, and new varieties such as Jasper Hill Farm Aspenhurst (page 181). Many of these artisanal cheeses are made on the same farms where the animals are milked, and that contributes to their unique flavor.

It is not hard now to find grass-fed beef and free-range chicken. And we are starting to ask the questions that Jean-Louis would have asked: Where and how were these animals raised? What did they eat? What does "natural" mean? As David Scribner, a Washington chef (page 167), told me, "Industrial agriculture robs food of its life. Conscientious chefs today feel that they are rescuing the soul of food."

Americans no longer have to go to Italy for estate-bottled extra-virgin olive oil, because boutique olive oil is being pressed in California (page 160). John Scharffenberger (page 367) is making high-quality American chocolate in Berkeley. Exotic fruits, like pomegranates and mangoes, are now grown in California and Florida, and all over the country varietal apples (page 400) are being reintroduced and sold at local farmers' markets, grocery stores, and even university cafeterias.

As chefs try out ingredients like baby artichokes (page 223) and portobello mushrooms (page 192), their customers want to cook with them as well. Today, Ocean Mist Artichokes and Phillips Mushrooms, in response to requests from home cooks, have brought these vegetables to the general public.

For my family, I make pasta with pesto and string beans one day, Moroccan chicken with olives and lemons the next, Tex-Mex fajitas on another, and Asian stir-fry with rice after that. My family's ethnic dishes may have less bite than they would in the Mexican or Thai communities, but our meals are still a far cry from those of my childhood, when each day of the week was assigned a particular dish—meat loaf, lamb chops, fish, roast chicken, spaghetti and meatballs, roast beef, and tuna casserole, with traditional family foods brought out on the Sabbath or on holidays.

Because I live in Washington, D.C., and summer in New England, I have naturally drawn more on these areas. Still, in interviewing people in forty-six of the fifty states, I've realized that what I discovered close to home pretty much represents what is happening across the country. I now look at food in a new light. I hope this book will open up new vistas for you as well. In many cases I have had to reconstruct recipes in my own kitchen for home cooks who might not be able to find a particular spice that was called for in the original recipe, or who might want to simplify by using fewer pots and pans. I've learned to be more flexible, more open to different ideas, and I hope that you will be, too.

Not long ago, at a particularly delicious luncheon at a friend's house, the hostess described the spread as an "American menu": heirloom tomatoes and mozzarella salad with a ribbon of fresh pesto; chicken satay with peanut sauce; Greek salad with feta cheese; and Asian sesame noodles. Since America has no deep culinary traditions of its own, this meal showed how we are not bound by convention. *The New American Cooking* is the story of our energy, ingenuity, innovation, and, above all, creativity. I pray the future holds many more satays and fresh heirloom tomatoes.

NOW WE
ARE SERVING
BREAKFAST
FROM 6 TO 10 AM.
DESAYUNOS
FREE CUP OF COFFEE

Breakfast and Brunch

Clockwise from top right: *A bilingual breakfast in Tucson; Huevos rancheros; Marion Spear picks arugula in the Ozarks; A tropical breakfast bar in Miami; Pam McKinstrey with her famous Morning Glory Muffins; Washington Youth Garden at the U.S. National Arboretum*

Breakfast, once the most ordinary of meals, has become big business. When I was growing up, weekday breakfast meant oatmeal, farina, and, sometimes, Wheatena. The dominant cold cereals were Cheerios, cornflakes, and Rice Krispies. Eggs, which occasionally stood in for cereal, were poached, sunny-side up, or scrambled (whoever heard of omelets in those days?), and lay on the plate beside bacon or sausage, toast or English muffin. New Yorkers were the only ones who had even heard of lox and bagels. The only really exotic breakfast item was eggs Benedict. Of course, in the South they loved their grits, and in Philadelphia, their scrapple.

But after thirty years of food and diet fads, new ethnic tastes, and the variety of choices supermarkets now offer for breakfasts on the run, breakfast is a new and exciting experience. Manufacturers have developed more than fifty kinds of cold cereal alone in the last ten years; instant oatmeal, breakfast bars, kashi, frozen waffles, instant cocoa with marshmallows, and breakfast smoothies packed with a whole day's supply of vitamins and minerals are all readily available. Wander today through the breakfast section of a supermarket and you'll find biscuits, croissants, sticky buns in a tube (just open, pull apart, bake, and serve) exactly like homemade (well, not quite, but close enough for many shoppers).

In his book *The Great Good Place*, Ray Oldenburg laments the fact that there are too few places in America to visit with friends or find some inner quiet. With cold, impersonal malls and copycat restaurants moving people in and out as quickly as possible, until recently it was hard to find somewhere that welcomed you to just sit awhile.

But in many cities, a countermovement is trying to slow the pace of breakfast. Starbucks, reproducing at a rabbit's pace, independent coffee shops, and even teahouses are popping up all over, offering a place to sip coffee or tea peacefully, to write, to meet friends.

In New York City, Maury Rubin thinks of his City Bakery as rekindling the neighborhood meeting place. "When I came back from Paris in 1987, I was obsessed with creating a place where people could have yogurt, oatmeal, granola, great baked goods, and, of course, good coffee," he said over coffee in his bakery. "It was the very last days of neighborhood bakeries here, like Greenberg and Dumas. The old guard was dying out, and no one thought of replacing them with new blood."

Hotels and restaurants have also discovered the charm and profit of breakfast as a full-fledged meal. "The power breakfast at the Regency Hotel [in New York City] is a sober hour for tycoons to start dealing over coffee and granola," Michael Batterberry, editor of *Food Arts* magazine, told me. San Francisco also has its power breakfast. In 1983, when chef Bradley Ogden opened Campton Place, he put such dishes on his breakfast menu as blue cornmeal pancakes (page 32) and sour cherry muffins, as well as old-fashioned oatmeal and cocoa. At Zov's Bistro, an Armenian-inspired restaurant in Orange County, open for three meals a day, I tasted delicious scrambled eggs with fresh feta cheese, tomatoes, and basil, served with Armenian sausage in a tortilla.

In some families, breakfast is the one meal of the day when the entire family can eat together. "We have breakfast together because we don't have time to eat dinner together," said Helen Pearson of Chevy Chase, Maryland, a mother of two. "It's easy to get up a half hour earlier. What we eat is not as essential as that we have time to talk." Like many mothers, Helen is busy and often buys ready-made sausage patties and biscuits in a tube. She fries the sausage, scrambles the eggs, and makes sandwiches of them, which she serves with cut-up fruit. She also prepares grits and cheese with bacon or sausage.

Then there's brunch, that wonderful meal peculiar to America that gives us time to slow down on nonwork days and savor our food. Although this late-morning meal combining breakfast and lunch has been around for years, it has now taken the place of the more formal Sunday lunch. At hotels, brunch can include anything, from omelets to a whole roast pig that I saw at one such meal. Brunch can also be quite simple, with a few items like huevos rancheros (page 26), French toast casserole (page 25), and fresh fruit salad (page 15). Eggs are served in a variety of ways: Japanese-style, filled with healthful greens (page 22), or Chinese egg foo yung (page 24), among many others.

No one seems to eat ordinary pancakes anymore; now it's Ogden's blue cornmeal pancakes and ricotta pancakes with lemon and poppy seeds (page 31). Supermarkets and bakeries sell sourdough baguettes as well as oversize, multiflavored muffins, bagels, scones, and croissants. These days scones are flavored with cardamom and ginger (page 38), bagels are covered with all kinds of seeds (page 33), and quick breads include banana with macadamia nuts (page 39). Tropical smoothies (page 18) are all the rage, as well as Asian dim sum (page 113), South American burritos filled with eggs and beans, Vietnamese hearty meat soups (page 152), and breakfast buns of all persuasions, expanding our global menu to farther and farther reaches.

The recipes here reflect my discoveries across the country in the last few years. If you are planning a brunch, look in the Bread, Salads, and Vegetables chapters for more ideas.

Granola from Emandal Farm

Granola is one of those breakfast items that we take for granted these days. Although it's been around since Sylvester Graham's health movement in the nineteenth century, crunchy granola became very popular in the 1970s when a freelance baker named Layton Gentry—called by many Johnny Granola-Seed—experimented with recipes to develop what is known today as crunchy granola and sold it to supermarkets across America. At a time when healthy breakfast cereals like Swiss muesli were coming into vogue, granola was often served with the new accompaniment called yogurt instead of milk.

Jenny Guillaume, program coordinator of the Washington Youth Garden at the U.S. National Arboretum, uses granola to teach inner-city children what to do with the pumpkin and sunflower seeds they harvest from their arboretum garden. Jenny learned to make this formula at Emandal, a farm at a children's camp in California, where she prepared it for breakfast with farm-fresh yogurt. Your hands may get sticky mixing it, but that's part of the fun.

YIELD: ABOUT 14 CUPS

7 cups rolled oats
1 cup shredded, dried, unsweetened coconut
1 cup unsalted sunflower seeds, hulled
1 cup pumpkin seeds
1 cup chopped walnuts
1 cup very coarsely chopped almonds
1 cup honey
½–1 cup vegetable oil
1 cup raisins or other dried fruit (optional)

1. Preheat the oven to 350 degrees.

2. Toss the oats, coconut, sunflower seeds, pumpkin seeds, walnuts, and almonds in a large bowl, with your hands. Drizzle on the honey and

Washington Youth Garden children at the National Arboretum

½ cup of the vegetable oil, blending them with the seeds and nuts. Add more vegetable oil if needed. Spread the granola out in 2 jelly-roll pans.

3. Bake in the oven for about 20–30 minutes, until golden brown, stirring the granola with a spatula every 10 minutes and reversing the pans halfway through the baking time. Remove from the oven, stir in the raisins, if desired, and let cool. Store in an airtight container.

Cooking class at the National Arboretum

Breakfast Fruit Salad with Ginger and Mint

I especially like this breakfast salad inspired by one that I ate at Prune, a tiny, homey restaurant on New York's Lower East Side. The fruits you use can change with the season. If you don't want to bother with ginger syrup, just sprinkle crystallized ginger over the fruit.

YIELD: ABOUT 8 SERVINGS

GINGER SYRUP
1 cup water
½ cup sugar
One 2-inch piece fresh gingerroot, peeled

FRUIT SALAD
1 apple, diced
1 pint blueberries
1 cup diced honeydew melon
1 cup diced cantaloupe
1 cup red or green grapes
2 tablespoons chopped fresh mint

1. To make the syrup, put the water, sugar, and gingerroot in a saucepan. Bring to a boil and simmer uncovered to reduce the liquid by half, for about 20 minutes. Set aside.

2. To make the fruit salad, toss the apple, blueberries, honeydew, cantaloupe, and grapes together in a large bowl. Add a few tablespoons of the ginger syrup and sprinkle the mint on top.

Pomegranate, Mango, and Papaya Fruit Salad with Lime

The only challenge with tropical fruits like pomegranates and mangoes is learning how to cut them, a skill that I have described below. If a pomegranate is supposed to be a symbol of fruitfulness and a papaya is good for whatever ails your stomach, what happens in this salad? Taste it and see!

YIELD: 6 SERVINGS

1 pomegranate*
1 papaya
2 mangoes (for instructions on how to cut, see page 17)
Juice of 2 limes
2 tablespoons honey, or to taste
12 mint leaves (optional)

1. To peel the pomegranate without staining yourself with juice, gently score the outer skin in quarters. Then place the entire pomegranate in a large bowl filled with water. With your hands under the water, gently pull off the skin and remove the arils (the seeds, with their fleshy covering), which will fall to the bottom. Drain off the water and discard everything but the arils. Dab them dry and leave on paper towels until ready to serve. You can also cut the pomegranate in two, then holding one half in your hand with seeds down over a bowl, whack the outer shell with a mixing spoon, letting the seeds fall through your hands and into the bowl. Keep whacking the shell until all the seeds are out; remove any pith that falls into the bowl. Repeat with the other half of the pomegranate.

2. Cut the papaya in half, scoop out the seeds, and reserve them if you like. Score the papaya in long strips, then score the strips in half. Gently remove the pieces with a spoon and combine them with the cut-up mango.

3. Sprinkle the fruit with the lime juice and honey, then dot with ½ cup of the pomegranate seeds. (If you have more, eat them as a snack.) Garnish with mint leaves, if using.

POMEGRANATE PUNCH

If you'd rather drink pomegranate juice straight from the source, try this method taught to me by a Persian immigrant: Roll the fruit along a countertop until all the crunchy sounds stop. Then pierce it with a skewer, insert a straw, and drink.

* Pomegranates can be stored whole in the refrigerator for up to a year. You may also substitute dried cranberries or cherries for the fresh pomegranate arils.

POMEGRANATES

Long known as a symbol of fruitfulness, the pomegranate was a favorite of the prophet Muhammad. In the last fifteen years new immigrants from the Middle East, especially from Iran, have increased our awareness of this bulbous red fruit. Once an occasional find in ethnic markets, pomegranates are now available in most supermarkets from October to the beginning of January.

Much of that is thanks to Lynda and Stewart Resnick, owners of the successful POM Wonderful label. In the late 1980s they acquired some land in southern California's San Joaquin Valley with a few pomegranate trees on it. As they learned more about the mythology and the health benefits of the plump red fruit, their interest grew. Today the Resnicks are America's largest growers of pomegranates. Lynda, who eats a bowl of pomegranate arils (the fleshy, tasty covering of the seed) every day for breakfast, told me, "We're doing God's work. And we're helping people clean out their arteries."

PEELING AND CUTTING MANGOES

A mango is a pain in the neck to peel because of its large, oddly shaped pit and slippery texture. Since the mango and its pit have a naturally flattened shape, you have to follow the natural contours of the fruit when cutting. Hold the mango flat, with the stem side in the palm of your hand. Using a sharp knife, slice from the stem end down over the pit. Open the mango up, score one half carefully crosswise into 6 or 7 thin strips, and pull the peel back, releasing the strips so they fall into a bowl. You might need your knife to help scrape the flesh from the pit. Repeat with the second half.

Mango Lassi from the Mango Man

Richard Campbell, whose job is to oversee about 250 varieties of mangoes from around the world at Fairchild Gardens in Coral Gables, Florida, doesn't just eat mangoes. He inhales their aroma and savors their flesh with almost every meal. Mango salads, mango juice, and mango lassi start his day. Dried mangoes are his snack, glacéed mango his candy, green mangoes his salad. He uses mango chutney on flatbread for lunch, squeezes a mango and lemon to marinate meat, and feeds his bread starter with mango juice. Mangoes perfume his house, and one of his children hugged a tiny mango as a security blanket.

One of the most beloved smoothies in America today is the Indian mango lassi, a mango drink with yogurt. Although fresh mango and homemade yogurt are used in India, most Indian restaurants here use canned sweetened mango imported from India.

YIELD: 2 SERVINGS

2 large ripe mangoes
1 cup plain lowfat yogurt
½ cup water
6 ice cubes
1 tablespoon sugar, or to taste
Dash of salt

1. Peel the mangoes, following the instructions in the box on page 17.

2. Put the mango pieces, yogurt, water, ice cubes, sugar, and salt in a blender. Process until smooth. Pour into 2 glasses and serve.

MANGO MINUTIAE

Although most mangoes eaten in the United States today are grown in Central and South America, Campbell told me, the varieties we get were originally selected from South Florida stock brought there from all over the world. Some of his favorites are Ataulfo, also called honey mango or champagne mango, a small, yellow Mexican variety; Keitt (pronounced "Kit"), a large yellow or green mango with fiberless flesh; Kent, a medium-size round variety; and Tommy Atkins, the most common American mango, firm and finely fibrous.

THE ULTIMATE CUBAN JUICE BAR

Whenever Miami Cubans feel nostalgic, they visit El Palacio de los Jugos, a small carryout store in northwest Miami. The store, owned by Cuban immigrants, opened twenty-six years ago, at a time when many Cuban refugees arrived in Miami. From seven a.m. to nine p.m. every day the juice bar serves at least twenty different kinds of juices, including a drink made with tamarind and cane sugar.

Once when I was visiting the bar, a woman

who was waiting in line had driven four hours from Smyrna Beach just to drink *guarapo*, sugar cane juice, and to taste the store's Haitian mangoes, which are sweeter and yellower than other varieties. Born in Nicaragua, she learned about the store on *Despierta América*, the Spanish version of *Good Morning America*. Outside, with a drink in hand, she joined a couple who were sitting at a table nestled under the palm trees, sipping coconut milk and inhaling the pungent smell of a Haitian mango.

California Date Shake

For years I wanted to taste a date shake. I knew I would have to go to California's Coachella Valley, located in the southern desert near Palm Springs, to try the genuine article. Accompanied by my cousin Bill Bloch, who has been coming to the desert since 1946, we found Shields Date Gardens, a nondescript white wooden building flanked by date palms on Highway 111 in Indio. Bill said that in the early days, all you could see for miles around was date palms.

Not indigenous to the California desert, dates were first introduced to the New World by Spanish missionaries in the eighteenth and early nineteenth centuries. Although most of the world's dates still come from the Middle East, California produces 99 percent of the U.S. crop, the majority being two varieties: *medjool,* meaning "unknown" in Arabic and called by many the Cadillac of dates; and *deglet noor,* meaning "finger of light."

According to Juanita Barbo Ottoman, now in her eighties, who has been making date shakes for the past sixty-plus years, the drink originated during World War II. In those days there was no air-conditioning in the desert, and little ice cream was available during the war. Since it was hot, people wanted cold drinks. So someone came up with the idea of combining frozen milk, a little vanilla, and some dates for thickening and flavor.

Having tasted date shakes throughout Palm Desert, and then playing around with the recipe at home, I prefer this version, made, ideally, with fresh dates.

YIELD: 1 SHAKE

10 dates, pitted
¾ cup vanilla frozen yogurt or ice cream
1 cup lowfat milk
6 ice cubes

Cut the dates into small pieces. Put them in a blender with the frozen yogurt, milk, and ice cubes and blend until smooth. Pour into a tall glass and serve.

When I started working on this book, I wanted to visit a part of the country where, I thought, maybe nothing had changed in the past thirty years. I suspected I would find that in Fox, Arkansas, but Marion Spear, who prepared breakfast for me in her hideaway home there, proved me wrong.

An herbalist, Marion teaches herbal cooking at the Ozark Folk Center in nearby Mountain View, the old-time country music capital of the world. To get to her house, at the bottom edge of the Ozark plateau, she drove me down the rockiest dirt road I had ever been on.

Her cookbook collection alone should have given me a hint about her: Diana Kennedy, André Simon, and James Beard. "I like James Beard because he gives you a basic recipe and lots of cooking possibilities, then he turns you loose, he sets you free," said Marion.

> If there is anything you need, we'll show you how to do without it.
>
> —AN OZARK SAYING

An experienced home brewer, Marion has papered her kitchen with colorful labels from the sides of six-packs. Jars of pickled eggs, hot pepper jelly, and wild plum shrub line the walls. Iron skillets decorate another wall in front of a Home Comfort Range made in 1881, which Marion told me cost $37 new. Always up for an adventure, she often packs her stove on a truck for demonstrations of cornmeal doughnuts for the Ozarks Foothills Handicrafts Guild.

As we talked, she prepared the greens for our breakfast omelet from her latest inspiration, Japanese cooking. She ran out to the garden and cut some arugula, mustard greens, and cilantro that were growing near the bok choy and other Asian greens, all good winter vegetables. "I'm a top-of-the-stove, scratch cook," she said apologetically. She turned on an electric skillet and poured the eggs in. Then she piled the greens on top and steamed them in the eggs. She served the omelet with a grilled bagel and her pepper jelly—it was a breakfast I will never forget.

Marion (far right) and the other members of the trio she sings with

Omelet with Mixed Greens and Cilantro

This delectable omelet tastes best with absolutely fresh herbs and vegetables steamed in a thin layer of egg in a minimal amount of oil. You can substitute spinach, dill, basil, or parsley for the herbs, and bitter greens and tomatoes for the mushrooms. Serve the omelet alone for brunch or for lunch with, if you want, fresh homemade salsa and bread. Although Marion uses a rectangular nonstick electric frying pan, I make it in a ten-inch nonstick frying pan.

YIELD: 2–3 SERVINGS

5 large eggs

1 tablespoon unsalted butter

2 ounces grated cheddar cheese

1 handful
(about ½ cup, or 1½ ounces)
chopped mustard greens

1 handful
(about ½ cup, or 1½ ounces)
chopped arugula

¼ cup chopped fresh cilantro

3 scallions, minced

3 shiitake mushrooms, diced

Salt and freshly ground
pepper to taste

1. Break the eggs into a medium bowl and mix well.

2. Heat the butter in a 10-inch nonstick frying pan and swirl it around to coat the bottom. Carefully pour the eggs into the pan and turn the heat to medium-high. Sprinkle the cheese on one half of the omelet 2 inches from the edge.

3. When the eggs are cooked on the bottom and around the edge but still a bit liquid in the middle, arrange the mustard greens, arugula, cilantro, scallions, and shiitake mushrooms on top of the cheese. Gently fold one half of the egg mass on top of the other half. Remove from the heat and let steam for 3–5 minutes, until the greens are wilted. Then return to the heat for 1–2 minutes to make sure the omelet is warmed through.

4. Season with salt and pepper and serve immediately. You can accompany the omelet with salsa (page 96).

Toni's Caramelized Onions with Apples

When we were preparing breakfast one misty morning at our home on Martha's Vineyard, my good friend Antonia Allegra started sautéing tangy apples with onions and grapes—an unusual combination. It was surprisingly delicious and is now one more guest breakfast staple in our family. Toni likes to pair it with sausages or eggs and waffles for brunch or crunchy fried chicken when she's cooking at home in St. Helena, California.

YIELD: 6 SERVINGS

¼ cup (½ stick) butter

3 tablespoons canola or vegetable oil

1 large yellow onion, thinly sliced in rings

6 Granny Smith or other tart apples (about 3 pounds), unpeeled, cored, and cut into 16 slices

1 cup red seedless grapes

1. Heat the butter and oil in a large frying pan.

2. Sauté the onion rings slowly over medium-low heat until they become limp.

3. Add the apple slices, stirring as you incorporate them with the onions, and cook for about 15 minutes.

4. When the apples have softened, toss in the grapes, stirring for a few minutes until everything is warmed through. Turn onto a serving platter and serve.

TO SALT OR NOT TO SALT

And every meal-offering of thine shalt thou season with salt; neither shalt thou suffer the salt of the covenant of thy God to be lacking from thy meal-offering; with all thine offerings, thou shalt offer salt.
LEVITICUS 2:13

At a dinner at the French Laundry in northern California, I was served a tray of seven different kinds of salt to sample. Today, we have so many kinds of salt—coarse kosher, sea salt, gray salt, lowly table salt—that sometimes we don't know where to turn. Here's how I choose my salt: For brining chickens and other meats, I use coarse-grained kosher (really, though, all salt is kosher). I prefer to use fine-grained table salt for baking because it sifts easily with flour and dissolves quickly. Prized—and expensive!— coarse sea salt, mined from seas around the world, is reserved in my kitchen for sprinkling on top of salads and already-cooked food; you can really taste the briny salt, and the large crystals add a nice crunch. I keep it in a little bowl to use whenever I need it.

Green Mountain Egg Foo Yung

If the Chinese ever created an American dish in this country, it's egg foo yung. Steve Bogart of A Single Pebble Restaurant in Burlington, Vermont, makes this egg dish with vegetables in the classic way for staff meals and for his family for brunch. When I make it, I sometimes substitute eggplant or corn for the meat, or whatever I might have in the refrigerator.

YIELD: 4–6 SERVINGS

SAUCE
1 teaspoon vegetable oil
1 teaspoon finely minced ginger
2 tablespoons finely minced green pepper
2 tablespoons finely minced peeled carrot
2 tablespoons finely minced onion
2 tablespoons finely minced scallion
2 tablespoons soy sauce
1 teaspoon sugar
¾ cup chicken stock
½ teaspoon Maggi (liquid MSG with flavor) (optional)
1 tablespoon cornstarch
2 tablespoons water
½ teaspoon Asian sesame oil

7 large eggs
1 cup diced barbecued pork, fresh baby shrimp, cooked chicken, sausage, tofu, or vegetable of your choice
2 minced scallions (about ½ cup)
1 cup bean sprouts
½ cup water chestnuts, sliced in thin rounds
1 tablespoon vegetable oil

1. To make the sauce, put the vegetable oil in a wok or saucepan. Sauté the ginger in the oil over medium heat to release its flavor. Add the pepper, carrot, onion, and scallion and stir-fry a minute. Stir in the soy sauce, sugar, chicken stock, and Maggi (if using) and bring to a boil. Mix the cornstarch and water in a small bowl and stir into the liquid. Lower the heat and continue stirring until the sauce thickens, coating the back of a spoon. Turn off the heat, add a squirt of sesame oil, and keep warm.

2. To make the omelet, beat the eggs, meat, shrimp, or tofu, scallions, bean sprouts, and water chestnuts with a whisk in a medium bowl.

3. Heat the vegetable oil over medium heat in a 10-inch nonstick frying pan. Add all of the egg mixture and cook about 2 minutes on each side or until crisp and cooked through. Serve immediately or keep warm in the oven set to a very low temperature. Just before serving, pour the sauce over the eggs.

Baked French Toast with Caramelized Fresh Fruit

When making French toast with egg-rich breads like challah (page 71) and brioche (page 68), you can slice the bread as thick as you want. I learned from my daughter Merissa to scatter apples and bananas on top of the butter and brown sugar. This make-ahead dish is wonderful for a brunch. You can substitute strawberries or apples for the banana if you prefer. Serve with bacon or just lots of fresh fruit.

YIELD: 8–10 SERVINGS

½ cup (1 stick) unsalted butter
¾ cup dark brown sugar
2 tablespoons maple or corn syrup
4 bananas
Six 1½-inch-thick even-size slices of bread, like challah or brioche
1½ cups half-and-half
6 large eggs
1 teaspoon vanilla extract
Confectioners' sugar for garnish

1. Melt the butter, brown sugar, and maple or corn syrup in a saucepan, stirring to break up the brown sugar. Bring to a boil and continue to cook for 2 minutes without stirring. Then coat the bottom of a 9-by-13-inch pan with this syrup and cool.

2. Cut the bananas in half-inch-thick circles. (To use apples, peel and core them, then slice in rings; cut strawberries lengthwise.) Scatter the fruit over the syrup in the pan.

3. Trim the crust from the bread if you wish to make the slices uniform (I don't usually bother) and arrange the bread over the fruit.

4. Blend together the half-and-half, eggs, and vanilla in a large mixing bowl and carefully pour the mixture over the bread in the pan, making sure that all the bread is well soaked. You might have to use a spatula to pat the bread down or spoon some of the egg mixture over the pieces. Refrigerate overnight.

5. When ready to bake, preheat the oven to 350 degrees and remove the casserole from the refrigerator. Bake for 30–40 minutes or until golden brown on top. Let cool 10 minutes before serving. Run a knife around the inside of the pan. Invert a platter on top and carefully flip the pan over onto it. There will be a lovely fruit pattern on top. Sprinkle with confectioners' sugar, cut into portions, and serve immediately.

Santa Fe Huevos Rancheros

Perhaps it's the altitude or the air, but no place seems more of a breakfast town than Santa Fe. As Katharine Kagel, owner of the popular Cafe Pasqual's, says, "Everything comes together in Santa Fe. Native Americans, Hispanics, and Anglos have been mingling in the city for centuries and make it unique and lively." Because Santa Fe is a mountainous and remote city inhabited for centuries, the food is neither Tex-Mex nor border Texan food. "The food is New Mexican," insists Katharine, as she rattles off the list of red and green chili sauces, posole, tortillas, tamales, and pinto beans that are served in the New Mexican manner at her trendy yet homey restaurant. She also considers her food to be equatorial cuisine, with shared ingredients of the southern latitudes. "We use coconuts, chilies, garlic, and cilantro from all across the equator."

Huevos rancheros, a hearty breakfast dish served here and in Mexico and other parts of Central and Latin America, is made of tortillas, eggs, beans, and chili sauce. This dish is at its best in restaurants like Cafe Pasqual's. Huevos rancheros, like breakfast burritos, originated as a peasant food.

While in Santa Fe, I tasted many versions of huevos rancheros in search of one I could serve for brunch in my own home. Most restaurant versions make eggs to order, but I wanted a dish that could be made in advance so all I have to do is stick it under the broiler when the guests arrive. Here it is.

YIELD: 6–8 SERVINGS

1 cup black beans or pinto beans, cooked and drained (page 226), or 2 cups canned

1 cup red chili sauce (page 27)

6 blue or yellow corn tortillas

2 tablespoons vegetable oil

¼ cup (½ stick) butter

10 large eggs

¼ cup milk

Salt and freshly ground pepper to taste

1 cup grated Monterey Jack cheese

1. Preheat the broiler and grease a 9-by-13-inch casserole.

2. Heat both the beans and the chili sauce separately, either in a saucepan or in the microwave.

3. Brush each tortilla on both sides with the vegetable oil. Set a dry skillet over high heat. When the pan is hot, add the tortillas, 1 at a time, and heat, turning once, until soft, about 5 seconds on each side. Wrap the tortillas in a cotton towel to keep them warm.

4. Melt the butter in the skillet. Mix the eggs with the milk, salt, and pepper and pour into the pan. Cook slowly, stirring, until the eggs are lightly scrambled and still moist. Remove from heat.

5. Place the tortillas in the prepared casserole, overlapping them to cover the entire bottom. Scatter the beans over the tortillas and top

1 cup salsa (page 96)
½ cup sour cream
½ cup chopped cilantro

with the eggs. Ladle dollops of the chili sauce over the eggs and sprinkle the cheese over all. You can make this dish an hour or so ahead of time up to this point.

6. Place the casserole under the broiler for a few minutes, until the cheese melts and bubbles. Garnish with dollops of salsa, sour cream, and the chopped cilantro and serve immediately on a trivet.

Red Chili Sauce

Katharine Kagel, from Cafe Pasqual's in Santa Fe, gave me her chili sauce recipe. The long, narrow New Mexico or Hatch chilies are similar to Big Jims, poblano, and Anaheim; use any of them dried for this dish. It is not necessarily true that the heat is in the seeds of peppers. Some are hotter than others, and the seeds just increase the heat.

YIELD: ABOUT 1½ CUPS

15 dried red New Mexico chilies,
about 2 packed cups,
stemmed, seeded, and rinsed
½ onion, coarsely chopped
2 cloves garlic
1 teaspoon dried oregano
1 teaspoon kosher salt
½ teaspoon ground cumin

Katharine Kagel

1. Place the dried chilies in an enameled or other nonreactive stockpot and cover with about 2 cups water. To keep the chilies submerged, cover them with a plate slightly smaller than the circumference of the pot and soak them until they're soft, about 20 minutes.

2. When the chilies are fully rehydrated, remove the plate and add the onion, garlic, oregano, salt, and cumin to the pot. Bring the water to a boil over high heat, then reduce the heat to low and simmer, uncovered, for 20 minutes.

3. Drain the contents of the pot, reserving the liquid. Working in batches, place the chilies, onion, and garlic in a blender, filling it about ¾ full. Add about ½ cup of the reserved liquid and blend to a thick, ketchup-like consistency. (You may need to adjust the amount of liquid you add.)

4. When the sauce is thoroughly blended, pass it through a fine-mesh strainer to remove unblended chilies and seeds. The finished chili sauce should be smooth and thick. Repeat until all of the chilies are used. Add more salt to taste.

5. Store the sauce in a plastic container in the refrigerator for up to 4 days or freeze it for up to 2 months. To heat, put the sauce in a nonreactive pan over medium-low heat, stirring frequently to prevent scorching.

Wild Rice Breakfast Quiche

Minnesotans are very protective of true wild rice. Like many of them, Daniel Biever, who lives in the southwestern part of the state, hopes to rejuvenate local wild foods that used to grow in the Plains. "People don't know about one of the most degraded ecosystems," he told me as we drove through northern Minnesota. "All the native foods got turned under by the plow when the Europeans came. When the first settlers arrived in the central part of America, they traded goods and supplies with the Indians for wild plums, wild clammy ground cherries [similar to a cape gooseberry], and other wild foods that the Indians ate. It was food they could have picked themselves."

In northern Minnesota, Daniel tracked down Indians who harvest beds of natural wild rice that was taken back to Europe by the French as a delicacy three hundred years ago. He sells this hand-harvested and hand-parched wild rice by mail order through his company, Coteau Connoisseur. This recipe that Daniel makes on Sunday mornings for his family is a great way to use leftover wild rice from the stir-fry on page 208. Cooked white rice or diced potatoes are good substitutes for the wild rice. Serve the quiche for brunch with *fattoush* salad (page 168), fresh fruit salad, and ginger-cardamom scones (page 38). I often make two of these quiches, one with bacon and one with sautéed mushrooms or zucchini.

YIELD: 8 SERVINGS

10 slices turkey bacon or other bacon

One 9- or 10-inch prebaked pie crust (page 405)

2 teaspoons Dijon mustard

4 large eggs

1 teaspoon Worcestershire sauce

Salt and freshly ground pepper to taste

1 cup milk or light cream

1 cup cooked wild rice (see page 208)

1 cup shredded Swiss cheese

¼ cup minced scallions or green onions

1 tablespoon chopped fresh dill

1. Preheat the oven to 425 degrees.

2. Fry the bacon in a frying pan, drain, and crumble.

3. Brush the bottom of the baked pie crust with the mustard.

4. Break the eggs into a bowl and beat well with the Worcestershire sauce, salt and pepper to taste, and the milk or cream. Fold in the bacon, rice, Swiss cheese, scallions, and dill, mixing well. Pour into the crust.

5. Cover the top of the pie loosely with aluminum foil and bake for 10 minutes. Reduce the heat to 325 degrees and bake for 25–30 more minutes or until a knife comes out clean when inserted into the center. Serve from the pan.

The Real Deal—a Holistic Farmer Who Grows Rhode Island Flint Corn

Here's another example of a return to regional ingredients, in this case Rhode Island flint corn. "I am a holistic farmer," Harry Records told me. "Indians grew flint corn, high in starch and low in sugar, before those three boats ever arrived in Plymouth. The Indians used it as barter with the traders."

Dipping his hands into a barrel of corn kernels, Harry described what makes flint corn unique. It's not a hybrid (which has been genetically altered), and Harry goes to a lot of trouble to keep it that way. "I take the best of the ears and keep them a mile away from any other corn," he told me. "That helps keep it pure and to retain its distinctive flavor, different from any other corn on the market."

He added, "The only way you can legally use the spelling 'jonnycake' is if you use Rhode Island white-cap flint corn. If you see the spelling 'Johnny,' with an 'h,' then you know that southern dent corn is being ground instead. There is a huge difference in the flavor of the two corns."

According to Harry, few people bothered with flint corn until health foods became popular. "With pure foods, this stuff took off," said Harry. "I like to think that my flint corn goes from the ground to the griddle."

But there's a little more to it than that. Harry dries his flint corn in a corn crib for a year before he grinds it into meal. He uses a grindstone, which gives the corn its unique texture. (Most corn and flour today are ground with steel rollers.) Flint corn grows slowly, and its yield is less than any other type of corn by almost half. Its individual kernels are bigger, and they come in all white, all yellow, with an occasional red ear.

Like many of the other people in this book, Harry feels a somewhat mystical connection to his calling: his career, chosen late in life, was simply meant to be. "I feel that someone is guiding me," he said. "Somebody put me into this position to help preserve this old tradition." As I was leaving, he added, "We're all either going to wear or rust out."

Rhode Island Cornmeal Jonnycakes

Some believe that *Jonny* is a corruption of the Indian name Shawnee; others say that it refers to the durability of these little cornmeal pancakes, which at one time may have been called "journey cakes." In the last thirty years jonnycakes have almost replaced traditional blinis as an hors d'oeuvre wrapper for smoked salmon or caviar, a trend initiated by Boston chef Jasper White.

Although jonnycakes are strictly a Rhode Island specialty, their popularity spills over to nearby southeastern Massachusetts, and Harry Records (see "The Real Deal," page 29) has even heard that jonnycake meal was used in Tennessee during the Civil War for breading fish. Today, much of Rhode Island's large Italian population comes to Harry for polenta, a coarser grind using yellow flint corn. Grits, usually made from dent corn, are ground even thicker.

I add an egg and a little baking powder to my jonnycakes, which holds them together and makes them lighter. Any way and any thickness, nothing beats them. Just remember, you cannot hurry jonnycakes. They should cook very slowly.

YIELD: ABOUT 10–12 JONNYCAKES

1 cup jonnycake meal or other stone-ground cornmeal
1 tablespoon sugar
1 teaspoon salt
1½ cups boiling water
1 teaspoon baking powder
1 large egg, lightly beaten
¼ cup milk
Bacon drippings or vegetable shortening
Maple syrup, warmed

1. Sprinkle the jonnycake meal, sugar, and salt into a large mixing bowl.

2. Stir in the boiling water and mix well, working out any lumps. Let sit for a few minutes, until the meal absorbs the liquid and returns to room temperature.

3. Stir in the baking powder, egg, and milk, adding more milk if you want thinner jonnycakes.

4. Heat a griddle over medium-high heat until it sizzles when you test it with a splash of water. Turn the heat down to low, add enough drippings or shortening to coat the pan, and spoon on heaping tablespoons of batter, leaving about 2 inches in between the pancakes to let them spread. Cook slowly, about 6 minutes on the first side, patting them down until brown around the edges. Flip them over and cook another 6 minutes, until golden brown on both sides. Repeat until all the pancakes are cooked. Serve hot on a platter with warm maple syrup.

Four Seasons' Lemon-Ricotta Poppy Seed Pancakes

When I was growing up, we had pancakes, period, usually made with Aunt Jemima mix. Because breakfast has become a destination meal, creative chefs have put their stamp on the ordinary pancake. The Four Seasons Hotel in New York serves my favorite, made from a recipe developed by former executive chef Susan Weaver. "The recipe had a life of its own," says Susan, who now works for Lettuce Entertain You Enterprises in Chicago. "In the mid-1980s, when breakfast started to be 'in,' we wanted to develop a pancake of the day. We found that ricotta worked very well with lemon. The poppy seeds came later."

YIELD: 16 PANCAKES

6 large eggs, separated
1½ cups whole-milk ricotta cheese
¼ cup (½ stick) unsalted butter, melted and cooled
1 teaspoon vanilla extract
½ cup all-purpose flour
1 teaspoon baking powder
¼ cup sugar
½ teaspoon salt
Grated zest of 2 large lemons
1 tablespoon poppy seeds
Vegetable oil for frying
Maple syrup, warmed
Berries for garnish

1. Whip the egg whites with an electric mixer until they form firm, glossy peaks.

2. Beat the ricotta, butter, egg yolks, and vanilla together in a large mixing bowl.

3. Mix the flour, baking powder, sugar, salt, lemon zest, and poppy seeds in a medium bowl, using a rubber spatula, then stir them into the ricotta mixture.

4. Fold a large spoonful of the whipped egg whites into the batter and mix, then gently fold in the remainder. Mix gently.

5. Grease a griddle with oil and heat it over high heat until quite hot, then lower the heat. Drop about ¼ cup of batter for each pancake on the griddle, allowing space for them to spread. If you want, flatten each pancake lightly with a greased spatula.

6. Cook until golden and the tops show a couple of bubbles, about 2 minutes. Gently flip them over and cook until the undersides are light brown. Remove to a serving plate and keep warm while you make the rest of the pancakes. Serve with warm maple syrup and top with berries.

Note: This batter needs to be used immediately. While it is unlikely that you will have leftovers, the cooked pancakes can be wrapped in plastic and frozen for up to a month.

Blue Cornmeal Pine Nut Pancakes

I first tasted these pancakes at the Campton Place Hotel in San Francisco, and more recently at the Plaza Restaurant in Santa Fe. This is an example of a recipe that people wrongly attribute to American Indians. Although my friend Ramus Suina of Cochita Puebla grew up picking pine nuts off the local piñon trees, he never ate them in pancakes, much less blue cornmeal pancakes. Regardless of its actual origins, this delicious recipe now evokes the Southwest. You can substitute yellow or white stone-ground cornmeal for the blue.

YIELD: 12 PANCAKES

1¼ cups pine nuts
1 cup all-purpose flour
½ cup blue cornmeal
2 tablespoons sugar
1 teaspoon baking powder
¾ teaspoon salt
2 large eggs
1 cup buttermilk
2 tablespoons unsalted butter, melted
Vegetable oil for frying
Maple syrup, warmed

1. Heat a frying pan over medium-low heat and stir-fry the pine nuts for a few minutes to brown them slightly and release their flavor. They burn easily, so keep shaking them as they cook.

2. Put ¾ cup of the pine nuts in a food processor along with the flour, cornmeal, sugar, baking powder, and salt. Pulse just to blend. Remove to a bowl.

3. Beat together the eggs, buttermilk, and melted butter in a separate bowl. Stir the buttermilk mixture into the dry ingredients and add the remaining pine nuts. Let the batter sit for a half hour.

4. Heat a griddle over medium heat. Pour enough oil onto the griddle to coat the surface. Pour about ⅓ cup of the batter into the pan for each pancake, leaving space between.

5. Cook the pancakes until bubbles form on the top surface, about 1–2 minutes. Flip them over and cook for another minute or so or until the bottoms are golden brown.

6. Repeat with the remaining batter, adding a bit more oil to the griddle as needed. Stack the pancakes on a plate as you go along and keep warm in the oven as you cook. Serve immediately with warm maple syrup.

Almost Everything Bagels

The original bagel, a round yeast roll with a hole in the middle, is cooked in two steps: first by boiling the shaped dough in water, then baking it. Boiling reduces the starch content and gives the bagel its outer sheen.

Retired Los Angeles baker Izzie Cohen taught Nancy Silverton of La Brea Bakery how to make bagels. "Nothing beats a fresh bagel, even if it's lousy," Izzie told me as he rolled out bagels in Nancy's bagel factory. What I like about Izzie's recipe is that you can make the dough and form the bagels ahead, then refrigerate or freeze them and bake them on weekends for breakfast with a shmear of cream cheese.

YIELD: 16 BAGELS

2 cups lukewarm water
3 tablespoons sugar
5 teaspoons active dry yeast
1 tablespoon salt
3 tablespoons malt powder* (optional)
6½–7 cups high-gluten bread flour
Cornmeal for dusting
½ cup roasted white sesame seeds†
½ cup black sesame seeds
2 tablespoons coarse kosher or coarse sea salt

* Some bakers consider malt powder, a derivative of roasted barley, to be the secret ingredient in bagels. It supposedly adds 2 properties to them: it flavors and firms up the dough, and, later, thrown into the boiling water, it helps add a little sheen to the boiled bagel before it is baked. Malt powder can be purchased in some health food stores and online at sites like King Arthur (see Mail-Order Sources).

† To roast sesame seeds, stir-fry them in a nonstick frying pan over medium heat for a few minutes, until they are golden and aromatic.

1. Using an electric mixer fitted with a dough hook, mix together the water, sugar, and yeast on low speed until the yeast dissolves. Add the salt, 2 tablespoons of the malt powder (if using), and 2 cups of the flour, mixing well. Gradually add enough of the remaining flour to make a smooth and relatively firm dough. Let the dough rest in the bowl for 10 minutes, covered with a towel.

2. Turn the dough out onto a floured work surface and shape it into an oblong mass. Divide it in half with a sharp knife or dough cutter, then divide it in half once more. Cut each of these pieces into 4, so that you have 16 pieces. On a wooden countertop or marble slab, flatten 1 of the dough pieces, then roll it up into a short, stubby cigar about 3 inches long. Repeat with the remaining balls. Starting with the first piece you rolled, roll each dough piece under your palm into a 5-inch length. Finally, roll each again, this time to a 7-inch strand. Take

1 of the strands and wrap it around 3 or 4 fingers with the ends over-lapping by about 1½ inches. With the dough still wrapped around your fingers, roll it on the table until the overlapping portion is sealed and is the same thickness as the rest of the bagel. Gently remove the doughnut-shaped bagel from your fingers and place on a floured board. Cover while you make the rest.

3. Let the bagels rise for about an hour or until doubled in volume. If you want to wait to cook them, place them on 2 jelly-roll pans dusted with cornmeal and wrap the pans in 2 large plastic bags—kitchen trash bags work well. Refrigerate them if you are going to bake them the next day. Otherwise, put them in the freezer (you will have to defrost them in the refrigerator the night before you bake them). Remove from the refrigerator and let them warm up, for about 1 hour.

4. Preheat the oven to 450 degrees. Line 2 baking sheets with parchment paper and sprinkle with cornmeal.

5. Bring a 5-quart pot with 4 quarts of water to a boil and add the remaining tablespoon of malt powder (if using). Drop 1 bagel into the boiling water, then drop 3 more into the water and boil them for 20–30 seconds, stirring at least once and turning over. Remove them with a slotted spoon and put them on a cooling rack set over a pan to let the water drain. Repeat with the remaining bagels.

6. As soon as they have cooled enough so that you can handle them, dip each bagel into the black and white sesame seeds and the kosher salt. Arrange on the baking sheets. Bake in the oven for 8 minutes, then turn the pans back to front and switch racks. Continue baking for about 8 minutes more or until the bagels are golden brown. Remove them from the oven and cool on racks.

THE BAGEL—THE BOILED AND BAKED ROLL WITH A HOLE

These days, nothing is more American than the bagel. A French toast bagel, advertised in—of all places—Plymouth, Massachusetts, has its dough infused with cinnamon chips and maple syrup before being boiled and baked. The Great American Bagel Company of Chicago advertises an award-winning bagel dipped in pizza sauce and topped with mozzarella cheese. The bagel, which may be green on St. Patrick's Day, filled with blueberries during the summer, or spicy with jalapeños, is one more example of how American cooks put their stamp on almost everything. Today, bagel bakeries are no longer the province of Jewish bakers, who brought this humble bread to America from Eastern Europe. The *New York Times* rated Absolute Bagels near Columbia University the best in New York. It happens that the owners are Thai. Bruegger's Bagels are Swedish, Marx's Hot Bagels in Cincinnati are German, and H&H Bagels in New York are Puerto Rican. Einstein Brothers Bagels alone boasts bagels topped with spicy nachos and power bagels with peanut butter. Gone is the simple snack food of Eastern Europe, usurped by bagel dogs, bagel chips, bagel pizzas, and now even French toast bagels.

MUFFIN TOPS

In a popular *Seinfeld* episode, Elaine convinced her old boss, Mr. Lippman, who had gone into the muffin business but was not doing as well as he had hoped, to sell only muffin tops. The muffin tops sold like hotcakes, but Mr. Lippman didn't know what to do with the unused muffin bottoms. He and Elaine tried to give them to the homeless, but they didn't want them. In fact, no one wanted them, and Elaine had to hire someone to dispose of the unwanted muffin bottoms. Thankfully those who like muffin tops can now buy muffin-top pans at kitchenware stores. When baking, one muffin top equals one regular muffin.

Cynthia Gerlach and her muffins

Bottletree Bakery's Orange, Carrot, Oat, and Bran Muffins

In Oxford, Mississippi, in the early 1990s, there was no place to get a decent cup of coffee or a loaf of bread. So Cynthia Gerlach, a native of Portland, Oregon, who had just graduated from Ole Miss, teamed up with Martha Foose, who had worked at Nancy Silverton's La Brea Bakery in Los Angeles, and together they opened the Bottletree Bakery.

"The Bottletree is a symbol of my appreciation of southern folk art," said Cynthia, who was a Southern Studies major at Ole Miss. "In the South, bottles are used essentially like a good-luck charm. The spirit would get caught in the bottle, and you knew your house was safe. Bottles are round, and all our bread is circular, a symbol of life.

"I was twenty-five years old when I started this crazy endeavor," she said, "but it took off right away. It was something the community needed, a kid-friendly place, a smoke-free environment." Here is Cynthia's bran muffin recipe—one that friends in Oxford have wanted for years.

YIELD: 12 MUFFINS

1¾ cups rolled oats
1¼ cups whole-wheat flour
1¼ cups bran
½ cup currants
¾ cup sugar
1½ teaspoons baking soda
1 tablespoon baking powder
½ teaspoon salt
2 large eggs
¾ cup orange juice
1½ cups carrots, grated coarsely in food processor (about 2½ carrots)
1¼ cups buttermilk
3 tablespoons vegetable oil

1. Toss the oats, flour, bran, currants, sugar, baking soda, baking powder, and salt together in a large mixing bowl.

2. Beat the eggs well in another large bowl and fold in the orange juice, grated carrots, buttermilk, and oil.

3. Stir the wet ingredients into the dry until blended. Refrigerate for a few hours or overnight.

4. Preheat the oven to 350 degrees and grease a 12-cup muffin tin. Fill the tins ¾ full with batter, almost to the top, and bake 25–30 minutes or until golden.

Morning Glory Muffins

Wanting to learn the source of these muffins, I tracked down their creator, Pam McKinstrey, who now lives in Carmel, California. It all started in 1979 on Nantucket's Old South Wharf when Pam converted a former sandal shop into the Morning Glory Café. Her neighbors, two artists, decorated the interior of the café to look like a barn. There were brightly colored tables with morning glories painted on the legs as well as growing along the split-rail fence.

"What I wanted to do was come up with a café menu that had signature items," she said. "I kept thinking that when you make a muffin, it isn't good the next day, and I wanted to make one that had shelf life for two or three days to sell to the boats."

So she worked with zucchini bread and carrot cake doughs because they were moist, adding crushed pineapple and apples, coconut, and raisins to the mix. This marriage of vegetables and fruit became the original morning glory muffin. Within a year, word of the muffin had spread far beyond the harbor. The *New York Times* published the recipe, and *Gourmet* magazine named the muffin one of its "50 Baking Favorites" in 1991. Starbucks serves morning glory muffins today, as do bed-and-breakfasts and cafés across the country.

YIELD: 12–15 MUFFINS

2¼ cups all-purpose flour
1 tablespoon ground cinnamon
2 teaspoons baking soda
½ teaspoon salt
1¼ cups sugar
½ cup unsweetened shredded coconut, loosely packed
½ cup raisins
2 cups grated carrots (3–4 large), loosely packed
1 apple, shredded
1 cup canned crushed pineapple, drained
½ cup chopped pecans or walnuts
3 large eggs
1 cup vegetable oil
1 teaspoon vanilla extract

1. Preheat the oven to 350 degrees and grease a 12-cup muffin tin or line it with paper or foil baking cups.

2. Sift together the flour, cinnamon, baking soda, and salt into a large bowl. Stir in the sugar. Add the coconut, raisins, carrots, apple, pineapple, and chopped nuts and mix well.

3. In a separate bowl whisk the eggs with the vegetable oil and the vanilla, then pour into the bowl with the other ingredients. Stir well.

4. Fill each muffin cup to the brim. Bake for 35 minutes or until a toothpick inserted in the center of a muffin comes out clean. Cool the muffins in the pan for 10 minutes and turn out onto a rack to finish cooling. Eat immediately—or, better yet, wait 24 hours.

Small World Coffee's Ginger Scones with Cardamom

I am always in search of a good scone, a breakfast bun that I first tasted in England slathered with Devonshire cream and jam. American scones today are bigger than their English cousins and come in almost as many flavors as muffins and bagels do. One of the best I have tasted is the candied ginger and cardamom scone from Small World Coffee in Princeton, New Jersey.

Located just a block from the gates of Princeton University, the café is filled with students, professors, and ordinary citizens. Dogs are tied outside, knapsacks are tossed on the ground, and the *New York Times,* like a bible, is spread out on the tables.

Like their homemade granola and oatmeal, this scone is one of Small World Coffee's main attractions. Jessica Durrie, who with her partner, Brant Cosaboom, owns the café, told me how they came up with the ginger-cardamom scone. "We were developing the chai recipe that has a lot of both cardamom and fresh ginger in it," said Jessica. "Brant decided to add cardamom and ginger to the scone recipe, using crystallized ginger instead of fresh. The combination was an instant hit."

You can mix the scone batter by hand, with a food processor, or with a mixer. But be careful not to overblend the ingredients or the scones will be tough and chewy. And grind the cardamom yourself. The difference in flavor between freshly ground cardamom and the preground powder you buy in the supermarket is enormous.

YIELD: 12 SCONES

3 cups all-purpose flour
2 teaspoons baking powder
½ teaspoon baking soda
½ teaspoon salt
¾ teaspoon cardamom pods
1 stick (½ cup) unsalted butter
¼ cup crystallized ginger, chopped in ¼-inch bits
¾ cup sour cream
½ cup plus 4 teaspoons sugar
2 large eggs

1. Preheat the oven to 350 degrees and line a baking sheet with parchment paper.

2. Mix the flour, baking powder, baking soda, and salt by hand or in the bowl of an electric mixer or food processor for a few seconds.

3. Peel the cardamom pods—you'll need some nails for this—and then grind the tiny seeds inside. There will be about 17–20 seeds. Sift the cardamom and stir into the dry mix.

4. Break the butter into small pieces and mix with the dry ingredients until crumbs form.

5. Add the ginger, sour cream, ½ cup of the sugar, and one of the eggs. Rub with your hand—or blend or pulse—just enough to mix the ingredients; do not overblend.

6. Scoop up about ⅓ cup of dough (an ice cream scoop is good for this), form it into a plump ball, and place it on the baking sheet. Repeat with the remaining dough, leaving 2 inches between scones.

7. Mix the remaining egg with a little water and brush the scones with the egg wash, then sprinkle on the remaining 4 teaspoons sugar. Bake for 25–30 minutes or until golden brown.

Whole-Wheat Banana Bread with Macadamia Nuts

On a trip to the Big Island of Hawaii, I stayed with my family at a macadamia nut farm called Lions Gate. Not knowing what to expect, we drove down a driveway lined with bougainvillea, king palm trees, and coffee bushes. Farther along, the driveway was blanketed with fallen macadamia nut shells. Diane and Bill Shriner, who moved to Hawaii from California for a change in lifestyle, have planted mangoes, papayas, bananas, pineapples, limes, lemons, grapefruits, and Surinam cherries all around their hundred-year-old farm. At breakfast, sitting on their *lanai* (porch), we ate delicious papaya halves filled with home-grown diced fruits, huge, salted macadamia nuts, and a macadamia streusel coffee cake. But the best was this banana bread studded with salted macadamia nuts. I store my overripe bananas in the freezer and take them out as needed to make this bread.

YIELD: 1 LARGE LOAF

½ cup (1 stick) unsalted butter
1 cup sugar
2 eggs, slightly beaten
3 medium, ripe bananas
1 teaspoon vanilla extract
1 teaspoon baking soda
1½ cups all-purpose flour
1 cup whole-wheat flour
½ teaspoon salt
1 teaspoon baking powder
½ cup chopped salted macadamia nuts

1. Preheat the oven to 350 degrees and grease a 9-by-5-inch loaf pan.

2. Cream the butter with the sugar in a food processor equipped with a steel blade. Add the eggs, bananas, and vanilla and pulse until blended.

3. Dissolve the baking soda in 2 tablespoons water and add to the banana mixture. Process for a minute or so. Sift together the flours, salt, and baking powder and fold into the banana mixture, then pour the batter into the loaf pan.

4. Sprinkle the macadamia nuts on top, gently pressing them in. Bake for 60–70 minutes or until an inserted toothpick comes out clean.

Frank Ruta's White House Doughnuts

When Frank Ruta was a chef in the Reagan White House, First Lady Nancy Reagan requested that he make a special bread for the family's Christmas dinner.

After Frank opened a restaurant, he decided to turn the recipe into breakfast doughnuts. In this current epoch of designer doughnuts (à la Thomas Keller of Napa's French Laundry, for example), they have been a huge success.

Even busy people can make these doughnuts. The dough can be mixed ahead of time, refrigerated overnight, then cut, formed, and fried the next morning. After trying the doughnuts, your family will never want store-bought again. Believe me, any leftovers are eaten instantly.

YIELD: ABOUT 20 DOUGHNUTS

1 scant tablespoon (1 package) active dry yeast
1¼ cups lukewarm milk
2 tablespoons sugar
4¼ cups bread flour
1 teaspoon salt
Zest of ½ orange
2 whole eggs
¾ cup (1½ sticks) unsalted butter, softened, at room temperature
Equal parts canola and sunflower oil for frying, to fill the fryer by 3 inches
Sugar for rolling
¾ cup confectioners' sugar
About ¼ cup water or dark rum like Myers's

1. Dissolve the yeast in the milk. Add a pinch of the sugar and 1 tablespoon of the flour and let sit for about 20 minutes.

2. Mix the remaining sugar, 4 cups of the flour, salt, and orange zest in the bowl of an electric mixer fitted with the dough hook. Stir in the yeast mixture, then add the eggs, 1 at a time. Now switch to the paddle attachment and add the butter bit by bit. When the dough comes together and all the butter is incorporated, scrape it out onto a work surface floured with the remaining flour and shape into a nice ball. It will be so sticky you will have to cover your hands with flour.

3. Place in a greased covered bowl in a draft-free place for about 2 hours or until the dough doubles in volume. Covering your hands with flour, punch the dough down, fold it over onto itself a few times, shape it into a smooth oblong, put it back in the covered bowl, and refrigerate overnight.

4. The next day, remove the dough from the refrigerator and roll it out into a rectangle on a floured surface, about ½ inch thick. Using a doughnut cutter, cut the dough into doughnut shapes. You can also use 2 cookie cutters—a 3-inch and a 1¼-inch cutter. Place the doughnuts on a lightly floured cloth and let them proof in a warm place for about 30 minutes, making sure they remain cool to the touch. Don't let them rise too long or they'll absorb too much grease when frying.

5. Heat 3 inches of oil in a deep fryer or wok to 365 degrees. Carefully add a few doughnuts at a time. Do not crowd the pan or the oil will cool and the doughnuts will absorb too much of it. Fry a few minutes on 1 side until a nice golden brown, then flip over and fry on the other. Drain the doughnuts on paper towels.

6. Roll the hot doughnuts in granulated sugar. Or make a glaze using ¾ cup of confectioners' sugar mixed with rum or water (use only enough water or rum to make a paste, about the consistency of toothpaste), and dip the warm doughnuts into the glaze on both sides. Set them on a rack to drain, and cool for about 30 minutes before eating.

Potica

Iron Range Walnut Coffee Cake

Potica (pronounced "po-TEET-sa") is a paper-thin sweet bread filled with walnuts, honey, sugar, and butter. Croatians who came to Minnesota's Iron Range to work the mines at the turn of the century likely brought this delicacy with them, but now just about everyone in Hibbing, Minnesota, serves it at Christmas, weddings, and other celebrations.

For years, most people in Hibbing bought *potica* at the Sunrise Bakery, which still makes it the old-fashioned way: stretching the dough until you can read through it, then sprinkling the nut filling on top and rolling it up. But recently, a slightly different *potica* has entered the scene. When Jan Latick moved to the Iron Range from Slovakia (via Flushing, New York), he brought with him a regional variation of the same cake. After trying his recipe, friends urged him to start baking on a larger scale.

While working in the Hibbing Hospital's maintenance department, Jan baked on the side. And he baked well—his *potica* won a blue ribbon at the local Balkan Fair. "I felt so horrible," he told me. "All these ladies come every year, and I get the ribbon."

After winning more blue ribbons, he decided to go into business, and in 2000, he opened Andrej's Bakery, named for his father. Now he is making between two hundred and three hundred loaves of *potica* a day, six days a week.

This easy version, which uses puff pastry dough instead of strudel dough, won accolades from a friend who was raised on the Iron Range and on the *potica* there.

Potica (continued)

10 ounces walnuts (3 cups)

⅓ cup granulated sugar

¼ cup light brown sugar

2 tablespoons honey

1 teaspoon cinnamon

1 large egg

4 tablespoons light or heavy cream

2 sheets prepared puff pastry dough (about 17.3 ounces)

1 egg yolk

1. Preheat the oven to 350 degrees and grease a 9-by-11-inch jelly-roll pan.

2. To prepare the filling, put the walnuts in a food processor fitted with a steel blade. Add both sugars, the honey, cinnamon, egg, and 3 tablespoons of the cream, and pulse a few times, until the mixture is the consistency of a chunky paste.

3. Flour a table or other flat surface and roll out 1 sheet of puff pastry dough to form a 12-by-16-inch rectangle. Smear half the filling all over the dough, leaving a 1-inch border all around.

4. Starting at the narrower 12-inch end, roll up the puff pastry like a jelly roll, tightly but gently, tucking in the sides as you roll. Place the dough in the baking pan. Repeat with the second sheet and the remainder of the filling. Mix the egg yolk with the remaining tablespoon of cream and brush the glaze over the *potica*. Bake in the oven for about 45 minutes or until golden brown. Cool slightly and transfer to a serving plate. Serve warm or at room temperature.

Chai at Teaism

Teaism, an Asian-inspired tea café in Washington, D.C., is a wonderful place to relax. Seated upstairs, you may see Leon Wieseltier, who wrote his book *Kaddish* surrounded by Teaism's protruding ducts and unadorned lightbulbs. In the background, sitar music and the whir of the black fans soothe customers as they wait in line for Japanese bento boxes filled with brown rice, salmon, cucumber salad, and edamame (soybeans) or a cup of authentic chai, Indian black tea boiled with milk, sugar, cardamom, cinnamon, star anise, and nutmeg.

"Make yourself a nice pot of tea to enjoy while you work," Linda Orr, the owner, suggested as we sat together in the tiny café. Linda's romance with tea began about fifteen years ago, when her business partner, Michelle Brown, married an Indian restaurateur. "Michelle would make wonderful meals with ginger and cilantro and serve such exotic teas," said Linda.

In 1997, Michelle and Linda decided to open a teahouse. They selected fifty different loose teas and chose a site near the D.C. embassies, where they thought the employees would be a receptive audience for real tea. "Michelle was more optimistic than I was," Linda told me over a cup of chai. "Lots of people whispered that they were tea drinkers but would never admit it out loud.

"Our mission became to promote loose-leaf tea," Linda said. "After 9/11 people were looking to carve out time for themselves. They would put their hands on the warm pot, savor the tea, and look out the window."

YIELD: 2 SERVINGS

2½ cups cold water

1 cinnamon stick, broken into pieces

5 whole cloves

5 green cardamom pods, smashed with the flat side of a knife and peeled

2 teaspoons loose-leaf black tea, such as Assam

½ cup whole milk

1½ tablespoons sugar, or to taste

1. Bring the water to a boil in a small pot. Add the pieces of cinnamon stick, cloves, and cardamom. Let boil for 1–2 minutes.

2. Sprinkle on the tea. Add milk and sweeten to taste with sugar. Leave the pot on the stove just until it returns to a boil, then pour the tea through a strainer into mugs and serve.

Kaldi's White Chocolate Latte

Although Kaldi's uses espresso in its latte, you can use regular coffee. If you have an espresso maker with a steamer, you're all set. Otherwise, try a milk frother to froth the hot milk or put the milk in the microwave for a minute and then whip it well.

YIELD: 2 SERVINGS

2 ounces white chocolate, grated
½ cup of espresso
(about 4 shots), heated
1¼ cups hot milk
2 dollops of whipped cream

1. Stir the white chocolate into the hot espresso.

2. Add the hot milk and pour into coffee mugs. Then top each mug with a dollop of whipped cream.

A GREAT PLACE—KALDI'S COFFEEHOUSE

Everything about bread that is true is true about coffee, and most of the coffee people drink in America is the coffee equivalent of Wonder Bread. Like bread, coffee is at its peak one day after roasting. People should seek out and learn from their local coffee roasters.

—DAVID STRYMISH, coffee roaster, Biscuit Brand coffee

Kaldi's Coffeehouse in St. Louis, Missouri, is the kind of place where you want to sip great coffee, nibble on a muffin, read, work on your computer, meet friends, or just sit back and listen to the soft jazz playing in the background.

Even the decor feels homemade. Soothing orange marbled walls and a winding hall separate the relaxing rooms from the steady stream of people ordering carryout (the reason these coffeehouses can afford lingerers like me). Sacks of coffee leaning against the wall are as much a part of the aesthetic as they are the café's life-blood. A blackboard announces the day's menu with colorful chalk. The scene is completed with ceiling fans, a fern or two, and mismatched Parisian café chairs covered with burlap coffee bags.

Kaldi's is named after the Ethiopian goatherd who supposedly discovered coffee when he found his goats prancing by a coffee bush, having eaten its stimulating red berries. "Now we roast our own coffee," Suzanne Langlois, one of the owners, told me. "In the beginning we burned coffee and made mistakes, before we mastered the skill."

As we sipped their white chocolate latte, Suzanne, who manages the coffeehouse, explained Kaldi's philosophy: "At a restaurant you're expected to leave after a certain spell so that the management can turn the table. We didn't want that. We want people to lose their concept of time here."

Bread

For us, bread is fundamental to our civilization. It is almost biblical.

—JULES RABIN, PIONEER AMERICAN BREAD BAKER IN MARSHFIELD, VERMONT

A fine loaf of plain French bread, the long crackly kind a Frenchman tucks under his arm as he hurries home to the family lunch, has a very special quality," wrote Julia Child in *Mastering the Art of French Cooking II* in 1970. "Its inside is patterned with holes almost like Swiss cheese, and when you tear off a piece it wants to come sideways; it has body, chewability, and tastes and smells of the grain." Those of us lucky enough to have spent time in France, tucking those baguettes under our arms and breaking off the crusty end for a snack along the way home, have come to know how good a baguette from a neighborhood bakery can taste.

Now Americans no longer have to go to France for good bread. Today our baskets are bursting with rustic sourdough baguettes, olive breads, seven-grain breads, and flatbreads like naan, pita, tortillas, and, of course, pizza. Handmade, slow-rising breads like the Italian *ciabatta* and the French baguette are all the rage, as are egg breads such as brioche. Produced in small artisanal bakeries, they are available in supermarkets in many corners of America. Bakeries that once catered to a small neighborhood ethnic group are now mass-producing their Lebanese pita, Afghani naan, and tortillas for the ever-increasing and ever-expanding American appetite.

Home bakers have access today to flour of all kinds, bread machines, countless recipes on the Internet, and television shows guiding novice bakers and giving old hands some new and inventive ideas. With the increased interest in and demand for good bread, those who once experimented at home often become professional baking entrepreneurs, like Mal Krinn, a retired ophthalmologist who now bakes at his son's restaurant, 2941, in northern Virginia.

This explosion of breads has a tasty fallout—a host of new sandwiches and reimagined classics. You can still get your ordinary grilled cheese sandwich and pepperoni pizza, but creative cooks are putting new spins on old standards: fillings of grilled eggplant and/or roasted pepper, toppings of portobello mushrooms and goat cheese for

Clockwise from top right: Primo Lombardi's palette—the pizza; Brian Kingsford teaching Rhode Island children how to make pizza; Nuns at a Vietnamese bakery in New Orleans; Taco Loco—a find on the Pacific Coast Highway; Lynn Banister's dream, her own bakery

Susan Sullivan and Ana Barbosa at Acme Bread

pizzas; a lobster-meat taco; and wrappings of everything from bagels and flatbreads to no-carb breads and even lettuce.

On a trip to the Vietnamese farmers' market in New Orleans, I was given a locally famous Vietnamese "po' boy," also known as *banh mi*: slivered roast pork served Asian-style with oyster sauce, garlic, cilantro, pickled carrots, cucumbers, onions, and very hot peppers. The crisp baguette, unlike the softer white bread often found at New Orleans restaurants, comes from Dong Phuong, a nearby Vietnamese bakery.

"We had these sandwiches in Vietnam," the owner of the bakery told me. "The French brought good bread to Vietnam."

Although many artisanal bakeries use starters, which leaven bread without commercial yeast, most home cooks rely on active dry yeast from the supermarket. So I have adapted the recipes for some of the artisanal breads for home cooks accordingly.

I also suggest using an all-purpose, unbleached flour to bake most breads. But if you really immerse yourself in bread making, you'll want to experiment with the many different flours available today. Bread flour, which has more gluten than all-purpose, is preferable for whole-wheat breads and bagels, but all-purpose also works fine. And, by all means, buy yourself a large rectangular baking stone. It is indispensable for producing artisanal breads and pizzas.

In addition to the breads mentioned above, I have included in this chapter old favorite recipes, some with a new twist: anadama bread flavored with maple syrup rather than molasses; a delicious griddle corn bread made with mayonnaise, its secret ingredient; and my favorite challah.

Acme Bread Company's Rustic French Baguette

One thing that makes Acme Bread so good is its bakers' ability to vary a bread's formula (a baker's term for *recipe*) when it isn't working quite right. They know their dough so well, keeping a journal of each batch's behavior as it ferments, that they can catch and correct the slightest departure from the usual standard. Bake often enough, and you'll develop the same intuition, even at home.

A good baguette is crusty with an inside that is, when you break it open, light, springy to the touch, and filled with holes. To achieve that state, you must have a long fermentation and handle the dough lightly, adding just the flour you need to roll and shape it. It may take more than one try to master the baguette's shape, but your bread will taste great no matter what it looks like.

YIELD: 2 LOAVES

¾ teaspoon active dry yeast

3 cups water

5½ cups (about) unbleached all-purpose flour

1 teaspoon salt

1. Sprinkle ¼ teaspoon of the yeast over 1½ cups of the water and stir to dissolve.

2. Stir in 1 cup of the flour, mixing well for a few minutes, until smooth. Cover the bowl tightly with plastic wrap. Let what is now called the sponge rise at room temperature for about 3 hours. At this point continue making the bread or refrigerate the sponge overnight, returning it to room temperature before you proceed.

3. Pour the remaining 1½ cups water onto the sponge and stir to loosen it from the bowl.

4. Stir in the remaining ½ teaspoon yeast, then put 4 cups flour and the salt into the bowl of a standing mixer. Stir the sponge into the flour and mix with the paddle. Now, switch to the dough hook and knead on low speed for a few minutes to mix the dough thoroughly.

5. Transfer the dough to a very large greased bowl and cover tightly with plastic wrap. When it is light and bubbly and has doubled in volume, about 3 hours, it is ready.

6. Turn the dough, which will be very sticky, out onto a lightly floured work surface. Sprinkle as necessary with the remaining ½ cup flour, to keep the dough from sticking, and cover with plastic wrap. Let the

dough rest for 30 minutes. The dough will be puffy with gas and very soft.

7. To shape the dough into a baguette, divide the dough in half and lightly flatten out each half portion. Fold the bottom third of 1 piece of the dough up to the center, then fold the top third down over to the middle—as you would fold a letter. With the side of your hand gently press a crease down the entire length of the dough.

8. With 1 hand on top of the other, roll the dough gently but firmly back and forth on the floured board, slowly moving your hands apart as the dough lengthens. Keep rolling until the dough is about 18 inches long. Use a little extra pressure at the ends of the dough to make them more pointed. Holding a cookie sheet covered with parchment paper or a baguette mold on the side of the counter, gently roll the loaf onto the sheet or into the baguette mold, seam side down. Shape the other piece of dough the same way.

9. Preheat the oven to 425 degrees. Place the rack on the second-to-top shelf.

10. Let the dough rise for about 30 minutes, uncovered. Just before baking, cut 3 slits diagonally across the loaves with a razor, a very sharp thin-bladed knife, or scissors.

11. Place the baguettes in the oven. Then toss a few ice cubes onto the bottom of the oven. The steam from the ice will help develop a better crust. Bake the bread for 25–30 minutes or until golden brown, rotating the pan halfway after 20 minutes. Remove the bread from the oven and let it cool completely on a wire rack before slicing.

It is people like Steve Sullivan, the founder of Acme Bread Company in Berkeley, California, who have helped Americans learn to appreciate good bread. While on a bicycling trip in Europe in the summer of 1977, Steve stumbled on the just-published *English Yeast and Bread Cookery*, by Elizabeth David. "I spent the rest of my trip reading the book," Steve told me in his living room in the Berkeley hills. "When I got back I started making bread all the time. My co-op apartment was a mess. There was bread dough on the doorknobs; it was a continually spreading experiment. I was learning about bread dough and bread baking."

In 1979, when Alice Waters was planning to open an upstairs café at Chez Panisse, she asked Steve, who had been working for her as a busboy, to bake bread for the restaurant. "At that point, I dropped out of Berkeley," he says. Little by little,

Steve's bread baking got too demanding for the restaurant. "We had baguettes upstairs and down. Sometimes the restaurant needed the oven for a leg of lamb or something, and I'd say, 'Sorry the bread has to go in.' "

Realizing the time had come, Steve and his wife, Susan, bit the bullet and opened Acme Bread Company in late 1983. "We never had any problem selling bread, and people were willing to pay a few extra cents to get it," Steve relates. "We've been really fortunate doing what we do at the time when we were doing it." Acme Bread Company's three local bakeries are a huge success, but Steve refuses to go national. "We were so fortunate that people paid attention to us from the beginning," says Steve, who recently returned to the University of California at Berkeley after twenty years to finally get his bachelor's degree.

Ciabatta

In bakeries around the country I have tasted Italian *ciabatta*, a crusty bread whose shape supposedly resembles a man's nine-inch slipper. In a way, it is more like a crustier, lengthier pita or pocket bread. The formula for it is allegedly two thousand years old, but until recently I had never tried to make it. It sounded intriguing, so I went to the Internet and immediately struck gold with a Colorado cooking school site. Note that you will need a baking stone, bricks, or tiles on your oven racks to make this *ciabatta* successfully.

It was Carol Field, one of my favorite cookbook writers, who probably first introduced this bread to Americans in her 1985 book, *The Italian Baker*. After that, bakers like Nancy Silverton and Peter Reinhardt developed their own versions. With artisanal bakeries proliferating around the country, this bread, found all over Italy but especially near Lake Como, is off the popularity charts.

YIELD: 2 LOAVES

SPONGE

⅛ teaspoon active dry yeast

½ cup warm water

1 cup bread flour

DOUGH

½ teaspoon active dry yeast

5 tablespoons warm milk

½ cup warm water

2 cups bread flour plus flour for dusting

1½ teaspoons salt

2 tablespoons extra-virgin olive oil

½ cup sun-dried tomatoes packed in oil, diced pitted olives, or a combination of both, drained (optional)

1. To make the sponge, stir the ⅛ teaspoon yeast and warm water in a small bowl until smooth.

2. Pour the 1 cup flour into the bowl of an electric mixer, add the dissolved yeast, and stir with the paddle for a few minutes. Cover the bowl with plastic wrap and let sit for 12 hours, until the dough rises and deflates. This happens more quickly in the summer than the winter. When it collapses it will be very bubbly.

3. To make the dough, stir the ½ teaspoon yeast, 5 tablespoons milk, and ½ cup water together in a small bowl, then into the sponge in the mixer bowl. Add the 2 cups flour and the salt and knead for about 5 minutes, using the dough hook. Stir in the olive oil and, if you like, the sun-dried tomatoes and/or chopped olives. Continue kneading for 1 more minute. Scrape the dough into a greased clean bowl and cover with plastic wrap. Let the dough rise at room temperature for about 1½ hours, until it has doubled in bulk. It will be very sticky and loaded with air bubbles.

4. Place two 12-by-6-inch sheets of parchment paper on 2 cookie sheets and sprinkle flour on top. Flouring your hands well, turn the dough onto a well-floured work surface. Divide the dough in half with a pastry cutter and transfer each half to the parchment sheets. Using

your fingers, well covered with flour, press the dough down and form ovals about 9 inches long. Dust the tops with flour and cover the loaves lightly with a dampened kitchen towel. Let rise another 1½–2 hours, until they are doubled in bulk.

5. Cover both racks of your oven with bricks or tiles or a baking stone and preheat the oven to 425 degrees. When ready to bake, slide the parchment papers with the loaves carefully onto the bricks or baking stone and bake about 20 minutes or until the loaves are very pale golden. Using a large spatula, transfer the loaves to a rack to cool.

Mark Furstenberg's Focaccia with Onions

Like its thinner cousin, pizza, focaccia was often made on bread-baking days. A hunk of dough would be extracted from the big mixing bowl, flattened and topped with leftovers, then baked on the hearth. It made a meal that was often carried to workers in the fields.

More than anyone else, Mark Furstenberg is credited with bringing good bread and focaccia to Washington, D.C. Mark, an avid home cook, opened Marvelous Market in 1990. "In retrospect it was really quite arrogant to think that I could open a bakery," Mark told me over lunch at his new venture, Bread Line, where he is producing innovative breads and stuffed sandwiches from around the world. "Handheld foods that people buy on the streets are ubiquitous everywhere: empanadas, samosas, *briques, piedini,* focaccia. I am trying to offer a fast-food restaurant that re-creates the traditional bread-based foods eaten in primitive cultures."

Focaccia is quite easy to make, but it takes planning to prepare the sponge a day in advance. I have used Mark's onion topping, but you can also use thick goat cheese or sun-dried tomatoes with other leftover vegetables. Basically anything you like on pizza you'll like on focaccia. Serve it with a salad, and everyone will be happy.

YIELD: I LARGE FOCACCIA

½ teaspoon active dry yeast

3 cups cool water

5½ cups (approximately) all-purpose flour

1. To make the sponge, mix the yeast with 2½ cups of the water in a medium bowl. Stir in 2 cups of the flour and leave it for about 3 hours. The sponge is ready when the top is covered with bubbles and you can shake the container without having the mass of dough fall. (If you

2 teaspoons fine sea salt

½ cup plus 2 tablespoons (approximately) olive oil

A few tablespoons coarse cornmeal

2 large red onions, chopped

1 teaspoon coarse sea salt

refrigerate the sponge for later use, take it out of the refrigerator at least 4 hours before it is to be used.)

2. To make the dough, put the remaining 3½ cups flour in the bowl of an electric mixer with a paddle. Add the sponge and remaining ½ cup water. Turn the mixer to low and leave it on until all the flour has been mixed in. Add the fine sea salt and continue mixing for 4 to 5 minutes. Pour in ¼ cup of the olive oil and mix that in, perhaps 3 minutes more. The dough will be shiny and very wet.

3. Transfer the dough to a bowl very lightly rubbed with oil. Cover the bowl with plastic wrap and leave it for an hour at room temperature. You will be able to see tiny air bubbles below the surface of the dough. At that point, dip your fingers in water to keep the dough from sticking, remove the dough to a lightly floured surface, and fold it over with your wet fingers. Grease the bowl lightly again, place the dough back in, cover, and let rise for another half hour.

4. Meanwhile, preheat the oven to 425 degrees, slide a baking stone onto the rack, and heat it for at least 30 minutes. If you do not have a baking stone, put a sheet pan upside down in the oven and preheat that.

5. Put a piece of parchment paper on the back of a baking sheet, about 12 by 16 inches. Sprinkle the parchment liberally with coarse cornmeal and dip your hands into cold water. Now gently coax the dough out of the bowl onto the parchment and spread it to the full length and width of the parchment. You should have a large rectangle of dough approximately ¼ inch thick. Dimple the dough firmly all over with your fingertips.

6. Heat ¼ cup of the olive oil in a medium frying pan and sauté the red onions until soft. Cool the onions to room temperature.

7. Drizzle the dough with about 2 more tablespoons olive oil, spoon on the sautéed onions, then sprinkle with the coarse sea salt.

8. Slide the focaccia on its parchment with a quick motion onto the stone or baking sheet. Bake it for about 25 minutes or until golden brown. Remove, let cool partially, and slice into squares.

By now "California pizza," synonymous with Wolfgang Puck's pizzas, is part of our everyday vocabulary. Puck's pizzas can be found in supermarkets coast to coast, and California Pizza Kitchen has more than 130 restaurants nationwide. But it was Ed LaDou, dubbed "the prince of pizza" by *Gourmet* magazine restaurant critic Jonathan Gold, who started it all.

A self-taught cook, Ed was working at a Bay Area Italian restaurant in 1975. "I was concerned about the slow lunch business," said this soft-spoken man when I met him at Caioti Pizza Cafe, his humble Studio City pizza parlor, "so I started creating specials with pizza." LaDou began pilfering ingredients from the pasta station—eggplant, zucchini, and chopped garlic—and sprinkling them on the pizzas. "Customers liked the new creations, like pizza with onions, garlic, and clams instead of the plain red sauce. Although the restaurant was successful, the owners weren't very encouraging: my pizzas never made it to the menu because they were not conventional."

A few years later, Ed found himself making pizzas at Wolfgang Puck's newly opened Spago. "Wolfgang was always bringing in new ingredients, so I could create a pizza with scallops, fish roe, zucchini flowers, tomato, and red onion, seasoned with fresh dill. I would get there an hour before the rest of the cooks did and look at the day's ingredients. I took pizza out of its static form, opened the door, and applied creative Pacific Rim, Greek, and Mediterranean flavors. In my mind, I Americanized it by using all those different ethnic cultures. The wood-burning pizzas were such a novelty, and an even greater novelty was Wolfgang's association with them, so he got the credit."

In 1985 two lawyers approached LaDou to help them create the first California Pizza Kitchen, in Beverly Hills. "The chef bailed out before the restaurant opened," said Ed, "so I put together the original menu of pastas, pizzas, and salads. My barbecued chicken pizza with smoked Gouda is still on the menu." The restaurant was so successful that Ed was given a small share of the profits before it went nationwide. He used the money to open Caioti Pizza Cafe in 1987.

California Pizza

As I watched Ed LaDou make pizza, I listened. "It's the feel of the dough," he told me. "You give ten chefs the same recipe, and the touch will be different. The longer you let the dough rest, the better your pizza will be. You have to make sure that the dough is round, remove and shape it carefully. Consistency, like with anything else, is important." For home cooks, Ed advises making the dough the day before and refrigerating it.

Ed also suggests buying a pizza stone. "Bake it dry," he urges. If you have only a baking sheet, make sure it is heavy. Although this recipe makes dough for four crusts, I give only two toppings. Experiment with others, or make what Ed considers pure indulgence: his addictive pizza nuts. He cuts a ball of pizza dough into ten pieces, rolls them into snakes, that he twists into knots, and bakes them for about ten minutes. Before serving he tosses them with olive oil, crushed garlic, a sprinkling of oregano, and kosher salt.

YIELD: FOUR 10-INCH PIZZAS

1 scant tablespoon (1 package) active dry yeast
1½ cups warm water
1½ tablespoons sugar
1 tablespoon salt
3 tablespoons olive oil
4½–5 cups all-purpose flour
½ cup plus 2 tablespoons semolina
1–2 tablespoons extra-virgin olive oil

1. Dissolve the yeast in the warm water in the bowl of an electric mixer. Using the dough hook, add the sugar, salt, olive oil, and enough all-purpose flour and semolina to form a soft dough; mix until it is smooth and still somewhat sticky.

2. Scrape the dough out onto a lightly floured surface and knead for at least 10 minutes, until smooth, adding flour if sticky.

3. Place the dough in a bowl, cover with plastic wrap, and let it rest at room temperature for at least 40 minutes or, if the room is cold, 1½ hours; it will increase in volume by about 20 percent.

4. Divide the dough into 4 equal parts. Form each into a smooth, tight ball; place them with space in between on a cutting board or flat sheet; cover with a damp towel; and let them rise for an hour. You can make the pizzas right away, but it is better if the dough rests in the refrigerator overnight. When you're ready to bake, remove the dough and allow it to rise at room temperature for about an hour.

5. Place a pizza stone in the oven, if you have one. (Ed would not make pizza without one.) Preheat the oven to 500 degrees.

6. Now you have to work fast. Roll, pat, or stretch each ball of dough into a 10-inch circle, creating a frame around the circumference with your fingers: press with your fingers from the center of the dough to the edge, patting out the bottom and leaving about a half-inch-thick border around the sides. You want the bottom to be as thin as possible and the lip to be doughy and breadlike. Transfer the circle to a pizza paddle or a heavy baking sheet sprinkled with a tablespoon of the remaining semolina and flour.

7. Brush the top of the pizza round with olive oil, then add the topping of your choice (see below).

8. Thrust the pizza paddle into the oven, jerking it back with enough force for the pizza to land on the pizza stone. Otherwise, just place the baking sheet in the middle of the oven. Bake for about 8–10 minutes, until the crust is golden brown. Repeat with the same topping or other ingredients of your choosing for the remaining pizzas.

Portobello Mushroom Topping with Spinach, Brie, Tomato, and Sliced Almonds

YIELD: ENOUGH TOPPING FOR ONE 10-INCH PIZZA

When the pizza dough is rolled out and brushed with oil, scatter 1 cup shredded mozzarella, 2 handfuls spinach, 1 thinly sliced portobello mushroom, 1 tomato cut in 1-inch chunks, and 2 ounces Brie cut in 1-inch pieces over the pizza. Sprinkle ½ cup slivered almonds on top.

Barbecued Chicken with Smoked Gouda Topping

YIELD: ENOUGH TOPPING FOR ONE 10-INCH PIZZA

Smear ½ cup barbecue sauce over the dough. Scatter almost 1 cup shredded mozzarella, 1 cup cooked chicken, 2 tablespoons chopped cilantro, 2 ounces shredded Gouda cheese, and ¼ red onion, sliced thin. Then sprinkle a little more mozzarella over the top.

Primo's Whole-Wheat Pizza with Vegetables and Goat Cheese

Primo Lombardi, pizza maker to vacationing stars on Martha's Vineyard, told me as he formed a pizza, the smell of garlic wafting through the air, that he uses only extra-virgin olive oil, King Arthur high-gluten white flour, and Gold Medal stone-ground whole-wheat flour for his dough. "I decided that if I worked this hard, I wanted the ingredients to be the best. The dough is 80 percent of the pizza. When you take a slice of pizza off the tray and the slice stays up and doesn't collapse, that's the sign of a good pizza. Pizza is my canvas."

Depending on a number of variables—the brand of flour you use, the weather at the time you bake, and the altitude you live at—your results will vary. Don't be afraid; just feel your dough. Add a little more water if it's too dry or more flour if it's too wet.

YIELD: 3 PIZZAS, OR 6 SERVINGS

DOUGH

1¾ cups very cold water

2 teaspoons sugar

4 tablespoons extra-virgin olive oil

1 scant tablespoon (1 package) active dry yeast

2 teaspoons dried basil

3½ cups all-purpose flour (approximately)

2¼ cups stone-ground whole-wheat flour

2 teaspoons salt

2 tablespoons cornmeal

TOPPING

1½ cups coarsely grated mozzarella cheese

1½ cups coarsely grated provolone cheese

1. To make the dough, mix the water, sugar, 2 tablespoons of the olive oil, and the yeast in a standing electric mixer using the dough hook on the slowest speed for 3 minutes.

2. Add the basil, 2½ cups of the all-purpose flour, the whole-wheat flour, and the salt, and continue to mix and knead for 5 minutes.

3. Divide the dough into 3 equal balls and place on a greased pan. Cover and refrigerate overnight.

4. The next morning, remove the balls of pizza dough from the refrigerator, work in about ½ cup of flour or as needed, and let the dough rise, covered, for 1 hour.

5. When the dough has doubled in volume, preheat the oven to 500 degrees; if you have a pizza stone, put it in the oven to heat.

6. Mix the remaining ½ cup of flour with the cornmeal and sprinkle a bit on a pastry board. Dip 1 ball of dough into the flour and cornmeal, slap the dough down, and, using the palms of your hands, press it into a 10-inch circle, dusting as needed with the cornmeal-flour mixture to keep it from sticking. Make a lip all around the outer edge of the pizza

6 cloves garlic, chopped
(about 6 teaspoons)

1 cup chopped fresh basil

3 cups vegetables: cooked,
if using broccoli or asparagus;
raw, if green or red pepper, or
fresh tomatoes; or cured, such
as canned artichoke hearts or
sun-dried tomatoes

1½ cups crumbled feta
or goat cheese

dough. Transfer the dough to a floured wooden pizza peel or baking sheet, dusted with the cornmeal-flour mixture to keep it from sticking.

7. Toss the mozzarella and provolone together in a small bowl. Line up the rest of the topping ingredients on a counter or board. Starting at the outer edge brush the dough with the remaining 2 tablespoons of olive oil, then sprinkle with ⅓ of the garlic. Add a third of the basil and the vegetables of your choice. Using your hands, sprinkle on ⅓ of the mozzarella-provolone mixture and then ⅓ of the feta or goat cheese. Carefully transfer the pizza to the hot stone or the baking sheet, nudging it with a spatula if necessary, and set the pizza in the oven. Throw a few ice cubes on the bottom of the oven to create steam. Bake in the oven for 10–15 minutes or until golden. Repeat with the other 2 pizzas and other toppings. (If you have a big enough oven, bake all 3 at once; otherwise, bake 1 at a time.)

Al Forno's Grilled Pizza

My favorite pizza is irregular-shaped, crusty, and thin. The just barely cooked topping looks like a painting when it comes off the grill. This so-called grilled pizza comes from Al Forno Restaurant in Providence, Rhode Island. In developing the recipe, chef-owners Johanne Killeen and her husband, George Germon, wanted to reproduce the taste of traditional Italian pizza they had tasted in Italy, without a wood oven. So George took his chances on getting a pizza to cook on a wood-burning grill. Since they were away when I visited, Brian Kingsford, who has been an apprentice and is now the chef and chief of operations at Al Forno, showed me how to make it. He stressed that the pizza can be cooked only on a charcoal or wood grill. Timing depends on the heat of your grill, but two things are certain: you don't want the bottom of the dough to burn, and you don't want to overcook the topping.

YIELD: 2 LARGE PIZZAS, SERVING ABOUT 6 PEOPLE EACH

DOUGH

1¾ cups warm water

1 scant tablespoon (1 package)
active dry yeast

1. To make the dough, place the water and yeast in the bowl of an electric mixer. Then add 3 cups of the flour and the salt. Using the dough hook, mix the dough for about 5 minutes or until you have a cohesive yet relatively sticky dough, adding more flour if needed.

3⅓–4 cups all-purpose flour

1 teaspoon salt

TOPPING

2 cups tomato chunks,
fresh or canned

4 cloves garlic

½ cup grated fontina cheese

¼ cup grated pecorino cheese

6 tablespoons (about) extra-
virgin olive oil

4 tablespoons chopped
fresh basil

4 tablespoons slivered scallions

Remove the dough from the mixer and press into a ball. Let it rise once, covered in a greased bowl, for about an hour.

2. Press the dough down, divide into 2 pieces, and let it rise again on a floured board, covered, or in the refrigerator if you're not using it immediately. Let it come to room temperature before proceeding.

3. Before making the pizza, prepare the tomato topping. Pulse the tomatoes and the garlic in a food processor fitted with a metal blade.

4. Toss the fontina and pecorino cheeses together in a small bowl.

5. Prepare a grill fueled by charcoal or wood. Make sure that you have a cool area on the grill to slide the partially baked dough onto while you distribute the toppings, and have the topping ingredients ready because you will have to move quickly.

6. Punch the dough down, then press it out to a free-form rectangle that will fit on a cookie sheet. Make sure not to make it so thin that holes appear. Gently place the pizza dough on the grill; grill for a minute or two, until the dough bubbles up.

7. Quickly remove the pizza from the heat with tongs and flip it over. Using tongs, move the pizza to a cool spot, sprinkle on half the cheese, spoon dollops of half the tomato over the crust, and sprinkle with olive oil. Return to the heat for a few minutes or until the cheese melts, moving the pizza with the tongs. Remove from the heat, sprinkle with half the fresh basil and half the slivered scallions, and serve. Repeat with the second pizza.

8. Serve whole or cut up for a first or main course.

George Germon and Johanne Killeen,
owners of Al Forno and creators of the grilled pizza

Taco Loco's Lobster Taco

Taco Loco, a Mexican seafood bar on the Pacific Coast Highway in Laguna Beach, California, is not much more than a shack with a few tables outside. The staff of this tiny kitchen is always busy taking orders for tacos, burgers, fajitas, and quesadillas. Four plastic bins containing serious-looking hot peppers are perched on a high shelf. Chopped avocado, cilantro, tomatoes, green peppers, and onions wait to be sandwiched into the soft tacos.

Although it calls itself a Mexican seafood bar, this place is very California, with fillings ranging from blackened tofu and mushrooms to calamari. I ordered a lobster and blackened fish taco. After rolling the seafood in a spice combination, the chef quickly stir-fried it. Then he wrapped a warm, soft tortilla around the fish and tucked fresh chopped guacamole salad inside. These tacos can easily be made at home (a great way to use leftover fish), but you won't get the atmosphere of Laguna Beach and Taco Loco's seafood bar.

YIELD: 4 TACOS

1 avocado

1 tomato

1 onion

1 cup chopped cilantro

2 tablespoons commercial or homemade blackened spice seasoning (page 269)

Salt and freshly ground pepper to taste

2 tablespoons vegetable oil

1 pound cooked or uncooked lobster or other seafood, such as swordfish, shrimp, or bluefish, cut into bite-size pieces

4 soft flour tortillas

1 cup hot or medium commercial or homemade salsa (page 96)

1. Dice the avocado, tomato, and onion and put in a bowl with the cilantro; toss to combine.

2. Put the blackened spice mix and salt and pepper in a small bowl. Heat a frying pan and add the vegetable oil when hot. Quickly roll the seafood in the spice combination, then sauté it in the pan over high heat for a few minutes, until heated or cooked through. Remove from the pan and set aside.

3. Heat the tortillas in the pan on both sides and wrap ¼ of the seafood in each tortilla. Sprinkle on the fresh avocado mixture and add mild or hot salsa. Repeat with the remaining tortillas.

Flour Tortillas from Montana

Named by Spanish conquistadors, the tortilla, a thin pancake made from flour or cornmeal, is a key part of the Mexican diet as well as that of the people of South and Central America. Used as bread, these flat rounds often serve as scoops or wraps.

Susan Castaneda and her husband, Bob, live in rural Libby, Montana, far from Bob's Mexican family. When they first moved, Susan tried her best to learn how to make flour tortillas, a staple of Bob's childhood and a specialty of his native Sonora. For many years, every time she visited his family in Arizona, Susan would ask her mother-in-law for tortilla-making lessons. But when Susan returned to her own kitchen in Montana, the tortillas never tasted the same. She decided to create her own recipe, using buttermilk and vegetable shortening rather than lard. Her flour tortillas are easy to prepare and delicious. Just remember to keep them wrapped in a tea towel to keep warm.

YIELD: ABOUT 18 TORTILLAS

3 cups all-purpose flour plus extra for dusting the board
2 teaspoons baking powder
1 teaspoon salt
5 tablespoons vegetable shortening
1–1¼ cups buttermilk

1. Put the flour, baking powder, and salt in a bowl. Cut in the shortening until the dough forms crumbs, then gradually stir in 1 cup of buttermilk, adding more if needed to make a soft dough. Knead for a few minutes until a pliable, soft, and sticky dough is formed.

2. Coating your palms lightly with shortening, shape the dough into about 18 rounds the size of golf balls and let rest for about 15 minutes.

3. Dust a board with flour and, using a rolling pin, start to roll the dough as thin as possible, rolling from the center out until you have a disk about 8 inches across. Flip it over, making sure you always dust with flour, and roll it out again. If the dough contracts, it needs to rest for a while. Don't worry if your tortillas are not perfectly round. Stack the formed tortillas and cover them.

4. Place the tortillas, 1 at a time, in a heated skillet over medium heat. Within 15–20 seconds you should see bubbles begin to form. Using your fingers or a fork, turn the tortilla over and let it cook for a few more seconds on the other side until bubbles form again. Lift the

tortilla out of the skillet to a plate lined with a towel. Stack them up as you make them and cover with a tea towel so they won't dry out. Serve immediately. You can also wrap the tortillas in a towel and reheat, for just a few seconds, in the microwave.

From India to Amagansett—the Hampton Chutney Company

Dosas—a slightly sour, paper-thin bread made from fermented lentils and rice—are very popular in Indian restaurants today, generally with vegetarians. Primarily a breakfast food in India, they are eaten plain or folded around a filling. But at the Hampton Chutney Company in Amagansett, Long Island, and its tiny, eighteen-seat counterpart in New York's SoHo district, *dosas* serve as a wrap for lunch and dinner as well.

Tasting a *dosa* at Hampton Chutney is quite an adventure. This two-foot-long sandwich comes in about a dozen versions, including grilled chicken breast with cucumber, romaine lettuce, and mango chutney; curried chutney chicken with roasted red peppers and arugula; and tuna mixed with cilantro chutney, grape tomatoes, and arugula. Except for a tiny photo of an Indian guru on the wall and the peaceful sitar music that's piped into the restaurant, no one would know what a journey these designer *dosas* have made.

Gary MacGurn spent twelve years working in an ashram kitchen in India, answering both his spiritual and his culinary callings. It was there, while doing Indian devotional chanting, that he met Swami Muktananda. "Muktananda was the one who taught me how to cook," Gary told me. "His teaching was, Food is God."

Gary also met his wife, Isabel, in the ashram's kitchen. "We were a southern California surfer and a New York Jew," he told me. "In the ashram, I saw how everybody loved *dosas*. I cooked with all these people from all over the world who never tired of the *dosa*." Together Gary and Isabel had fun coming up with fillings: chilies, avocados, portobello mushrooms, fresh grilled corn, and cheese.

When the two married and left the ashram to work in New York, they devised a business plan for selling dosas. "We always felt that people would love *dosa* sandwiches here. They're fast, affordable, yeast-free, wheat-free, and different," said Gary. "We get a lot of Indians coming here who are blown away by the quality of the *dosas*. They know that it's an art."

Dosas

Indian Lentil Crepes

You can make this Indian crepe out of fermented lentils and rice. If that's too much trouble, use a Philippine *lumpia* wrapper, available at Asian stores and many supermarkets. I like to make *dosas* with this traditional potato filling, topped with the jazzy mango chutney that follows. You can also use whatever's in your refrigerator. Have fun with your fillings.

YIELD: 5 DOSAS

½ cup urd dal *(white lentils), available in Indian grocery stores*
2 cups short-grain rice
1 tablespoon fenugreek *(optional)*
½ tablespoon salt
Vegetable oil for frying

1. Soak the lentils, rice, fenugreek, and salt in a bowl of cold water to cover, for about 3 hours. Grind the rice and the lentils in a food processor, using just a little of the water but reserving the remaining water. Place in a bowl, cover, and leave to ferment at room temperature for at least 12 hours. When the lentils start to smell sour they are ready. Otherwise, wait another few hours. The mixture should be the consistency of crepe batter. Add water if too thick.

2. Heat a griddle or large heavy skillet to medium, then sprinkle with water and wipe clean with a towel. Spray oil on the griddle. Scoop up about ¾ cup of batter in a measuring cup. Pour a little on the center of the griddle and continue to pour in a circle outward, gently flattening the batter and swirling around and around with the bottom of the measuring cup, until a large paper-thin circle about 12 inches in diameter is formed. Cook until crisp and golden in color. Do not turn.

3. Place about ½ cup of filling down the center, then roll and serve immediately.

Potato Masala

¼ cup vegetable oil

1 dried red chili

1 teaspoon black mustard seeds

4 curry leaves

½ cup fresh or frozen peas

2 jalapeño peppers, seeds removed and sliced into julienne strips

2 inches gingerroot, peeled and sliced into julienne strips

1 large onion, sliced into julienne strips

1 tablespoon ground turmeric

1 tomato, sliced thinly

1 teaspoon salt

2 large potatoes, peeled, cooked, and coarsely mashed, about 1¼ pounds

2 tablespoons chopped cilantro

Heat the oil in a frying pan and add the chili, mustard seeds, curry leaves, peas, jalapeños, ginger, onion, and turmeric. Cook until the onion is soft, then add the tomato and salt and heat through. Fold in the potatoes and heat through. Sprinkle with the cilantro and stir in.

Mango Chutney

Slathered on Gary MacGurn's *dosas* are six kinds of chutneys, made and marketed by his Hampton Chutney Company. These chutneys, first sold at the Amagansett Farmers' Market, are now produced for supermarkets around the country. This fresh, slightly sweet chutney is not like the sweet mango chutney I remember from my childhood. If Gary's home version of his commercial sauce isn't sweet enough for you, add a little brown sugar. I serve it on sandwiches and with chicken or fish; it's delicious and very refreshing.

Mango Chutney (continued)

4 ripe mangoes (about 4 pounds)

1 jalapeño pepper
(seeds removed if desired)

½ ounce fresh gingerroot
(about 2 inches), peeled

½ cup apple cider vinegar

Juice of 2 lemons

½ cup chopped fresh cilantro

1 teaspoon salt

2 tablespoons vegetable oil

½ tablespoon cumin seeds

½ tablespoon black mustard seeds

1 tablespoon brown sugar
(optional)

1. Peel and chop the mangoes coarsely. (See page 17 for instructions on peeling and cutting mangoes.) Place in the bowl of a food processor with the jalapeño, ginger, apple cider vinegar, lemon juice, cilantro, and salt. Do not pulse yet.

2. Heat the oil almost to smoking in a small skillet. Toss in the cumin and mustard seeds and cook for a few minutes, stirring. Drain most of the oil and add the spices to the food processor.

3. Using the steel blade pulse just to combine; you do not want a purée. Taste, and if the chutney is too bitter, add a little brown sugar.

Bukharan Flatbread

Flatbreads are eaten either topped with onions, cheese, and tomatoes, like pizza, or formed into sandwich wrappers. Traditionally, they are slapped onto the inside wall of a tandoori clay oven and cooked very quickly. I learned to make this bread at the Uzbek-istan Tandoori Bakery in Queens. As soon as Arye Barayev got his green card, he returned to Uzbekistan and brought back an authentic Uzbek oven. He also brought back with him a baker whose family has been crafting this flatbread for generations. Although expert bakers tend to bring their own secret nuances to each production, a fair adaptation of the *lepeshka* (Bukharan flatbread) can be made at home in a conventional oven with a baking stone.

2½ cups lukewarm water

1 package (1 scant tablespoon)
active dry yeast

2 teaspoons sugar

1 tablespoon salt, or to taste

1. Mix the water, yeast, and sugar in a large bowl or the bowl of a mixer equipped with a dough hook. Gradually add the salt and 5 cups of the flour, a cup at a time, mixing well after each addition.

2. Knead by hand or with the dough hook until the dough is smooth and elastic, adding enough of the remaining flour to prevent sticking.

6½–7 cups high-gluten or bread flour

2 teaspoons white sesame seeds

2 teaspoons black sesame seeds

Ice cubes

3. Shape the dough into a ball and place in a greased bowl, turning to coat. Cover with plastic wrap and let rise in a warm room until doubled in bulk, at least 1½ hours.

4. Divide the dough into 4 pieces and shape each piece into a ball. On a floured surface, roll out each ball into a round about 8 inches in diameter. Using a pastry brush, brush each round with cold water. Cover with a towel and let stand for 30 minutes.

5. Line the lowest rack of the oven with a baking stone or bricks and set a baking sheet on top, or 2 sheets if you have a large oven. Preheat the oven to 500 degrees.

6. Brush the dough with a little oil. Using the heel of your hand, press the dough down in the center to make a round of about 10–11 inches, then prick it with the tines of a fork to make a design (use a clean flower-arranging frog if you have one—it is perfect for this). Brush the rounds with water, then sprinkle each round with the white and black sesame seeds.

7. Remove the baking sheet or sheets from the oven. Carefully place 2 rounds on one sheet, leaving space between, and sprinkle lightly with cold water. Bake one sheet at a time on the lowest rack of the oven, and just before you shut the door, put a few ice cubes in a pan on the oven floor to create steam. Bake until the breads are golden, 12–15 minutes. Remove from the oven. Let the loaves rest 10 minutes, while you preheat the second baking sheet and repeat. Eat immediately, if possible.

Jean-Louis Palladin's Brioche

When you sat down at the restaurant Jean-Louis at the Watergate Hotel, the first thing the waiter used to bring out was a slice of warm brioche and two ramekins: one filled with anchovy butter, the other with plain good French butter at room temperature. The flavor of the light, rich brioche in contrast with a tiny slab of anchovy butter was pure nirvana.

I was lucky enough to learn how to bake this brioche from the master. When Jean-Louis made brioche, he let the loaves rise for hours right next to pots of simmering stock. He was always generous in sharing his energy and enthusiasm. I have been told that Anna Ramos, a woman from El Salvador whom he taught, is still making his brioche for the Watergate. Thank you, Jean-Louis!

YIELD: 2 LOAVES

2 scant tablespoons (2 packages) active dry yeast
¾ cup warm water
8½ cups all-purpose flour
¾ cup sugar
4 teaspoons salt
10 large eggs
2½ cups (5 sticks) unsalted butter, softened

1. Dissolve the yeast in the warm water.

2. Place the flour in the bowl of a heavy-duty electric mixer, then add the sugar and salt and start beating slowly, with a dough hook, adding the dissolved yeast mixture.

3. Add the eggs one by one and continue beating, on the slowest speed, for about 10 minutes. (This may seem like a long time, but it takes that long for the eggs to mix with the flour and to attain a smooth, shiny texture. Let the machine rest briefly if it begins to overheat.) Add the butter, little by little, continuing to beat until the butter is totally absorbed and the dough is smooth, about 3 minutes. Sprinkle with additional flour.

4. Let the dough rise, covered, in the mixing bowl for 6 hours at room temperature. Punch it down and let it rise, covered, in the refrigerator overnight.

5. The next day, form the dough into 3 cylinders. Then divide each cylinder into plum-size pieces, about 2 ounces each. Roll each piece into a log 3 inches long and fit them crosswise in 2 layers in two 9-inch loaf pans. You should have 7 or 8 logs per row.

6. Let the dough rise, covered, for about 3 hours in a very warm room or in the oven with a pilot light, until it reaches the top of the pans.

7. Preheat the oven to 350 degrees and bake for about 25 minutes or until the loaves are golden on top.

Anchovy Butter

Herb butters with fresh basil or dill are quite commonplace these days. But this anchovy butter was one of the first butter spreads. To make an herbed butter, substitute about two ounces of fresh herbs for the anchovies.

YIELD: 1 CUP

1 cup (2 sticks) unsalted butter, at room temperature

16 large anchovy fillets (about 1⅓ ounces), packed in oil

Purée the butter with the drained anchovy fillets in a food processor. With a plastic spatula transfer the mixture to a ramekin. Cover and chill. Soften to room temperature before serving.

THE BUTTERING OF AMERICA

Good American butter is back on the table. With the farmer-to-restaurant movement, chefs often make a point of telling customers what boutique butter they are using in their restaurants, usually higher in butterfat and lower in moisture than regular brands. At Chanterelle's twenty-fifth-anniversary dinner in New York, the owners served their homemade artisanal breads with two butters: unsalted, light, creamy Plugra from Pennsylvania, and salted Devonshire double-cream from England. When I asked why they did that, the general manager said that the option of two good butters is a nice indulgence.

Typical of many producers of good American butter is Alison Hooper, who spent her junior year of college in France, working on a dairy farm. Then she returned to America knowing she wanted to be a cheese and butter maker. It was natural that she would go to Vermont, a dairy state, where she had summered as a child. After a stint at the Vermont Department of Agriculture, she was in business. Alison's butter, with its 86 percent fat content (most American butter has a lower fat content and more water), is close to good French butter.

Incidentally, it turns out that butter is less of a health hazard than margarine and other hydrogenated vegetable oil spreads, which contain trans-fatty acids, an artery-clogging fat.

Swedish Cardamom Bread

Douglas Stieber got hooked on baking when he worked washing dishes as a teenager at Frederick's Bakery in Sheboygan, Wisconsin. He married the baker's daughter, Geralyn, and baked there until it closed a few years ago. Instead of working at a large supermarket in-store bakery, he now runs a state-of-the-art bakery at Kohler's America's Club, making high-end artisan-style rustic baguettes as well as the traditional semmel rolls with the help of his son and apprentice, Nicholas.

To honor his area's Scandinavian immigrants, he makes this cardamom bread every holiday season. No wonder it's a local favorite. For an even more intense cardamom flavor, peel and grind the cardamom pods yourself.

YIELD: 2 LOAVES

1 scant tablespoon (1 package) active dry yeast
½ cup warm water
¾ cup lukewarm milk
½ cup sugar
1 teaspoon salt
3 large eggs
2 teaspoons freshly peeled and ground cardamom
6¼–6½ cups all-purpose unbleached flour, plus extra for kneading
½ cup (1 stick) unsalted butter, melted and cooled
2 tablespoons coarsely chopped almonds
2 tablespoons pearl sugar or granulated sugar

1. Dissolve the yeast in the water in a small bowl. Put the milk, sugar, salt, 2 eggs, cardamom, and 2 cups of the flour in the bowl of an electric mixer equipped with the paddle. Beat until smooth. Add the melted butter and blend well. Switch to the dough hook and blend in the remaining flour, 1 cup at a time, until the dough is satiny smooth.

2. Remove the dough, wash out the bowl, and grease it with vegetable spray. Return the dough to the bowl, cover, and set in a warm place for about 1½–2 hours or until about doubled in volume.

3. Punch the dough down and knead on a lightly floured board.

4. Divide the dough into 6 equal portions. Roll each portion between your hands to make a 14-inch-long strand. Place 3 strands side by side in the center of a greased baking sheet; braid from the center to each end, pinching the ends to seal and tucking them slightly under the loaf. Repeat to make the second loaf.

5. Preheat the oven to 350 degrees.

6. Cover lightly with a towel and set in a warm place about 45 minutes.

7. Beat the remaining egg and gently brush over the tops and sides of the loaves. Sprinkle each loaf with half of the coarsely chopped almonds and half of the sugar. Bake until richly browned, approximately 25 minutes. Cool on wire racks. Slice to serve.

Holiday Challah

When a bread goes mainstream, like Jewish challah, you can buy it 365 days a year. People eat it because it tastes good. Homemade challah, which I make each week for the Sabbath, is simply scrumptious. The dough, similar to Portuguese sweet bread, can also be rolled out and spread with onions and poppy seeds, sprinkled with salt, and rolled up into delicious onion rolls, or it can be made into equally delicious hamburger rolls for Danny Meyer's tuna burgers (page 73). You can also cut the challah thick for fabulous French toast (page 25). This is my favorite recipe, one that I learned from Chasidic Jews who carried the religious tradition with them from Eastern Europe to Brooklyn and Jerusalem. Some people like raisins in their challah. I prefer them cut into very small pieces in the food processor. You will need about ½ cup raisins.

YIELD: 2 CHALLAHS

1½ tablespoons (1½ packages) active dry yeast
1 tablespoon plus ½ cup sugar
1¾ cups lukewarm water
½ cup vegetable oil
3 large eggs
1 tablespoon salt
8–8½ cups all-purpose flour
Poppy or sesame seeds for sprinkling

1. Dissolve the yeast and 1 tablespoon of the sugar in the water in a large bowl.

2. Whisk the oil into the yeast mixture, then beat in 2 of the eggs, 1 at a time, along with the remaining sugar and the salt. (You can also use a mixer with a dough hook for both mixing and kneading.) Gradually add 8 cups of flour and stir. When the dough holds together, it is ready for kneading.

3. Turn the dough onto a floured surface and knead until smooth. Clean out the bowl and grease it, then return the dough to the bowl. Cover with plastic wrap and let the dough rise in a warm place for 1 hour. (You may put the dough in an oven that has been warmed to 150 degrees then turned off.) When the dough has almost doubled in volume, punch it down, cover, and let it rise again in a warm place for another half hour.

4. To make a 6-braided challah, take half the dough and form into 6 balls. With your hands, roll each ball into a strand tapered at the ends, about 12 inches long and 1½ inches wide. Pinch the strands together at one end, then gently spread them apart. Next, move the outside right strand over 2 strands. Then, take the second strand from the left and move it to the far right. Regroup to 3 on each side. Take the outside left

strand and move it over 2 to the middle, then move the second strand from the right over to the far left. Regroup and start over with the outside right strand. Continue until all the strands are braided, tucking the ends underneath the loaf. The key is always to have 3 strands on each side, so you can keep your braid balanced. Make a second loaf the same way. Place the braided loaves in greased 10-by-4-inch loaf pans or on a greased cookie sheet with at least 2 inches between them.

5. Beat the remaining egg and brush it on the loaves. Let rise another hour.

6. Preheat the oven to 350 degrees and brush the loaves with egg again, then sprinkle on poppy or sesame seeds.

7. Bake for 35–40 minutes or until golden. Tap to make sure the loaves sound hollow. Remove from the pans and cool on a rack.

Note: To make rolls, take some dough, about the size of a tennis ball, roll it out to about 12 inches, and swirl into a roll. Place on a greased cookie sheet and bake for about 20 minutes in a 350-degree oven.

Union Square Cafe's Tuna Burger

Sometimes the best recipes happen almost by accident. "Take the tuna burger," says Danny Meyer, the owner of the Union Square Cafe in New York City. "It was an outrageous thing."

Every day, after prepping the tuna filet mignon, a menu mainstay, Danny's staff was stumped over what to do with the leftover tuna. They tried everything: tuna sloppy joes, tuna club sandwiches, even a sashimi salad niçoise. Then one day the late cookbook author Pierre Franey walked into the restaurant and suggested, "Why don't you do a burger topped with a ginger mustard glaze on a bun?" The tuna burger has been on the café's menu ever since. It's even sparked other outrageous burgers: foie gras burgers, lobster burgers, even an ostrich burger. Here is the Union Square Cafe's tuna burger. I've tried grilling these burgers. Don't make that same mistake. Grilling makes the tuna tough. Fry them instead; the flavor is in the caramelization. Use a heavy-bottom pan to get the entire surface of the burger nice and brown. I have also included recipes for two sauces: the ginger-mustard glaze used at Union Square, and a ginger-wasabi mayonnaise that I tasted at Butterfield 9, a Washington, D.C., restaurant. Try them both!

YIELD: 4 SERVINGS

1½ pounds yellowfin tuna, skin removed

2 teaspoons minced garlic

3 tablespoons Dijon mustard

½ teaspoon cayenne

¼ cup extra-virgin olive or grapeseed oil

1 teaspoon kosher salt

¼ teaspoon freshly ground black pepper

4 fresh hamburger buns with seeds

½ cup Japanese pickled ginger, available in Japanese specialty food shops (optional)

1. Grind the tuna in a grinder or chop with a large sharp knife to the texture of tuna tartare or ground beef. Don't use a food processor, which will shred the tuna rather than chop it. Remove as much gristle as possible.

2. Transfer the ground tuna to a bowl and mix thoroughly with the garlic, mustard, and cayenne. Divide the tuna into 4 equal portions. Using your hands, roll each portion into a smooth ball, then flatten it into a compact patty.

3. Heat the oil in a large heavy skillet over medium-high heat, sprinkle the patties with salt and pepper, and sear until browned and medium-rare, 3–4 minutes on each side—they should be almost raw in the center. Slice 1 open if you are not sure of the 3 minutes on each side. Serve each burger on a buttered, toasted bun and spread with a tablespoon of warm ginger-mustard glaze or ginger-wasabi mayonnaise. Garnish the burgers with equal amounts of pickled ginger slices, if you like.

Ginger-Mustard Glaze

This is the classic topping from the Union Square Cafe.

YIELD: ½ CUP

⅓ cup teriyaki sauce
2 teaspoons minced ginger
½ clove garlic, minced
(about ½ teaspoon)
1 tablespoon honey
1 tablespoon Dijon mustard
½ teaspoon white wine vinegar

Stir the teriyaki sauce, ginger, garlic, honey, Dijon mustard, and white wine vinegar together in a 1-quart saucepan and bring to a boil. Lower the heat and simmer until the glaze coats the back of a spoon, about 5 minutes. Reserve in a warm place until the tuna burgers are cooked. The glaze can be prepared up to 2 days ahead and stored, covered, in the refrigerator.

Ginger-Wasabi Mayonnaise

I tasted this mayonnaise at Butterfield 9 in Washington, D.C., on their tuna burger, and it was fabulous. Made like an aioli, it can also be used on crab cakes (page 272).

YIELD: ½ CUP

1 large egg yolk
1 teaspoon Dijon mustard
½ cup grapeseed, peanut,
vegetable, or other
neutral-flavored oil
1 ounce or 1 medium-size knob
of gingerroot
1–2 tablespoons fresh
wasabi paste

1. Mix the egg yolk and the mustard in a medium bowl. In a steady stream, whisk in the oil to make an emulsion.

2. Peel and grate the ginger fine. (A microplane, a grater like those used by carpenters and engineers, is fabulous for this.) Whisk into the mayonnaise, along with 1 tablespoon wasabi. Taste; if you like it stronger, as I do, add another tablespoon of wasabi paste.

WHY WASABI?

Wasabi—that Japanese flavoring that burns your nose and tastes great in mashed potatoes has nothing to do with horseradish. It's not even a root; it's a member of the mustard family, actually a rhizome that grows aboveground rather than in the ground like horseradish. But most so-called wasabi powders sold today are made of ground horseradish, mustard, and green food coloring. Until Pacific Farms in Eugene, Oregon, started growing wasabi in 1991, the plant was always imported from Japan. Roy Carver III, a southern California real estate developer, started the farm after a long search for a new agricultural product. He chose wasabi because it wasn't cultivated in the United States. And he chose Oregon because its growing conditions are closest to those of Japan. Now he ships his paste throughout the United States and abroad.

"He doesn't have wasabi, dear."

GOOD CALIFORNIA GOUDA

Lots of American companies make processed Gouda cheese, but how many make boutique Gouda cheese from raw milk? Jules Wesselink, a dairy farmer from Haarlem, Holland, came to southern California after World War II to seek a better life. In an area with many dairy farmers, he, too, became a dairy farmer, selling his milk to a cooperative. In 1995 he took a trip to Holland and, just for fun, brought back a Gouda cheese–making kit—talk about a souvenir!

Back in California, he made two cheese wheels. His friends thought they were so good they asked him to make more. Now his Winchester Cheese Company makes eight hundred pounds of cheese per day, from the milk of his five hundred Holstein cows. He sells his cheese mostly at southern California farmers' markets and, occasionally, to stores like Murray's in Manhattan.

Grilled Cheese Sandwich with Eggplant and Tomatoes

What's more American than a grilled cheese sandwich? I like mine fried in a frying pan and weighted down so the bread is browned and the cheese oozes out. These days there are so many varieties: Stilton with pears and walnuts on pumpernickel, or cheddar and bacon with caramelized onions on rye. My new favorite grilled cheese sandwich comes from the Galley, a tiny takeout shack in the fishing village of Menemsha on Martha's Vineyard. In 1999, Barbara Fenner, a 1976 Culinary Institute of America graduate, changed the menu slightly. "When I took over the Galley, the only vegetarian alternatives we had on the menu were a veggie burger and a grilled cheese sandwich," she told me while grilling her last eggplant sandwich of the summer season. "I knew I had to make sandwiches fast and quick, and I didn't have a lot of room to make them in. I was in the kitchen fooling around and I came up with the grilled eggplant sandwich idea." Barbara knew it would be a hit when an Italian taxicab driver told her, with tears in his eyes, that he hadn't tasted anything like it since his grandmother died.

This is my take on her recipe, using fresh tomatoes and Vermont cheddar cheese. In winter, I substitute sun-dried tomatoes preserved in oil.

YIELD: 4 SANDWICHES

¾ cup vegetable oil
1 teaspoon salt
½ teaspoon black pepper
1 garlic clove, minced
1 medium eggplant
(about 1 pound),
cut in ½-inch-thick rounds
1 tomato, sliced, or 1 cup
sun-dried tomatoes,
in olive oil, drained
8 thick slices of Vermont
cheddar cheese
8 slices whole-wheat bread
(page 78)
2 tablespoons butter

1. Preheat the broiler and set the rack 4 inches below the top. Cover a baking sheet with aluminum foil.

2. Mix the oil with the salt, pepper, and garlic in a small bowl. Dip the eggplant slices in the oil, shaking to get rid of any excess oil, and place on the baking sheet. Place under the broiler for 5 minutes or until the eggplant is golden. Flip the eggplant over, continue cooking until golden, remove, and cool on the cookie sheet.

3. Place the eggplant and tomatoes in a medium mixing bowl. Don't worry about the excess oil.

4. When ready to make the sandwiches, place a piece of cheese on each slice of bread, and add about ¼ of the eggplant and tomatoes on each of the 4 slices. Top with the other 4 bread slices.

5. Melt the butter in a skillet or griddle over medium heat and grill the sandwiches a few minutes on each side, until the crust is a crisp, golden brown.

Rancho La Puerta Spa Bread

In the 1940s Deborah Szekely, the daughter of a vegetarian-fruitarian family, and her husband, Edmund, founded a tent colony in northern Mexico, just south of San Diego, known as Rancho La Puerta. Eating healthy, mostly raw food, including organic vegetables and cheese made from their own goats, they germinated their own grain, ground it, and formed it into crackers, baked in the sun in the summer and in ovens in winter.

Little by little, Rancho La Puerta grew, its reputation spreading by word of mouth. Today it is known, with its sister spa, Golden Door, as a world-class spa. "It is still luxurious in its simplicity," Deborah Szekely avowed. "Retreats reflect and redirect your life." The spa serves healthy soups and salads with herbs from the garden. "People come not to lose weight but to have an annual tune-up." This dense bread recipe is a specialty of Rancho La Puerta and is still served there. It is delicious toasted by itself or as a base for sandwiches. Add some flaxseed, if you like.

YIELD: 2 LOAVES

2 scant tablespoons (2 packets) active dry yeast
2 tablespoons honey
3½ cups lukewarm water
2 tablespoons cold-pressed or other vegetable oil
2 tablespoons dark molasses
1 tablespoon salt
1 cup wheat bran
¼ cup flaxseed (optional)
6–6½ cups whole-wheat flour, plus more for dusting

1. Use an electric mixer fitted with a dough hook, if you have one. Dissolve the yeast and honey in the warm water in the mixer bowl. Add the oil and molasses.

2. Combine the salt, bran, flaxseed (if using), and 6 cups of the whole-wheat flour. While the mixer is running at slow speed, add the flour mixture, 1 cup at a time, and mix until the dough pulls away from the sides of the bowl. If the dough is too sticky, add the extra ½ cup of flour. Continue mixing until the dough is smooth and elastic.

3. Place the dough in a clean, lightly floured mixing bowl, cover with a damp towel, and let rise in a warm, draft-free spot for 30–40 minutes, until doubled in volume.

4. Preheat the oven to 350 degrees and grease two 9-by-5-inch loaf pans lightly with vegetable oil.

5. Turn the dough onto a lightly floured work surface; knead for a minute or so, until smooth. Form into 2 loaves and place them in the prepared pans. Cover again with a towel and let rise for 20–30 minutes.

6. Bake for 50 minutes or until browned on top and firm on the bottom. Turn out of the pans onto a wire rack and let cool.

My Favorite Multigrain Oatmeal Bread

The oatmeal bread that I have been making for years is a descendant of the "health" bread popularized in the nineteenth century. Today, health breads are more in demand than ever. Just look at supermarket shelves: multigrain, seven-grain, low-carb, all "healthy" packaged breads.

The late Edna Rostow, an avid cook, taught me to make her signature bread, which she always set out on a wooden board for her family. Through the years, making the bread for my own family, I have simplified the recipe. Sometimes I add leftover cooked cereal, flaxseeds, wheat berries (soaked first in water), or any whole grains that I happen to have in my kitchen.

YIELD: 2 LOAVES

2 tablespoons (2 packets) active dry yeast
3 cups lukewarm water
⅓–½ cup honey
2 cups old-fashioned oatmeal
1 tablespoon kosher salt
1 cup toasted wheat germ
1 cup bran, oat, or soy flakes
2 cups whole-wheat flour
4 cups (approximately) all-purpose flour

1. Dissolve the yeast in the lukewarm water in a large bowl. Stir until well mixed.

2. Stir in the honey, then add the oatmeal, salt, wheat germ, and bran, oat, or soy flakes. Mix well. Stir in the whole-wheat flour and 3½ cups of the all-purpose flour to form a smooth dough. (This can also be done in a standing mixer.) Turn out of the bowl and knead until a firm, slightly sticky dough is formed, adding more all-purpose flour if needed.

3. Put the dough in a greased bowl and cover. Let it rise for at least 1 hour or until it is doubled in volume.

4. Preheat the oven to 375 degrees and grease two 9-by-5-inch or equivalent baking pans. If you have a baking stone, insert it in the oven.

5. Punch down the dough and divide it in half. Form 2 loaves and place them in the prepared bread pans. Let rise another half hour.

6. Bake for 40 minutes or until the loaves sound hollow when tapped. Turn out of the pans and let cool on a rack. This bread is great for sandwiches.

An Asparagus Bacon Sandwich

There are many variations on the classic bacon, lettuce, and tomato sandwich. When I went to the farmers' market in San Francisco at Ferry Plaza, a long line was forming for the grilled salmon BLT at the Hays Street Grill stand.

I tried this asparagus and bacon sandwich recipe in Hadley, Massachusetts, a town that was once called the "asparagus capital of the world." Located north of Springfield in the Pioneer Valley, the area is still known today for the green spring spear, referred to locally as "Hadley's grass." My friend David Nussbaum, a food writer who lives nearby, got the recipe from Marion Zuchowski, a third-generation asparagus grower, and published it in *Saveur* magazine, when he did a story on the Zuchowski family and others who've been asparagus growers there for three generations. I like a little mayonnaise on my sandwich, but you can use just butter, or both if you wish.

YIELD: 4 SANDWICHES

1 pound asparagus
2 tablespoons butter
Salt and freshly ground black pepper to taste
8 pieces buttered toast
12 slices cooked bacon
2 tablespoons mayonnaise (optional)

1. Bring about 4 inches of water to a boil in the bottom of a steamer pot.

2. Prepare the asparagus by bending the spears gently until they break naturally. Discard the ends. Cut the asparagus into 2-inch pieces and rinse.

3. Steam asparagus in a steamer basket over the pot of simmering water until soft, but not mushy, 8–10 minutes.

4. Transfer to a bowl, toss with the butter, and season to taste with salt and pepper.

5. To make the sandwiches, divide the spears equally among 4 pieces of buttered toast, then arrange slices of cooked bacon on top of each. Smear mayonnaise on the remaining pieces of toast, if you like, and top the sandwiches with them.

Tempeh Reuben Sandwich

"I'll have the corned beef, please."

"Oh, yeah, I'll have pastrami on white bread with mayonnaise, tomato, and lettuce."

—ANNIE HALL

In 1977 Woody Allen got a lot of laughs from this now famous line after he ordered the conventional corned beef on rye. In those days, corned beef and pastrami went with rye bread and mustard, period. But today anything goes, even vegetarian corned beef. Like eggplant, tempeh takes on the flavor of its seasonings. Try this sandwich, similar in flavor to the Reuben sandwich, which is, of course, traditionally made with corned beef.

YIELD: 3 SANDWICHES

1 package (8 ounces) tempeh*

4 tablespoons olive, sesame, or canola oil

6 slices Swiss cheese

6 slices pumpernickel or rye bread†

3 tablespoons Russian dressing

3 tablespoons yellow mustard

6 tablespoons sauerkraut, well drained

1. Cut the tempeh in half and fillet each piece into 3 thin squares, giving you 6 pieces total.

2. Heat the oil in a large frying pan, and fry 1 side of the tempeh squares in oil until golden brown on the bottom. Flip the tempeh over and place 1 slice of cheese on each piece while the other side is browning. When the cheese begins to melt, flip 1 piece of tempeh onto another, so the cheese sides are touching. Repeat for the other slices of tempeh, giving you 3 pieces. Continue to cook to melt the cheese completely. Remove the tempeh from the pan and drain on a paper towel.

3. Fry the 6 slices of bread on both sides in the frying pan. Once the bread is a nice golden color, remove it from the pan and spread Russian dressing over 3 pieces and mustard over the remaining 3.

4. Place the tempeh squares on each of the dressing-smeared bread slices and top with 2 tablespoons of sauerkraut. Put the remaining bread, mustard side down, on each sandwich. Cut and serve.

* If tempeh is not available in your local market, or if you are a meat lover, just use corned beef in place of tempeh.

† See my *Jewish Cooking in America* or *Joan Nathan's Jewish Holiday Cookbook* for recipes for pumpernickel and rye breads.

In the late 1960s Michael Cohen dropped out of college and by the early seventies had moved to Greenfield, Massachusetts. A hippie hangout during that period of alternative lifestyles, Greenfield was a place where people were looking for meaningful ways of saving the planet. Cohen, like everyone else, was a member of the local co-op, which today looks surprisingly like an upscale Whole Foods Market.

"We wanted to change the way people thought about the food they ate, to eliminate world hunger, to show people how to have a healthier body and a healthier planet," Michael told me as we toured his home near Greenfield. In the mid-seventies Michael became a founding partner of one of this country's first non-Asian tofu factories. "Four of us started a tofu company called Laughing Grasshopper Tofu," he said. The tofu was "aged" in handmade oak barrels and delivered twice a week to health food stores and cooperatives in the Pioneer Valley and Boston.

By 1978, customers began to ask for tempeh, a soy-based protein staple from Indonesia. Tempeh, a product that was first developed two thousand years ago, is sold in sheets and looks like a bumpy cutlet; it is made from boiled, cultured soybeans. Cohen decided he would produce tempeh in the United States. With a small loan from his father, he started Tempehworks in 1979, and he met his wife and business partner, Chia Collins, there in 1980.

Since tempeh does not have much flavor of its own, the Cohens' challenge was to give it some. With the help of the food science department at the University of Massachusetts at Amherst, they used taste enhancements—pickling spices, coriander, garlic, fennel, and mustard—to add a meaty flavor. Their first product was veggie burgers.

In a brilliant move, the two vegetarians contracted with a small meat hot dog factory in Pittsfield to make "Tofu Pups," the first vegetarian hot dogs. Tofu Pups made the front page of *USA Today*, Peter Jennings mentioned them on *World News Tonight*, and they were a "hot pick" in *Newsweek*. "Literally the nature of our business just changed overnight," said Michael.

Five years later a consumer wrote the Cohens asking why they couldn't make Tofu Pups without fat. Soon Smart Dogs appeared. "Smart Dogs took off like a wildflower in Colorado," said Michael. "Supermarkets were calling us 'truly an overnight sensation.' It was the first totally fat-free hot dog in the world." In 2000 ConAgra, the food conglomerate, purchased Lightlife for millions of dollars. And Cohen and Collins still shop at their local food co-op.

Pita Bread

The name for this thickish pocket flatbread comes from the Greek *petta,* meaning "a flat bread." Replicating authentic pita is not difficult if you have a baking stone or tiles. To refresh the bread, pop it into the microwave or a medium oven, slice, and stuff. This is a great bread for sandwiches.

At Samos Restaurant in Baltimore's Greek Town, I tasted a delicious Greek feta cheese pita pizza. Nick Loukourgo, who runs the restaurant started by his late father, told me that he created this pizza because his sons wanted American pizza. Top your pita with leftovers and feta or goat cheese. Just heat the oven to 450 degrees and bake the pita pizza for about ten minutes.

YIELD: 12 PITA BREADS

1 scant tablespoon (1 package) active dry yeast
1½ cups warm water
1 tablespoon olive oil
1 teaspoon salt
3½ cups (approximately) all-purpose flour

1. Sprinkle the yeast into a large bowl and pour the warm water on top. Stir until the yeast is dissolved; add the olive oil and salt and mix well. Mix in enough of the flour so that the dough is difficult to stir. You can use a food processor or an electric mixer with a dough hook.

2. Turn the dough onto a floured surface and knead for about 10 minutes, adding more flour as necessary to make a firm, elastic dough, or continue to knead in the food processor or mixer. Place the dough in a greased bowl and let rise, covered, for about 1½ hours or until it has doubled in volume.

3. Preheat the oven to 500 degrees. Line 1 rack with baking tiles or a baking stone. (If you don't have either, heat a baking sheet.)

4. Turn the dough onto a large floured surface and cut into 12 equal pieces. Using your hands, form each into a ball about the size of a Ping-Pong ball. Let rest, covered with a towel, for 5 minutes.

5. Flour the work surface lightly. Using a rolling pin, roll each ball out to a disk 6 inches in diameter. The dough will be very elastic, so roll firmly, sprinkling a little more flour as necessary to keep it from sticking. Cover the circles and let rest for 15 minutes.

6. If you have a pizza paddle, dust it with flour and transfer 2 of the rounds to it, then slide them onto the hot tiles or stone. Otherwise, gently pick up the disks with your fingers and toss them onto the tiles. Bake for 3 minutes. The pita disks will have puffed up into balloons. Remove them with tongs or a spatula to a rack, where they will quickly deflate. Repeat with the remaining rounds.

PITA PIES IN FALL RIVER, MASSACHUSETTS

The story of Sam's Meat Pies, located in a low-slung brick building on a side street in Fall River, Massachusetts, is the story of many immigrant bread bakeries across America. Inside the bakery, lines form for meat pies made out of pita, the mountain bread first brought here by Lebanese immigrants early in the twentieth century.

The bakery's founder, Saleen Yamin, was born in Fall River. But he went back to Lebanon every summer, returning after World War II with his childhood sweetheart, Georgette, as his bride. Together they opened a bakery specializing in pita for the immigrant population who lived and worked in the textile mills of Fall River.

"At the beginning of the McDonald's era, all of a sudden there was a need for fast food, and we went from a bread bakery to a meat pie bakery," Dora Yamin, one of the owners' six daughters, told me. Soon Sam's (the family felt *Sam* sounded more American than *Saleen*) started making triangular and open-face meat pies. Now their repertoire includes broccoli, spinach, and cheese pies for vegetarians and chorizo pies to satisfy Fall River's Portuguese community. When I visited the bakery, a long line of people formed, ordering pies by the dozen for relatives as far off as Florida.

"Our pies are like chow mein and coffee syrup," Dora continued. "People come back to Fall River for nostalgic food."

In Belden Place, a crowded side street in down-town San Francisco informally known as the French Quarter, stood, until recently, a tiny restaurant called Café 52. The restaurant served French and Middle Eastern food. Most of the regulars had no idea that Setrak Injaian, the chef-owner, was the originator of that San Francisco classic the Aram sandwich.

> Our favorite item (taste it once and you're hooked) is called the Aram sandwich. It's roast beef, cream cheese, lettuce, and tomato rolled in Armenian lavash bread.
> —FROMMER'S SAN FRANCISCO, 1981–1982

"My mother used to bake bread at home," said Setrak, a man with a big smile, whom I met shortly before his death. "She would roll the dough, open it up really thin, then put it on a wok turned upside down to bake it, and we'd have this cracker-type bread called lavash. Then she would moisten the lavash, wrap it like a cone, and put feta cheese, tomatoes, and olives in it, and that was breakfast."

When Setrak came to America from his native Haifa, he owned the Caravansary Restaurant, a simple sandwich, tea, and spice shop. "I got tired of people ordering turkey sandwiches on dark bread with mayonnaise. We started getting very busy, and people asked for weird things like 'hold the mayo, hold the lettuce,' or they'd put 'ketchup on everything.' So I figured out the best thing for me. One day a customer was ordering a sandwich with white turkey meat on dark bread and dark turkey meat on white bread. I got very upset and I thought, 'I am not making it.' I pulled down the menu from the wall and I put up a chalkboard with a few sandwiches on it."

The next day, on his way to work, Setrak bought two packages of lavash bread at a deli and wet them down, the way he remembered his Armenian mother doing. He softened up the cream cheese, added slices of roast beef and marinated cucumbers, rolled it all up like a burrito, and sold them all. "One of my partners had a new baby boy named Aram, so I named the sandwich after him," Setrak told me.

After watching Setrak prepare his roll-up using the original hard cracker bread, I found a more practical way to make it, with the soft lavash available in many grocery stores. If the lavash gets dry, sprinkle it with water to make it more pliable. You can also use a double layer of the lavash so it won't tear, but be sure that both pieces are softened with sprinkles of water.

The ingredients are not set in stone, so use your imagination and what's available in your refrigerator. I used goat cheese, olive spread, sun-dried tomatoes, mozzarella, and chopped fresh basil. Roll gently but tightly—a second set of hands is helpful. Then wrap in plastic wrap and place the rolled sandwich in the refrigerator until it's time to serve it. Trim the ends, and cut in slices to serve. This is great for parties and potlucks!

Vermont Anadama Bread

Carol Reynolds, a teacher and the wife of a maple syrup producer in East Hardwick, Vermont, uses her husband's grade B, dark amber maple syrup instead of molasses in her anadama bread. She also tears off a piece of the dough to make pizza. I tried it, sprinkling it with Vermont goat cheese, peppers, tomatoes, and fresh basil. It was delicious.

YIELD: 2 LOAVES

2½ cups water
½ cup stone-ground cornmeal
1 scant tablespoon (1 package) active dry yeast
½ cup maple syrup, preferably dark
1 tablespoon vegetable oil
2 teaspoons salt
5½–6 cups all-purpose flour

1. Bring 2 cups of the water to a boil. Put the cornmeal in a mixing bowl or the bowl of a standing mixer, if you plan to use that, and pour the boiling water over it, letting the cornmeal absorb the water for 30 minutes or until cooled to lukewarm.

2. Stir the yeast into the remaining ½ cup water. Add the maple syrup, vegetable oil, and salt. Stir into the cornmeal mixture.

3. Stir 5 cups of the flour into the cornmeal, adding more as necessary to make a soft dough that does not stick to your hands when you try to knead it. Turn the dough out and knead well until it is soft. You can also knead it with a dough hook in your standing mixer or use a food processor. Put the dough into a greased bowl, cover, and let rise for 2 hours or until doubled. (Or you can cover the bowl and let the dough rise overnight in the refrigerator.)

4. Grease two 9-inch bread pans and turn the dough into the buttered pans. Let them rise another half hour, uncovered.

5. While the bread is rising, preheat the oven to 350 degrees. Slash the tops of the loaves a few times with a sharp knife, then bake for 45–50 minutes. Turn the bread out of the pans and cool on racks.

Herb Onion-Rosemary Bread

Lynn Joyner Banister has been baking all her life. But it wasn't until age forty-eight that she realized her lifelong dream, installing a commercial kitchen in her two-car garage in Chesterfield, Massachusetts, and starting the Work of Art Bakery. "My baking is different from that of my grandmother [from whom she learned the art]," she told me. "She baked for the family. I also bake for my children and grandchildren, but I do mostly professional baking and use new gadgets like the food processor and convection ovens. I believe that what makes my grandmother and me the same is that we both put our love in our work, that 'magic ingredient'; if it's only for one person or a whole school, the recipient feels special." Here is the recipe for her popular onion-rosemary bread.

YIELD: 2 LOAVES

1 large onion, coarsely chopped

3 tablespoons olive oil

1 tablespoon dried rosemary or 3 tablespoons coarsely chopped fresh rosemary

1 tablespoon dried thyme or 3 tablespoons coarsely chopped fresh thyme

2 cups lukewarm water

2 tablespoons (2 packages) active dry yeast

1 tablespoon kosher salt

4½–5 cups all-purpose flour

1 egg, well beaten

1. Sauté the onion in the olive oil in a small frying pan over medium heat until soft. Remove from the heat, stir in the herbs, and let cool.

2. Pour the water into the bowl of an electric mixer. Dissolve the yeast in the water and mix with the dough hook. Add the salt and the onion and herb mixture, then mix in enough flour to make a firm dough, adding more flour if necessary, kneading until the dough holds together.

3. Remove the dough to a floured work surface. Clean out and grease the bowl. Return the dough to the greased bowl, cover, and let rise for 1 hour.

4. Grease two 8½-inch loaf pans.

5. Remove the dough to a floured work surface and punch it down. Divide in half, shape it into 2 loaves, and put it into the prepared pans. Let the loaves rise for 1 hour, covered, or until the dough has doubled in volume. Carefully brush the loaves with the beaten egg a few times while they are rising.

6. Preheat the oven to 400 degrees. Just before baking cut 4 slits on the top of each loaf and dust lightly with flour. Bake for about 30 minutes or until the breads are nicely browned and sound hollow when tapped.

7. Remove the loaves from the pans and let them cool on a rack.

Appalachian Griddle Corn Bread

The way I see it, corn bread is all about crust. The color of the corn, yellow or white, is determined by where you live. I'm from the white country in southwest Virginia, where the corn bread tends to be dense and dry. The key to moist corn bread is a liquidy batter. Sugar is the other sore point with folks. Most of us in the South are adamant about it: this is corn bread, it isn't cake. You can cause a riot along the Mason-Dixon Line, whether to add sugar or not to corn bread. In Texas you gob it up with creamed corn, chilies, and cheese. You need a really hot, well-greased skillet; heat the skillet first, then dump the batter in and bake it and get a beautiful crust. I like my corn bread to be an inch thick."

These are the words of Fred McLellan, owner of Hillbilly Food Stores, in Bristol, Virginia. Fred comes from a family of musicians: his father was a mountain fiddler who played at the Grand Ole Opry, and his mother, of Scottish descent, was a classically trained pianist. Although he learned the love of food from his mother, it was an Appalachian mountain woman who taught him the secret to corn bread that's crisp on the outside and moist inside—mayonnaise. Yes, mayonnaise. It makes it nice and moist. This delicious bread has now become a staple in my family. If you don't have a nine- or ten-inch cast-iron skillet, just use a heavy frying pan. Serve it in the pan straight from the oven.

YIELD: ABOUT 8 SERVINGS

2 tablespoons bacon drippings or vegetable oil
1 cup self-rising flour*
1 cup yellow cornmeal
2 tablespoons sugar
1 teaspoon salt
2 teaspoons baking powder*
½ teaspoon baking soda
¼ cup mayonnaise
1½ cups buttermilk
2 large eggs

1. Preheat the oven to 400 degrees. Heat a heavy 9- or 10-inch oven-proof frying pan with the bacon drippings or vegetable oil, then place the frying pan in the oven and start preparing the batter. Take the pan out when the drippings or oil starts to sizzle.

2. Mix the flour, cornmeal, sugar, salt, baking powder, and baking soda together in a large bowl.

3. Blend together in a small bowl the mayonnaise, buttermilk, and eggs. Stir the wet ingredients into the dry with a few rapid strokes.

4. Pour the batter into the hot frying pan and bake it in the oven for about 25 minutes or until golden brown on top.

5. Place the frying pan on a trivet, cut corn bread into wedges, and serve.

*Note: If you don't have self-rising flour, use 3½ teaspoons baking powder (add 1½ teaspoons more baking powder to the recipe).

SMOKEY HOLLOW FISH CO.
218-568-FISH
SMOKED FOODS   SEAFOOD   CATERING   ANTIQUES

Starters and Small Plates

Clockwise from top right: Ecuadorean ceviche in New Jersey; A yuca treat; A smoked-fish shack in Pequot Lakes, Minnesota; Anthony Uglesich making the stuffing for his oysters; Dining al fresco in New Orleans; Mike Rogers, a master oyster shucker

At the opening of Per Se, a posh new restaurant overlooking Central Park in New York City, the waiters passed around some of chef Thomas Keller's signature hors d'oeuvres: "pop tarts," ice cream cones, grilled cheese, and popcorn. But instead of vanilla ice cream, cheddar cheese, and raspberry jam, the ice cream cones had smoked salmon and crème fraîche inside, the grilled cheese sandwiches were filled with goat cheese and guava jelly, and the pop tarts and popcorn were infused with truffles. Whatever you call this food—haute whimsy or whimsical gourmet—it was delicious and precisely executed. A chef has time for fun once he has reached perfection. But even for those who haven't, starters are a place for experimentation. Appetizers today are a far cry from the shrimp cocktail, grapefruit, or celery and olive plate featured at restaurants fifty or sixty years ago. For one thing, we don't even call them appetizers anymore.

These days sushi, foie gras, and calamari (once known as a trash fish) are the top palate teasers. I remember when the only place you could find calamari was in Italian sections of cities like Providence's Federal Hill. Today we have calamari Caesar salad, and every restaurant has a different dipping sauce for deep-fried squid.

"Everything tastes so divinely artisanal."

Most home cooks won't go to the trouble to execute Thomas Keller's state-of-the-art hors d'oeuvres, but even so, this is the part of the meal where cooks can take risks, trying to awaken the appetite with new and often bold flavors. In this chapter, I have included Americanized versions of small plates eaten around the world, dishes scooped up with a chip, a piece of pita, or a fork; Middle Eastern *mezze*, Spanish tapas, and Russian *zakuski*, hummus, guacamole, salsa, and the phyllo savories of Greece and Turkey. First courses today resound with experiment. And we Americans love it.

Black Bean Hummus with Red Peppers

In the 1960s and early '70s, when Americans started traveling in the Middle East, they came back with the garlicky taste of hummus on their breath. It was a delicious, exotic mix, and later, with the food processor, easy to prepare. When I got married, in 1974, I gave the caterer a recipe for this purée of chickpeas and tahini that I had learned to love in Jerusalem, where I met my husband. One person who had never tasted hummus thought my recipe—with its hint of cumin—was so good I could sell it to Zabar's. Others heeded the call (I didn't), and today hummus is marketed all over the world.

In the early 1970s, the only ones to sell hummus (a word that means "chickpeas" in Arabic and Hebrew) were Middle Eastern specialty stores like Sahadi's Specialty and Fine Foods in Brooklyn, which has been catering to the Arab community since 1895. "In the early 1970s we had outside contractors making hummus and baba ghanouj for us or we would buy it already prepared from the Middle East," Charlie Sahadi told me as we browsed through the shelves of his food emporium. "In 1985 our hummus and baba ghanouj were so popular that we put a deli in the store. Today you go to a specialty food store and you see seven varieties of Americanized hummus: sun-dried tomato, basil, pepper, black bean . . . I don't know what [it is], but it isn't hummus." Here is an American-ized version Charlie Sahadi might not approve of, made with New World black beans. You can, of course, use the original biblical chickpeas instead.

YIELD: ABOUT 4 CUPS OR 6–8 SERVINGS

1 cup dried black beans

2 teaspoons salt, or to taste

1 cup tahini (sesame seed paste)

½ cup lemon juice, or to taste

2–3 cloves garlic

½ preserved lemon (see page 171), optional

Freshly ground pepper to taste

½ teaspoon ground cumin, or to taste

2 red peppers, pith and seeds removed, quartered

1. Drain and rinse the black beans and put them in a pot of boiling water for 2 minutes. Then let the beans soak in the hot water for about an hour and a half, or simply leave overnight in water to soak.

2. Drain the beans and put them in a heavy pot with enough cold water to cover. Bring to a boil, add 1 teaspoon of salt, then simmer, partially covered, for about 1 hour, or until the beans are soft. Add more water as needed.

3. Drain the beans again, reserving about 1½ cups of the cooking liquid and ¼ cup of the cooked beans for garnish. Process the beans with the tahini, lemon juice, garlic, preserved lemon (if using), 1 teaspoon of the salt, pepper, cumin, and at least ½ cup of the reserved cooking liquid in a food processor fitted with a steel blade. If

3 tablespoons extra-virgin olive oil

2 tablespoons pine nuts, toasted

Dash of paprika or sumac

2 tablespoons chopped fresh parsley or cilantro

Raw cut-up vegetables and/or warm pita bread

the hummus is too thick, add more reserved cooking liquid or water until you have a pastelike consistency.

4. Add the red peppers and pulse to chop, leaving flecks of pepper throughout the hummus. Taste and adjust the seasonings.

5. Heat 1 tablespoon of the olive oil in a small frying pan. Toss the pine nuts in and stir-fry, browning all sides, for about 5 minutes.

6. To serve, transfer the hummus to a large, flat plate, and make a slight depression in the center with the back of a spoon. Drizzle the remaining olive oil on top and sprinkle the reserved black beans, toasted pine nuts, paprika or sumac, and parsley or cilantro over the surface.

7. Serve with raw vegetables and/or warm pita bread cut into wedges.

Note: Sometimes leftover hummus tends to thicken; just add some water to make it the right consistency and adjust the seasonings.

THE ADVENT OF THE ELECTRIC SUPERBLENDER— THE FOOD PROCESSOR

I have a distinctly negative reaction to the food processor, which has become a kitchen shrine and will cause the next generation of Americans to grow up without teeth.

—GEORGE LANG, FOOD & WINE, JANUARY 1979

While Americans were stirring packaged instant soup into sour cream, cooks throughout the world were using mortars and pestles to pound. They ground chickpeas and garlic into hummus, avocados into guacamole, and peppers into salsa.

In the early 1970s, Carl Sontheimer, an American inventor who had spent his youth in France, decided, at the age of fifty-seven, to turn to cooking, a longtime hobby, for his next inspiration. He went to a trade show in France and saw an industrial blender that he thought could be adapted for home cooks. He soon reached a licensing agreement with the company, Robot Coupe, modified the machine for home cooks, and called it the Cuisinart. There were other similar appliances at the time, like the small Moulinex, but none so remarkable as Cuisinart. In addition to chopping, grinding, and puréeing, the Cuisinart could slice, grate, knead, and mix pie crusts, with the flick of the switch.

Mahammar

Pepper, Pomegranate, and Walnut Dip

This full-flavored dip of peppers, pomegranates, and walnuts, as prepared by Syrian native Sakina Shahadi, graces the tables of many Washington dinner parties. It is a winning combination, and one that would never have been made in this country before the food processor. I make this dip year-round, substituting dried cranberries if pomegranates aren't in season. I have also seen it lately in restaurants as an accompaniment to roast chicken.

YIELD: 2 CUPS

2 red peppers, pith and seeds removed, quartered

2 cloves garlic

1 cup walnuts

½ cup bread crumbs

Dash of cayenne

½ teaspoon salt, or to taste

¼ cup extra-virgin olive oil

1 tablespoon pomegranate syrup

¼ cup fresh pomegranate seeds (see page 16 for peeling)

2 tablespoons chopped fresh mint

¼ cup chopped black Greek-style olives, optional

·Raw cut-up vegetables or toasted pita bread

1. Put the peppers and the garlic in a food processor fitted with a steel blade. Pulse until the peppers are in little pieces.

2. Add the walnuts, bread crumbs, cayenne pepper, and salt and pulse a few times until the walnuts are processed but still have some crunch to them.

3. Stir in the olive oil and pomegranate syrup. Adjust the seasonings and gently fold in the fresh pomegranate seeds, mint, and olives. Turn into a brightly colored serving bowl and serve with cut-up vegetables or toasted pita bread.

Susie's Avocado and Pepper Salsa

When Susie Almendarez's son-in-law, who was stationed in Iraq, came home on leave, he asked for one recipe: her salsa. Susie, who comes from a Mexican-American family and is married to a military man in Flagstaff, Arizona, developed this recipe over the years, using peppers available in Arizona and some that were brought over the border from New Mexico. It doesn't matter which peppers you use, as long as you have a mix of some hot and some mild. I have toned the heat down a bit for my family by leaving out some of the seeds. Each time I make this salsa, I think there will be too much, but it always gets eaten immediately. Try it on top of grilled fish, with huevos rancheros (page 26), or as a dip with chips.

YIELD: ABOUT 4 CUPS SALSA

1 green chili (mild like the New Mexico Anaheim or Hatch), or a green bell pepper

2 yellow sun chilies

2 jalapeño chilies (medium-hot)

2 serrano chilies, medium to medium-hot

1 bunch cilantro, chopped (about 1 cup), plus 2 tablespoons for garnish

2½ tablespoons fresh chopped or 1 tablespoon dried oregano

2 cloves garlic

1–1½ cups homemade tomato sauce (page 273) or jarred

Salt to taste

1 large tomato

½ large onion

2 firm avocados, peeled and pit removed

Chips for dipping

1. Take the stems off the chilies and cut them up, removing the seeds if you want. Put them in a food processor equipped with a steel blade and add the cilantro, oregano, and garlic. Pulse until chopped.

2. Stir in 1 cup of the tomato sauce, then sprinkle on salt to taste.

3. Turn into a serving bowl, cover, and refrigerate. Just before serving, chop the tomato, onion, and avocado and stir them in. Adjust the seasonings, and if the salsa seems a bit dry, add the remaining ½ cup of tomato sauce. Garnish with cilantro. The salsa will keep for a week. Serve with chips.

Directly across from the tiny Santuario de Chimayó, a spiritual center for New Mexicans, sits a shop with the simple sign "Léona's Restaurante de Chimayó." Léona Medina-Tiede's family has lived across from the church for six generations. Her ancestors, like many others, came here from Spain via Mexico in the seventeenth century.

Chilies and corn are in her blood. When she isn't molding the best tamales I have ever tasted, she is gathering the bright red chilies that hang outside her shop or preparing meals for the priests in the church. For a long time she also made flavored tortillas with spinach and red chili, a technique she claims to have invented.

Léona explained to me that most of the long southwestern peppers are of the same genus, but have different names depending on the region they come from. Although it used to be that peppers grew all over New Mexico, today most are cultivated around Hatch, located in the southeast corner of the state. Léona gets hers delivered from a little farm there. "In Chimayó a lot of people used to grow peppers," she told me. "Now they grow mobile homes."

All kinds of American chilies hang outside her tiny store. The large red ones, Anaheims or Big Jims, are medium-hot, and she sells them dried, crushed, or ground. The dried Anaheims are soaked for red chili sauce; the dried black, smoky ones, like poblanos and ancho chilies from Mexico, are especially nice for stuffing. Tiny, thinner chilies, like those used in Asia, are crushed for pizza and ground for what we call cayenne pepper.

Like tomatoes, peppers start out green. By the end of the summer they are yellow, and then, finally, red. "When I was growing up, we'd harvest the chilies," Léona told me. "My mother would roast I don't know how many chilies a little bit in a three-hundred-degree oven. Then she would peel them, string them on a string, and hang them in the attic to dry. They smelled real good. Then she would grind some with an old-fashioned grinder." Léona's mother planted by memory, using no labels. She used to taste the seeds she was planting to see how hot the chilies would be. "The trick was to remember where she planted each of the hot ones," Léona said.

El Nopalito's Kentucky Guacamole

Driving through southern Indiana, my daughter Merissa and I were looking for a good mashed-potato-and-meat kind of place. We saw people gathered at El Nopalito in Corydon, not your typical, quaint American restaurant, but what the heck—we were on a road trip. The restaurant, which was housed in an old "Dog and Suds" drive-thru, is one of three restaurants in the Louisville area owned by Mexicans from Michoacán. They use a mortar and pestle to crush the flavorings for their guacamole, a dip that has become as American as apple pie. We loved the guacamole and learned later that it is considered the best in the area.

YIELD: 3 CUPS

½ white medium onion, cut in 4 pieces

1–2 serrano chilies, seeds removed

3 cloves garlic, minced (about 3 teaspoons)

1 teaspoon sea salt, or to taste

3 tablespoons fresh chopped cilantro

4 avocados, peeled and pit removed

Juice of 1–2 limes

Sour cream for garnish (optional)

Chips for dipping

1. Put the onion, chilies, garlic, sea salt, and 2 tablespoons of the cilantro in a food processor or mortar and pestle and pulse or mash until partially blended and still chunky. Add the avocados and pulse 1 or 2 seconds or if you like your guacamole chunky and more if you like it smoother.

2. Transfer to a bowl, pour the lime juice over all, adjust seasonings to taste, and sprinkle with the remaining tablespoon of cilantro. Top with a dollop of sour cream, if you like, and serve with chips.

VARIATION: It is very American to add mayonnaise or a little salsa. You can also substitute 2½ tablespoons of apple cider vinegar for the lime juice.

Rancho La Puerta's Broccoli and Pea Guacamole Dip

> *Why should I get cancer? I eat broccoli, I do everything right.*
> —WOODY ALLEN, *DECONSTRUCTING HARRY*

Some dips just have a life of their own. This unusual broccoli and pea guacamole dip from Rancho La Puerta spa (page 77) is one of them. I have tasted it at many parties, modified by home cooks.

YIELD: ABOUT 2½ CUPS

¾ cup broccoli flowerets

1 cup fresh or frozen peas, defrosted

2 medium avocados (about 8 ounces each), peeled and pit removed

1 medium tomato, diced

½ red onion, finely diced

1 scallion, trimmed and thinly sliced

1 jalapeño pepper, seeded and minced

4 garlic cloves, minced (about 4 teaspoons)

¼ cup chopped fresh cilantro, plus more for garnish

Juice of 2–3 limes (4–6 tablespoons fresh lime juice)

Salt to taste

Raw cut-up vegetables for dipping

1. Steam the broccoli until tender but still a little crunchy, or put it on a plate, sprinkle some water on top, cover with plastic wrap, and cook on high in the microwave for about 5 minutes or until soft.

2. Transfer the broccoli and peas to a food processor, add the avocados, and process until smooth. Scrape the purée into a bowl, then add the tomato, red onion, scallion, jalapeño, garlic, and chopped cilantro, and season with lime juice and salt. You really have to keep tasting until you reach the right balance of lime juice and salt. Mix well and serve in a bowl or cover and refrigerate for up to 2 hours. Garnish with cilantro.

Burt Lancaster pulling bread from the oven at Rancho La Puerta

Minnesota Salmon Dip

Gene Peterson is the quintessential Minnesotan: a big, burly guy with an infectious grin and a Garrison Keillor accent. Ask him about lutefisk, the traditional lye-preserved cod dish of his Swedish ancestors, and he'll say, "Does anybody want it? Not me. I don't like the stuff myself, but my father, he goes to every Lutheran church lutefisk feed. Why ruin good cod? You don't have to do that anymore." Ask him about smoked salmon, and he'll talk your ear off about the different ways of smoking, while letting you taste his smoked salmon dip.

YIELD: ABOUT 2½ CUPS

8 ounces cream cheese

¼ cup chopped onion

½ cup sour cream

6 dashes Tabasco sauce, or to taste

2 tablespoons lemon juice

1 pound smoked salmon, sliced

Put the cream cheese, onion, sour cream, Tabasco, lemon juice, and smoked salmon in the food processor. Pulse until the salmon is chopped but not puréed. Taste and adjust the seasonings, and serve slathered on crackers or toasted bread.

VARIATION: I sometimes substitute smoked or lemon-peppered smoked bluefish for the salmon, and I often use capers, with some mixed in and the rest on top as a garnish.

Nuegado de Yuca

Yuca Fritters

Americans have always eaten hush puppies and crab cakes, but I had never tasted yuca fritters until I visited Pupuseria Dona Azucena, a Salvadoran restaurant in Silver Spring, Maryland. The restaurant's owner, Ceta Azucena, came to this country as a housekeeper on a diplomatic visa. When the diplomatic family moved, she decided she could make more money cooking the food Salvadoran immigrants grew up on than cleaning houses. At first she ran a *pupuseria,* a store where *pupusas,* thick Salvadoran tortilla sandwiches, were made on a makeshift stove and sold from a truck, and later she turned her truck into two very successful restaurants, still operating a few *pupuseria* trucks on the side.

Also known as manioc, yuca is a starchy root vegetable used in South America. Salvadoran cooks pound it by hand, but Maria Gudiel, another great cook from El Salvador who helps me in the kitchen, showed me how to do it with a food processor. Although Maria serves the fritters as a dessert, with a syrup made from dark brown sugar, I serve them as a savory appetizer, eaten alone or dipped in tamarind chutney. I love the taste of the yuca with the cornmeal.

YIELD: ABOUT 50 FRITTERS

2 pounds yuca, peeled and cut into 3-inch chunks
4 large eggs
½ cup water
1 cup masa harina (corn flour)
1 teaspoon salt, or to taste
Vegetable oil for frying

1. Put the yuca, eggs, and water into the bowl of a food processor fitted with a steel blade and process to a purée.

2. Transfer the yuca mixture to a bowl. Using your hands, mix in the masa harina and salt. Let sit for about 10 minutes.

3. Heat about 3 inches of oil in a heavy pot (I use a wok) until it is about 375 degrees or sizzling. Scooping up about ¼ cup of the batter in a ladle at a time, drop the yuca balls into the oil and deep-fry a few minutes until golden, then turn and fry for another minute or so. Repeat until all the batter is used up. Drain on paper towels and serve.

Ecuadorean Shrimp Ceviche

I recently tasted a ceviche with Asian pear and grapefruit, sweet shrimp, orange clams, and scallops. It's hard not to be amazed how far ceviche has come from the coast of South America, where there are literally hundreds of versions.

In order to taste an authentic Ecuadorean version of this popular dish, I visited Josephina and Alfredo Vizueta of Passaic, New Jersey. Rather than using the blender and the food processor her daughters gave her, Josephine cuts everything by hand with a knife and grinds spices with a stone mortar and pestle. Although she always loved cooking, Josephine, born in a small Andean village and married at thirteen, never wanted to work as a cook. "Cooking is what I do for the family," she says. "The tradition of ceviche depends on your parents," she continued. "The shrimp holds its color better when it is cooked in its shell." Red coloring is important in Ecuadorean ceviche, I learned, and thus the ketchup. I have added some avocado, which keeps its nice green color with so much lime added.

YIELD: 8 SERVINGS

2 pounds unpeeled medium shrimp, washed

3 tablespoons extra-virgin olive oil

1 orange, peeled and cut in half

1 cup plus 1 tablespoon roughly chopped parsley

1 cup plus 1 tablespoon roughly chopped cilantro

1 tomato, chopped

1 red onion, cut into small dice

1 tablespoon sugar

1 teaspoon salt, or to taste

3 limes

2 heaping tablespoons ketchup (approximately)

1 avocado

Hot sauce for garnish

Plantain chips

1. Rub the shrimp with 1 tablespoon of the olive oil. Then squeeze the orange halves over the shrimp and simmer in a large frying pan, covered, for 5 minutes.

2. Remove the shrimp to a bowl and add a few ice cubes to prevent the shrimp from discoloring or shrinking. Strain the juice from the frying pan and pour into the bowl of a blender or food processor. Add 1 cup each of the parsley and cilantro as well as the tomato to the juice, then pulverize.

3. Peel the shrimp, cut in half lengthwise, and return to the bowl.

4. Stir the diced onion, sugar, and salt in a bowl with the herb mixture.

5. Cut the limes in half. Stick the tines of the fork in the center of a lime and rotate it as you squeeze it over the shrimp and onions, discarding any seeds. Stir in the remaining 2 tablespoons of olive oil and the ketchup and mix with a spoon then toss with the shrimp.

6. Refrigerate for a couple of hours, until cold. Just before serving, dice and add the avocado. Serve the ceviche in individual bowls, topped with dabs of ketchup or hot sauce and sprinkled with the remaining parsley and cilantro. Pass the plantain chips.

Skewered Cherry Tomatoes with Olive Oil and Basil

At the stately Blue Hill at Stone Barns restaurant on the eighty-acre Rockefeller Estate in Pocantico Hills in Tarrytown, New York, chef Dan Barber served us a tomato-tasting menu. It was early fall, when tomatoes were still at their best. The menu and the restaurant work on the premise that food is sustainable even in the Northeast, and thus the first two courses were listed as "Tomatoes" and "More Tomatoes." Dan's menu was filled with them: heirloom tomato salad, tomato water extracted from the tomatoes, and my favorite, roasted cherry tomatoes, cooled and then gently skewered on a bamboo stick with a small basil leaf tucked in between. Leftover tomatoes would be put up for the long winter.

Before dinner, Dan took me on a tour of the garden. He patted his favorite pig, we listened to chickens, occasionally seeing one strutting about, and we went through a twenty-thousand-square-foot state-of-the-art greenhouse set up by Eliot Coleman, a four-season farmer in Maine. Dan, who must never sleep, works at his New York restaurant Blue Hill on Mondays and Tuesdays, then travels to Stone Barns the rest of the week, carrying his leftovers from the restaurant for compost.

YIELD: ABOUT 12 SKEWERS OF TOMATOES

1 pint cherry or pear tomatoes
1–2 tablespoons olive oil
1 teaspoon kosher salt
Freshly ground pepper to taste
Handful fresh basil leaves, preferably small leaves
Long wooden skewers

1. Preheat the oven to 300 degrees and line a baking sheet with parchment paper or a Silpat mat.

2. Place the cherry tomatoes in a small bowl with the olive oil. Roll the tomatoes in the oil, coating them well, then sprinkle with the salt and a few grinds of pepper. Place on the baking sheet and bake for 90 minutes or until dried out a bit. Remove from the oven and let the tomatoes cool.

3. Just before serving, gently poke a hole in each tomato with a toothpick. Skewer each tomato on a wooden skewer. Then thread a basil leaf (if small; otherwise tear a larger leaf neatly in quarters) and a second tomato on the skewer, leaving about a half inch in between. Serve as a first course.

The California roll, according to *Gourmet* magazine's restaurant critic Jonathan Gold, was developed in the early 1960s by an unknown chef from the Old Tokyo Kaikan restaurant in Los Angeles. The chef was trying to come up with something for his customers who refused to eat raw fish. He probably thought snow crab, cucumber, and avocado would be a good substitute for raw tuna or other fish.

Today, there are many kinds of American sushi: Hawaiian rolls with avocado, tuna, and pineapple; Cajun rolls with deep-fried crawfish and cucumber; and Philly rolls (also known as bagel, or Great Neck, rolls) with smoked salmon and cream cheese, served with wasabi on the side.

Sushi Philly (or Bagel) Roll

This sushi roll undoubtedly got its name because it includes Philadelphia cream cheese in the filling . I watched Kenji Akiho making the roll one night as I sat at his sushi bar, Café Japone, in Washington, D.C.

You'll need a bamboo sushi-rolling mat to make this, something obtainable from Asian stores. The instructions are for one roll, which makes six pieces of sushi, usually enough for one person. Make as many as you'll need.

YIELD: 6 SLICES, WHICH SERVES 1 OR 2 PEOPLE

One 8-by-7½-inch sheet of dried nori seaweed

¾ cup cooked short- or medium-grain rice, plus extra cooked rice for garnish

2 tablespoons cream cheese

2 teaspoons diced white onion

2 ounces smoked salmon, cut into 1-inch-long strips

Salmon roe for garnish (optional)

Soy sauce, pickled ginger, and wasabi paste for accompaniment

1. Place the sushi-rolling mat on a flat surface in front of you so that the bamboo strips run horizontally. Place the seaweed sheet on the mat with the shiny, smooth side down.

2. Spread the cooked rice in a thin layer over the entire area of the seaweed sheet, leaving bare a 1-inch strip along the edge that is closest to you, and a 2½-inch strip along the opposite edge.

3. Arrange 1 layer each of cream cheese, onion, and smoked salmon in a 1-inch horizontal strip along the center of the rice.

4. Dip your fingertips in water and dab the edge of the seaweed closest to you to serve as an adhesive later on. Pinching the seaweed to the edge of the bamboo mat closest to you, roll it over, jelly-roll fashion,

releasing the mat and keeping the roll perfectly tight and round. Once the shape is set, press the wet edge of the seaweed onto the roll to glue it. Then sprinkle more water at the remaining end to keep it tight. Take the bamboo mat and fold it over on top of itself away from you, using the mat to help form the sushi roll, then pull back on the newly formed roll. Now, with the palms of your hands, roll the sushi firmly away from you. Peel off the mat, and the roll should be nice and tight.

5. Roll the sushi in more sticky rice and sprinkle with salmon roe for garnish. Cut the roll in half and put the halves side by side. Cut each half into thirds and serve with soy sauce, pickled ginger, and wasabi paste.

Mushrooms Stuffed with Mozzarella and Fresh Herbs

When I came here in 1979 from Italy and started to cook, one of the biggest problems I had was finding the right mushrooms: porcini, cremini, or *finferli* [chanterelles]," Genoveffa Franchini, a scientist at the National Institutes of Health, told me. "I used to joke with my husband that the only thing I could find was the 'national' white mushroom." Now, with so many kinds available, Veffa uses a combination of commercial white and larger cultivated brown cremini, stuffing them with mozzarella and basil. The beauty of this recipe is that you can prepare the mushrooms in advance, then bake them later.

YIELD: 2 DOZEN STUFFED MUSHROOMS

1 pound (2 dozen) medium cremini or white mushrooms

4 ounces mozzarella cheese

2 tablespoons Parmesan cheese

1 clove garlic, peeled and smashed

3 tablespoons chopped fresh basil

3 tablespoons chopped fresh parsley

Salt and freshly ground pepper to taste

2 tablespoons extra-virgin olive oil

2 tablespoons fine bread crumbs

1. Preheat the oven to 350 degrees. Grease a rack and place it on top of a baking pan.

2. Clean the mushrooms, separating the caps from the stems and setting aside the caps.

3. Place the stems in the bowl of a food processor equipped with a steel blade, along with the mozzarella, Parmesan, garlic, basil, and parsley. Pulse until finely chopped but not puréed. Add salt and pepper to taste.

4. Gently fill the mushroom caps to the top with the filling. Place the filled mushroom caps on the rack in the baking pan. Drizzle the olive oil over them, then sprinkle the tops with bread crumbs. Bake for about 30 minutes. If they haven't formed a nice crust by then, put them under the broiler for a few minutes.

Drago's Charbroiled Oysters

Oysters casino and oysters Rockefeller have both long been staples of New Orleans cuisine. A few years ago, when Tommy Cvitanovich took over Drago's from his father, he wanted to try something new. Through trial and error, he came up with another classic: charbroiled oysters.

YIELD: 4–6 SERVINGS

24 Louisiana oysters

¼ cup (½ stick) butter

4 cloves garlic, minced

Salt and freshly ground pepper to taste

2 tablespoons grated Romano cheese

2 tablespoons grated Parmesan cheese

4 tablespoons chopped fresh parsley

1. Make a fire in your grill or heat the broiler of your oven.

2. Wearing a glove, poke a knife or oyster shucker into the shell of each oyster, then twist the muscle which attaches it to the shell and open up the oyster, running the knife around the rim. Discard the empty shell.

3. Melt the butter with the garlic, sprinkle with salt and pepper, and spoon equal amounts over the half-shells containing the oysters. Sprinkle the cheeses and the parsley over the oysters.

4. Before grilling, have a spray bottle of water ready to squirt on any flames and be mindful of possible popping oyster shells. Watching carefully, put the oysters on the grill or in the broiler, and cook for 3–5 minutes, until they are charbroiled.

Roy Scheffer and his floating oyster nursery

DRAGO'S—A CROATIAN NEW ORLEANS INSTITUTION

Sitting at the bar in Drago's, a restaurant in Metairie, Louisiana, I met Drago (Charley) Cvitanovich, the patriarch of this huge seafood emporium. Retired now, Drago watches as his wife and son Tommy manage his empire. Over the bar is a mural of the Croatian coastal town from which Drago came in 1958. "Every house in that town had oystermen coming to Louisiana," said Drago, who still speaks with a heavy accent. Unlike most Croatians who emigrated to Louisiana, Drago did not become a fisherman or an oysterman. Instead, he opened a small restaurant near the French Quarter.

According to Drago, the summer months were when oyster fishermen went back to Croatia to visit their families, make babies, and tend their boats. When I asked if oysters were really an aphrodisiac, he laughed and offered me one of the oyster shells he decorates as a hobby. It read, "Love New Orleans, love oysters."

FULFILLING OUR OYSTER CRAVINGS WITH FARMED OYSTERS

Martha's Vineyard has always had its share of wild oysters, most of which grow in brackish oyster ponds. But recently a few entrepreneurs have begun farming oysters on the island. I talked with Roy Scheffer, a fisherman from Edgartown who traces his lineage back to Sir Francis Drake, to learn more about oyster farming.

In 1995, with fishermen going out of business due to government restrictions and dwindling stock, a National Marine Fisheries Service grant reeducated Roy and a handful of other fishermen to grow fish instead of catching them. One of the first to take advantage of the government grant, Roy is now seeing the results of his work.

Roy starts with oyster seed (small oysters) spawned at the Martha's Vineyard Shellfish Hatchery in Vineyard Haven. "Ten thousand of them, as tiny as grains of sand, can fit in the cup of your hand. Wild shellfish are the most vulnerable when small," he said. "If they don't have the right conditions, they'll die. By going to the hatchery, I'm keeping them from any harm."

Like a farmer, he "plants" these seeds in a tidal-powered nursery bathed in seawater rich with microscopic algae. The floating nursery catches the tide and force-feeds the baby oysters until their shells are half an inch in diameter. "It's all graduation," he said. "They get food from the tide running through there all the time. The oyster picks the food, and the food makes the flavor." When they reach three inches in size, Roy harvests and sells them.

"From Newfoundland to Texas, you have the same American oyster," Roy explained to me. As for the old wives' tale about not eating oysters in months that end with "r," he added, "it used to hold weight, but that was before the big 'r' for refrigeration."

Uglesich's Baked Stuffed Oysters

After meeting Drago, I wanted to meet Anthony Uglesich, another New Orleans Croatian restaurateur. At ten thirty, when I arrived at his popular no-frills, no-coffee, no-dessert, cash-only restaurant, Uglesich's, there was already a line forming outside. Uglesich was seated at a table, a three-by-five-inch recipe card beside him, making the dipping sauce for his crawfish balls.

While Uglesich peeled the carrots and squeezed the limes, Mike Rogers, who has been shucking oysters there for thirty years, was busy getting ready for the onslaught. "Shucking is all in the wrist," this champion Louisiana shucker said, deftly opening the shells.

Except for Asian fish sauce, which he purchases at the outdoor Vietnamese market (page 201), Uglesich uses only Louisiana products in his restaurant. When Paul Prudhomme made Cajun food famous in the early 1980s, Uglesich got braver. "You got to change with the times," he told me as he ground his spices with a mortar and pestle. When I asked why he didn't use a food processor, he said, "It's all done by hand. I don't know, we still are old-fashioned."

Uglesich's popularity grew when he appeared on Emeril's and Martha Stewart's TV shows. "The power of the TV thing is tremendous," he said as he surveyed the crowd.

YIELD: 4–6 SERVINGS

18 oysters

½ cup seasoned bread crumbs

¼ cup grated imported Parmesan cheese

1 tablespoon fresh lemon juice

¼ teaspoon salt

2 cloves garlic, minced

1 tablespoon chopped fresh parsley

¾ teaspoon crushed red peppers

⅓ cup regular olive oil

1. Shuck the oysters, using the method on page 106.

2. Preheat the broiler.

3. Mix the bread crumbs, Parmesan, lemon juice, salt, garlic, parsley, crushed peppers, and olive oil.

4. Place a heaping teaspoon of the filling on top of the oyster in the shell and broil for about 5 minutes. Serve immediately.

Michel Richard's Porcupine Shrimp

Shrimp enclosed in crisp *ketaifa* (shredded phyllo-like dough available in Greek stores and many supermarkets) is a dish that I have tasted at many restaurants throughout the United States. Whenever I ask the chef where he got the recipe, the answer is that he learned it from Michel Richard, chef-owner of Citronelle, in Washington, D.C. "But," Michel told me, "I didn't create *ketaifa*. I just used a Middle Eastern ingredient, which a French chef can do in America."

In the Middle East, *ketaifa* is used primarily for desserts, but Michel instinctively knew it would be good with savories like shrimp. When he opened Citrus, in Los Angeles in 1987, he put this dish on his menu and called it "Shrimp Porcupines." You can also make it with lobster, oysters, scallops, langouste, or any firm white fish.

YIELD: 24 SHRIMP

24 large raw shrimp, peeled, deveined, and tails intact

Salt and freshly ground pepper to taste

1 cup cake flour

1 large egg

2 ounces ketaifa*

24 bamboo skewers

Vegetable oil for deep-frying

Coconut-curry sauce (recipe follows) or red pepper pesto sauce

*Available in the frozen food section of many supermarkets or at Greek grocery stores. If you can't find *ketaifa*, just substitute shredded phyllo.

1. Season the shrimp with salt and pepper and place in a bowl. Put the flour in 1 bowl and the egg in another. Beat the egg well with a little water.

2. Holding the shrimp by the tail, dip into the flour, shake off the excess, then dip the shrimp in the egg mixture.

3. Take a tablespoon or so of the *ketaifa* and spread it with your fingers on the table. Roll the dipped shrimp in the *ketaifa*, gently covering the entire shrimp. Again holding the shrimp by the tail, shake off any excess *ketaifa*. (Cover the remainder of the *ketaifa* with a wet towel.) Repeat with the remaining shrimp and then thread each shrimp onto a bamboo skewer and lay them on a tray lined with parchment paper. The coated shrimp can be refrigerated up to an hour before frying.

4. Bring the shrimp to room temperature and heat 3 inches of vegetable oil to 365 degrees in a wok or other deep frying pan.

ABOUT LEMONGRASS

A popular flavoring these days, lemongrass is a bit difficult to learn to use. I peel off the fibrous outer leaves and smash the inside leaves with a hammer. Then I insert the entire stalk into my soup or whatever else I'm making, and remove it when I'm done. Young, fresh stems taste best. Today in many Asian stores and certain supermarkets, you can buy frozen or jarred lemongrass, already diced.

5. Dip the skewered shrimp into the hot oil. Hold in the oil for about 3 minutes, to brown the *ketaifa* and cook the shrimp. Then drain on paper towels and serve the skewers as a first course on a plate with coconut-curry sauce (see below) or pass around as an hors d'oeuvre with the sauce for dipping.

Note: *You can also fry the shrimp an hour in advance and reheat briefly in a 450-degree oven when ready to serve.*

Michel Richard's Coconut-Curry Sauce

Michel serves this sauce with his shrimp. It's so good you can use any leftovers as a dip for vegetables or a sauce for pasta.

YIELD: ABOUT 1½ CUPS

½ medium onion, diced (about ½ cup)

2 tablespoons butter

½ cup apple juice

One 13-ounce can unsweetened coconut milk

1 cup fish stock, clam juice, or water

¼ cup heavy cream

1 tablespoon curry powder

1 pinch saffron thread

½ ounce (about 2 inches) sliced lemongrass

2 Kaffir lime leaves (optional)

Salt and freshly ground pepper to taste

Juice of ½ lime, or to taste

1. Sauté the onion slowly in the butter in a medium-large sauté pan, until the onion is translucent.

2. Pour on the apple juice and boil to reduce until the pan is almost dry.

3. Add the coconut milk and the fish stock, clam juice, or water and let simmer, uncovered, for 15 minutes, until the sauce is reduced by half. Turn off the heat and stir in the cream, curry powder, saffron, lemongrass, and lime leaves (if using). Cover and let sit for 10 minutes. Adjust seasoning with the salt and pepper. Add lime juice to taste, remove the lemongrass, and strain the sauce.

4. Heat just before serving, pour a bit on each individual serving plate, and top with the shrimp, or serve in a bowl as a dipping sauce.

Cambodian Lettuce Wraps with Noodles and Fresh Herbs

I once visited a group of Cambodian women farmers working at the Nesenkeag Farm outside of Litchfield, New Hampshire. It was an amazing sight, seeing them crouched down, picking pumpkin tendrils and mesclun and talking to one another in Khmer. I wondered what stories these women, who have witnessed so much horror, were sharing as they worked. They use the new land to connect to what they knew before Pol Pot desecrated their families' lives.

At the lunch break, we all sat down at a table near the field. The women spread out leftover rice, chicken, and meat, which we wrapped with fresh Thai basil and mint in lettuce leaves and ate dipped in a pungent sauce.

The night before, at a Cambodian restaurant, I had tasted something similar, wrapped also in damp rice paper. They're called summer rolls, and I like their rustic look. When I make them, I use rice noodles sparingly, filling them with bean sprouts, fresh mint, basil, vegetables, and leftover chicken, meat, or shrimp. They make a beautiful starter for a dinner party.

YIELD: 24 WRAPS

3 heads Boston lettuce or any easy-to-wrap lettuce leaves

1½ pounds shrimp, chicken, or pork, cooked and shredded in 1-inch-long pieces

Accent to taste or 2 teaspoons MSG (optional)

2 ounces rice noodles

1 cup bean sprouts

1 packed cup fresh mint and/or basil leaves

½ cup rice vinegar

3 tablespoons sugar, or to taste

1 onion, sliced in julienne strips

24 sheets rice paper, available at Asian markets and many supermarkets

1. Wash and dry the lettuce well. Taste the meat or shrimp; if it needs seasoning, add Accent or MSG, if desired.

2. Soak the rice noodles in lukewarm water for about 5 minutes. Remove, drain, and set aside.

3. Place a few pieces of meat or shrimp down the center of a lettuce leaf. Add a few tablespoons of bean sprouts and a few sprigs of mint or basil.

4. Put the vinegar and sugar in a bowl. Dip a slice of onion in the vinegar to give the onion a sweet-and-sour taste, then place the onion on top of the mint. Roll up the lettuce leaf like a jelly roll.

5. Wet the rice papers in a bowl of water, 1 at a time, and cut each in half with scissors to make half circles. Handle the papers very carefully to avoid breaking when dry or tearing when wet. Lay a rice paper on a towel on a flat surface. In a couple of seconds, it will become soft enough to roll. Place the rolled-up lettuce leaf on the

half circle of rice paper. Roll up tightly and clip the ends if you wish, so the rolls look like filterless cigarettes. Place on a large platter and cover until serving time to preserve the softness of the rice paper wrapping. Serve as is, or dip in nuoc cham sauce.

Nuoc Cham Sauce

Nuoc mam, a Southeast Asian fish essence from anchovy extract, adds a salty flavor. It is to Southeast Asian cooking what Worcestershire sauce, also made from anchovies, has long been to Western cooking. I got this recipe from a Vietnamese woman in Bowie, Maryland, one of the first Vietnamese boat people to come to the Washington area.

YIELD: 1 CUP

1½–2 tablespoons fish sauce (nuoc mam)
¼ cup water
¼ cup rice vinegar
¼ cup sugar, or to taste
1 small hot red pepper, crushed, or crushed red pepper to taste
2 cloves garlic, minced
Juice of 1 lime
¼ carrot, sliced in julienne strips

1. Mix all the ingredients together in a small bowl and stir.

2. Serve in small bowls as a dip with lettuce wraps or spring rolls. If you like, add a few tablespoons of crushed salted and toasted peanuts. You can store this sauce, covered, in the refrigerator for several months.

Cambodian Hoisin Shrimp Spring Roll

One day Eero Ruuttila, a farmer in Litchfield, a town in southern New Hampshire, was eating in a Cambodian restaurant in Lowell, Massachusetts. The food reminded him of his time as a student in Thailand, where he fell in love with the culture and the food. "The ingredients were utterly fresh," he told me at his farm. "They were not dumbed down for American clients." When a new wave of Cambodian immigrants came to Lowell, Eero hired some of the women as field- and farmworkers, and soon they began planting their own seeds for their personal use. Eero and the women then started selling these herbs and vegetables to the Cambodian restaurants and grocery stores in Lowell, where there is the second-largest Cambodian population in America. He then introduced the greens to high-end chefs in the Boston area.

When Eero invited me to lunch with a Cambodian family in Lowell, I was delighted. There, in a house with several families living and cooking together, I tasted this delicious shrimp, coated with hoisin sauce, wrapped in wontons, and deep-fried.

YIELD: 8 SERVINGS

½ cup hoisin sauce
1 tablespoon sugar
1 teaspoon salt, or to taste
¼ teaspoon black pepper, or to taste
Sixteen 3½-inch-round or 3-inch-square wonton wrappers
16 jumbo or regular shrimp, peeled and deveined, tails left on
Vegetable oil for deep-frying

1. Stir together the hoisin sauce, sugar, salt, and black pepper in a small bowl.

2. Lay a wonton wrapper flat on the counter and put a teaspoon or so of the seasoned hoisin sauce in the middle of 1 side. Place 1 shrimp on top with the tail extending above the wrapper. Fold the wrapper into a triangle and press the edges down, sealing with a little water.

3. Heat the vegetable oil in a wok to 350 degrees. Fry the rolls a minute or so on each side. Serve, using any extra sauce for dipping.

Chilean Empanadas

Food is becoming a tool to teach history in many universities around the country. "What we eat, how we prepare it, and how our meals are presented at the table is a most important part of people's lives," Professor Hernan Vera of the University of Florida told me over dinner. In a class on Latin American civilization he ends the course with a meal of some typical dishes cooked by his Latino students. Hernan always brings empanadas, a filled turnover that varies from country to country.

Recounting the journey of this one dish and examining its different components, he teaches the story of Latin American culture. According to Hernan, the Arabs, who occupied Spain for nine hundred years, taught the Spanish how to make this dish, probably prepared with lamb, a variation that is seldom found in Latin America today. But the same spices, the olives, and the raisins in the filling are still there, all of which Spanish conquerors brought to Latin America, where they have taken on regional flavors, based again on local ingredients and culture. "Food preparation is also an important part of a family's heritage," he added. "The empanada from Chile will be a part of my children's inheritance." Hernan got this recipe from his great-aunt. He has changed it slightly, substituting vegetable shortening for the lard and occasionally chopped artichoke hearts for the meat. If you have leftover filling, serve it with rice.

You can use prepared empanada dough or frozen puff pastry instead of making your own dough.

YIELD: 24 EMPANADAS

FILLING

4 tablespoons vegetable oil

4 cups finely chopped Spanish onions

2 cloves garlic, finely minced

1 tablespoon sweet paprika

2 teaspoons ground cumin

2 teaspoons dried basil or oregano

1 teaspoon ground coriander

½ teaspoon ground cayenne pepper, or to taste

1. To make the filling, heat the oil in a large skillet over medium-high heat. Add the onions and garlic, stirring often, until the onions are transparent and soft, but not browned, about 5 minutes.

2. Stir in the paprika, cumin, basil, coriander, cayenne, the meat, and the raisins. Cook, stirring, for 5 minutes, then sprinkle with the flour and mix well. Stir in the broth and cook, uncovered, for about 5 minutes, or until most of the juices have evaporated. The mixture should be moist but not runny. Season with salt and pepper to taste. Remove from the heat and cool. This is best when made a day ahead.

3. To make the dough, toss the flour and salt into the bowl of a food processor. Add the vegetable shortening or butter in small pieces and

¾ pound ground beef, or
mixed pork and beef
½ cup raisins
1 tablespoon unbleached
all-purpose flour
½ cup beef broth
Salt and pepper to taste
3 hard-boiled eggs, peeled and
roughly chopped
⅓ cup Calamata olives, pitted
and halved
1 egg yolk, beaten with
1 tablespoon water

DOUGH
4 cups unbleached
all-purpose flour
½ tablespoon salt
¾ cup vegetable
shortening, or butter
1 cup lukewarm water

process just until crumbly. Add the water in a stream and process for about a minute, just until the dough is pliable but firm. Do not over-process, because the dough will get tough. Cover the dough tightly with plastic wrap and refrigerate for a few hours.

4. When you are ready to make empanadas, remove the dough or prepared puff pastry dough from the refrigerator. Dust your board or counter generously with flour so the dough will not stick. Pat the dough into a sausage and slice into 24 pieces. Roll each slice of dough into a circle roughly ⅛ inch thick and 4 inches in diameter. If you do not have a rolling pin, a wine bottle will do.

5. Preheat the oven to 425 degrees and line a baking sheet with parchment paper or a Silpat baking mat.

6. Remove the filling from the refrigerator and place the eggs and olives in bowls. Place 1 tablespoon of filling, a little egg, and 2 pieces of olive on each disk of dough. With your fingers wet the space around the filling with water. Fold the circle in half, sealing the dough securely all around to make a half circle. Seal the edges by crimping the dough.

7. Place on a baking sheet and brush with the egg yolk glaze. Prick 4 holes in each empanada with a toothpick or a fork to let the steam escape while baking. Bake for 15–18 minutes or until golden. Serve hot as an appetizer you pass around or as finger food for a casual party or family dinner.

Zucchini Blossoms Stuffed with Goat Cheese

When the late Jean-Louis Palladin came to Washington, D.C., we had a huge garden in our backyard with loads of zucchini. One day, he rode out to our house on his motorcycle, walked into the garden, carefully plucked the male squash blossoms (female ones, with the seeds, are slightly more bulbous), and took them to serve at his restaurant stuffed with black truffles and lobster *mousseline*. That may be overdoing it for home cooks, but this appetizer is easy to make and delicious.

YIELD: ABOUT 10 STUFFED ZUCCHINI BLOSSOMS

8 ounces goat cheese

2 tablespoons heavy cream

2 tablespoons mixed chopped
fresh herbs, like rosemary,
thyme, and chives

Salt and pepper to taste

10 zucchini blossoms

Vegetable oil for deep-frying

2 tomatoes, diced

1. Mix the goat cheese and heavy cream in a small bowl. Fold in the herbs and season with salt and pepper to taste.

2. Spoon a heaping tablespoon of filling into each blossom. Press the tops to close, put on a plate, and refrigerate.

3. When ready to serve, heat 3 inches of oil in a wok or deep fryer. Gently lower the blossoms into the hot oil. When they puff up, remove, drain, and serve immediately as is or gently lay on top of cut-up tomatoes for a stunning first course.

Caramelized Cherry Tomato Tart with Olive Tapenade

This appetizer (or light main course . . . in this era of small plates), made with cherry or grape tomatoes, has that savory-and-sweet taste that Americans love so dearly. Grape tomatoes, first developed in America in the late 1990s, are a hybrid of cherry and Roma tomatoes, guaranteeing a uniform size and intense flavor, which chefs like. The tart is easy to make, especially if you have tapenade (a black olive spread) in your refrigerator and you buy a prepared crust. Or you can do as I do, make and mold a few extra crusts at a time and freeze them for use when needed. You can also make individual tartlets if you like.

YIELD: 12 APPETIZER SERVINGS OR 4 MAIN-COURSE SERVINGS

1–2 tablespoons olive oil

1 pint cherry or grape tomatoes

½ cup olive tapenade

1 baked 9-inch pie crust
(page 405)

¼ cup brown sugar

1. Preheat the broiler and place the rack one-third up.

2. Heat the olive oil in a medium frying pan large enough to hold all the tomatoes in 1 layer, toss them in, and sauté until they start to exude some of their juice, about 5 minutes.

3. With a spatula spread the tapenade carefully over the baked pie crust. Carefully spoon the cooked cherry tomatoes on top of the tapenade with their juice, sprinkle them with the brown sugar, and place the tart under the broiler for a few minutes, until the tomatoes become slightly caramelized. Remove from the oven and serve immediately as a first course or as a main course with a green salad.

A Single Pebble's Szechuan Red Oil Vegetarian Dumplings

The term *dim sum* means to please the heart with little bites, Steve Bogart, the chef-owner of A Single Pebble in Burlington, Vermont, told me. We were eating a dim sum breakfast at the Nice Restaurant in New York's Chinatown. According to Steve, who cooks classic Chinese food at his restaurant, dim sum started out in southern China, in tea-houses that are open only until lunch. "Of course, in America, Chinese restaurants now serve dim sum all day long," he said.

Steve was on one of his frequent trips to New York to taste Chinese dishes. Unlike most other chefs, who head to the upscale restaurants of Manhattan, Steve, armed with his small notebook (he has over a hundred of them), goes to tiny restaurants in the back streets of Chinatown. Between tastes of *har gow* (tiny shrimp dumplings in the shape of a prairie bonnet) and *gau-choy-gau* (translucent round garlic chive dumplings), which he ordered in Cantonese, he told me that he fell in love with Asia as a little boy. Instead of going to college, he moved to Vermont, and worked as a painter, mail carrier, town assessor, and contractor. Weekends and evenings, he cooked, studying Chinese language, culture, and cuisine until he was able to open a restaurant.

Steve learned how to make dim sum by eating the various dishes and analyzing their ingredients. He makes his own wrappers for some dumplings. For others, he orders them from a food supplier in New York's Chinatown. "Everything I serve, including this classic Szechuan dumpling, has a history," he said. "It's just like classical music. I try to reproduce only classical food."

YIELD: 2 DOZEN DUMPLINGS AND ½ CUP DIPPING SAUCE

DUMPLINGS
1 tablespoon vegetable oil
1 tablespoon finely diced ginger
1 tablespoon finely minced garlic
2 tablespoons chopped scallions
1 cup small-diced firm tofu
½ cup minced carrots
½ cup minced water chestnuts
¼ cup minced bamboo shoots
1 pound fresh spinach, stems removed, and blanched for 1–2 minutes and squeezed dry

1. To make the filling, heat the vegetable oil in a wok or skillet. Add the ginger, garlic, and 1 tablespoon of the scallions and stir-fry 1–2 minutes or until aromatic. Add the tofu, carrots, water chestnuts, and bamboo shoots. Stir-fry for 1 minute. Slowly add the spinach, stirring to incorporate, and stir-fry for 2 minutes.

2. Mix the sugar, soy sauce, and hoisin sauce, adding a tablespoon or so of the water if too dry. Pour over the vegetables and stir-fry 1 minute. Let cool.

3. Stir the cornstarch into the remaining 4 tablespoons of water in a cup. Take a wonton wrapper and, holding it with a point toward you,

1 tablespoon sugar

2 tablespoons soy sauce

2 tablespoons hoisin sauce

5 tablespoons water

2 tablespoons cornstarch

1 package 2-inch-square wonton skins, yellow if available

RED OIL SAUCE

1 teaspoon finely minced garlic

4 tablespoons soy sauce

½ teaspoon sugar

¼ teaspoon ground cinnamon

1–2 tablespoons chili oil, or more to taste*

put 1 tablespoon of filling on the lower half. Fold once, then bring each point around so they meet. Brush with the dissolved cornstarch and pinch the points together.

4. Bring 2 quarts of water to a boil. Add the dumplings in 1 batch and stir immediately to separate. As soon as the water comes to a boil again, lower to a simmer for 15 minutes.

5. Meanwhile, make the sauce. Stir together the garlic, soy sauce, sugar, cinnamon, and 1 tablespoon of the chili oil in a small bowl. Add more chili oil according to your taste. Mix well. (This sauce keeps in the refrigerator, covered, indefinitely.)

6. When the dumplings are done, drain them. Place a dumpling on a plate, pour a little red oil sauce over, and garnish with remaining scallions.

*You can easily make your own chili oil. Just take a teaspoon of pepper flakes and heat them in a tablespoon or so of vegetable oil for a few minutes. Drain out the chilies and you have your chili oil.

TOFU TIPS

I asked Steve Demos, founder of Silk Soy, to talk about tofu, the custard-like curd made from soybeans. As a serious meditator and vegetarian in the 1970s, he came up with a business plan to Americanize tofu. He started by borrowing $500 and buying a blender and a pot. "I started making tofu in my kitchen and sold it at my tai chi class," he said. "I opened a shop, and away I went." Thirty years later, Steve sold his soy milk business to Dean Foods for $295 million.

Tofu is made from curdled soy milk, extracted from ground cooked soybeans. "You create the same result as when you squirt lemon on top of milk," he told me. "We take the curdle, which is similar to farmer cheese, remove the whey, and press the curd. Alone it's almost as flavorless as plain ground beef or chicken. So you use flavor enhancers with tofu as the base," he added. "In addition, tofu and soy products generally are good for the lactose-intolerant and they are good for the environment."

Today we see tofu in many forms. But the most common are soft, firm, and extra firm. Soft tofu is generally for soups and sauces. Americans mainly use firm and extra firm as a meat substitute or sliced, pan-fried, and seasoned as a side dish. The tofu we buy in supermarkets is packaged in a container with water; just drain and it's ready to use. If you have leftover tofu, replace the water with fresh tap water and cover.

Turkish Stuffed Grape Leaves

Y ou can learn a lot about someone's roots from the accompaniments found on his or her Thanksgiving table: stuffed grape leaves, Vietnamese spring rolls, empanadas, chicken soup, oysters, and so on.

Katie Buyukunsal, a traditional Turkish cook, serves stuffed grape leaves at every event, including Thanksgiving. Although she doesn't grow grapes in her own garden, her friends do. She picks the tender leaves in the spring, blanches them, and freezes them in plastic freezer bags, thawing them the night before she needs them. When she runs out, she uses jarred grape leaves, which she soaks first in cold water to remove some of the salt.

YIELD: ABOUT 50 STUFFED GRAPE LEAVES

¾ cup extra-virgin olive oil

3 medium onions, diced (about 2 cups)

2 cups medium-grain rice

⅓ cup pine nuts

⅓ cup currants

4½ cups water

4 tablespoons minced fresh or 1 tablespoon dried mint

2 tablespoons dried dill

1 teaspoon cinnamon (optional)

1 teaspoon allspice

1 teaspoon black pepper

1 tablespoon salt

2 tablespoons sugar

60 fresh grape leaves or one 16-ounce jar (dry weight) grape leaves

2½ lemons

1. Heat the olive oil in a pot and sauté the onions for about 5 minutes, until they are translucent. Add the rice and the pine nuts and cook for 10 minutes, stirring. Add the currants and 3½ cups of the water, bring to a boil, cover, and simmer slowly over low heat for another 15 or so minutes or until the water has evaporated. Add the mint, dill, cinnamon (if using), allspice, black pepper, salt, and sugar and stir.

2. Cover the pot with a paper towel, then the lid, and let sit for about a half hour.

3. If using fresh leaves, just rinse them in water. If using leaves bottled in brine, drain and soak them in cold water for about 5 minutes to get rid of some of the saltiness, changing the water a few times. Drain the leaves in a colander, then squeeze the juice of 1 lemon over them. Line a heavy 6-quart pot with 5 leaves, dull side up. Place 1 leaf on a flat surface, dull side up and with the stem away from you. Spoon 1 tablespoon of filling near the stem end of the leaf and flatten the filling to the width of the leaf. Fold the stem over the filling, then fold the sides into the center and roll toward you. Repeat with the remaining leaves and stuffing.

4. Arrange the stuffed grape leaves, seam sides down, in rows along the bottom of the leaf-lined pot, then stack them on top of one another. Pour the remaining 1 cup of water over the leaves, squeeze another half a lemon over all, top with a few of the remaining leaves, and place

a small plate on top to keep the leaves weighted down. Cover the pot and bring to a boil; reduce the heat and simmer slowly for 30 minutes. Allow to cool in the pot and chill for a day.

5. Before serving, slice a second lemon to decorate the grape leaves.

Malaysian Swordfish Satays

Satay, which seems to be served at every cocktail party these days, originated in Southeast Asia. The skewers of meat or fish are especially popular in Malaysia, where making them has been raised to a high art. In Washington they are served each year at the Malaysian embassy's Independence Day celebration. What guests do not know is that the Malaysian women associated with the embassy voluntarily prepare the food for weeks ahead: marinating, skewering, chopping, stuffing, and rolling the ingredients for their satays, spring rolls, rice cakes, and curry puffs. The satays, assembled a week in advance and bundled in bunches of fifty, are covered in foil and frozen uncooked.

I like to make them with swordfish, chicken, and sirloin. I half-freeze the fish or meat for easier cutting, then marinate the pieces and skewer them in advance. The delicious peanut sauce will last a long time refrigerated.

YIELD: ABOUT 30 SATAYS

3 pounds swordfish, boneless chicken breasts, or sirloin steak (excess fat removed)

2 tablespoons coriander seeds

1 teaspoon fennel seeds

½ teaspoon cumin seeds

4 cloves garlic, peeled and left whole

Two 2-inch stalks lemongrass, outer fibers removed

1. If using swordfish, cut horizontally with the grain into 3-inch strips, then cut against the grain and shave the strips into ⅛-inch slices. With chicken and beef, cut carefully into 2-by-3-inch strips, ¼ inch thick.

2. Toast the coriander, fennel, and cumin seeds in an ungreased frying pan over medium-high heat for about 3 minutes or until you can crack the coriander seeds easily with your fingers. Grind all the seeds together, using a spice grinder, and sprinkle over the meat or fish.

One 1-inch piece fresh
gingerroot, peeled and
sliced thinly
3 tablespoons soy sauce
5 tablespoons vegetable oil
Pinch turmeric powder
½ teaspoon salt (optional)
6 tablespoons sugar
Thirty 8-inch bamboo skewers
Peanut sauce (recipe below)

3. Pulse the garlic, lemongrass, and ginger together in a mini-chopper or mortar and pestle and rub into the fish or meat with your fingers. Put into a bowl or plastic container with a lid and add the soy sauce, vegetable oil, turmeric powder, salt, and sugar. Marinate the fish or meat for at least 1 hour, or overnight, in the refrigerator.

4. Soak thirty 8-inch bamboo or wooden skewers in cold water for 15 minutes. Thread the fish or meat onto the skewers lengthwise, using 3 or 4 pieces of meat per skewer and allowing 4 inches of space at the handling end of each skewer but keeping the fish or meat close to the sharp end for easier eating. (If you wish, you may freeze the threaded skewers for later use.)

5. Grill or broil the skewers over high heat for 1 minute on each side for the fish and 2 minutes on each side for the meat. Serve with peanut sauce for dipping.

Peanut Dipping Sauce

YIELD: ABOUT 3 CUPS

7 ounces (1⅓ cups) roasted
peanuts
1 tablespoon hot chili powder,
or to taste
2 cups warm water
½ onion, quartered
2 teaspoons tamarind paste
¼ cup vegetable oil
½ stalk lemongrass, split in half
lengthwise and coarse outer
skin removed
1½ tablespoons brown sugar
¼ cup granulated sugar
1 teaspoon salt, or to taste

1. Pulse the peanuts and chili powder coarsely in the bowl of a food processor equipped with the steel blade. Remove to a bowl and stir in 1 cup of the water.

2. Purée the onion, remaining water, and the tamarind paste in the food processor.

3. Heat the vegetable oil in a medium-size frying pan. Add the puréed onion and heat over medium heat until it comes to a boil. Stir in the lemongrass, brown sugar, granulated sugar, salt, and the peanut mixture. Simmer for about 15 minutes or until the mixture is thick and bubbly. If it is too thick, stir in 1–2 tablespoons more warm water. Remove the lemongrass stalk. Cool, then pour into a serving bowl and serve as a dipping sauce with the satays. This sauce can keep in the refrigerator, covered, for at least a week.

Memelitas

Tortillas Topped with Refried Beans and Salsa . . . a Taste of Mexico on the Jersey Shore

As soon as I stepped inside Mexico Lindo, a restaurant in Point Pleasant, New Jersey, I smelled the aroma of *memelitas*—little handmade tortillas filled with beans and topped with a tomato-based salsa, shredded cheese, and minced fresh cilantro. The owner, Abel Guerrero, who hails from Puebla (as do more than half of the Mexicans in the New York area), offered me a glass of tamarind juice made with fruit he had brought from his uncle's garden in Tehuixtla.

The Guerrero family came across the border in 1963 and then took a bus from San Antonio to New Jersey. "My mother used to make tortillas for the young men who immigrated alone," he said. "She'd buy the masa, which came in a can from Mexico for fifteen cents, and make dozens of tortillas at a time." In 1965, the Guerreros started selling *masa tamalina* locally, and soon his mother was making tamales and selling them on Fourteenth Street in New York City.

Watching Abel's mother and aunt molding these little pielike tortillas and filling them with creamy black beans, I had the sense that the hearts of these first-generation immigrants were still in Mexico. The daily rhythm of cooking, as they prepare these delicious *memelitas*, takes them back to their roots. "All our dishes are natural," said Abel as he glanced at his mother. "And all our dishes have been homemade for generations."

YIELD: 5 MEMELITAS

2 cups instant masa harina (corn flour)

1⅓ cups water

Canola oil for deep-frying

2 cups creamy refried beans (page 225), or canned

½ cup salsa (page 96)

1 cup grated queso (Mexican cheese)

½ cup chopped fresh cilantro

1. Put the masa in a bowl, pour on the water, and, using your hands, knead well. Form into 5 balls. Using the heel of your hand, flatten each into a circle 4 inches in diameter and less than ¼ inch thick. Cook the tortillas on a very hot griddle (about 450 degrees) for 4–5 minutes on each side. Let cool.

2. Heat about 2 inches of oil to 375 degrees in a wok or deep fryer.

3. Holding each *memelita* in the palm of your hand, form a lip about ½ inch in from the edge, then press it into a round mold like a small pie tin for a few seconds to keep the shape. Deep-fry the shaped *memelitas* 2 or 3 at a time, for at least 1½ minutes. Repeat with the remaining *memelitas*. Serve each as an appetizer topped with warm creamy refried beans, salsa, grated *queso*, and cilantro.

Soups

The soup pot is a good barometer of American cooking. These days, hot peppers are replacing paprika, and Thai basil and lemongrass are becoming as common as dill and parsley. I remember, when I attended a luncheon years ago at the home of a food writer, eating an almond gazpacho with grapes and garlic. I had never tasted anything so exotic. Today we have watermelon gazpacho, vichyssoise with blue potatoes (page 129), and cold ginger carrot soup. We also have tricolored soups, cappuccino-foamed mushroom soup, and soups served in demitasse cups.

This chapter reflects the many different kinds of soup that have entered our repertoire since the early 1960s: pho, a hearty meat soup from Vietnam (page 152), chicken lemongrass soup from Cambodia (page 144), sashimi gazpacho from Japan (page 130), and, of course, a variety of chicken-based coconut soups from Southeast Asia (page 153).

Modern food science has perfected the art of canning and freeze-drying soups. Indeed, some packaged soup mixes are so good that many chefs use them as bases in their restaurants. Throughout this chapter, I sometimes call for vegetable or chicken broth. You can use bouillon cubes or, if you like, use vegetable peelings and scraps to make your own vegetable stock.

Clockwise from top right: Alice Waters's edible schoolyard; Roberto Donna, Wolfgang Puck, and Jean-Louis Palladin; Cliff Wharton at rest; A rainbow of tomatoes; Suad Shallal molding meatballs; A ripe artichoke

Francis's Fresh Mesclun Greens and Herb Soup

"Thirty years ago, when I came to America, I couldn't get fresh herbs or the selection of greens that I can today," Francis Layrle, the chef at the French ambassador's residence in Washington, D.C., told me. "Even if I can't use all the different ingredients from so many influences in America, I use many of the new techniques, like sautéing instead of blanching. That way you don't lose the nutrients. All French chefs who come over to America overcook vegetables."

If the top invitation in Washington is the White House, then the second is to dine at the French ambassador's table. Eager to have those fresh herbs on hand, Francis encouraged Richard Ober, a friend who had just retired from the foreign service, to plant a garden, in which he eventually cultivated eighty-five different kinds of herbs and salad greens. Richard would deliver his goods daily to the embassy kitchen, often arriving just in time to join Francis for lunch.

Francis, whose tiny office is stocked with old French cookbooks, is the culinary representative of his country. Although he must often serve classic French food, he has been influenced by nouvelle cuisine and the American culinary revolution. This wonderful herbal soup, made with a mesclun mix, is typical of his new style—lighter, fresher, and with no cream. It can easily be prepared with those bagged mixed greens one finds at the supermarket.

YIELD: 6 SERVINGS

2 cups vegetable or chicken broth (pages 290, 146)
½ sweet onion, such as Vidalia or Walla Walla, chopped
½ leek, chopped, white part only
1 bay leaf

1. Pour the broth into a large pot and bring to a slow simmer. Add the onion, leek, and bay leaf and simmer, uncovered, for about 10 minutes. Remove the bay leaf.

2. Coarsely chop the mixed greens and the herbs. Heat 4 tablespoons of the olive oil in a large sauté pan and sauté the garlic until golden. Toss

10 ounces of spring greens or other mesclun mix

2 cups chopped fresh mixed herbs such as chervil, cilantro, flat parsley, mint, tarragon, thyme, and basil

6 tablespoons olive oil

2 cloves garlic, chopped

Salt and freshly ground pepper

2 tablespoons unsalted butter

2 tablespoons grated Parmesan cheese for garnish (optional)

in the mixed greens and herbs and sauté for another 2 minutes. Drain everything in a colander, pressing out any excess liquid.

3. Place the vegetables and the broth in a blender and purée. Taste, adding salt and pepper if needed, and blend again.

4. Pour the soup through a coarse sieve, a colander, or a food mill placed over a bowl.

5. To serve hot, pour the puréed soup into a saucepan and heat, stirring in the butter. Pour into warm soup bowls and drizzle a ribbon of olive oil on top of each serving and, if you like, a little grated Parmesan cheese. To serve cold, omit the butter, and chill.

FOOD WITH FASHION FLAIR

Han Feng, a fashion designer and artist born in Nanjing, China, lives in a simple loft in New York City's Flower District. To me, she is the ultimate New York entertainer. Sensing her hand in every creative touch in her apartment, down to the dining table and the food, I only wanted her to dress me as well! Walking into her long white dining room, where the table was set for ten, I met a wonderful array of guests—among them, a musician, an artist, a literary agent, and NPR's Scott Simon. Rocks and pebbles plucked by Han Feng from Long Island, Iceland, and New Zealand decorated the apartment.

Even though the eight-course meal was served by a Russian helper, you had the feeling that Han Feng was very much in charge. Several days in advance of the meal, she'd gone to Chinatown to see what was fresh and in season—fresh peas, halibut, exotic fruits, and lime leaves. My favorite courses were tuna poached in carrot juice, halibut cooked with sake (page 278), and this simple pea soup, now a regular at my summer dinner parties. Han Feng clearly loves to cook, to bring people together. Her motto is "Life is for loving, loving is for life." When I left her home at midnight, the party was still going on, and I felt she very much represented the spirit of the new century.

Han Feng's Pea Soup

> "The hue of this soup is a crisp light green reminiscent of a nubile spring palette. The aroma is a subtle bouquet top, noted with fresh lime. In order to punctuate these unique aspects in presentation, I suggest placing each soup serving in a delicate white rice bowl—dropping in a single ice cube, which will look like a bit of glass, and garnishing each bowl with a few finely chopped chives or a fresh lime leaf."
>
> —HAN FENG

M ost cold pea soups have mint and lots of heavy cream. I love this simple East-West fusion with fresh lime leaves.

YIELD: 6–8 SERVINGS

4 cups chicken broth (or 4 cups water and 1 cube of Star Ai Funghi Porcini mushroom-flavored bouillon)

1 pound fresh sweet peas, shelled, or two 10-ounce packages frozen peas

Sea salt to taste

Pepper to taste

4 fresh Kaffir lime leaves plus chopped lime leaves for garnish

2 tablespoons chopped chives

1. Pour the chicken stock or the water and bouillon cube into a large pot and bring to a boil.

2. Add the peas. Sprinkle on salt and pepper to taste and simmer for 3–5 minutes, covered, until the peas are just cooked. Remove from the heat, allow to cool, then purée the peas and the 4 lime leaves with 1 cup of the stock in a blender or food processor. Pour the purée into a bowl, stir in the rest of the broth, and cover. Chill in the refrigerator until ready to serve.

3. The moment before you serve the soup, plop an ice cube into each bowl and garnish with chopped lime leaves and the chopped chives.

Pickity Place Blue Potato Vichyssoise
with Loads of Fresh Herbs

This is a new wrinkle on an old theme—using blue potatoes and lots of fresh herbs to make a nouvelle vichyssoise.

Pickity Place, a charming lunch restaurant hidden in the hills of southern New Hampshire, serves an especially good vichyssoise with blue potatoes flavored with fresh herbs and decorated with edible flowers, all picked from their sprawling garden.

YIELD: 8–10 SERVINGS

2 Spanish onions, roughly chopped

2 leeks, both green and white parts, roughly chopped

2 tablespoons pure olive oil

2 cloves garlic, minced (about 2 teaspoons)

4–6 blue potatoes (about 1¼ pounds), peeled and halved

4 cups chicken broth (page 146)

2 tablespoons chopped fresh dill

2 tablespoons chopped fresh chives

2 tablespoons chopped fresh or 2 teaspoons dried thyme

2 tablespoons chopped fresh parsley

½ cup heavy cream

Salt and freshly ground pepper to taste

1. Sauté the onions and leeks in the olive oil in a soup pot for a few minutes, until translucent. Add the garlic and sauté for a few minutes more.

2. Add the potatoes, chicken stock, 1 tablespoon of the dill, and 1 tablespoon each of the chives, the thyme, and the parsley, and bring to a boil. Reduce heat and simmer for about 15 minutes or until the potatoes are soft, then purée the soup using either a food mill or a food processor. Stir in the heavy cream and add salt and pepper to taste. Just before serving, toss in all the remaining herbs, give the soup a quick stir, and ladle into soup bowls. This soup can be eaten hot, but I prefer it cold, especially in the summer.

Kaz Sushi's Sashimi Gazpacho

Of all the exotic gazpachos I have tasted recently, this one stands out. Kaz Okochi at Kaz Sushi Bistro in Washington, D.C., made this simple Spanish soup with jalapeño peppers, sashimi, wasabi, and Meyer lemon oil from California. "We are constantly thinking of how to serve fish and soup," he told me. "I know ceviche and I know gazpacho—all very Spanish. Being in America frees me to do whatever I want to do—to be freestyle Japanese." When I made this recipe for my family, we realized how great the gazpacho was on its own, even without the sashimi. So dress it with sashimi, or just eat it alone, garnished with the remaining jalapeño and a little Meyer lemon oil.

YIELD: 6 SERVINGS

1 large jalapeño pepper

2 pounds ripe plum tomatoes, seeded

¼ medium onion, coarsely chopped

¼ red pepper, chopped in large chunks

¼ cucumber, unpeeled, chopped in large chunks

¼ cup rice vinegar

¼ cup freshly squeezed lemon juice

1 teaspoon wasabi or to taste

¼ cup extra-virgin olive oil

Salt and white pepper to taste

¼ pound tuna (optional)

¼ pound salmon (optional)

¼ pound fresh sea scallops (optional)

Splash of Meyer lemon oil (optional)

1. Cut the stem off the jalapeño, then cut in half vertically and remove the seeds. Cut a ½-inch piece off the pepper, dice, and reserve.

2. Put the remaining jalapeño in a blender, along with the tomatoes, onion, red pepper, cucumber, rice vinegar, lemon juice, and 1 teaspoon of the wasabi. Slowly add the olive oil as the blender purées everything, blending at high speed until smooth. Season to taste with salt and pepper. Remove to a bowl, cover, and chill well.

3. If you want to add sashimi, slice the raw fish into paper-thin slices that are about an inch long. Before serving, place a few slices of each fish on the bottom of each soup bowl and sprinkle with some of the diced jalapeño. Ladle the gazpacho over the fish. Garnish the servings with a little more minced jalapeño, a dab or two of wasabi, and, if you like, a squirt of Meyer lemon oil.

Turkish Cucumber Yogurt Soup

During my junior year abroad in France, in the 1960s, I discovered yogurt. I loved sprinkling sugar over the soured custard sold then in individual glass bottles, or blending it in but tasting the sweet and the tangy on my tongue. It was delicious. When I returned home, very few people had heard of it. Now we have chocolate yogurt, yogurt ice cream, pourable yogurt, even bright blue "go-gurt" for kids on the go. Sometimes it's hard to find plain whole milk yogurt.

We have learned a lot recently, from our exposure to Indian and Middle Eastern cuisine, about how to use plain yogurt in our cooking. We now make Indian mango lassi drinks (page 18), salads with yogurt dressing, and even cakes with yogurt instead of sour cream.

Katie Buyukunsal (page 119) of Turkey served me this refreshing cold cucumber soup, a recipe that I have varied throughout the years, substituting mint for dill or adding raisins, nuts, and eggs in a Persian adaptation. The key to this recipe is the cucumbers: you don't want them too big, and you need to get rid of the seeds.

YIELD: ABOUT 6 SERVINGS

2 medium cucumbers, peeled, cut in half lengthwise, and seeded

One 32-ounce container of plain yogurt

2 cloves garlic, mashed

1 tablespoon salt

1 teaspoon dried dill or dried mint

1 tablespoon extra-virgin olive oil

2 tablespoons chopped fresh dill or mint

1. Grate the cucumbers through the large holes of a grater, or dice.

2. Place the cucumber in a bowl and stir in the yogurt, garlic, salt, and the dried dill or mint. Refrigerate the soup, covered, until very cold. If it is thicker than the consistency of heavy cream, add a little water to thin it out.

3. To serve, ladle the soup into soup bowls, drizzle with olive oil, and finish with a sprinkling of fresh dill or mint.

Yin-Yang Lovage/Celery and Carrot Soup

This delightful cold soup, actually two soups in one, comes from Linda-Marie Loeb. I met Linda at a food writers' symposium and later visited her eighty-acre farm in Calistoga, California, where she cultivates at least one hundred kinds of unusual herbs, including burnet, borage, angelica, lovage, and lemon verbena.

She gave me this recipe calling for combining lovage, an herb that is similar to but more intense than celery, with carrots—two flavors, she said, that are opposite yet complementary, like yin and yang in Chinese philosophy. I often use celery instead of the lovage, selecting some of the larger, more mature leaves on the outside tops of the stalks, rather than the tender interior fernlike leaves. I also add some celery and fennel seeds. I have listed the ingredients and preparation for each soup separately. You can serve them as two soups on their own or as Linda does, positioning the lovage or celery and carrot soups on either side of a shallow soup bowl with a flat lip. To do this, simultaneously scoop a ladleful of each soup with your right and left hands, and then pour the soups into the bowl at the same time, gradually moving each ladle slightly clockwise to form a yin-yang pattern. Garnish each serving with a dollop of crème fraîche in the center of each bowl and top with a sprig of fennel leaf. Either way you serve them, these are two refreshing summer soups.

Carrot Soup

YIELD: 4 SERVINGS

5 tablespoons butter
½ medium onion, coarsely chopped
1 stalk celery, coarsely chopped (about ½ cup)
7 carrots, peeled and coarsely chopped in ¼-inch pieces (about 3 cups)
2½ cups chicken broth
1 teaspoon salt
3 sprigs tarragon
½ cup crème fraîche or sour cream

1. Place the butter, onion, celery, and carrots in a medium saucepan. Sauté over medium heat for about 8 minutes, stirring frequently to avoid sticking or burning.

2. Pour on the chicken broth and salt. Bring to a boil, reduce the heat to low, and simmer for about 10 minutes.

3. Sprinkle on the tarragon and continue simmering, stirring occasionally, until thickened slightly and the vegetables are soft enough to be mashed with a spoon against the side of the pan, roughly 30 minutes. Remove the saucepan from the heat when done and allow the soup to cool for about 5 minutes, removing and discarding the tarragon sprigs.

4. In a blender or food processor, with the lid on tightly, purée the soup, 1–2 ladlefuls at a time. After puréeing each ladleful, empty the soup into a deep bowl.

5. Serve immediately, garnished with a dollop of crème fraîche or sour cream, or cool and refrigerate until ready to serve.

Lovage/Celery Soup

YIELD: 4 SERVINGS

5 tablespoons butter

½ medium onion, coarsely chopped

½ cup chopped lovage leaves and stalks (if lovage is not available, use ½ cup chopped celery plus ¼ teaspoon fennel seed and ¼ teaspoon celery seed)

3 cups fennel bulb sliced in ⅛-inch slivers (approximately 2 bulbs)

2½ cups chicken broth

1 teaspoon salt

¼ cup anise-flavored liqueur like Pernod or arak

½ cup crème fraîche or sour cream

A few fennel leaves (optional)

A few grinds of pink peppercorns (white or black will do)

1. Place the butter, onion, lovage or celery, and fennel in a saucepan. Simmer over medium heat for about 8 minutes, stirring frequently to avoid sticking or burning.

2. Pour on the chicken broth and salt. Bring to a boil and reduce the heat to low and simmer for about 10 minutes.

3. Sprinkle on the anise-flavored liqueur and continue to cook, stirring occasionally, until reduced to a nice soup consistency and the vegetables are soft enough to be mashed with a spoon against the side of the pan, roughly 20 minutes. Remove the saucepan from the heat when done and allow the soup to cool for about 5 minutes.

4. In a blender or food processor, with the lid on tightly, purée the soup, 1–2 ladlefuls at a time. After puréeing each ladleful, empty the soup into a deep bowl.

5. Serve immediately, or cool and refrigerate until ready to serve.

6. Garnish each serving with a dollop of crème fraîche or sour cream in the center of each bowl and top with a sprig of fennel leaf. Take 3 or 4 peppercorns between your thumb and middle finger, gently crush them, and sprinkle around the lip of the soup bowl.

Miso Soup with Vegetables and Noodles

Like many young cooks today, my daughter Daniela determines her menu by what is fresh at the market. Living in Fort Greene, Brooklyn, she shops in Korean bodegas and green markets. Daniela often makes this soothing miso soup for Sunday night dinner and brings the leftovers to work during the week. Being of the tofu generation, she combed vegetarian cookbooks for a good, all-purpose miso-vegetable recipe until she arrived at her own formula, one that evolves according to what is available at the market. For Daniela, this soup is as wholesome as chicken soup is for me.

Be careful when using miso. Some mixtures, like soybean and brown rice, are stronger than others. So start with a little, taste, and gradually add more.

YIELD: 6–8 SERVINGS

4 quarts water

2 garlic cloves, cut in half

2 inches fresh gingerroot, unpeeled and sliced in big chunks

4–5 tablespoons brown miso paste

2 tablespoons soy sauce, or to taste

8 ounces firm tofu

2 scallions, chopped

3 carrots, peeled and cut in rounds

1–2 broccoli flowerets

8 ounces white mushrooms, sliced

4 ounces Asian rice or soba noodles

4 ounces fresh spinach, chopped

3 tablespoons chopped fresh cilantro

1. Pour the water into a soup pot and bring to a boil with the garlic cloves and the ginger. Simmer, uncovered, for about 10 minutes while preparing the vegetables.

2. Remove the garlic and ginger with a slotted spoon and stir in 4 tablespoons of the miso paste, continuing to simmer.

3. Drain the water from the tofu, sprinkle with soy sauce, and set aside.

4. Add the scallions, carrots, and broccoli to the pot and cook a few minutes. Add the mushrooms and the noodles and simmer, uncovered, for another 5 minutes or until noodles are cooked.

5. Stir in the spinach and heat 1–2 minutes. At the last minute, dice the tofu and stir it into the soup. Adjust the seasonings, adding more soy sauce and miso, if necessary. Ladle into soup bowls, sprinkle with cilantro, and serve.

MISO

"Miso is like cheese," said Kazuhiro Okochi, one of the chefs at the forefront of Japanese cooking in America. "There are so many varieties, you have to try them out to see which one suits you." A thick, salty paste of fermented soybeans and grain, miso has been used by Japanese chefs for centuries in soups, marinades, dressings, and dips, and as a leavening agent. Although here it is known mainly in vegetarian circles, some chefs use it as a meat tenderizer. Nobu Matsuhisa, the chef at Nobu, in New York, started a craze with his miso-marinated sea bass.

There are three main types of miso, ranging in color from pale white to dark brown: sweet golden, yellow, or white miso, made of rice and soybeans; brown rice miso, which also has some barley in it; and red miso, the one most commonly served at Japanese restaurants in miso soup. Similar to yogurt in that it contains live cultures, which aid digestion, miso is rich in vitamins, minerals, and amino acids. It is also a very strong antioxidant.

ALICE WATERS'S EDIBLE SCHOOLYARD

Every town should have an Alice Waters. The chef-owner of Chez Panisse, Alice has spearheaded a very successful program called The Edible Schoolyard, located a stone's throw from her home in Berkeley, California. Like so many great ideas, it began as a mix of chance and inspiration. One day in 1995, as she was walking across a vacant lot attached to Martin Luther King Middle School, Alice found herself thinking how wonderful it would be for schoolchildren to learn to grow the food they eat. A brainstorming session with the principal of the school soon followed. Now, that once-vacant lot is filled with sunflowers, corn, raspberries, onions, lavender, and vines crawling every which way—a splendid garden and classroom.

"Some of the local children hadn't ever tasted a fresh raspberry," said Beebo Turman, director of the Berkeley Community Gardening Collaborative, whose husband, an architect, provided Alice with expert help. In fact, as far as I could see as I wandered through the garden, practically the whole neighborhood was and is involved in some way. One parent, another architect, had just designed and helped construct a fabulous chicken coop with fennel growing right in the middle of it.

While I was visiting, Esther Cook, a chef and teacher, was preparing the cooking curriculum. When the students are learning Middle Eastern history, for example, they can cook the Egyptian lentils; when studying the Neolithic period, they can grind and cook millet. "Not only do they cook with the foods from the garden," said Esther, "but they learn how they fit within history."

Edible Schoolyard's Autumn Harvest Soup

This harvest soup from Esther Cook—as colorful as a confetti of fall leaves—is a perfect, and delicious, example of what Alice Waters and her team of cooks and gardeners are trying to accomplish. The children learn where each of the ingredients comes from, when each is at its peak, and how to make a vegetable stock and soup. They try new ingredients, like Swiss chard and bulgur—and learn that maybe they taste good!

YIELD: 10–12 SERVINGS

2 leeks

1 medium onion

3 carrots

3 ribs celery

1½ pounds pumpkin

1½ pounds winter squash, such as acorn, butternut, hubbard, or kabocha

4 tablespoons pure olive oil

5 sprigs fresh thyme

3 teaspoons minced garlic (about 3 cloves)

3 tablespoons finely chopped fresh parsley

¾ cup coarse bulgur

1 bunch Swiss chard (about ½ pound), trimmed and chopped

5 medium tomatoes, diced small

Salt and freshly ground pepper to taste

1. Cut the leeks lengthwise and clean them with lukewarm water to remove any grit. Slice the white part, saving the green stalks. Peel and trim the onion and carrots and chop, saving the peels and skins. Cut the celery into small dice and save the ends. Peel the pumpkin and the squash, cube the flesh, and save the peels. You will use all the scraps to make a vegetable stock.

2. Place the scraps in a stockpot. Cover with about 12 cups cold water and bring to a boil. Reduce the heat and simmer, uncovered, about 15 minutes while you prepare the rest of the vegetables, then strain the stock into a bowl and discard the scraps.

3. Heat the olive oil in a sauté pan and sauté the leeks, onion, carrots, and celery for 5 minutes. Add the pumpkin, squash, thyme, garlic, and parsley and sauté a few minutes longer.

4. Transfer everything to the stockpot. Bring to a boil, then reduce the heat and simmer the soup, uncovered, until the pumpkin and squash are tender, about 10–15 minutes.

5. Meanwhile, cover the bulgur with 2 cups water and let sit for about 15 minutes, while the squash is cooking.

6. Add the bulgur, Swiss chard, and tomatoes to the soup and simmer for another 10 minutes. Season with salt and freshly ground pepper. If the soup is too thick, thin it by adding vegetable broth or water, a ladleful at a time.

7. Serve in warm bowls to friends and family along with a loaf of crusty bread.

Cream of Tomato Soup at Second Sunday Supper at Six

Potlucks and communal meals are a part of American life. Diane Ebersole, a financial planner and single mom from California, decided, when she moved to Minneapolis, to start Second Sunday Supper at Six. Here is how Diane describes this extraordinary monthly tradition: "I am the Sunday supper that people come home to, which is why I felt that it would be a standing invitation. We started with a dozen people, who were free to invite other people. The rules are simple: I make soups in the winter, salads in the summer. If I come back from a trip with a new recipe, like yak stew that I learned in Bhutan, we'll have that."

When I asked Diane what her most popular soup is, she immediately said this tomato soup, with quantities reduced here.

YIELD: 10 SERVINGS

1 tablespoon unsalted butter

4 cloves garlic, minced

1 large onion, minced

1 cup red wine

One 48-ounce jar nonmeat spaghetti sauce

One 28-ounce can whole tomatoes, chopped up, with juices

½ cup finely chopped fresh basil or 2 tablespoons dried basil

2 cups half-and-half

1 cup heavy cream

Salt and freshly ground pepper to taste

1. Heat the butter in a soup pot, add the garlic and onions, and sauté until they are golden. Pour in the red wine and simmer for 5 minutes.

2. Add the spaghetti sauce, tomatoes, and half of the basil and simmer very slowly, uncovered, for 1 hour. Add the half-and-half and heavy cream and continue simmering over low heat for a few more minutes. Add a little salt and pepper, tasting to see if you need more. Ladle into soup bowls, sprinkle with remaining basil, and serve immediately.

Lentil Soup with Swiss Chard and Lemon

This soup, using Swiss chard and Middle Eastern spices, is quite different from the lentil soup that many of us grew up with. A typical Middle Eastern *iftar* (the Ramadan fast-breaking meal) dish, it can be eaten year-round. Lentils have been the poor man's protein since biblical times. Middle Eastern immigrants tend to like this soup puréed, but I prefer to leave the lentils whole. You can serve it as is or with the meatballs that follow. Try some of the colorful lentil varieties available in Indian and health food markets.

YIELD: 8 SERVINGS

8 cups water
2 cups lentils
1 onion, diced
1 stalk celery, diced
1 carrot, peeled and diced
1 recipe meatballs (next page), optional
2 tablespoons pure olive oil
¼ pound Swiss chard or spinach, chopped
1 teaspoon salt, or to taste
¼ teaspoon freshly ground pepper, or to taste
1 teaspoon ground cumin, or to taste
½ teaspoon ground allspice
Juice of ½ lemon, or to taste
1 pita bread, toasted (optional)
½ cup plain yogurt
1 tablespoon ground sumac (available in Middle Eastern markets)

1. Bring the water to a boil in a soup pot. Add the lentils, reduce the heat, and simmer for 20 minutes. Then add the onion, celery, carrot, and, if you like, some of the cooked meatballs, and cook another 10 minutes, uncovered, until the lentils are almost tender.

2. Heat the oil in a frying pan, then add the Swiss chard or spinach and sauté for a few minutes. Transfer the greens to the soup. Season with salt, pepper, cumin, allspice, and lemon juice, adjusting the seasonings to your taste. To serve, ladle into soup bowls and, if not using the meatballs, top with broken-up pieces of toasted pita bread, a dollop of yogurt, and a sprinkle of sumac.

Meatballs

1 onion, chopped

1 pound ground beef or lamb (or a combination of the two)

½ cup finely chopped fresh parsley

1 cup soft bread crumbs

1 teaspoon salt

¼ teaspoon pepper

¼ teaspoon allspice, freshly ground from about 2 whole allspice

1. Preheat the oven to 400 degrees and line a baking pan with parchment paper.

2. Place the chopped onion, the ground meat, the parsley, the bread crumbs, salt, pepper, and ground allspice in a medium mixing bowl. Using your hands, blend the ingredients together and form into balls the size of a walnut. Arrange the meatballs on the parchment-covered baking pan and bake for 10 minutes. Remove the meatballs from the oven and drain on a paper towel.

Haitian *Soupe Jaune* with Butternut Squash, Beef, and Cabbage

Alain Joseph is one of the new breed of indispensable chef's assistants. He is the person who makes Emeril Lagasse look good on television and at demonstrations. Trained at the New York Restaurant School, he now lives in New Orleans. After hearing his story about how this fragrant yellow squash became a symbol of Haitian independence, I asked Alain to give me a modernized version of the dish using some slightly different techniques and ingredients but still holding true to the essence of the dish.

YIELD: ABOUT 8–10 SERVINGS

3½ pounds butternut squash

1 tablespoon kosher salt, or to taste

2 teaspoons cracked black pepper, or to taste

4 tablespoons pure olive oil

1. Preheat the oven to 400 degrees and cover a baking sheet with aluminum foil.

2. Slice each butternut squash in half lengthwise. Scoop out the seeds with a spoon and discard them. Place the squash, cut side up, on the baking sheet and season it lightly with salt and pepper. Drizzle 2 table-

1½ pounds beef stew meat, cut into 1½-inch cubes

1 tablespoon Creole seasoning

1 large onion, diced small (about 2 cups)

One 3-pound cabbage, shredded (about 4 cups)

3 fat garlic cloves, minced

1 tablespoon minced ginger

3 quarts chicken broth or water

1 tablespoon chopped fresh or 1 teaspoon dried thyme

1 tablespoon kosher salt

1½ teaspoons cracked black pepper

¼ teaspoon ground allspice

8 carrots, peeled and cut into 1-inch pieces (about 3 cups)

2 cups farfalle (bow-tie) pasta (optional)

¼ cup chopped fresh parsley

spoons of the olive oil over and roast in the oven for 1 hour or until tender. Remove the squash from the oven and allow it to cool for 15–20 minutes or until cool enough to handle. Use a spoon to scoop the pulp from the skin, then discard the skin.

3. Season the beef with the Creole seasoning and heat the remaining 2 tablespoons olive oil in a wide-mouthed stockpot over medium-high heat. Scatter the meat into the pan and sear the pieces, stirring often, for 5 minutes. Remove the beef with a slotted spoon and set aside. Sauté the onions and cabbage in the same pan, adding a little more oil if necessary and stirring occasionally, for 5 minutes. Toss in the garlic and ginger and cook for another 2–3 minutes.

4. Pour the chicken broth or water over the onions and cabbage and bring to a boil. Reduce the heat to a simmer and add the squash, beef, and thyme. Season with the salt, black pepper, and allspice. Simmer the soup, covered, for 1 hour, stirring occasionally to ensure that nothing sticks to the bottom of the pan. Add the chopped carrots. Simmer 30 minutes more, then stir in the pasta, if using, and cook for another 12–15 minutes or until the pasta is al dente. If the soup should get too thick, you can thin it out with more stock or water, starting with no more than a half cup and adding more if needed. Serve in large individual serving bowls garnished with chopped fresh parsley.

As a child growing up in Queens, New York, I can clearly recall every New Year's Day having a bowl of *soupe jaune* [yellow soup]. It didn't matter if we ate at home, or at my aunt's house or with family friends, there was always yellow soup being served on New Year's Day. Being no stranger to good food, I eat it gleefully each and every year, not particularly concerned about its origins. It was only very recently that I learned of the reason behind the tradition of eating yellow soup on New Year's Day.

"My father, a journalist and authority on Haitian culture and traditions, told me that during the late 1700s, when Haiti was a colony of the French empire, and many French citizens had plantations in Haiti, *soupe jaune* was a dish prepared by the French landowners for special occasions. The combination of butternut squash, cabbage, beef, and carrots produced a mélange of odors that were well known to the noses of the slaves, but the flavor of it was unknown to them and forbidden.

"In 1804, at the end of the Haitian revolution—which marks the liberation of the Haitians from their French masters—the citizens of this newly formed nation decided that now they too would enjoy the spoils of this once forbidden food. Now, in remembrance of their oppression and in celebration of their liberation and freedom, Haitians in Haiti, New York, Miami, Montreal, and throughout the world eat yellow soup on New Year's Day. Understanding now as I do, who would I be to break with tradition and try to replace yellow soup with something with far less importance and history? I now understand, and I now too will keep the tradition. And I hope, after trying this soup, that you will too." —ALAIN JOSEPH

Jean-Louis Palladin's Corn Soup with Lobster

Jean-Louis Palladin will be remembered for his amazing soups. In 1979, Jean-Louis, the youngest chef ever to receive two Michelin stars, left France to come to the Watergate Hotel in Washington, D.C., and create its flagship Jean-Louis Restaurant. Since his death in 2001, other chefs have used his soups as points of departure for their own creations.

When I tried to think of one recipe that shows how he embraced food, this soup immediately came to mind. Jean-Louis finished the soup off with a *mousseline* of lobster, oysters, and red caviar. I have simplified the recipe for home cooks, most of whom don't have his legions of kitchen helpers.

YIELD: ABOUT 8 SERVINGS

2 lobsters (about 3 pounds),
heads included if possible

2 tablespoons vegetable oil

4 carrots, peeled and finely
chopped (about 1½ cups)

4 stalks celery, finely chopped
(about 1½ cups)

4–6 leeks, depending on size,
roughly chopped (mostly white
part) (about 1½ cups)

3 unpeeled turnips, roughly
chopped (about 1½ cups)

1 large onion, roughly chopped

6 tablespoons roughly
chopped shallots

½ cup chopped fresh parsley

1 tablespoon coarse salt

1 teaspoon whole black
peppercorns

1 cup chardonnay or other dry
white wine

5 cups heavy cream

8 ears of corn

Fine sea salt and freshly ground
black pepper to taste

Lobster coral for garnish
(optional)

Chopped fresh dill for garnish

1. Bring a large pot of salted water to a boil, then plunge the lobsters into the water, cover, and bring to a boil again. When the water returns to a boil, turn off the heat and let the lobsters sit in the water for 8 minutes. Using tongs, remove the lobsters from the water and let cool. When the lobsters are no longer too hot to handle, break off the claws and crack them, removing the claw meat and cutting it into ½-inch pieces. Next, break off the tails from the bodies, place on a cutting board, and slice along the hard shell side, cutting the tail in half lengthwise. Remove the meat and set the shells aside. Then halve the bodies of the lobsters, remove the meat, and cut it into ½-inch pieces. Set aside the lobster meat for the soup, and the shells, plus the heads, for the stock.

2. Clean the pot or use another 6-quart saucepan, add the oil, and heat over high heat for about 1 minute. Add the carrots, celery, leeks, turnips, onions, shallots, parsley, salt, and peppercorns and cook until the onions are transparent, about 5 minutes. Add the lobster shells and cook for an additional 5 minutes, stirring occasionally.

3. Pour in the white wine and simmer slowly for 10 minutes, stirring occasionally. Add the cream, bring to a boil, and simmer slowly for another 15 minutes.

4. Remove the pot from the heat. Pluck the shells out of the pot and throw them away.

5. Shuck the corn and cut kernels off the cob. Add the corn to the soup base and heat for about 5 minutes or until the corn is cooked. Season to taste with salt and pepper. Using a slotted spoon, remove about ¼ cup of corn and set aside.

6. Place the soup in a blender and purée. Strain through a chinoise or other strainer, using the bottom of a sturdy ladle to force through as much of the pulp as possible. To serve, place the lobster pieces and a few corn kernels in the middle of a soup bowl. Ladle some soup over, sprinkle with lobster coral and dill, and serve.

Sancocho

Latin Vegetable and Meat Soup

To immigrants from Venezuela, Ecuador, Colombia, and other Latin American countries, *sancocho* means not only soup but comfort. With so many immigrants today coming from Latin America and Africa, it is more and more common to find plantains, cassava, and Latin squashes in grocery stores. (If you can't, I have suggested substitutes for some of the ingredients.) This is my sister-in-law Ilse's version, which she learned in her native Venezuela. You can substitute stew beef for the chicken, in which case, cook for two hours before adding the other vegetables and omit the cumin.

YIELD: 6—8 SERVINGS

One 3-pound chicken, cut into 8 pieces

3 quarts cold water

2 garlic cloves, minced

1 medium onion, diced

1 leek, cleaned and chopped

2 stalks celery, chopped

1 large red or green pepper, diced

4 medium carrots, 2 diced small and 2 cut into ¼-inch rounds

1 teaspoon salt, or to taste

½ teaspoon freshly ground pepper

½ teaspoon ground cumin

1 green plantain, in 2-inch chunks

1 winter squash, such as butternut or acorn (about 1½ pounds), peeled, seeded, and cut into 2-inch pieces

3 medium potatoes or cassava, peeled and cut into 2-inch cubes

1 jalapeño pepper, stem removed, diced, with or without seeds

½ cup chopped fresh cilantro

1. Put the chicken in a soup pot with the water and bring to a boil, removing the fat and foam as they rise to the top. Add the garlic, onion, leek, celery, red or green pepper, the 2 diced carrots, salt, pepper, and cumin. Simmer, uncovered, until the chicken is tender, about 1 hour.

2. Stir the plantain into the pot and simmer for another 5 minutes. Add the remaining carrots, the squash, and potatoes or cassava and simmer, uncovered, until all the vegetables are tender, about 10 more minutes. Adjust the salt and pepper to taste. Stir in the diced jalapeño pepper (along with the seeds if you want it hotter), and serve sprinkled with the cilantro.

Cambodian Chicken Soup from Massachusetts' Pioneer Valley

When Sokhen Mao isn't farming, he's cooking. He suggested that I try his chicken soup, so fresh and very different from my own Jewish chicken soup. He uses no onion, seasoning instead with Thai basil, lemongrass, and Kaffir lime leaves, now easily obtainable at ethnic markets and even at some supermarkets. Savor this soup fresh; it is delicious. If you are keeping it overnight, leave the lemongrass in the pot to retain the lemony flavor. But discard it when serving, as the heavy stalks are too fibrous to eat.

YIELD: 10 SERVINGS

*1 chicken, approximately
4 pounds*

10 cups cold water

¼ cup chopped Thai basil leaves

5–6 cloves garlic, crushed

*3 stalks lemongrass, outer layers
removed and stalks pounded
with a hammer*

5–6 Kaffir lime leaves

1 teaspoon salt, or to taste

2 teaspoons sugar

*½ cup each blanched snow peas,
bean sprouts, shredded carrots,
and/or blanched bok choy*

1. Place the chicken in a soup pot and cover it with the water. Bring the water to a boil. Add the basil, garlic, lemongrass, lime leaves, salt, and sugar. Cover and simmer for about an hour or until the chicken easily pulls away from the bone.

2. Remove the pot from the heat and let everything cool slightly in the stock. When the chicken is no longer too hot to handle, take it out and

pull the meat away from the bone, tearing it into thin strips. Remove the lemongrass, return the chicken strips to the soup, reheat, and serve immediately, alone or over rice noodles. Garnish each bowl with the snow peas, bean sprouts, carrots, and/or bok choy.

We may bitch all day long about the distress of being Hmong, but at the end of the day we will always return home to a bowl of warm rice and chicken soup flavored with fresh blades of lemon grass picked from our humble backyard garden.

—BEE CHA, BAMBOO AMONG THE OAKS: CONTEMPORARY WRITING BY HMONG AMERICANS

The comfort that chicken soup provides takes on new meaning for those, like the Hmong or the Cambodians, who can no longer return to their native homes. When I first met Sokhen Mao, he was darting around the five-acre field leased by the Khmer Growers of Western Massachusetts, showing me snow peas (which he and a group of other Cambodian refugees use for the leaves, not the pods), Chinese broccoli, and oddly shaped gourds. A high school history teacher and community organizer, he told me that his father, brother, and other family members were slaughtered in the 1970s. He described how he watched the Khmer Rouge collect the severed heads of people from his village and how he was forced to leave his homeland at eighteen, escaping to Thailand and, finally, after being interned in two refugee camps, to the United States.

Sokhen handles many tasks at once. Through the New American Farmers Enterprise Initiative, he connects with a local farmer who distributes the Cambodian farmers' bounty directly to chefs in New York City. In addition to the more commonplace corn and tomatoes, the Khmer farmers introduce chefs to unusual kinds of basil, gourds, and pea leaves.

Dad's Chicken Onion Soup

It used to be that fathers cooked on Mother's Day, and that was about it. Paul Bogaards, the executive director of publicity at Alfred A. Knopf, my publisher, is a very hands-on suburban dad. He loves to cook with his children (mostly on weekends) and told me he feels there is an added benefit for his wife: it makes Dad a more responsible cleaner-upper. He lets the kids make a mess, which is part of the fun, and at the end they all clean up the kitchen together. "I used to cook and not clean up," says Paul, "and that is not a recipe for marital bliss." Of course, the most important thing that Paul is giving his children, Michael, Sarah, and Isabel, is the model of a father in the kitchen. "We help him cook and it's kind of fun," said Isabel, six. "It's spending time with my daddy and I get to smell the great smells."

When I attended a weekday family dinner of steak and mashed potatoes prepared by Paul, I asked the children what dish they liked best. "Daddy's chicken onion soup," piped up Sarah. "It tastes so buttery."

Paul waits until he has enough chicken parts stashed away in the freezer to make his stock base for the chicken soup or the onion soup. He puts the rest of the base in ice trays so that the cubes are readily available whenever he needs some. Paul's advice to chicken soup newbies: "Watch the stock, look at the color, and if there is a lot of fat coming to the top, by all means skim."

YIELD: 6–8 SERVINGS

CHICKEN STOCK

4–5 pounds assorted chicken parts, necks and backs, thighs, wings, and/or legs

About 4 quarts water

2 whole medium yellow onions

3 garlic cloves, unpeeled, cut in half

2 carrots, cut on the diagonal

10 peppercorns

2 bay leaves

2 stalks celery, cut on the diagonal into 6 pieces

1. First make the chicken stock. Toss the chicken parts into an 8-quart deep stock pot. Fill it with about 4 quarts water—to about 2 inches below the top of the pot. Bring to a boil, skimming off the fat or the foam as it rises to the surface. Reduce the heat and simmer, uncovered, for about 2 hours. You will have about 8 cups of broth at this point.

2. Add 2 whole onions, the garlic cloves, carrots, peppercorns, 1 bay leaf, the celery, leek, salt to taste, parsley, and dill. Simmer, uncovered, for another hour.

3. Set a fine strainer over a large bowl and carefully strain the stock. Chill, then skim off any fat that rises to the surface.

4. To make the onion soup, peel the 6 onions, cut them in half, and then slice them into ½-inch slices. Heat the butter in a large sauté pan

1 leek, cleaned well and
cut in half

1 teaspoon kosher salt,
or to taste

1 sprig of fresh parsley

1 sprig of fresh dill

ONION SOUP

6 whole onions

2 tablespoons unsalted butter

1 tablespoon flour

1 cup dry white wine

1 teaspoon white wine vinegar

2 sprigs fresh thyme

Salt to taste

6 slices French bread (optional)

½ cup grated Gruyère cheese
(optional)

and sauté the onions over medium heat, until they are tender and straw-colored, about 20 minutes.

5. Stir in the flour. Add the wine, wine vinegar, and thyme. Keep cooking over medium heat until the wine has reduced by a third or so, about 5 minutes, then remove the thyme sprigs.

6. Transfer the onions to a soup pot and pour in the chicken stock along with the remaining bay leaf. Bring to a boil and then reduce the heat and simmer, uncovered, for 1 hour. Remove the bay leaf and add salt to taste.

7. Serve as is, or for each serving broil a slice of French bread with 1 tablespoon grated cheese on top until the cheese melts, then top each bowl of soup with the toasted bread.

My Mother's Chicken Escarole Soup

My ninety-year-old-plus mother loves order and hates chaos. She is precise and unwavering about everything—the way she runs her family, her house, her kitchen. And for her, there is only one way to prepare for holidays. She cooks a week, two weeks, sometimes a month in advance, freezing the rugelach, the chicken, and the plum pies—but never the matzo balls.

Just before she turned ninety, my mother started using chicken legs, which give more color to the soup and are easier to handle—and are often on special in her supermarket. She learned from an Italian restaurant in Providence to swirl in escarole at the last minute, just before she adds her matzo balls.

YIELD: ABOUT 10 SERVINGS

4 quarts water
6 whole chicken leg-thigh quarters
2 stalks celery, sliced into 2-inch chunks
2 whole carrots, cut into chunks
1 large onion, quartered
1 parsnip, cut into chunks
2 tablespoons chopped fresh dill
2 tablespoons chopped fresh parsley
Salt and pepper to taste
About 1 pound escarole, chopped
Matzo balls (recipe follows)

1. Bring the water to a boil in a soup pot. Add the chicken, return to the boil, skimming off the foam that accumulates at the top. Reduce the heat to low and cook for 2 hours, uncovered.

2. After 2 hours, add the celery, carrots, onion, parsnip, dill, and parsley. Continue cooking slowly, uncovered, for another hour.

3. Set a strainer over a large bowl and strain the soup. Season it to taste with salt and pepper. Refrigerate the soup, covered, overnight.

4. The next day skim the layer of solid fat that has formed on the soup's surface. Bring the soup to a boil, or freeze it for another day. Before serving, after bringing the soup to a boil, swirl in the escarole and add the cooked matzo balls. Cook for a few minutes, until the escarole is just tender.

Matzo Balls

3 tablespoons chicken fat or
vegetable oil
6 large eggs, well beaten
1 teaspoon salt
¼ teaspoon grated nutmeg
1¼ cups matzo meal
1 tablespoon chopped
fresh parsley
3 quarts water

I suppose that, being who I am, I cannot write a cookbook without a recipe for matzo balls. We have all heard about the properties of chicken soup, but the curative effects of matzo balls are less well known. Whenever friends are suffering from the effects of chemotherapy, one of the foods that they ask me to bring is chicken soup with matzo balls.

YIELD: ABOUT 12

1. Mix the chicken fat or vegetable oil with the eggs, salt, nutmeg, matzo meal, and parsley in a medium bowl. Cover and refrigerate for a few hours or overnight.

2. Bring the water to a boil in a large pot. Take the matzo mix out of the refrigerator and, after dipping your hands into a bowl of cold water, gently form balls the size of large walnuts. Add salt to the water and drop in the balls. Simmer slowly, covered, for about 20 minutes, then remove from water with a slotted spoon and add to the soup.

"A Jewish deli—second only to a Jewish mother's matzo ball soup."

Oven-Roasted Squash Soup

This recipe comes from Christian Thornton, who, while working at Nora Pouillon's restaurant Asia Nora, prepared it for a crowd at the Dupont Circle Farmers' Market in Washington, D.C. Everybody loved the marriage of squash and coconut milk. Today, Christian makes the soup at Atria, his restaurant on Martha's Vineyard.

YIELD: 4–6 SERVINGS

1½ pounds autumn squash, such as acorn, butternut, or kabocha, cut into large pieces, and seeds removed

2 tablespoons vegetable oil

½ teaspoon sea salt, or to taste

¼ teaspoon freshly ground pepper, or to taste

3 cloves garlic, chopped (about 1 tablespoon)

1 inch gingerroot, peeled and grated (about 1 tablespoon)

1 large onion, coarsely chopped

2 carrots, peeled and coarsely chopped

1 stalk lemongrass, cut in 2 pieces (see page 110)

1–2 teaspoons sambal or other hot Thai chili paste

2 quarts vegetable stock, chicken stock, or water

1 cup coconut milk

Soy sauce to taste

1. Preheat the oven to 350 degrees.

2. Toss the squash with the vegetable oil, salt, pepper, garlic, and ginger. Roast the squash for 1 hour or until it is soft and the edges have begun to brown. Remove the peel.

3. Transfer the pieces of roasted squash to a large soup pot along with the onion, carrots, lemongrass, 1 teaspoon chili paste, and stock or water. Bring to a boil, reduce the heat, and simmer for 20 minutes or until everything is soft and cooked through.

4. Pluck out the lemongrass stalk, add the coconut milk, and purée the soup in a food processor fitted with a steel blade or with a handheld blender. Add soy sauce to taste and, if you like, the second teaspoon of chili paste, and serve.

The word *organic* no longer raises eyebrows in America. Today, people often don't even realize when they are eating organic food and when they aren't. This wouldn't be the case if it weren't for people like Nora Pouillon, the chef-owner of Restaurant Nora in Washington, D.C., which opened over twenty-five years ago. "For the first fifteen years no one understood it," she told me in her restaurant. Her fans urged her not to call the food organic. "Your food is so good and tasty, you don't want to ruin the image by calling it organic," they said.

Nora came to this country in 1965, a young bride from Austria, where food in the years after the war was sometimes scarce but wholesome. Here, she became interested in cooking and food. "But food in the United States had no flavor: garlic, tomatoes, Wonder Bread or Pepperidge Farm," she said. "I found the food so processed and artificial." When Nora started questioning the farmers she got her produce from, she was surprised. "They were using pesticides for the vegetables and grains, they sprayed fruit trees a million times, they used artificial or chemical fertilizers instead of composting," she said. "By more asking around the more I realized how far away from nature agriculture had gone. It is so important what you put in your body. Food grown organically is full of life and energy, and conventional food for me is dead, has no life force in it. People don't understand that everything is connected, we are all part of this earth."

Once Nora realized what she wanted, she took the next step: finding farmers who would grow heirloom tomatoes and fingerling potatoes and raise free-range chickens. She encouraged her chefs to visit the farmers who were growing food for them. After visiting New York's Greenmarket in Union Square, she spearheaded the movement for farmers' markets in Washington. Twenty-five years later, Restaurant Nora became the first certified organic restaurant in America.

Faux Pho

Vietnamese Beef Soup

Innovative cooks have many different cookbooks and visit different markets and restaurants where they look for inspiration. Always searching for new ideas, David Osterhout, a Washington attorney and the cook in his family, checks cookbooks and local ethnic stores. A family favorite is what David calls "faux pho," his version of Vietnamese soup. "I call it 'faux' because if it were real I would use a whole cow, as they often do, making the broth first from the bones of the cow and then cutting the meat paper thin."

If David doesn't have time to go to an Asian supermarket he improvises, using eye of round, which he sticks in the freezer until it is very firm, but definitely not frozen, and then cuts paper thin. For the noodles, he sometimes uses angel hair instead of rice noodles, and he has substituted Tabasco for Vietnamese hot sauce. I have included several different garnishes. Use all of them or whatever is easily available. This is a great dish for kids because they feel they have choices.

YIELD: 8 SERVINGS

4 quarts canned beef broth
1 tablespoon crushed fennel seed
1 tablespoon grated fresh ginger
1 pound very thinly sliced beef
12 ounces thin Japanese rice noodles
A handful of shredded hearts of romaine lettuce
A handful of shredded hearts of celery with the leaves
A handful of bok choy, sliced (or shredded Chinese cabbage)
A handful of bean sprouts
4 scallions, sliced lengthwise and then crosswise
8 cilantro sprigs
8 fresh whole basil leaves

1. Pour the beef broth into a large pot and bring to a boil. Put the fennel and ginger in a tea ball or wrap in cheesecloth and drop into the pot. Reduce the heat and simmer for 20 minutes. If you don't have a tea ball or cheesecloth, just add the spices to the broth.

2. Return the broth to a boil and remove the tea ball or the cheesecloth or strain the spices from the broth. Add the thinly sliced beef, stir to separate the slices, then add the noodles.

3. Reduce the heat to a simmer again and cook for 3–5 minutes, until the noodles are al dente.

4. Scatter the romaine lettuce, celery, bok choy, bean sprouts, scallions, cilantro, and basil leaves in an attractive pattern on a platter. Serve the pho very hot in large bowls, passing the platter of garnishes at the table for everyone to choose what they wish to add. Add as much or as little of the Vietnamese hot sauce and/or soy sauce as you like. Garnish each bowl with slices of the jalapeño pepper and the

2 jalapeño peppers,
cut into 4 pieces, stems and
seeds removed

Vietnamese hot sauce

Soy sauce to taste

2 limes, quartered

limes. Offer chopsticks to anyone who wants them. Eat the beef and vegetables and then drink the broth straight from the bowl.

Note: David recommends the Tuong ot Sriracha brand of hot sauce and any Asian soy sauce. You can also add star anise, cinnamon, and cardamom to your pho.

Ten Penh's Coconut Soup with Lime

After I read about Ten Penh's fabulous coconut-lemongrass soup, mentioned as the ultimate comfort food in the *Washington Post,* I made a beeline for the restaurant. There, I met chef Cliff Wharton. The son of an American naval officer and a Filipino mother, Cliff grew up on Filipino basics like *lumpia* and chicken adobo as well as the meat and potatoes of his father's culture. "My dad was a total meat man," he told me over lunch at Full Key, his favorite Chinese joint in Washington's Chinatown. "If I didn't get into cooking, I'd probably be a meat-and-potatoes guy, too, with all the barbecue in Kansas City."

Cliff decided to become a chef after working in a restaurant while he pursued his first love, music. This soup, served in a hollowed-out coconut, incorporates strips of chicken *adobo,* as well as portobello mushrooms, lemongrass, and lime juice. Galanga, a Southeast Asian rhizome often substituted for ginger, is used in this dish. Ginger is often substituted for galanga because it is easier to find. Cliff loves Kaffir lime leaves in this dish—their aroma is extraordinary. If you can't get them, use the lime zest.

YIELD: 10 SERVINGS

Six 13-ounce cans coconut milk

5 inches of galanga or
gingerroot, peeled and chopped

2 stalks of lemongrass, cut in
2-inch lengths and pounded

6 Kaffir lime leaves, or the grated
zest of 1 lime

½ cup lime juice

½ cup fish sauce

⅓ cup sugar

Salt to taste

¼ cup minced chives

1. Mix the coconut milk, galanga or ginger, lemongrass, lime leaves or zest, lime juice, fish sauce, and sugar together in a small pot. Bring to a boil, reduce the heat, and simmer for 15 minutes. Strain the soup, add salt to taste, then set it aside while making the garnishes (see next page).

2. When the garnishes are finished, place a few pieces of chicken adobo and a few slices of mushroom in individual soup bowls. Add the coconut soup and garnish with the minced chives.

Chicken Adobo

4 chicken thighs, boneless
and skinless
Flour for dredging, about ¼ cup
2 tablespoons vegetable oil
1 cup rice vinegar
1 cup soy sauce
10 black peppercorns
3 bay leaves
3 garlic cloves, chopped

1. Lightly dredge the chicken in the flour, shaking off any excess.

2. Heat the oil in a sauté pan. Sear the chicken on both sides until golden brown. Add the rice vinegar, soy sauce, peppercorns, bay leaves, and garlic cloves and simmer, partially covered, for 20 minutes. Remove the cooked chicken and dice for the soup garnish.

Roasted Portobello Mushrooms

4 medium portobello
mushrooms, sliced
½ cup oyster sauce
½ cup vegetable oil
½ cup soy sauce

1. Marinate the mushroom slices in a large bowl with the oyster sauce, vegetable oil, and soy sauce for 30 minutes.

2. Preheat the oven to 350 degrees.

3. Remove the mushrooms from the marinade and spread them out, in 1 layer, on a baking sheet. Roast in the oven for 15 minutes or until cooked through. Dice the mushrooms and add to the soup.

Salads

W hat a difference fresh greens make. Years ago, salad, particularly in winter, meant either canned fruit; a Waldorf salad with apples, walnuts, celery, and mayonnaise; or iceberg lettuce with a blob of Russian dressing on top. Larger, lunch-size salads might be a chef's salad with ham, cheese, chicken, and hard-boiled eggs; a Cobb salad, the same ingredients with bacon bits and avocado; chicken or tuna salad with lots of mayonnaise; or seafood salads. But in recent years America's salad bowl has been tossed with Asian green papaya and cilantro, French greens and goat cheese, and Middle Eastern *fattoush* and tabbouleh. Today what is called Caesar salad is ubiquitous, topped with grilled chicken, grilled salmon, or grilled calamari, and flavored with balsamic vinegar, Chinese black vinegar, chili-garlic paste, and lemongrass. One fan even has a Caesar salad website, found at www.caesar-salad.com.

"It was the arrival of nouvelle cuisine that rescued the salad," wrote the late Craig Claiborne in the *New York Times* in 1983. Perhaps. But it started on the West Coast with Alice Waters's green mâche salad with California goat cheese.

The most important ingredient in a salad is, of course, what's grown on the farm. And all over the country now there are farmers like Morse Pitts, from Windfall Farms, in Orange County, New York, who have made a difference. Morse grew up on Long Island watching *Modern Farmer* on television; he was an amateur gardener and musician until 1980, when his father inherited 142 acres of rural land. After receiving this windfall (hence the farm's name), Morse and his sisters moved onto the land and began cultivating it, growing vegetables, particularly salad greens, which he has sold at New York's Greenmarkets since 1989. Then he went to a conference on organic farming in California, where a woman showed him micro salad greens, which hadn't been seen on the East Coast. He thought that New York chefs would love a mix of tiny field greens, so he started growing them. He was right; they did.

Clockwise from top right: The Kehler brothers at their cheese farm in Vermont; Minh and Anh-Thu Cao at their restaurant in Gretna, Louisiana; A raw food lunch with Shanti and Gabriel Cousens; Jose Andres and his daughters picking pumpkins; Nan McEvoy and her olive trees

Morse and other farmers like him have rediscovered field greens (also known as spring mix), sprouts, mustard greens, mustard shoots, arugula, mizuna, chard, amaranth, radicchio, and dandelion greens, some of which were widely cultivated during our country's early years. Myra and Drew Goodman, owners of Earthbound Farms, two health food hippies, started with an organic raspberry stand on two and a half acres in Carmel, California. Now they have thousands of acres growing organic vegetables and field greens. They were the ones who had the idea of packaging fresh, washed organic greens for busy consumers. Today Earthbound Farms is one of the largest produce companies in the United States, and it's all organic. Following the Goodman example, other huge companies now wash your spinach and lettuce for you, but their greens are not always organic or as carefully grown. "Organic was just a value added to our product," Myra Goodman told me. "Quite simply, our greens first had to be good, and *then* we turned the farm organic."

Americans' salads have become inventive, using creative combinations of greens, vegetables, fruits, meat, cheese, and seafood. Store-bought salad dressings, vinegars, and designer olive oils have proliferated. It's hard to keep up with the many kinds of vinegars there are—sherry, raspberry, and various balsamic vinegars.

Have fun with these globally influenced salad recipes.

Salad Greens with Goat Cheese, Pears, and Walnuts

One of the most appealing recipes to come out of Alice Waters's restaurant Chez Panisse in Berkeley, California, is a salad of tiny mâche topped with goat cheese. How revolutionary this salad seemed to Americans in the 1970s! Alice got her cheese from Laura Chenel, a Sebastopol, California, native who was trying to live off the grid, raising goats for milk, and had gone to France to learn how to make authentic goat cheese. When she came back, she practiced what she had absorbed, and it wasn't long before a friend tasted her cheese and introduced her to Alice. "All of a sudden the demand was so great," Laura told me, "that I had to borrow milk from others." Beginning with its introduction at Alice's restaurant at the right moment in 1979, the goat cheese produced at Laura Chenel's Chevre, Inc., became a signature ingredient in the newly emerging California Cuisine. Today, artisanal cheese (made by hand in small batches with traditional methods), along with farmstead cheese (made on the farm where the milk comes from), is one of the largest food movements in the United States. Chevre, Inc., has become synonymous with American chevre, and Laura still tends her beloved herd of five hundred goats herself.

YIELD: 6–8 SERVINGS

½ cup walnuts
1 teaspoon Dijon mustard
2 tablespoons balsamic vinegar
¼ teaspoon sugar
2 tablespoons walnut oil
2 tablespoons canola or vegetable oil
Salt and freshly ground pepper to taste
2 ripe Bosc pears
5 ounces goat cheese
6 slices French bread, cut in thin rounds
8 cups small salad greens

1. Preheat the oven to 350 degrees. Spread the walnuts out on a small baking pan and toast them in the oven until lightly browned, 5–7 minutes. Remove the walnuts but leave the oven on.

2. Mix the mustard with the vinegar and sugar in a large salad bowl. Slowly whisk in the walnut and canola or vegetable oil. Season with salt and pepper to taste. Set aside.

3. Core and cut 1 pear into thin rounds. Peel and core the second pear, slice it in half lengthwise, and cut into thin strips.

4. Spread some of the goat cheese on the rounds of French bread and top with a pear round. Then spread some more cheese on top of the pear. Bake in the oven a few minutes, until the cheese has melted.

5. While the cheese is baking, mix the salad greens and pear slices gently in the salad bowl. Divide the salad among 6–8 plates.

6. Place the hot pear-cheese rounds on top of the greens, scatter the walnuts around, and serve.

Olive oil has become quite the thing in America. We've always had Spanish olives and oil, produced by Spanish padres from Mexico. But now, especially in California, American olive oil has been taken to a new level. One of the pioneers in planting Tuscan olives is Nan McEvoy, heir to the *San Francisco Chronicle* fortune. I went to visit the McEvoy ranch and had lunch with Nan, considered to be the American Medici of Tuscan oil. A no-nonsense, take-control woman, Nan was looking for a weekend getaway in the early 1990s and fell in love with a property in the Marin Hills near Petaluma. The only problem was that it was zoned for agriculture.

Not wanting to be a farmer, she thought about bringing Tuscan olive trees to the area . . . which she did, to the tune of several thousand. (The numbers differ depending on who is telling the story.) She also brought over a state-of-the-art Italian cold press, and a professional to show her how to make the olive oil and how to care for the trees. Today, on a hillside covered with olive trees, she is turning out emerald-green, richly aromatic, peppery oil that proves Americans can produce olive oil as good as that in Italy. Nan sells her certified organic oil on the ranch and at a store in the Ferry Building Plaza Marketplace in San Francisco.

Use the best virgin olive oil for salad dressings and lesser, more inexpensive versions for cooking.

Caprese Tomato-Mozzarella Salad with Pesto

When I was growing up in Providence, Rhode Island, you ate this salad only if you were lucky enough to live near the Italian section, Federal Hill, where you could purchase fresh mozzarella, basil, tomatoes, and Parmesan cheese.

Today, with more than 3,100 farmers' markets in the United States (a 79 percent increase since 1994), there's no excuse not to use fresh tomatoes and basil for this salad. Oh, those summer tomatoes! At the San Francisco Farmers' Market, I tasted dozens of heirloom varieties: New Zealand Pink Paste, Green Zebra, Purple Calabash, Black Brandywine, and Mortgage Lifter, to name just a few.

Even mozzarella cheese, made by American cheese makers like Paula Lambert of the Mozzarella Company in Dallas, can now easily be bought fresh. Near Sacramento, a farmer is using real buffalo milk for his buffalo mozzarella. Pine nuts are no longer imported only from Italy; we get them from Turkey and China as well.

I love this colorful twist on a classic recipe: instead of dressing, drizzle a little pesto sauce over the cheese. And if you can, use ripe, multicolored tomatoes.

PESTO

2 cups finely chopped fresh basil leaves

¼ cup pine nuts

2 cloves garlic

2 tablespoons Parmesan cheese

¼ cup extra-virgin olive oil

DRESSING

3 tablespoons balsamic or red raspberry vinegar

¼ cup extra-virgin olive oil

Sea salt to taste

Freshly ground black pepper to taste

2–3 large ripe tomatoes (about 1 pound), cut into chunks

2 balls fresh standard-size mozzarella, cut in half, then sliced (about 8 ounces), or ciligiene (little balls)

1. To make the pesto, place the basil, pine nuts, garlic, Parmesan cheese, and ¼ cup extra-virgin olive oil in a food processor fitted with the steel blade. Pulse until everything is finely chopped but not quite puréed. You'll want a little crunch in the pesto.

2. To make the dressing, pour the vinegar into a small bowl and whisk in the oil. Season with sea salt and freshly ground black pepper to taste.

3. Toss the tomatoes and mozzarella in a large bowl. Drizzle on a little of the dressing and toss. Just before serving, drizzle the pesto on top. Toss at the table.

Jose Andres's Orange and Endive Salad with Goat Cheese, Garlic Dressing, and Almonds

This very American combination is the most popular of all the tapas in Spanish-born Jose Andres's restaurant Jaleo in Bethesda, Maryland. This very imaginative chef told me, "I remember the first time my father picked up two endives at our local market. They were so expensive that he made me treat them very special."

I like the play of orange, endive, and almond in this salad because it is colorful, flavorful, and crunchy. Plus, it's really easy to make.

YIELD: 6–8 SERVINGS

DRESSING

5 whole peeled garlic cloves

4 shallots, peeled and thinly sliced

1 cup extra-virgin olive oil

2 tablespoons sherry wine vinegar

Salt and pepper to taste

2 whole Belgian endives (½ pound)

4 oranges

8 ounces goat cheese

½ cup slivered almonds

2 tablespoons chopped fresh parsley

1. To make the dressing, gently sauté the whole garlic cloves and shallots in ¼ cup of the olive oil in a small frying pan. When the garlic cloves have lightly browned and softened, remove the pan from the stove.

2. Transfer the garlic, shallots, and olive oil mixture to a blender or food processor. Add the vinegar and the remaining ¾ cup of the olive oil. Pulse until the dressing becomes almost homogenous but with small pieces of garlic and shallot remaining. Tasting as you go, season with salt and pepper, and then set the dressing aside.

3. To make the salad, separate the endive leaves and put them in a bowl.

4. Using a sharp knife, cut off the top and the bottom of each orange. Then, slice off the skin from the sides of the orange. (By peeling and cutting the orange in this manner you will avoid leaving any of the white pith on the orange slices.) Holding the orange in your hand with the sections parallel to your fingers, use the knife to cut out and separate individual orange sections.

5. Divide the endives among 6–8 salad plates. Top each endive slice with 2 orange sections, then dot each orange section with about 2 teaspoons of goat cheese. Scatter about a teaspoon of slivered almonds on top and sprinkle with 1–2 teaspoons of parsley.

6. Just before serving, drizzle 1–2 tablespoons of dressing over each plate.

"You think I'm a raw-foodist by choice?"

Interest in the raw food movement has recently been increasing. Gourmet raw food restaurants are sprouting up all around the country. Wanting to see for myself what and how raw foodists eat, I visited the Tree of Life Rejuvenation Center in Patagonia, Arizona, an almost biblical setting in the cactus-filled Sonora Valley. Dr. Gabriel Cousens, the director of the center, eats only organic live (raw) foods, high in minerals and fiber and low in sugar.

The meals at Tree of Life, which serves as a spiritual retreat and a consciousness-raising center, contain neither eggs nor milk. Whenever possible, vegetables straight from the center's own organic garden are used. The cooks rely on a powerful blender and a dehydrator instead of a stove. Bread is made from almond flour, flaxseeds, and coconut water, and is not baked. The prima "pasta" is prepared with raw, julienned butternut squash, and topped with a sun-dried tomato marinara sauce and almond "cheese." The abundant green salad is topped with a chipotle dressing made out of blended vegetables, tahini, and pumpkin seed

oil—no fermented vinegar is allowed. Everything I tried was delicious.

Dr. Cousens, now in his early sixties, came to what he calls "conscious eating" during the 1960s. He has studied the Bible, sun-danced with Native Americans, and spent time with Swami Muktananda, a well-known Indian guru. His wife, Shanti, who lived in India for many years and leads yoga classes at the center, is the author of many of the raw food recipes they use.

"We see live foods as a connection with nature," Dr. Cousens told me as he sipped herb juice on a sunny terrace. "We see ourselves as a community holding the light of well-being as a model of how people can live their lives."

Tree of Life Salad with Red Pepper Dressing

I love Shanti's spicy red pepper, tahini, and garlic dressing and use it on this colorful salad. Whatever is left over I store to have later as a dip for raw vegetables.

YIELD: 6–8 SERVINGS

1 red pepper, halved, seeds and white membrane removed

1 green pepper, halved, seeds and white membrane removed

1 head endive, leaves separated and torn into bite-size pieces

1 cup thinly sliced red cabbage

4 cups mixed salad greens

DRESSING

2 oranges, peeled, seeds and membranes removed

¼ cup tahini (sesame seed paste)

½ tablespoon sea salt

One 1-inch piece fresh gingerroot, peeled

1 large clove garlic

½ tablespoon black peppercorns

½ tablespoon chipotle or other pepper flakes

½ Catarina pepper or other medium-hot chili pepper

1 tablespoon pumpkin seed or vegetable oil

¼ cup raisins

1. Slice half of the red pepper and half of the green pepper into julienne strips. Toss in an attractive serving bowl with the endive, red cabbage, and mixed greens.

2. To make the dressing, place the remaining halves of the red and green peppers with the oranges in a powerful blender or food processor, along with the tahini, salt, ginger, garlic, peppercorns, pepper flakes, chili, and pumpkin seed or vegetable oil. Blend until smooth, taste, and adjust the seasonings. This makes about 2 cups of sauce.

3. Pour enough dressing on the salad to lightly coat it. Add raisins, toss, and serve.

Tree of Life cooks displaying their bounty

Asparagus Salad with Blood Orange Mayonnaise

Even though we can get asparagus from Peru and Mexico any time of year, I still think of it as one of the first signs of spring, and that's when I serve it. Sometimes I prepare this salad as a first course with smoked salmon or as finger food to dip in the orange mayonnaise dressing, made with blood oranges whenever possible. To intensify the orange flavor, I frequently add a bit of dried granulated orange peel found at Middle Eastern markets and many supermarkets.

YIELD: 6–8 SERVINGS

2 pounds asparagus
Salt to taste

BLOOD ORANGE
MAYONNAISE
2 egg yolks
1 teaspoon Dijon mustard
Juice and grated zest of
1 blood orange
1 cup extra-virgin olive or good
vegetable oil
Salt and freshly ground pepper
to taste
Dried granulated orange peel
(optional)

1. Break off the ends of the asparagus with your hands. Bring a large pot of water to a boil and add a little salt, then drop the spears in. Lower the flame and simmer the spears until they are tender, about 5–7 minutes. Remove with tongs and quickly transfer to a large bowl of ice water, so the asparagus will retain its brilliant green color. When chilled, drain the spears on paper towels and refrigerate, wrapped in a towel, up to 4 hours before serving.

2. To make the mayonnaise, put the egg yolks, mustard, and orange zest and juice in a food processor fitted with the steel blade. With the processor turned on, gradually add the oil in a thin, steady stream, processing until the mayonnaise is thick. Taste and season the mayonnaise, adding salt and pepper and optional dried orange peel.

3. Lay the asparagus on an attractive plate and drizzle with the mayonnaise.

Goodbye, baby lettuce. Hello, petite brussels sprouts and mâche. At the Chef's Garden in Huron, Ohio, Bulgarian, Laotian, and Romanian workers wear white lab coats that sport the slogan "Wow Team." They want their customers, the nation's finest chefs, to say "wow" when they open the boxes of salad greens and baby vegetables picked less than twenty-four hours before they arrive. Using hybridization, staggered planting, and experimental crops from seeds given to them by chefs from around the world, this seventy-acre farm is at the forefront of the micro-greens movement.

Lee Jones, dressed in his signature overalls and bow tie, greeted me at his farm, a flat site about three miles from Lake Erie with a balmy microclimate. He told me how, when he was deciding to run a farmers' market in Cleveland in the early 1980s, he ran into a food writer who asked him for some squash blossoms. "I didn't even know what they were," he said. To accommodate her, as well as his own curiosity, Lee started to study and grow squash blossoms, as well as the thin French green beans haricots verts. Word of this spread among local chefs, who quickly became regular customers. "We reached a point where we had to pick chefs or farmers' markets. We took a gamble and picked chefs," Lee told me as he guided me through the high-tech greenhouses where he raises and cultivates designer vegetables and greens.

Now, twenty years later, this high-tech, high-priced farm sells fifteen varieties of squash to twenty-five hundred chefs around the country. "We like to think of ourselves as chefs' personal gardeners," said Lee. In the salesroom, an account executive, one of eighty-six full-time workers, was on the videophone, tempting chefs with the most exciting product of the week: a beautiful purple cauliflower.

As we wandered through the greenhouses, Lee showed me pea tendrils as well as an experiment to produce a white-gold blush beet. The day after I left the Chef's Garden, I received a package at home. "Wow" was the word I uttered when I opened the box to find petite golden and red carrots, fennel, lettuce, and scallions.

Panzanella

Summary Tomato and Bread Salad

In recent years I've noticed that Americans are eating more salads like *fattoush* (page 168), a Middle Eastern bread salad, and *panzanella,* this rustic Italian salad consisting of tomatoes and stale bread.

"The character of the salad is determined by the quality of the tomatoes and the texture or bite of the torn bread pieces," David Scribner, chef at Smith Point in Washington, D.C., told me as he tossed tomatoes in my kitchen. "I like to think of the bread as little sponges absorbing all of the residual juices of the tomatoes. The texture should be slightly chewy and depends on the type of bread you use, how stale it is, and the amount of tomato juice available for absorption. A good rustic, slightly stale farm bread combined with seasonal ripe tomatoes works best." While traditional *panzanella* uses bread and tomatoes with capers and anchovies, David likes to add some pesto to his and uses white balsamic vinegar, which he feels has a nice sugar-acid balance.

YIELD: ABOUT 4 SERVINGS

1 loaf day-old farm or other rustic-style white bread, torn into irregular pieces, crusts included (about 2 cups)

2–3 ripe, juicy tomatoes, cut into ½-inch pieces

1 cucumber, peeled and diced, seeds removed, and cut into ½-inch cubes

½ red onion, cut into ¼-inch dice

1 cup torn greens, like frisée, arugula, and watercress

3 tablespoons pesto (see page 161)

¼ cup extra-virgin olive oil

1 tablespoon white or other balsamic vinegar

Sea salt and freshly ground pepper to taste

1. Toss the bread and tomatoes in a mixing bowl. Wait a few minutes while the bread absorbs the juices.

2. Using your hands, blend in the cucumbers, onions, greens, and pesto and remove to a colorful plate.

3. Drizzle the olive oil and vinegar over the salad. Add salt and pepper to taste and serve.

Fattoush

Lebanese Tomato and Pepper Salad with Mint and Pomegranate

Ilove this Lebanese salad made with roughly cut tomatoes, green peppers, onions, scallions, fresh mint, parsley, lemon juice, garlic, and olive oil. The flavors are unusual and the texture varied. Every Middle Eastern restaurant now makes its own version. Lebanese-born Ramzi Osseiran showed me some of the vegetables he uses, and I incorporated them into my own recipe. Like *panzanella* (page 167), *fattoush* was created as a way to use up day-old bread, soaking it in the dressing and serving it with vegetables. I sprinkle sumac on top, a tangy spice from a red berry. Start with a teaspoon and work your way up, flavoring to taste. When fresh pomegranates are available, sprinkle the seeds on top.

YIELD: 6–8 SERVINGS

1 whole pita bread

1 large tomato, diced, seeds removed

¼ red onion, diced

1 yellow pepper, halved and cut into long strips

1 red pepper, halved and cut into long strips

1 cucumber, peeled and cut in rounds

1 bunch radishes (about 5), sliced

2 scallions, chopped, both white and green parts

1. Preheat the oven to 350 degrees. Separate the pita into 2 rounds and bake on a cookie sheet for about 5 minutes or until very crisp but not browned. Set aside.

2. Put the tomato, red onion, peppers, cucumber, radishes, and scallions into a large salad bowl. Add the romaine or purslane and the fresh mint and sprinkle over the dried mint. Toss with your hands.

3. To make the dressing, whisk together the garlic, olive oil, lemon juice, pomegranate syrup, and salt and pepper in a small bowl. Just before serving, give the dressing another quick whisk and then pour it over the vegetables and work it in with your hands.

4. Break the pita halves into roughly 1-inch pieces and, at the last

1 head of romaine lettuce, purslane, or other wild greens, torn into bite-size pieces

1 handful (about ¼ cup) coarsely chopped fresh mint

1 teaspoon dried mint

DRESSING

2 cloves garlic, minced (about 2 teaspoons)

⅓ cup extra-virgin olive oil

Juice of ½ lemon

4 teaspoons pomegranate syrup

1 teaspoon salt, or to taste

¼ teaspoon freshly ground pepper, or to taste

1–3 teaspoons ground sumac (available in Middle Eastern markets)

moment before taking the bowl to the table, sprinkle with some of the sumac and toss the pita gently into the salad. Taste, add more sumac or other seasonings if you want, and serve right away; otherwise the pita chips will get soggy.

Raw Sweet Potato and Dried Cranberry Salad from Arkansas

This autumnal raw sweet potato salad is an excellent source of vitamins and minerals.

YIELD: 6 SERVINGS

2 cloves garlic

8 sprigs (½ bunch) fresh parsley, stems removed, plus 2 tablespoons chopped fresh parsley

1 pound sweet potatoes, peeled and cut into 2-inch chunks

4 tablespoons orange juice

Zest and juice of 1 lemon

¼ cup extra-virgin olive oil

1–2 tablespoons honey

½ teaspoon salt

Several grinds of black pepper

¼ cup dried cranberries

1. Put the garlic, parsley sprigs, sweet potatoes, orange juice, lemon zest and juice, olive oil, 1 tablespoon of the honey, salt, and pepper in the bowl of a food processor equipped with a steel blade. Pulse until the sweet potatoes are well chopped but not puréed. Remove to an attractive serving bowl.

2. Taste and adjust the seasonings, adding more honey if desired. Arrange the salad on a platter, sprinkle the dried cranberries and chopped parsley on top, and serve.

Lobster Salad with Avocado and Preserved Lemon

"There's a big lobster behind the refrigerator. Maybe if I put a little dish of butter and a nutcracker on the floor, he'll run out the other side."

"I'm making excellent progress. Pretty soon when I lay down on the couch I won't have to wear the lobster bib anymore."

—ANNIE HALL

Keith Korn, a larger-than-life character who died too young, was a very talented chef who opened the Ice House Restaurant on Martha's Vineyard. Having worked with many well-known chefs, he learned from them all and then developed his own personal American style. This is one of his signature dishes. I sometimes serve the salad as is, or make the lobster salad alone, adding a cup of corn, a diced avocado, a diced tomato, and a handful of lettuce. Substitute tuna or shrimp for the lobster if you like. And don't forget the preserved lemon!

YIELD: 4 SERVINGS

LOBSTER SALAD

1 pound of lobster meat from four 1½-pound live lobsters (see page 142 for cooking lobster), cut up

2 stalks finely chopped celery

2 cups cooked corn

1 tablespoon finely chopped fresh chives

1 tablespoon finely chopped fresh tarragon

2 heaping tablespoons mayonnaise

1 teaspoon ketchup

Salt and freshly ground pepper to taste

AVOCADO TOPPING

1 large ripe avocado, peeled, pit removed, roughly chopped

1. Place the lobster meat, cut in generous chunks, in a bowl and carefully stir in the celery, corn, chives, tarragon, mayonnaise, ketchup, and salt and pepper to taste.

2. For the topping, purée the avocado with the olive oil, lemon juice, and cilantro in a food processor. Sprinkle on salt and pepper to taste.

3. Slice the tomato into 4 half-inch-thick rounds. Put the flour in 1 bowl, the egg in a second, and the bread crumbs in a third. Dust the tomato with the flour, shaking off the excess. Dip the tomato in the beaten egg, then coat in the bread crumbs, shaking off the excess.

4. Heat about ½ inch of oil in a frying pan to sizzling. Pan-fry the tomatoes on both sides until golden brown and drain on a paper towel.

5. To assemble salad, place a spoonful of avocado purée on each plate. Lay the fried tomato on top of the purée and spoon the lobster salad on top of the tomato. Garnish with the preserved lemon.

Dash extra-virgin olive oil

Juice of ½ lemon

1 teaspoon chopped fresh cilantro

Salt and freshly ground pepper
to taste

FRIED TOMATO

1 large ripe tomato,
preferably yellow

½ cup pastry flour for dredging

1 egg, well beaten

1 cup bread crumbs

Corn oil for frying

GARNISH

1 preserved lemon, pith removed,
diced finely (recipe follows)

Classic Preserved Lemons

When I give cooking classes, I try to make at least one dish using Moroccan preserved lemons. After tasting their tart flavor, the students go right home and start putting up their own. I love the flavor of these lemons and include them in many dishes, like stuffed snapper with braised fennel (page 289) and quinoa salad with preserved lemon dressing (page 214).

Long ago the lemons were weighted down with stones to keep them submerged in the preserving liquid, but I find they eventually sink with the weight of the salt. I pickle a dozen lemons at a time and keep them on my counter throughout the year—they'll last that long—adding them to salads, fish, and meat.

I have tried quick methods but prefer the slow method, which can take up to a month to mature. Just think ahead and buy a bag of lemons. For a flavorful variation, I sometimes tuck two or three whole cardamom pods or some fresh bay leaves in the jar.

Classic Preserved Lemons (continued)

12 (or more if desired) lemons
1 cup (approximately)
kosher salt
½ cup extra-virgin olive oil

1. Leaving them intact at 1 end, cut 8 of the lemons lengthwise, almost into quarters.

2. Using your fingers, open up the lemons and stuff about 2 tablespoons of salt inside each one, then close them and put them in a sterilized 8-cup wide-mouth jar. Juice the remaining 4 lemons and pour the juice, along with half that amount in water, into the jar, making sure the liquid almost covers the lemons. Add more lemon juice if necessary. Allow to stand, half-covered, at room temperature for at least 2 days, shaking the bottle once each day. The second day add more cut lemons with salt if there is room, cover with more lemon juice, and, if you like, olive oil just to cover and seal in the lemon juice.

3. Close the jar and leave it out on the counter for at least 3 weeks before using. To use the lemons, shake off excess liquid, discard the seeds, and chop up the peel.

Farmers' market in Oxford, Mississippi

Vietnamese Coleslaw with Peanuts and Lime

I first tasted this exotic mix of shredded cucumbers, spearmint, bean sprouts, and crispy lettuce with a pungent peanut sauce at the home of a Vietnamese immigrant family years ago in Bowie, Maryland. They were among the first boat people to come here after the fall of Saigon in 1975. Since then I have tasted the salad in various versions at Vietnamese and other Southeast Asian restaurants throughout the country, but the dish wasn't the same. Then I visited Minh and Anh-Thu Cao's Pho Tau Bay, a restaurant in a strip mall in Gretna, Louisiana, and discovered the real thing again. The couple comes from Saigon, where Anh-Thu's family owned a restaurant. The *bun* (salad) sounds very American, listed on their menu as "vermicelli salad bowls." The Caos explained to me that they listed it this way so their customers can choose individual toppings for their salads: Vietnamese egg rolls, sliced pork, shrimp, chicken, or vermicelli noodles. Not a recipe cast in stone, it's a dish you can vary any way you want. I always add a little shredded green papaya, whenever it's available.

YIELD: ABOUT 10–12 SERVINGS

½ green cabbage (1 pound), shredded

½ red cabbage (1 pound), shredded

3 carrots, peeled and shredded

¼ green papaya or green mango (½ pound), peeled and shredded (optional)

1 medium red onion, shredded

1 red pepper, halved and shredded

2 cups bean sprouts

Nuoc cham sauce (page 112)

Juice of 1 lime

½ cup slivered fresh Thai basil, cilantro, or mint, or a combination of all 3

4 tablespoons crushed roasted peanuts

1. Put the cabbage, carrots, papaya or green mango, onion, and red pepper in a large bowl and toss with your hands.

2. Just before serving, scatter the bean sprouts over the vegetables. Pour some of the nuoc cham sauce over the vegetables, just to coat, sprinkle the lime juice over them, and toss the salad again. Scatter the Thai basil, cilantro, or mint, and the crushed peanuts over all, and serve.

Tunisian Turnip and Orange Salad

I learned how to make this salad from Sylvia Pryzant, a chicken farmer in Pennsylvania (page 305), who learned it from her mother years ago in Tunisia. It is particularly delicious if you can get sweet Macomber turnips from Massachusetts, which taste like radish, turnip, and cabbage combined. People say these recently revived turnips were first brought to America's shores on the *Mayflower* and grown on Clark's Island, across from Plymouth. The recipe calls for Tunisian harissa, for which I have provided a quick formula. However, you can use any store-bought harissa (it comes in tubes or small cans) or another hot sauce.

YIELD: 4 SERVINGS

2 small white turnips
(about 1 pound)

1 teaspoon salt

1 orange (about ¾ pound), peeled

Juice of 1 lemon

1 clove garlic, minced

¼ teaspoon harissa
(recipe follows)

Salt to taste

3 tablespoons extra-virgin
olive oil

2 tablespoons chopped
fresh cilantro

1. Remove the tops and bottoms of the turnips and peel just the top white part. Cut in half from top to bottom, then into slices about ⅛ inch thick, and put in a bowl. Sprinkle with 1 teaspoon salt and leave for ½ hour. Drain and squeeze out the excess liquid.

2. Cut the pulp of the orange into small chunks and toss with the turnips.

3. Stir the lemon juice, garlic, harissa, and salt to taste together with the olive oil. Pour the dressing over the turnips and orange, blend well, and sprinkle with cilantro. Serve alone, or with several other salads, such as the sweet potato salad (page 169).

Harissa

Tunisian Hot Chili Sauce

This hot sauce, which varies across North Africa, has become very popular in America. Today you can buy it in many supermarkets. According to Sylvia Pryzant, a teaspoon of it will cure the worst cold!

YIELD: ABOUT ¾ CUP

2 ounces small dried hot red chili peppers, like pequin or Thai
½ cup extra-virgin olive oil
7–8 cloves garlic
½ teaspoon ground cumin
½ teaspoon ground coriander
1 teaspoon coarse salt, or to taste

1. Cut the stems off the peppers and shake out the seeds. Soak the peppers for several minutes in warm water, until soft; drain and squeeze out any excess water. Transfer them to a food processor and process along with ¼ cup of the olive oil, the garlic cloves, cumin, coriander, and salt until you have a thick purée, the color of deep red salmon. Pour into a jar, add the remaining olive oil, cover, and refrigerate.

2. Let the sauce sit for a few days before using, until it becomes less opaque. Use sparingly; it's very hot.

Chayote Salad with Carrots

This recipe comes from Rebeca Esquenazi, whose parents were born in Turkey and moved later to Cuba, where Rebeca was born. Like many Cubans, she and her husband relocated to Miami in the late 1950s because of Fidel Castro. The recipe reflects the family's wanderings, adding Cuban chayotes (vegetable pears) to a basic Turkish dish.

YIELD: 6–8 SERVINGS

4 chayotes, peeled and diced into 1-inch pieces

4 large carrots, peeled and sliced into rounds

3 stalks celery, diced into 1-inch pieces

1 cup water

1 teaspoon salt

⅓ cup fresh lemon juice (about 3 lemons)

2–3 tablespoons sugar

2 tablespoons vegetable oil

¼ cup thick canned or homemade tomato sauce

1. Put the chayotes, carrots, and celery in a saucepan. Pour in water and salt and bring to a boil. Turn down the heat to a simmer and cook for 10 minutes, uncovered, or until the vegetables are almost soft.

2. Add the lemon juice, 2 tablespoons of the sugar, the vegetable oil, and the tomato sauce. Return to a boil, then simmer, uncovered, for about 15 minutes more or until the sauce reduces slightly. Adjust the seasonings to make a sweet-and-sour sauce, adding additional sugar if necessary. Serve warm or cold as a salad side dish.

SESAME OIL

Plain sesame oil is light and is used in salad dressings and for sautéing. Toasted sesame oil, also called roasted sesame oil and Oriental or Asian sesame oil, is darker, with a stronger flavor, because the whole sesame seeds are roasted before they are crushed into oil. This is used more for flavoring vinaigrettes, for steamed vegetables, and for all kinds of stir-fried dishes.

Greens with Wild Ginger–Maple Vinaigrette

Several years ago, Tom Bivins, the executive chef at the New England Culinary Institute in Burlington, Vermont, prepared a dinner with wild foods. This was the dressing he made, using a brilliant combination of flavors—maple syrup, soy sauce, and wild ginger, to name a few. Wild ginger, if you can find it in the wild, has a fairly pronounced flavor, with a peppery, floral scent, but you can also use fresh ginger. Because there is so much flavor in this marvelous dressing, use it with simple greens and tiny summer vegetables like baby beets or sugar snap peas. This is one of those salad dressings that age well.

YIELD: I CUP DRESSING, TO DRESS AT LEAST 6 CUPS OF GREENS

DRESSING

3 tablespoons peeled, roughly chopped wild ginger, or 2 tablespoons regular ginger

⅛ teaspoon salt

2 cloves garlic

1 shallot, chopped

1 tablespoon balsamic vinegar

1 tablespoon soy sauce

1 tablespoon sherry wine vinegar

1 tablespoon rice vinegar

1½ teaspoons Dijon mustard

¼ teaspoon coarsely ground black pepper

¼ cup maple syrup

2 tablespoons extra-virgin olive oil

2 tablespoons peanut, vegetable, or canola oil

2 tablespoons toasted sesame oil

6 cups mixed salad greens

A few enoki mushrooms

1 pound tiny beets, steamed and peeled

1. Put the ginger, salt, garlic, and shallot into the bowl of a food processor equipped with a steel blade and process until finely minced.

2. In a medium-size bowl, stir the ginger mixture together with the balsamic vinegar, soy sauce, sherry wine vinegar, rice vinegar, Dijon mustard, black pepper, and maple syrup. Set aside for 1 hour at room temperature to allow the flavors to marry. Taste it to see if it is either too sweet or too salty, and adjust accordingly.

3. Slowly whisk in the oils until the vinaigrette begins to emulsify. Check the seasonings again and correct to your taste.

4. Place the greens, mushrooms, and tiny beets in a salad bowl and toss. Pour the dressing sparingly over the greens and toss. You will have enough for your salad and then some.

Chinese Chicken Salad with Cashew Nuts

When I first tasted this Chinese-influenced salad, years ago at a catered event, it was so exotic I asked the caterer for the recipe. The recipe calls for iceberg lettuce, which in its supermarket-processed state has gotten a bad reputation. But it works well here, or try to find fresh iceberg lettuce at a farmers' market.

YIELD: 6–8 SERVINGS

CHICKEN
¾ cup soy sauce
1 clove garlic, minced
1 tablespoon sugar
2 teaspoons hoisin sauce
About 2¼ pounds boneless and skinless chicken breasts
1 cup all-purpose or rice flour
1 large egg
½ cup sesame seeds, toasted
2½–3 cups vegetable oil for frying

SALAD DRESSING
¼ cup white or rice vinegar
2 tablespoons sugar
1 teaspoon minced hot red pepper
2 cloves garlic, minced
1 scallion, finely chopped
¼ cup toasted sesame oil

SALAD
2 cups (4 ounces) rice sticks
½ head iceberg lettuce, finely shredded
2 bunches scallions, chopped
1 cup chopped cilantro leaves
1 tablespoon sesame seeds, toasted
½–1 cup roasted whole cashews

1. To make the chicken, stir together the soy sauce, garlic, sugar, and hoisin sauce in a medium bowl and add the chicken, turning to coat with the sauce. Cover and refrigerate in the marinade for several hours.

2. To prepare the salad dressing, stir the vinegar, sugar, red pepper, garlic, and scallions in a small bowl. Slowly whisk in the sesame oil and set aside until ready to serve.

3. To cook the chicken, put the flour in a shallow bowl, beat the egg in a second bowl, and put the sesame seeds in a third. Remove the chicken from the marinade and cut it into 1-inch cubes. Roll each chicken cube in the flour, shaking off any excess, dip in the beaten egg, and roll in the sesame seeds.

4. Pour the vegetable oil into a wok or a deep pot to a level of 3 inches and heat it to 365 degrees. When the oil is hot, carefully drop the coated chicken pieces, a few at a time, into the oil and fry them for 3–5 minutes, until they are cooked all the way through. Drain the chicken on a paper towel. Leave the wok over heat for the rice sticks.

5. Fry the rice sticks in batches or together for 2–3 minutes, until they turn brown and crisp. Drain them on a paper towel.

6. Assemble the salad. Toss the lettuce on a large serving dish with a slight lip, then arrange the rice sticks on top (can be done an hour in advance). Add the chicken and sprinkle on the scallions, cilantro, and sesame seeds, and scatter the cashews on top. Just before serving pour the dressing gently over the whole dish and serve at room temperature.

Maternity Salad with Romaine and Watercress

Perhaps more important than California pizza (page 55) is Ed LaDou's romaine and watercress salad. Also dubbed the "Maternity," "Labor," "Miracle," or "Pregnancy" Salad, it purportedly induces labor in overdue women. About fifty women visit Caioti Pizza Cafe in Studio City each week to sign the Pregnancy Book and order the salad.

The day I visited the restaurant, a very pregnant Patty Murphy had driven seventy miles from San Clemente to order a Maternity Salad to go. It seems that speculation about this simple watercress and romaine salad studded with Gorgonzola cheese and walnuts has gone national. The best and most expensive balsamic vinegars, which LaDou uses, are produced in wooden barrels and aged for years, and according to scientists at the National Institutes of Health, a fungus that grows on grain can produce derivatives that cause the uterus to contract. Watercress is a blood purifier, and Gorgonzola is a blue cheese that may have a chemical with the properties of oxytocin, the natural hormone in the woman's body that induces labor.

Whatever its chemical properties, this salad certainly has the magic. "We get six to twelve pregnant ladies a day," Ed told me. "The legend has been going on so long, there must be some merit to it." Although he showed me how to make his pizza, he wouldn't reveal the exact formula for his salad dressing, so I have improvised here.

YIELD: 2 SERVINGS

½ cup walnuts

1 bunch watercress, large stems removed (approximately 5 cups)

1 head romaine, leaves separated and torn (approximately 5 cups)

¼ pound Gorgonzola cheese, crumbled

2 tablespoons balsamic vinegar, preferably aged

¼ cup extra-virgin olive oil

Salt and freshly ground pepper to taste

1. Preheat the oven to 350 degrees. Scatter the walnuts on a baking pan and toast for 5–7 minutes. Remove and cool.

2. Place the watercress and romaine in a salad bowl and toss with the crumbled Gorgonzola and toasted walnuts.

3. Whisk together the balsamic vinegar and the olive oil in a small bowl. Add salt and pepper to taste, and pour over the salad.

Wheat Berry Salad with Peppers and Zucchini

One day at Krupin's, my local deli in Washington, D.C., I noticed a salad that looked too healthy for the heavily meat-laden place. But this wheat berry salad with diced vegetables has been on the menu, according to the deli owner, for years.

Wheat berries, also marketed as "spring wheat," are whole wheat kernels stripped of their husks. Because they are not processed, wheat berries retain many of their nutrients: vitamin E, riboflavin, thiamin, iron, and phosphorus.

I tried my own rendition of this dish with everyday garlic vinaigrette. You can vary it by adding feta cheese, fresh capers, and dill. This salad will last three to four days in your refrigerator. Freeze any leftover cooked wheat berries and throw them into your dough the next time you make bread (page 78).

YIELD: 6–8 SERVINGS

2 cups raw wheat berries
1 tablespoon salt
1 medium red pepper, diced
1 medium green pepper, diced
1 medium zucchini, diced
1 medium onion, diced
5 sprigs of parsley, chopped
2 tablespoons chopped or torn fresh basil
2 tablespoons chopped fresh chives
2–3 tablespoons goat or feta cheese

VINAIGRETTE
2 tablespoons balsamic vinegar
3 tablespoons extra-virgin olive oil
1 clove garlic, crushed
1 teaspoon mustard
1 or 2 pinches sugar
Salt and freshly ground pepper to taste

1. The night before you plan on serving the salad, put the wheat berries in a large pot, cover them with 4 inches of water, and soak them, covered, for 8 hours or overnight, in the refrigerator. This shaves an hour off the berries' cooking time.

2. The next day, pour out the soaking water, cover the berries with an inch or so of water, then add the salt and bring to a boil. Reduce the heat and simmer, covered, for about 1 hour or until the berries are tender but still very chewy. If you haven't soaked the berries overnight, simmer them for an additional 1 hour or until done. You will have about 5 cups of wheat berries.

3. While the berries are simmering, toss the peppers, zucchini, and onion in a large bowl.

4. Prepare the vinaigrette by briskly stirring together the vinegar, olive oil, crushed garlic, mustard, sugar, and salt and pepper in a small bowl.

5. When the berries are tender, drain the water and add them to the vegetables, stirring gently with a large spoon. Toss with the vinaigrette, parsley, basil, chives, and goat cheese and serve at room temperature.

Jasper Hill Farm, in the Northeast Kingdom of Vermont, is one of the outstanding producers of farmstead cheese (made from the milk on the farm) in America today. What gives the cheeses such distinct and unforgettable flavors is the milk of the Jasper Hill cows, which feed on local grasses and hay, resulting in cheeses as individual as the men and women who make them.

"What you are getting is a taste in time," Mateo Kehler, who owns and runs the Greensboro farm with his brother, Andy, told me. "As our season changes, our pasture, the weather, it all has an impact on each cheese. We are not looking to sameness in our production."

As children, the brothers vacationed in Greensboro and always wanted to return there. "This is where our heart and our home is," said Mateo, who apprenticed on a dairy farm in England while Andy bought the last chunk of dairy land in Greensboro and learned to tend cows.

When I visited, twenty-seven Ayrshire cows, a breed brought to America by Scottish settlers, were grazing on the 225-acre farm. "The most important thing in cheese making is the milk cows," said Mateo. "We are not stressing the cows to produce more and more. Farmers who use hormones to get every last drop out are like athletes who take performance-enhancing drugs. You breed them once, then they are off to a meat truck. We are hoping to have our cows for fifteen years."

Mateo Kehler and his Aspenhurst cheese

With a loan from the Vermont Economic Development Authority, the two brothers began making raw-milk cheese. As Mateo gave me a tour of the sparklingly clean facility where the cheese is made—we changed into plastic boots and donned hairnets before entering—he told me of the importance of raw milk, which gives their cheese a character you can't find in mass-produced, pasteurized cheeses. "When you pasteurize milk," Mateo told me, "you wipe out everything—the good, the bad, and the ugly. There is a movement to ban raw milk. This would be devastating to us. Our sanitation practices are working, so I can sleep at night."

And it would be devastating to anyone who has tasted any of their three raw-milk cheeses that have been aged for the mandatory sixty days. The Bayley Hazen Blue, a creamy blue-veined cheese, tastes like a cross between a Stilton and a Roquefort. The Constant Bliss is a mold-ripened creamy cheese. And the Aspenhurst is a hard cheese that tastes like a full-flavored cheddar. Said Rob Kaufelt of Murray's Cheese Shop in Manhattan, one of the first to start buying Jasper Hill cheese, "These cheeses have a complexity of flavor that most cheese makers aren't able to achieve."

Mateo showed us how the mold, like mushrooms, ripens the cheese from the outside in. "We try something and wait. The amount you stir cheese, the moisture content, these are all variables. I have learned in making mold cheese that all of the best things are controlled spoilage," Mateo told me as he pierced a wheel of Bayley Hazen Blue to increase the mold. As I tasted the latest batch, Mateo paused. "What you are getting is a taste in time."

Baby Spinach Salad with Blue Cheese, Bacon, Grapes, and Balsamic Vinaigrette

The relationship between chef and farmer seems to be getting closer every year. Steven Obranovich, executive chef of the Lakeview Inn and Restaurant in Greensboro, Vermont, gets his bacon from Winding Brook Farm, twenty minutes away; his cheese from Jasper Hill Farm in Greensboro (see page 181); and his vegetables from Pete's Greens in Craftsbury. Steve, who recently came to Vermont from his native California, where he was a chef at the Left Bank Restaurant in Mill Valley, says, "In California I would get produce from a nameless person. Here the farmer answers the phone. The sense of community is stronger in Vermont. It's something wonderful."

YIELD: 4–6 SERVINGS

4 slices bacon

7 ounces baby lettuce

1 cup red seedless grapes, cut in half

3 ounces Bayley Hazen or other blue cheese (such as Roquefort, Stilton, Gorgonzola), crumbled

2 tablespoons balsamic vinegar

2 tablespoons extra-virgin olive oil

Salt and freshly ground pepper to taste

1. Fry the bacon until crisp, drain on a paper towel, and break into bite-size pieces.

2. Wash and dry the lettuce thoroughly and toss in a bowl. Add the bacon, grapes, and cheese.

3. Mix the vinegar and oil in a small bowl and pour over the salad. Sprinkle with salt and a few grinds of pepper and toss again.

Japanese Spinach Salad

I got this recipe years ago from a Japanese friend. Today you can get sesame seeds already roasted.

YIELD: 4 SERVINGS

1 pound fresh spinach, thoroughly washed and stems removed

2 tablespoons sesame seeds

4 tablespoons rice vinegar

1 tablespoon soy sauce

1 tablespoon toasted sesame oil

1. Bring a large pot of salted water to a boil, stir in the spinach, and swirl around for just a minute, until it's wilted, then drain well and set aside to cool.

2. Toast the sesame seeds in a dry heavy frying pan over medium heat for 1–2 minutes or until fragrant.

3. Using a mortar and pestle or a small grinder, mash 1 tablespoon of the sesame seeds well. Mix the mashed seeds with the vinegar and soy sauce in a little bowl, then stir in the sesame oil. Toss the dressing with the spinach. Sprinkle on the remaining sesame seeds and serve.

Roasted Beet Salad with Cumin and Parsley

Fresh yellow, orange, and red beets not only add beautiful color to salads, they are also very tasty. For this typical Moroccan salad I roast the beets instead of boiling them, thus intensifying the flavor. Beets and cumin marry well and look beautiful sprinkled with lots of green parsley.

YIELD: 4–6 SERVINGS

6–8 medium beets of your choice

2 teaspoons plus 4 tablespoons extra-virgin olive oil

Juice of 1 lemon, or to taste

2 cloves garlic, minced

½ teaspoon sea salt, or to taste

¼ teaspoon freshly ground pepper, or to taste

½ teaspoon cumin, or to taste

½ teaspoon paprika, or to taste

¼ cup chopped fresh parsley

1. Preheat the oven to 350 degrees and oil a 9-by-13-inch pan.

2. Scrub the beets. Keeping them whole with the bottoms still attached, place on the baking pan. Drizzle with 2 teaspoons of the oil and bake for an hour or longer, uncovered, or until tender when pierced with a fork.

3. Cool, peel, and cut the beets into bite-size pieces and place in a serving bowl.

4. Sprinkle the lemon juice, garlic, salt, pepper, cumin, and paprika over the beets. Drizzle the 4 tablespoons olive oil over and toss with the beets. This can be done at least a day in advance.

5. Just before serving adjust the seasonings and sprinkle the parsley all over. Serve alone or with several other colorful salads, such as a roasted red pepper salad, the turnip and orange salad (page 174), or the sweet potato salad (page 169).

Pasta and Grains

In 1963, when Tony May came here from Italy, he was distressed to find that American spaghetti and meatballs was not the pasta with which he grew up. "They called it Italian, but I didn't recognize the spaghetti they served," he told me recently at San Domenico, his restaurant in New York City. "They cooked lasagna on Monday and still served the same mess on Saturday." Tony, who takes great pride in his national food, was determined to show Americans the real thing. So working with the Italian government he devised a plan to bring food writers to Italy to teach them about Italian products, like prosciutto, Parmigiano-Reggiano cheese, and high-quality pasta. It didn't hurt that Italian writers on Italian food for Americans, like Marcella Hazan and Giuliano Bugialli, were already making their mark. In those days the only way to get imported De Cecco pasta, for example, was at Italian grocery stores within Italian neighborhoods. Families like the Da Lallos of Greensboro, Pennsylvania, made weekly trips to New York to buy imported cheeses, olive oils, and pastas that they then brought home to the Italian coal workers near Pittsburgh. Today De Cecco and Da Lallo products are sold in supermarkets across the country. With the increased visibility of Italian food, Americans became more adventurous with their pasta and rice, embracing dishes like Joe Tropiano's pantry pasta (page 189) and mushroom risotto (page 193).

In 1975, a New York businessman named Henry Lambert became interested in fresh pasta, something he found in the Italian neighborhoods of San Francisco and Manhattan. He wanted to be able to buy it near his townhouse on the Upper East Side, and he also wanted to dabble in the food business. He found space in an abandoned cheese shop on Third Avenue between Seventy-eighth and Seventy-ninth Streets, and hired an out-of-work mime and a recent college graduate to make pasta with machines he acquired. This was the first Pasta & Cheese shop.

Mimi Sheraton, who was then a food writer for the *New York Times*, passed the store. A few weeks later she wrote a rave review of the shop. "Pasta cognoscenti who value the

Clockwise from top right: An Ann Arbor favorite; Add some grains to those veggies, and you have a meal; Provolone in Green Bay; Supreme comfort food; The makings of pistachio pesto

delicately tender delights of freshly made fettuccine and related noodle dough variations should waste no time in getting over to Pasta & Cheese," she wrote of the new store. "In the bright white open kitchen of this sparkling new shop, two pasta makers roll out a day-long supply of white or spinach-tinted noodles in widths that range from a standard fettuccine size to the finest, most gossamer *capelli d'angelo*, angel's hair, generally served in broth." Sheraton's review ensured an instant success for the store. One store led to a chain and, eventually, to refrigerated packages that were sold in supermarkets nationwide under the name of Pasta & Cheese, which Henry eventually sold to Contadina. Now Contadina sells the pasta and sauces under the name Buitoni.

But Italian pasta is not the only success story. Today, not only are there myriad Italian pastas in stores, but risotto, polenta, rice, and other grains are sweeping the country as we learn how good they are for us. Exotic rices used to be found only at health food stores or the occasional Greek or Indian market. Now, we have Korean grocery stores serving immigrants from South America, Asia, and Africa. We have new American standards like pad Thai (page 198), sesame noodles (page 200), and peanut basmati rice from the Ivory Coast (page 209). Jasmine, basmati, and *kao niow dahm*—unmilled black sticky rice that turns purple when cooked—all are now available, if not on your local market's shelves then on the Internet. And while rice is still brought in from abroad, unusual varieties are now grown in Missouri and Texas as well.

Despite Atkins and other trendy low-carb diets, pasta, rice, and ancient grains such as quinoa, bulgur, and couscous have earned a permanent place on the American dinner table.

Joe Tropiano's Pantry Pasta with Tuna, Tomato, and Hot Pepper

In the last thirty years, films about food have enticed the American public. To me, the most compelling feature about them is the picture of immigrants who cling to their food traditions as they try to find their footing here. "There is a tension in America between staying true to your culinary roots and adapting to the cooking," said Joe Tropiano, who wrote the 1996 film *Big Night* with his cousin, actor Stanley Tucci. Set in the late 1950s, it's the story of two southern Italian brothers who run a small restaurant. Primo (played by Tony Shalhoub) is a chef whose fanatical commitment to the authentic dishes of his homeland clashes with the visions that his brother Secondo (played by Tucci) has of the money to be made catering to Americans' narrow view of what's Italian.

"We didn't set out to write a 'food movie,'" said Joe. "It was really a movie about two brothers and their immigrant dream. After we made the movie and started showing it to people, the food stood out. We didn't realize that the food had become a character in the film."

While the two cousins were working on the film, from 1991 to 1995, they lived near each other in studio apartments in New York City. "We would work in Stanley's apartment or mine and cook pasta for lunch and drink wine my grandfather made. I like to think that what we cooked and ate helped us to get into the spirit of the film." The following recipe is one they often made from what was already in their refrigerator or pantry. Joe suggests serving this dish without grated cheese. I agree. It is delicious on its own or tossed with a little broccoli.

YIELD: 8 SERVINGS

2 cloves garlic, crushed (about 2 teaspoons)

¼ cup extra-virgin olive oil

¼–½ teaspoon hot red pepper flakes, or to taste

1 teaspoon anchovy paste

One 28-ounce can crushed Italian tomatoes

1 teaspoon salt, plus 2 tablespoons for cooking pasta

6 quarts water

1 pound dried spaghetti

One 6-ounce can olive oil–packed imported tuna

4 tablespoons chopped fresh parsley

1 tablespoon capers, rinsed (optional)

8–10 oil-packed black olives (preferably the tiny Gaeta ones), pitted and quartered (optional)

Freshly ground pepper to taste

1. Sauté the garlic in the oil in a medium skillet over medium-low heat until it is golden, being careful not to burn it. Take the pan off the heat and scoop out the garlic (it's used simply to flavor the oil). Toss the hot red pepper flakes into the oil and stir, then add the anchovy paste. Keep stirring until the paste has dissolved in the hot oil.

2. Return the skillet to the heat and pour in the crushed tomatoes along with 1 teaspoon of the salt. Stirring occasionally, let the tomatoes bubble gently over medium heat, uncovered, for 15–20 minutes. (Lower the heat if the tomatoes begin to splatter.)

3. Meanwhile, bring 6 quarts of water to a boil with 2 tablespoons of salt. Drop the spaghetti into the boiling water, stir, and cook until al dente—usually a minute or 2 less than what the package recommends.

4. While the spaghetti is cooking, break up the tuna with a fork and swirl it into the tomatoes. Add 3 tablespoons of the parsley and simmer for another 10 minutes. (If you're using the capers and olives, drop them into the sauce 5 minutes or so before it finishes cooking.)

5. Drain the spaghetti well and pour it into a serving bowl. Toss the spaghetti with the sauce, grind the pepper over, and sprinkle on the remaining parsley. Serve immediately.

Rigatoni with Tomatoes, Basil, and Asiago Cheese from an Italian Cheese Maker in Wisconsin

Wisconsin has long been a cheese-producing state. But when Eric Auricchio, whose great-grandfather started making provolone in Italy's Po Valley in 1879, decided to settle in Green Bay, he wanted to introduce a variety of authentic Italian cheeses to the American market at a time when America's taste for cheese was expanding.

So he sold his shares in the family business in Italy and changed his company's name from Auricchio Cheese to BelGioioso Cheese, after a town in Italy whose name means "beautiful and joyous."

Soon he was making Parmigiano, Asiago, mascarpone, mozzarella, and Gorgonzola—just five of the fifteen different kinds of cheese that Eric sells to supermarkets and, under private labels, to wholesalers like Costco and Trader Joe's.

Since Eric goes home for lunch every day, he invited me to accompany him. His wife, Patricia, made a simple pasta dish with summer tomatoes and basil followed by roast veal and salads. Instead of using the classic Parmigiano cheese, she uses Asiago, the nutty-flavored cheese her family has done so much to promote in this country. The slow cooking of fresh local tomatoes intensifies the flavor of this classically simple but delicious dish. Patricia often adds a little pesto too.

YIELD: 6 SERVINGS

6 tablespoons olive oil

14 plum tomatoes (about 2 pounds)

Coarse salt and freshly ground pepper to taste

1 pound rigatoni or other thick pasta

1 cup fresh basil leaves, torn in half

⅓ cup grated Asiago, American Grana, or Parmigiano cheese

1. Preheat the oven to 350 degrees and brush a tablespoon or so of the olive oil on the bottom of a 9-by-13-inch baking or jelly-roll pan.

2. After removing the stems, cut the tomatoes in half lengthwise from top to bottom. Place them cut side up in the baking pan, sprinkle them with about ½ teaspoon of the salt and a few grinds of pepper, and drizzle over 3 tablespoons more of the olive oil. Roast for 90 minutes or until the tomatoes have lost much of their liquid. Cool and then cut the tomatoes in half again.

3. Bring a pot of water to a boil with salt and cook the pasta until al dente—usually a minute or 2 less than what the package recommends. Drain it in a colander.

4. Transfer the pasta to a large serving bowl and toss with the remaining olive oil and the tomatoes.

5. Sprinkle with salt and pepper to taste, toss in the basil and cheese, and mix. Serve immediately.

MUSHROOM MANIA

In the 1970s, most mushrooms grown in the United States were the plain white button mushrooms. But in the early 1980s, Don Phillips, owner of Phillips Mushroom Farms in Kennett Square, Pennsylvania, looked to the future, and gambled that Americans would soon discover a taste for fresh exotic mushrooms.

Don got his hands on a Japanese spore to grow shiitake mushrooms commercially, using a new process that would cut the time for mushroom growth from six years to six months, thus enabling the business to change dramatically. At first he sold his shiitakes, and other new varieties, only to food services and chefs. But little by little, diners began asking those chefs where they could get these strange mushrooms. The answer: Don Phillips, who now sells royal trumpets, enokis, pompoms, and maitakes (hen of the woods), all grown commercially and organically.

But the most popular variety proved to be an ordinary white mushroom that just grew and grew. In 1985, a box of mushrooms labeled "portobello" was left on a Phillips truck by a vendor—perhaps Maria Venuti Forrest (see page 241), who had fallen in love with them in Italy and was instrumental in bringing them to America. Although Don and his general manager, Jim Angelucci, had seen similar mushrooms before, neither had heard them called portobello. One look convinced Don and Jim that the oversize mushrooms were something with which they should experiment. "We allow portobellos to mature on the bed much like vine-ripened tomatoes are allowed to ripen on the vine rather than using a ripening process," Jim told me. For a while Don and Jim were the only ones interested in portobellos: "In the beginning we threw them away because there wasn't the demand for the product," said Jim. That slowly began to change as chefs and later home cooks developed a taste for these full-flavored meaty mushrooms. Today, portobello—with its open veil, hardy texture, and long shelf life—is a household word.

Chanterelles, porcini, and morels still grow only in the wild, although attempts have been made at cultivating them. "Only one person can grow them," said Jim. "That is God."

Wild Mushroom Risotto

It is farmers like Mike Martin of Martin Rice Company, in the northern delta of southern Missouri, who have started cultivating in the United States arborio rice, that plump, pearly Italian white rice used for risotto. "My father grew rice for a long time. But we had to be innovative. The price of rice was so low here that we went into specialty rices," Mike told me. First the family started cultivating baldo, an Italian rice popular in Mediterranean countries. That led to arborio rice. Now they are also cultivating jasmine rice for Taiwan. The family's small Missouri-based business grows, produces, processes, and packages its own rice in the marshlands, where the conditions are similar to the region in Italy where arborio rice is cultivated. "Most knowledgeable chefs think the rice has to come from Italy, but it is the seed that makes it arborio, not where the rice is grown," Mike said.

Risotto is particularly popular today: wet risotto, dry risotto, risotto with seafood, risotto with asparagus, with mushrooms, with truffles—you name it. American chefs prepare it on television, numerous Italian cookbooks demystify techniques of making it. And now with arborio available in this country, anyone can make this elegant rice dish.

Charlie Pinsky, a producer of TV food shows, has watched the best of them making risotto in Italy and from coast to coast in America. When it comes to making risotto, Charlie thinks that it is like courting a woman: Either give it your full attention, or don't bother. And don't forget to keep stirring!

YIELD: 4–6 SERVINGS

4–6 cups homemade or canned chicken, veal, or vegetable stock

2 tablespoons extra-virgin olive oil (the better the oil, the better the dish)

4 tablespoons butter

1 pound mixed wild mushrooms, or a combination of regular button and wild, chopped

1 medium onion, finely diced

Coarse sea salt and freshly ground black pepper to taste

1½ cups arborio rice

1. Bring the stock to a boil in a medium saucepan, then turn the heat down to low to keep the broth warm.

2. Put the olive oil and 2 tablespoons of the butter in a wide skillet and turn the heat to medium. When the butter foam subsides, add the mushrooms and onions and cook, stirring. After a minute or so, sprinkle on a large pinch of salt to coax the liquid from the mushrooms. Continue to cook over medium or medium-low heat until the onions soften and the mushrooms have given up their liquid.

3. Add the rice and cook, stirring occasionally, until the rice is warm (feel it with the back of your hand) and coated with the fat and flavor in the pan. Turn up the heat to medium-high and pour in the white

Wild Mushroom Risotto (continued)

1 cup chardonnay or other dry white wine

1 cup freshly grated aged Gruyère cheese (about 4 ounces), or to taste

1 tablespoon truffle oil (optional)

4 tablespoons chopped fresh herbs such as chervil, tarragon, or flat-leaf parsley

wine. Cook, reducing the wine by two-thirds or more, until there's almost no liquid left in the pan.

4. Add enough warm stock to just barely cover the rice—a couple of ladlefuls should do. Stir the rice regularly, making sure it doesn't stick to the pan. When the pan is almost dry, add another couple of ladlefuls of stock, again to barely cover the rice, and cook, stirring constantly, then add another ladleful. I find that risotto usually takes 3 additions of stock. Start tasting the grains at this point—it should take about 15–18 minutes. It is done when the rice is soft but still offers a little resistance when you bite into it. Take the pan off the heat and stir in the cheese, the 2 remaining tablespoons of butter, and, if you like, the truffle oil. If the risotto seems too thick to you, stir in a few tablespoons of stock to loosen it. Divide the risotto between warmed serving bowls, scatter on the chopped herbs, and serve immediately.

A NOODLE IMPRESARIO

In Silicon Valley, across the street from a Chevy's Restaurant, Chef Wong's Chinese Restaurant & Bar looks like any old Sunday-night Chinese joint. If you didn't know better, you might drive right by it. But in the depths of the kitchen, Chiang Jung spins a magic dough.

I had seen Korean noodle making in the Chinatowns of New York and Washington, D.C. But I particularly wanted to watch Chiang Jung make Chinese noodles. Unfortunately, he was off on the Sunday I stopped in. But Thomas Liu, who owns the restaurant with his wife, Lucy, was more than happy to oblige—even though

he hadn't made noodles in twenty years. Laughing, he scooped up two kinds of flour—cake and all-purpose—mixed the flour with water and a little salt, twisted the dough, then stretched it, and swung it like a jump rope, twisting and stretching it at least twenty times, occasionally sprinkling flour on the dough, until long noodles were formed. As I watched him, Lucy told me that in ethnic Chinese families noodle making is a skill passed down from father to son. At least once a year, at New Year's and at life-cycle celebrations, noodles are stretched to ensure long life.

Chef Wong's Seafood Chow Mein

Many Chinese visiting America today are surprised to see chop suey and chow mein on restaurant menus. The dish chop suey does not exist in China, and chow mein means stir-fried (*chow*) noodles (*mein*) in Mandarin. Both recipes were improvised here to feed Chinese laborers who, in the late nineteenth century, built the railroads to the West. The dishes were invariably made with fried noodles, canned bean sprouts, some celery, and meat.

Today, new immigrants from China have brought us a more authentic chow mein, one with homemade noodles, stir-fried fresh vegetables, and fish or chicken. At Chef Wong's, in Mountain View, California, this stir-fry, not at all like the chow mein I grew up with, includes northern Chinese wheat-flour noodles, which can be bought fresh or dry at Asian and many mainstream supermarkets around the country. Linguini and fettuccine are good substitutes.

YIELD: SERVES 4–6

¼ cup vegetable oil

½ onion, sliced thin (½ cup)

1 carrot, peeled and sliced thin on the diagonal

4 enoki or white mushrooms, sliced

1 scallion, including white and green parts, cut into ½ inch slices

3–4 cloves garlic, slivered

3–4 dry pequin chilies, left whole

1 zucchini, sliced thin on the diagonal

½ pound shrimp, peeled

½ pound squid bodies, skin removed, cleaned, and sliced into 2-inch pieces

½ pound bay scallops

½ pound Chinese-style wide or round noodles

2 tablespoons toasted sesame oil

1. Set a pot of salted water on a hot burner. While waiting for it to boil, heat the vegetable oil in a wok or a large frying pan. Stir-fry the onion, carrot, mushrooms, scallion, garlic, and chilies for about 2 minutes, then add the zucchini and continue cooking a few more minutes, until the zucchini is cooked.

2. Add the shrimp, squid, and scallops and stir-fry 1–2 minutes, until just cooked.

3. Drop the noodles into the boiling water, cook until al dente (about 5 minutes), then drain in a colander.

4. Pour the sesame oil over the vegetables and fish, add the drained noodles, and stir-fry together to heat through. Serve at once.

Thomas Liu spinning and stretching his noodle dough

Pancit

Philippine Noodles with Chicken, Shrimp, and Vegetables

Asian noodles have worked their way into our home cooking. But most Americans do not realize that they can be the centerpiece for special-occasion dishes. When Mary Horcajo, a babysitter and cook for a diplomatic family, was growing up in the Philippines, *pancit* was an important part of her life. *Pancit,* meaning "noodles" in Mary's native Tagalog, are Cantonese noodles made from wheat flour, eggs, and coconut oil. Once commonly made by hand, *pancit* today come precooked. The noodles are softened in just a small amount of chicken broth.

When Mary came to the States in 1980, only one Philippine grocery store in nearby Virginia sold *pancit.* The proprietor, an employee of the World Bank, ran it part-time. Now Asian grocery stores are everywhere, including Asian-Hispanic supermarkets that sell every imaginable type of Asian noodle.

This delicate dish is a lovely centerpiece for a dinner party. The beauty of it, as with so many Asian recipes, is that you can do all your chopping in advance and stir-fry at the last minute. Remember to take time for the final presentation. If you want more punch to your *pancit,* serve it with an Asian hot sauce on the side. I like to serve Asian slaw (page 173) with it as well.

YIELD: AT LEAST 8 SERVINGS

3 boneless, skinless whole chicken breasts (about 3 pounds), cut into 2-inch strips about ½ inch wide

2 large onions, diced

4 stalks celery, sliced diagonally into 1-inch pieces

4 large carrots, peeled and cut into 2-inch julienne strips (about 3 cups)

1–3 teaspoons salt

1. Place the chicken, 1 of the onions, 1 stalk of the celery, 1 of the carrots, 1 teaspoon of salt, and several grindings of pepper in a saucepan. Cover with the water and bring to a boil. Simmer, covered, for about 30 minutes, or until the chicken is tender. Strain the broth and set aside; allow the chicken to cool. When it is cool enough to handle, dice the chicken and set aside.

2. Line up all the remaining onion, celery, and carrots, cabbage, and the chicken, shrimp, and snow peas nearby you at the stove.

3. Heat the vegetable oil in a wok. Stir in the garlic and stir-fry for a minute or so. Add the remaining onion and stir-fry until it is opaque.

Freshly ground pepper to taste

5 cups water

1 pound medium raw shrimp, peeled and tails removed

¾ pound snow peas or sugar snap peas, trimmed, or at least any strings removed

¼ cup vegetable oil

4 cloves garlic, chopped

3 tablespoons soy sauce, or to taste

2 tablespoons fish sauce (optional)

2 pounds cabbage, shredded (about 4 cups)

Two 8-ounce bags pancit, available at Asian markets

1 teaspoon toasted sesame oil

4 hard-boiled eggs, peeled and quartered (optional)

4 scallions, diced

½ cup chopped fresh parsley or cilantro

2 lemons, cut in wedges

4. Pour in the chicken broth, soy sauce, fish sauce (if using) or 2 teaspoons salt, and ¼ teaspoon black pepper and bring to a boil. Toss in the celery, carrots, and cabbage and simmer for 5 minutes.

5. Break up the noodle pieces and fold into the broth. Stir the noodles until they soften, about 5 minutes. Stir in the chicken, stir-frying for 1½ minutes, then add the shrimp and snow peas. Cook for a few more minutes, until the chicken turns white and the shrimp pink. Just at the end stir in the sesame oil. Do not overcook.

6. Turn the stir-fry onto a large serving dish. To decorate the *pancit*, arrange the quartered eggs, if using, around the dish. Garnish with the scallions, parsley or cilantro, and lemon wedges.

Pad Thai

Pad Thai, perhaps more than any other dish from Asia, has won over the hearts of Americans. Cecilia Tobler, a personal trainer in Washington, D.C., prepares pad Thai as a reward for her clients after they lose a few pounds. When you make this dish, it is important to prepare the various elements and mix them just before serving. If Cecilia can't find tamarind for the sauce, she will substitute lime juice but never, as many restaurants do, ketchup. Buy Thai products like tamarind, fish sauce—made from salted and fermented anchovies—and palm sugar from an Asian store whenever possible. The ingredients will keep indefinitely and are well worth the adventure.

YIELD: 2–4 SERVINGS

3 tablespoons palm sugar or soft brown sugar

3 tablespoons fish sauce

3–4 tablespoons compressed tamarind paste

⅛ teaspoon salt

8 ounces fresh bean sprouts (about 2 cups)

8 ounces medium flat rice stick noodles

4 tablespoons vegetable oil

3 cloves garlic, chopped

2 tablespoons diced fresh radish

1–2 teaspoons dried red pepper flakes, depending on taste

½ pound chopped chicken, pork, shrimp, or extra-firm tofu, diced

1 cup chicken broth or water

2 large eggs

½ cup chives or garlic chives, cut in 1-inch lengths

2 tablespoons lime juice, plus lime wedges for garnish

2 tablespoons chopped roasted peanuts

1. Prepare the pad Thai sauce by stirring together the sugar, fish sauce, tamarind paste, and salt in a small bowl. Set aside.

2. Meanwhile, soak the bean sprouts in a bowl of cold water for 30 minutes. Then drain and dry them.

3. Soak the noodles in warm water for 10–15 minutes or until soft, then drain.

4. Heat the oil in a wok or large frying pan. Add the garlic and stir-fry until golden. Add the radish, red pepper flakes, and meat, shrimp, or tofu and stir constantly for 2 minutes. If you are using shrimp, remove it after it turns pink to prevent overcooking and set aside.

5. Add the drained noodles and the chicken broth or water, stirring constantly. Add the sauce a few tablespoons at a time, stirring until blended. Adjust the amount of sauce to your taste. Cover and cook for another minute.

6. Slide the noodles to 1 side of the pan and break the eggs on the other side. Stir the eggs until they are nearly cooked, then quickly cover them with the noodles to finish cooking them. Break up the egg and stir into the noodles with the bean sprouts.

7. Spoon the pad Thai onto a serving platter and stir in the chives or garlic chives, lime juice, and the shrimp if you are using it. Sprinkle with the peanuts and serve with wedges of lime.

Israeli Couscous with Pine Nuts and Fresh Herbs

Israeli couscous, a large round toasted wheat pasta, was created by Osem, a Czech noodle company, at the request of David Ben-Gurion, Israel's first prime minister. "In the early 1950s there was very little couscous in Israel," Gad Propper, the president of Osem, now a subsidy of Nestlé International, told me. "Ben-Gurion asked my father if he could create a pasta product for immigrants from North African couscous-eating countries. So he made an extruded wheat pasta shaped like couscous." Today, this so-called "Ben-Gurion pasta," larger than the semolina-based couscous and one that holds its shape beautifully, is, for American chefs, a darling newcomer of the pasta world.

I prepare Israeli couscous as an accompaniment to chicken or fish, much as I would serve rice. If you can't find Israeli couscous, which is available both packaged and loose in many supermarkets, orzo pasta or arborio rice makes a nice substitute. I often replace the pine nuts with chestnuts and cooked brussels sprouts or pecans and Swiss chard.

YIELD: 6–8 SERVINGS

2 tablespoons extra-virgin olive oil
1 onion, diced
1 stalk celery, diced
2 cloves garlic, diced
2 cups Israeli couscous
4 cups chicken broth or water
2 tablespoons chopped fresh parsley
2 tablespoons chopped fresh mixed herbs such as lemon thyme and rosemary
Salt and freshly ground pepper to taste
½ cup toasted pine nuts

1. Heat the oil in a frying pan and sauté the onions, celery, and garlic until the onions are translucent. Add the couscous and stir until browned.

2. Stir in the chicken broth or water and half the parsley and fresh herbs. Bring to a boil, then lower to a simmer and stir occasionally for about 8–10 minutes or until the couscous is al dente and most of the water is absorbed. If you leave it in the pan after cooking, it tends to stick together, but it will return to its proper consistency if you fluff it up with a fork and add a little more hot liquid.

3. Season with salt and pepper to taste and turn onto a platter. Sprinkle with the remaining herbs and the toasted pine nuts and serve hot or at room temperature.

Soba Noodles with Peanut Butter, Sesame, and Ginger

When I think of sesame noodles, I think of Thai or other Far Eastern dishes made with peanut butter. I like to use the sturdy Japanese soba noodles made from buckwheat for this dish. I also buy big jars of roasted sesame seeds at Asian stores.

YIELD: 4–6 SERVINGS

¼ cup chunky or smooth peanut butter, preferably unsweetened

3 tablespoons brewed black tea

1 tablespoon hot chili oil, or to taste* (available in Asian markets)

3 tablespoons soy sauce

2 inches gingerroot, peeled

3 cloves garlic

1 tablespoon rice vinegar

2 tablespoons toasted sesame oil

1 tablespoon sugar (optional)

1 pound soba buckwheat or other sturdy noodles

TOPPING

2 scallions, chopped

2 tablespoons chopped cilantro

2 tablespoons roasted sesame seeds

*To make your own chili oil, add a teaspoon of crushed red pepper flakes to a tablespoon or so of vegetable oil and heat for 1–2 minutes over medium heat. Strain the resulting oil and cool before using.

1. Put the peanut butter, tea, chili oil, soy sauce, ginger, garlic, rice vinegar, and sesame oil in a food processor equipped with the steel blade. Process until smooth. Taste and add sugar depending on the peanut butter used. You want the sauce to taste slightly sweet.

2. Cook the noodles according to the directions on the package, then drain and transfer to a serving bowl. Stir in the peanut butter sauce and serve lukewarm or at room temperature, topped with the scallions, cilantro, and sesame seeds.

FLAVOR ENHANCERS

When I went to Quito, Ecuador, recently, I was surprised to see billboard murals advertising Maggi. A commercial flavor enhancer with MSG that originated in France, Maggi is used frequently in Africa, South America, and Asia. We use seasoned salt for the same purpose.

Squid with Fettuccine, Asian Peppers, and Onions

The Vietnamese outdoor market on the outskirts of New Orleans, a block away from real rice paddies, is more unusual than most markets in America. The day I went, a man with a truckload of geese was stationed outside the entrance. Nearby, women were selling greens grown just down the street in gardens that had special plots for Vietnamese vegetables.

Dickson Ogbomah, a Nigerian engineer who frequents the market each week, showed me around. "The Vietnamese are industrious people," he told me. "They eat all the foods that Third World people eat, cutting them up to stretch them into a meal." He finds many vegetables here that are also used in his own cooking in Africa. "These foods excite me," he said. "I feel like I am back at home." Dickson, who is married to an American, was buying squid and hot peppers for this fusion pasta dish. Depending on your tolerance for peppers, start with one or two.

YIELD: 4–6 SERVINGS

½ pound squid tubes or bodies, already cleaned, about 5–6 bodies, 5–8 inches long

3 tablespoons vegetable oil

3 cloves garlic, minced (about 3 teaspoons)

½ onion, diced

1 beef bouillon or Maggi cube

¼ cup water

12 ounces fettuccine

3 plum tomatoes, diced

1–4 diced hot peppers like pequin, seeds removed

5 tablespoons chopped fresh parsley

1 teaspoon kosher salt, or to taste

½ tablespoon butter

1. If using whole squid, twist off the head, and pull out the inside cartilage and discard. Save the tentacles for another dish. Then peel off the outer white skin of the squid body and slice the flesh into ½-inch rounds.

2. Heat the vegetable oil in a large skillet. Add the garlic and the onion and sauté until the onion is soft and translucent, about 5 minutes. Dissolve the beef bouillon or Maggi cube in the water and pour into the skillet. Simmer, stirring frequently, for about 5 minutes.

3. Meanwhile, cook the pasta according to the directions on the package.

4. While the pasta is cooking, add the squid, tomatoes, peppers, 4 tablespoons of the parsley, and salt to the skillet. Simmer for a few more minutes, then stir in the butter. Drain the pasta and toss in with the vegetables, sprinkling on the remaining parsley. Serve immediately.

Pistachio Pesto with String Beans

Nouvelle Italian restaurant, candles on the table. Jerry and Elaine are finishing dinner. George, sitting across from them, hasn't eaten a thing.

GEORGE: *Why do I get pesto? Why do I think I'll like it? I keep trying to like it, like I have to like it.*

JERRY: *Who said you have to like it?*

GEORGE: *Everybody likes pesto. You walk into a restaurant, that's all you hear—pesto, pesto, pesto.*

JERRY: *I don't like pesto.*

GEORGE: *Where was pesto ten years ago?*

—SEINFELD, "THE BUSBOY EPISODE,"
WRITTEN BY LARRY DAVID AND JERRY SEINFELD

Pesto is the quiche of the 80s.　　　　　　　　　　　　　—WHEN HARRY MET SALLY

Traditionally pounded with a mortar and pestle, classic Ligurian pesto has become both effortless and ubiquitous in this country with the introduction of the food processor and the availability of fresh basil, pine nuts, and garlic. With such exotic takes on pesto developed in recent years as ancho chili pesto, shiitake mushroom pesto, tarragon-walnut pesto, and black olive pesto, this version of pistachio pesto is really quite tame. It comes from Gail and Gene Zannon, who own the Santa Barbara Pistachio Company. I was introduced to their nuts at the Santa Monica Farmers' Market and later at their own stand at the farmers' market in Santa Barbara.

"At farmers' markets, the customers take ownership of the family," Gail told me. "Somehow customers feel they are helping to send our kids through college. They also give farmers lots of feedback. They'll tell us, 'When are you going to get a bigger bag?' or 'Why not have flavored pistachios like garlic or sprinkle some soy sauce on them?' "

One October when the pistachios were harvested, the Zannons hosted a Slow Food USA event at the farm. Not only did the members of this movement, dedicated to preserving old-fashioned ways, help harvest the nuts, but they also orchestrated an entire pistachio banquet in the fields, which included pistachio-stuffed chicken breasts, salmon with a pistachio crust, pasta with pistachio pesto, and apricot ambrosia with pistachios.

Always pushing pistachios, the Zannons suggest putting a spoonful of this pistachio pesto sauce in salad dressings, on coarse breads, focaccia, or crackers, and of course on pasta or potatoes. I like to toss string beans or broccoli in with some of the pesto and the pasta. It will keep, covered, in the refrigerator for up to two days.

2 cups chopped fresh basil leaves

3 garlic cloves

1 cup roasted, unsalted shelled pistachios

½ cup extra-virgin olive oil

½ cup grated Parmigiano-Reggiano cheese

1 teaspoon salt, or to taste

A few grinds coarse black pepper, or to taste

12 ounces linguine or other pasta

1 pound fresh string beans

1. Place the basil leaves, garlic cloves, and pistachios in a food processor equipped with a steel blade.

2. With the motor running, slowly pour the olive oil through the feed tube until you have a paste. Stir in the cheese, salt, and a good grind of pepper.

3. Cook the pasta according to the package directions. Halfway through, drop the trimmed string beans into the pasta pot and continue cooking until the pasta is al dente. Drain, place in a serving bowl, and gently fold in the pesto. If you have any leftover pesto, cover with a thin coating of olive oil so the basil retains its green color and refrigerate or freeze.

Zingerman's Macaroni and Cheese

Although I grew up on boxed Kraft macaroni and cheese, this stuff is about eighteen thousand times better," Ari Weinzweig told me. "It is amazing what happens when you use really great artisan-made macaroni and marvelously good farmhouse cheddar instead of industrially made noodles and cheese." Ari, a purist, uses a year-old cheddar, preferably one from Shelburne Farms or Grafton Village Cheese in Vermont, Martelli macaroni, and Tellicherry black pepper. Purist or not, you will like this recipe.

1 pound good-quality macaroni

2 tablespoons butter

1 medium onion, coarsely chopped (about ¾ cup)

1 clove garlic, mashed

1 tablespoon fresh thyme or 1 teaspoon dry thyme

1 tablespoon fresh rosemary or 1 teaspoon dry rosemary

1. Preheat the oven to 350 degrees and grease a 9-by-13-inch glass baking dish.

2. Bring a large pot of well-salted water to a boil. Add the pasta and stir. Cook until the pasta is 2–3 minutes from being al dente. You'll want it underdone so it doesn't get overcooked in the oven.

3. While the pasta is cooking, make the cheese sauce. Melt the butter in a large, heavy-bottomed pot over medium-high heat. Add the onion, garlic, thyme, and rosemary and sauté until the onion is soft, about

¼ cup white wine
2–4 tablespoons flour
3½ cups whole milk
2 tablespoons Dijon mustard
¾ teaspoon coarse sea salt
½ teaspoon freshly ground black pepper, preferably Tellicherry
4½ cups (about 12 ounces) grated good-quality aged cheddar

5 minutes. Add the wine and let it reduce until it has almost evaporated, about 3–4 minutes. Add 2 tablespoons of the flour and, stirring constantly, cook for a minute or so, adding more flour to thicken if needed. Slowly add the milk a little at a time, stirring constantly to avoid lumping, then stir in the mustard, salt, and pepper. Make sure to keep the sauce at a gentle simmer (not at a high boil).

4. When the sauce becomes thick, reduce the heat to medium. Working a handful at a time, stir in about 3 cups of the cheese. When all the cheese has melted in the sauce, remove the pan from the heat.

5. By this time the pasta should be ready. Drain the pasta and stir it into the cheese sauce.

6. Pour the macaroni and cheese into the baking dish and top with the reserved grated cheese. Bake for 20 minutes or until golden and crusty.

ZINGERMAN'S DELICATESSEN

Whenever I go back to Ann Arbor, Michigan, I make a pilgrimage to Zingerman's Deli. Too bad it didn't exist when I was a student at the University of Michigan! Ari Weinzweig, a graduate of the university, and his partner, Paul Saginaw, opened Zingerman's as a tiny deli, but today it has expanded into a bakery, mail-order business (see Mail-Order Sources), catering service, bakery, and Zingerman's Creamery. At the creamery, they make cream cheese from cream, milk, and vegetable rennet, the way the original upstate New York farmers in the nineteenth century did. The name "Zingerman's" is made up. "It just sounds like it should be a traditional deli," Ari once told me. Housed in two wooden buildings in a residential area of Ann Arbor, it is more than the quintessential delicatessen. Ari and Paul have an artistic and academic interest in products that once were in the classic delicatessen, but they take a step further, seeking out the masters of each product that they sell and adding an international selection to the traditional deli fare. Like New York's Zabar's or Eli Zabar's Vinegar Factory, Zingerman's has created a midwestern emporium of good food and excellent products. "We're like a family," said Ari as we munched cheese blintzes with chestnut honey and real vanilla at the deli. "We wanted to make something special happen," he continued. "Our place has become like the VFW hall, the church, or the tavern—a place to congregate. Hanging out here has become an integrated part of some people's lives."

Wild Mushroom and Goat Cheese Lasagna

This recipe shows the new relationship between cheese makers and markets. When Dan Lewis (see box, page 206) needed a soft and smooth goat cheese to spread on toast for hors d'oeuvres and to make his wild mushroom lasagna, he worked with Vermont Butter and Cheese, a small boutique cheese maker in Websterville, Vermont, to create a creamier yet full-flavored goat cheese. A year or so later they introduced a spreadable goat cheese.

This is definitely a winter recipe, one that will get oohs and aahs at your dinner party. The mushroom sauce is very versatile and can also be used as a filling for strudel or crepes or as a topping for prepared puff pastries. If you like, make the mushroom sauce and the cheese filling a day ahead. I have even assembled the entire lasagna one day ahead, baking it just before my guests arrive. Dan suggests serving this dish on top of a splash of tomato sauce. Don't expect a lasagna that holds together—this one is very soupy.

YIELD: 10–12 SERVINGS

One .35-ounce package dried porcini mushrooms

1½ pounds assorted mushrooms, such as portobello, cremini, oyster, chanterelles, shiitake, or hen of the woods

1 medium onion, diced

1 large clove garlic, chopped

2 tablespoons extra-virgin olive oil

½ cup dry white wine

1 tablespoon flour

1 cup heavy cream

1 teaspoon salt, or to taste

¼ teaspoon freshly ground pepper, or to taste

2 teaspoons chopped fresh or 1 teaspoon dried thyme

1 tablespoon chopped fresh or ½ tablespoon dried rosemary

1¼ pounds slightly creamy goat cheese or ¾ cup ricotta and 12 ounces goat cheese

1. To make the mushroom mixture, soak the dried porcinis in lukewarm water to cover—use at least 2 cups of water—until softened, about 30 minutes. Meanwhile, roughly chop the rest of the mushrooms. Drain the porcinis, reserving 1½ cups of the soaking liquid, and chop them roughly. Because there is often grit in the soaking water, I pour the water through a paper coffee filter to strain.

2. Sauté the onion and 1 teaspoon of the garlic in the olive oil until the onion is soft. Add the fresh chopped mushrooms and continue cooking for a few minutes. Add the drained dried mushrooms with the reserved water and heat for a few minutes. Add the wine and reduce the liquid for a few minutes more. Sprinkle on the flour and stir to prevent any lumps from forming. Pour in the cream and simmer slowly, uncovered, for about 15–20 minutes or until the sauce reaches the consistency of a thick ragout. Season with salt and pepper to taste, followed by the thyme and rosemary. Adjust the seasonings to your taste.

3. To make the cheese mixture, purée the goat cheese, and ricotta if you are using it, eggs, Parmesan cheese, the remaining ½ teaspoon garlic, and basil in a food processor equipped with a steel blade.

4. Preheat the oven to 350 degrees and grease a 9-by-13-inch baking pan.

2 large eggs

¼ cup freshly grated Parmesan cheese

1 tablespoon chopped fresh or ½ teaspoon dried basil

3–9 sheets of fresh lasagna (depending on the size) or 9 boxed lasagna noodles

¾ pound shredded mozzarella cheese

2 cups good-quality jarred tomato sauce or the sauce on page 273

5. Bring a large pot of water to a boil. Cook the lasagna noodles with a little salt until almost al dente. Drain and reserve.

6. Now assemble the lasagna, a step you can do a day ahead of time. If using fresh lasagna, you will have to cut it to fit your pan. Whichever you use, place a layer of the lasagna noodles on the bottom of your baking pan, then add a third of the cheese mixture, a third of the mushroom mixture, and a third of the mozzarella. Repeat with 2 more layers of pasta, ending with the mozzarella.

7. Bake the lasagna for 45 minutes. Ten minutes before it is done, heat the tomato sauce in a saucepan. Take the lasagna out of the oven and let it rest for 10 minutes so that it will better hold together when cut. To serve, spread a few tablespoons of tomato sauce on each plate and top with a square of the lasagna.

CHOOSING MUSHROOMS

Dan Lewis, the corporate chef for Balducci's food stores, took me to the colorful produce department of his upscale market to shop for mushrooms. Exotic and ordinary fruits and vegetables are perfectly ripened and arranged in such an artistic way that I didn't want to disturb the beauty while at the same time wanting to indulge in everything. "Depending on the market," he explained to me, "you can spend quite a bit or meet your budget just on mushrooms."

The day I was visiting, the mushroom prices ranged from four dollars a pound for cremini to forty dollars a pound for fresh morels. We chose cremini, portobello, shiitake, white button, hen of the woods, and oyster mushrooms. Dan suggested using a few portobellos and cremini—which are just smaller portobellos—for a meaty flavor and dark color, trimming off the bottoms and using the squat stems. He showed me how to tear the oyster mushrooms apart with my fingers instead of dicing them. He says they should be cut large so you really feel their texture. Since there were no fresh porcini mushrooms, whose flavor adds a delicious woodiness, Dan suggested soaking dried porcini in water and adding them—and the water—to the mix. "The soaking liquid from the dried mushrooms can add lots of flavor," he said. Not everyone has the selection of mushrooms that Dan has. As he surveyed the produce section of his store, he sighed. "Sometimes we will have seven kinds of mushrooms to choose from. Other times, just one."

Although Judy Harper no longer gathers wild rice, she is proud to tell you that her mother was born in a rice camp, an igloo-shaped hut made from reeds which is moved from lake to lake during the wild rice season. Judy, an Ojibwe Indian, lives in northern Minnesota, home of the true wild rice. These days, this grandmother of ten and mother of four is concerned with sustaining her American Indian culture. A cook with Head Start, she has introduced wild rice, the symbolic staff of life for her people, into the school lunch program. "When my kids were in school," Judy told me, "wild rice was not on Head Start school menus."

For the Ojibwe, harvesting wild rice is part of the cycle of their year. Dennis, Judy's husband, and two of her children, Jeff and Leslie, wanted to show me how they do it. Before we started out, Leslie sprinkled tobacco as an offering of thanks for the wild rice we would gather in late summer on the marshy Middle Sucker Lake. Once in the canoes, Jeff and Dennis stood erect, poling through the marshy water with long green and yellow grasses all around. The rest of us sat in the canoes, gathering the rice, using cedar hand-carved knockers about thirty inches long and weighing about a pound in each hand. One knocker held the blades of grass down, and the other whacked

the grass two times so that the wild rice would fall easily into the moving canoe. For several hours we did this, until the rice piled up in the hull of the canoe.

Once we had the rice scooped into sacks, we brought it back to be parched, jigged, and winnowed. In the olden days the rice was parched in an iron pot over heated logs. Now it is done by machine, as is jigging—that is, separating the rice from the shell.

"We used to dance on the rice to loosen the chaff from the grain," said Leslie, proudly describing this tradition of the Ojibwe people. "The old people drummed while the children danced on the rice," recalled Judy. "I remember watching my grandfather dance and sing all sorts of songs. Then the children would follow him and the rice would be jigged."

Stir-Fried Wild Rice with Vegetables

The Harpers (see page 207) sometimes add a contemporary touch of soy sauce and ginger or a jalapeño pepper to this stir-fry. Just remember that hand-harvested wild rice expands much more than commercial wild rice does when cooked. As Dan Biever of Coteau Connoisseur, a wild rice company (page 28), says, "This is Mother Nature straight out of the wild."

YIELD: 6–8 SERVINGS

1 cup wild rice
1 cup water
1 cup chicken broth
3 tablespoons vegetable oil
1 onion, diced
2 cloves garlic, minced
1 green pepper, diced
1 red pepper, diced
1 cup diced cremini, chanterelles, or other wild mushrooms
Salt and freshly ground pepper to taste
½ cup chopped pecans, preferably honey coated

1. Wash the wild rice several times while you bring the water and the chicken broth to a boil in a medium saucepan. Pour in the rice and simmer, covered, for about 30 minutes or until the rice is al dente and the water evaporated.

2. Meanwhile, heat the oil in a medium frying pan and add the onion and the garlic. Sauté for a few minutes or until the onion is opaque. Then stir in the peppers and the mushrooms, sautéing a few minutes, until the vegetables are soft.

3. Stir the vegetables into the rice and then season to taste with salt and pepper. Stir in the pecans and serve.

Cori Harper eating her grandma's wild rice

Peanut Basmati Rice

Chef Morou Ouattara (see page 251) makes this peanut basmati rice at his Washington, D.C., restaurant, Signatures. The dish has roots in Morou's native Cote d'Ivoire, where hot spices are commonly used. Like many chefs from abroad, Morou has had to adapt his cooking to American palates, in many cases turning down the heat of his dishes. Not here. The dish is as hot as he serves it at home. Feel free to cut the red pepper by half if you don't want to go native.

YIELD: 6–8 SERVINGS

½ cup vegetable oil

1 large onion, sliced

3 cloves garlic, chopped

1¼ cups basmati rice

1 teaspoon turmeric

1 curry leaf*

2 bay leaves

1 teaspoon–1 tablespoon crushed dried red pepper

¼ teaspoon ground cardamom

2½ cups homemade (page 146) or canned chicken broth

Salt and freshly ground pepper to taste

1 cup chopped roasted peanuts

1 teaspoon lemon zest

1. Heat the oil in a large pot over medium-low heat. Toss in the onion and garlic and sauté for 3 minutes. Stir in the rice, turmeric, curry leaf, bay leaves, as much of the crushed red pepper as you like, and cardamom and sauté for a few minutes.

2. Pour in the chicken broth, season with salt and pepper, and bring to a boil. Cover and reduce the heat. Simmer until the rice is cooked and the liquid absorbed, about 15–20 minutes, and then serve it right away in a colorful bowl, with the peanuts and the lemon zest sprinkled on top.

* Curry leaves are available at Indian markets.

Coconut Rice

I met John Phillips more than thirty years ago, when he was an urban designer with the Office of Midtown Planning in New York City. Together we created and implemented the Ninth Avenue International Food Festival—a two-day, mile-long street fair that has developed into an annual event attracting one million visitors.

This rice dish, colored with turmeric and flavored with cumin, cloves, and a cinnamon stick, was one John enjoyed when he lived with a family in India. It goes well with any of the spicy chicken dishes in this book or John's rum ribs (page 363). Sometimes, if John does not have turmeric and cumin, he will substitute curry powder.

YIELD: 6 SERVINGS

2 tablespoons butter

2 tablespoons vegetable oil

1 large onion, thinly sliced in half-moon shapes

1 teaspoon turmeric

1 teaspoon ground ginger

1 teaspoon ground cumin

3 whole cloves

1 cinnamon stick

1 cup grated unsweetened coconut

2 cups long-grain rice

4 cups chicken broth or water

1 teaspoon salt

1. Heat the butter with the oil in a large skillet. Add the onion and sauté until golden. Add the turmeric, ginger, cumin, cloves, cinnamon stick, and coconut. Fry, stirring constantly, for 1–2 minutes. Scatter the rice into the pan and stir constantly for about 2 minutes, until it is coated with spices and coconut.

2. Pour in the chicken broth or water and salt, bring to a boil, stir, and cover. Reduce to a simmer and cook slowly for about 15 minutes, until all the water is absorbed. Remove from the heat and allow to sit for 10 minutes before serving.

Iranian Rice

In recent years, I have tasted many delicious home-cooked rice dishes from Latin America, Asia, and the Middle East. Iranian cooks get top marks for their treatment of rice, managing through careful cooking to preserve the unique flavor and texture of their favored basmati rice, which is now cultivated in the States and so available to everyone. You can make this with rice alone or add potatoes to the bottom of the pan, producing the *tadig*, the always cherished portion of crusty, crunchy potatoes and sometimes rice. Nonstick pots make this dish almost effortless.

YIELD: 8 SERVINGS

2 quarts water

4 cups basmati rice

2 tablespoons salt

6 tablespoons vegetable oil

2 potatoes, peeled and sliced about ¼ inch thick

1. Fill a 4-quart saucepan with the water and bring to a boil. Add the rice and salt. Boil over high heat, uncovered, for 7–10 minutes, stirring gently every minute or so, being careful not to break the rice grains. Taste the rice after 7 minutes to see whether it is partially cooked. The long grains should be half done, still a little firm. If the rice is ready, remove it from the heat immediately, strain it in a colander, and rinse with lukewarm water to remove any excess starch; otherwise, cook 2–3 minutes longer, then drain. Serve as is or make a *tadig*.

2. After you have drained the rice, pour the oil into a nonstick pot. Cover with a layer of potatoes, then gently spoon in the rice. Poke a few holes in the rice and then cover with the lid of the pot. Steam slowly for about 15 minutes. Gently turn into a serving bowl, carefully removing the potatoes, and serve with *fesenjan* (see page 316) or other dishes.

Shirin Polo

Sweet Rice with Orange Peel, Saffron, and Carrots

Today cross-cultural weddings are quite common in America. At a recent Persian wedding I attended where the bride was Catholic and the groom of Moslem Persian descent, the other guests and I witnessed two ceremonies: one Catholic, and one Moslem. For me the most compelling was the Persian wedding ceremony, choreographed by the mother of the groom. The wedding platform was decorated with wishful symbols for their life together: a mirror, for clarity; candles, for a bright future; the Koran, for words of wisdom; apples and eggs, for fertility; candy and baklava, for sweetness; and bread and cheese, to remind them of the basics of life. After the bride and groom exchanged vows, they fed each other honey, using their fingers to put the taste of honey in each other's mouths.

The menu crossed cultures as well. Put together by both an American and a Persian caterer, the first course included traditional *kofta* (meatballs) and stuffed grape leaves, both symbolic dishes at a life-cycle event. But the most symbolic dish was the traditional *shirin polo,* sweet rice with orange peel and almonds, served on a bed of chicken, which I have adapted from *The Food of Life,* a cookbook written and self-published by my friend Najmieh Batmanglij, which links the American Persian community with their culinary past.

YIELD: 6–8 SERVINGS

3 cups basmati rice

2 cups orange peel in matchstick strips (about 4 oranges)

2 cups sugar

6 carrots, cut into strips 1 inch long and about ⅛ inch wide (about 1 pound)

½ cup slivered blanched almonds

2 tablespoons salt

½ teaspoon ground saffron

2 tablespoons hot water

¼ cup plus 2 tablespoons vegetable oil

1. Clean and wash the rice several times in cold water, until the water remains clear.

2. Put the orange peel and 3 cups water in a saucepan, and boil for 5 minutes. Drain the orange peel and place it, the sugar, carrots, and 3 cups water in the saucepan and simmer, uncovered, for 15 minutes. Drain, add the almonds, and set aside.

3. Bring 8 cups water with 2 tablespoons salt to a boil in a large non-stick pot. Add the washed and drained rice to the pot. Boil briskly for 6 minutes, stirring gently twice to loosen any grains that stick to the bottom. Drain the rice in a colander and rinse in lukewarm water.

4. Dissolve the saffron in the 2 tablespoons hot water.

½ teaspoon cinnamon
¼ teaspoon ground ginger
¼ teaspoon ground cardamom
⅛ teaspoon ground cloves
2 tablespoons chopped pistachio nuts

5. In the same pot used for the rice, heat ¼ cup of the oil and a drop of the dissolved saffron. Cover with a ½-inch layer of rice and a ½-inch layer of the carrot mixture (reserving ¼ cup of the carrot for garnish later). Continue layering in this manner until you have used up all the ingredients. End with a large layer of rice, forming it into a pyramid. Sprinkle the cinnamon, ginger, cardamom, and cloves over the rice, and pour the remaining oil and the dissolved saffron over the pyramid. Pour 1–2 tablespoons water over the pyramid.

6. Place a clean towel over the pot, and cover firmly with a lid to prevent any steam from escaping. Cook for 10 minutes over medium heat and another 50 minutes over very low heat. Remove from the heat, and without uncovering allow to cool for 5 minutes.

7. Remove the lid, and extract 2 tablespoons of the saffron-colored rice for garnish.

8. Gently spoon the dish onto a platter, shaping it into another pyramid. Garnish with the saffron rice and reserved carrot mixture. Sprinkle the pistachio nuts over all.

9. Using a wooden spatula, scrape up the bottom crusty layer from the pot, and serve on the side.

Quinoa Salad with Asparagus and Preserved Lemon Dressing

Cool rice and other grain salads are very popular today. I love this quinoa salad. The nutty taste of the quinoa marries well with the preserved lemon dressing. Preserved lemons are something I always have on hand now. They must be done ahead. You can use sugar snap peas in place of the asparagus.

YIELD: 6 SERVINGS

1 pound asparagus

2 tablespoons pure olive oil

1 red onion, finely chopped

1 cup quinoa

2 cups water

1 teaspoon kosher salt

5–6 sun-dried tomatoes, soaked in water, drained, and chopped

5–6 cherry tomatoes

Preserved lemon dressing (recipe follows)

½ cup toasted pine nuts

4 tablespoons slivered fresh basil

Peel of ½ preserved lemon, diced (page 171)

1. Prepare the asparagus by bending the spears gently until they break naturally. Discard the tough ends and cut the asparagus into 2-inch pieces.

2. Bring about 4 inches of water to a boil in the bottom of a steamer pot. Put the asparagus in a steamer basket and steam until it has softened slightly but is still crisp, about 10 minutes, then plunge into ice water to stop it cooking and drain. (Alternately, you can cook the asparagus in the microwave. Put the asparagus on a plate, sprinkle it with a little water, cover with plastic wrap, and microwave on high for about 4 minutes.)

3. Heat the olive oil in a large skillet over high heat and sauté the onion for about 2 minutes. Add the quinoa and cook, stirring constantly, for about 5 minutes. Add 2 cups water and the teaspoon of salt and bring to a boil. Reduce the heat, cover the skillet, and simmer for about 5 minutes, then shut off the heat and leave for 15 minutes. Let it cool completely.

4. Turn the quinoa onto a serving platter. Toss it with the sun-dried and cherry tomatoes and the asparagus. Pour the dressing over the salad and toss, then sprinkle with the pine nuts, basil, and diced preserved lemon peel. Serve at room temperature.

Preserved Lemon Dressing

YIELD: ABOUT 1 CUP

1 preserved lemon (page 171)

7–8 tablespoons extra-virgin olive oil

1 teaspoon ground cumin

1 teaspoon ground coriander

½ teaspoon freshly ground black pepper

1. Rinse the lemon in water, drain, and cut it in half. Remove the seeds and the flesh from 1 half and dice the rind into little pieces. Set aside.

2. Put the other lemon half (rind and all, minus any seeds), the olive oil, cumin, coriander, and pepper in a food processor or blender and blend until puréed. Add a little water if the dressing is too thick. Then add the diced preserved rind.

Couscous Salad with Dates and Almonds

Rozanne Gold has made her mark on American cooking with her 1-2-3 cookbooks. She made her mark on me with this easy couscous salad, which I tasted at a dinner at her home. Once exclusively a North African staple, couscous has become a familiar ingredient in American home kitchens. And no surprise—cooking the boxed couscous commonly available in supermarkets is nearly instant and effortless. This salad, which requires little work to prepare, has become a summer standby in our family.

YIELD: 6 SERVINGS

2 cups water

½ teaspoon salt

1½ heaping cups couscous (one 12-ounce box)

2 large lemons

¼ cup extra-virgin olive oil

1¾ cups cooked chickpeas, drained (or one 15-ounce can)

¼ cup finely minced scallions, white part only (about 4 scallions)

1. Bring the water to a boil in a large saucepan along with the salt. Add the couscous and stir for 30 seconds. Remove the saucepan from the heat, cover it, and let stand for 5 minutes. Fluff the couscous with a fork and transfer it to a large bowl to cool.

2. Grate the peel of the lemons to get 1 generous tablespoon zest. Cut the lemons in half and juice them. Whisk together 3 tablespoons of the lemon juice and the olive oil and drizzle it over the couscous. Add the lemon zest and gently toss.

3. Fold in the drained chickpeas, scallions, dates, almonds, minced cilantro, and cardamom. Season the couscous salad to taste with

⅔ cup finely chopped pitted dates

½ cup slivered almonds, toasted

½ cup minced fresh cilantro plus cilantro sprigs for garnish

1½ teaspoons ground cardamom

Freshly ground pepper to taste

additional salt and freshly ground black pepper. Let it stand at room temperature for at least 1 hour. Toss gently again and adjust seasonings, if needed. Garnish with the sprigs of cilantro.

COOKING IRAQI FOOD IN VIRGINIA

When Suad Shallal came from Iraq to Falls Church, Virginia, in 1966, she felt as if she had landed on another planet. She spoke no English, she didn't drive, and she cooked only Iraqi food. For ingredients like bulgur, tahini, or sumac, all staples of her native Iraq, she had to trudge fifteen miles to Thomas Market, the only Middle Eastern market in the area. When she wanted to go out to eat, her choices were either American food or Mama Ayesha's, a lone Middle Eastern restaurant in Washington. "For us it was Iraqi or McDonald's," recalled Andy Shallal, one of her sons. "It was the American thing. It was such fun when my father brought us McDonald's milkshakes. But we liked it when company came, because then my mother would bring out all her talents, the phyllo, the *burek,* the finger foods, all food reserved for company. Everyday meals centered around rice."

The Shallals came here because Ahmed Shallal was working as a diplomat in the Arab League. They decided to stay because of political changes back home. "Every year we said we would go back," Suad told me during a cooking session. "Then we acquired property, our children married, we had grandchildren. Everything has changed in Iraq, and now most of our people have left to go everywhere in the world."

When Ahmed lost his job, he opened a restaurant—a pizza parlor in Annandale, Virginia. "We always fought about the meatballs," said Andy. "My father made them like *kofta.* Even his sauce had a Middle Eastern flavor." The restaurant not only fed the Shallal family but put the children through school.

How quickly things have changed. Now there are more than one hundred Middle Eastern restaurants in the Washington area and about a dozen Middle Eastern markets, run by Armenians, Persians, Palestinians, and Egyptians, and many *hallal* butchers (who slaughter ritually in the Moslem fashion). And, what is more, bulgur, tahini, and sumac are now available almost anywhere.

Rice-Stuffed Vidalia Onions, Iraqi-Style

As I watched Suad Shallal deftly stuffing Vidalia onions, yellow bell peppers, and dark green zucchini with rice, she told me that in Iraq she never would have used these vegetables. The peppers there are red, the green squash are light green, and onions are less sweet than Vidalias. In Iraq, stuffed vegetables are a way of using up the bounty of summer. "When I make *dolma* [stuffed vegetables] at home, all the kitchen becomes a production line," she told me. "My husband helps chop, slice, he even does the grocery shopping."

YIELD: 8 SERVINGS

8 Vidalia onions

3 cups short-grain rice

½ cup chopped fresh cilantro

½ cup chopped fresh parsley

1 cup chopped tomatoes
(approximately 2 tomatoes)

1 cup shredded carrots
(approximately 3 carrots)

3 tablespoons tomato paste

2 tablespoons
pomegranate syrup

4 tablespoons lemon juice,
or to taste

½ tablespoon salt

½ teaspoon freshly ground
pepper, or to taste

½ teaspoon cayenne pepper

1 teaspoon turmeric

1 teaspoon ground cumin

1 teaspoon allspice

1 teaspoon curry powder

½ teaspoon cinnamon

½ cup olive oil

½ cup vegetable oil

4 cups water (about)

1. Bring 10 cups of water to a boil in a large pot. Cut the stem ends off the onions, peel, and immerse the onions in the boiling water for a few minutes. Remove with a slotted spoon, cool slightly, cut them in half horizontally, then carefully push out and reserve the inner rings, leaving 2–3 outer layers of rings together. (A grapefruit knife is useful for this task.) Sprinkle the exposed inner layer with salt.

2. Place the raw rice in a large bowl along with the cilantro, parsley, chopped tomatoes, shredded carrots, 1 tablespoon of the tomato paste, pomegranate syrup, 1 tablespoon of the lemon juice, salt, pepper, cayenne pepper, turmeric, cumin, allspice, curry, and cinnamon. Chop the reserved onion and add to the vegetables. Stuff the rings of onions with the rice filling, leaving about an inch empty at the top (you will need this for the rice to expand).

3. Arrange the stuffed onions snugly in 1 layer in a flameproof casserole. Add enough of the olive and vegetable oils and enough water to come ¼ inch up the sides of the pan.

4. Stir the remaining 2 tablespoons tomato paste into 1 cup of the water and add the remaining lemon juice. Pour over the onions, adding 1 cup more water to almost cover. Set a heatproof plate on top to weight the onions down, then cover the casserole and bring to a boil. Simmer for about 10 minutes, making sure the rice is submerged in water.

5. Lower the heat and cook for about 1 hour or until most of the water is evaporated. Taste and adjust the lemon juice.

Gratin of Zucchini and Rice with Cheese

Corinne Lewis has two full-time jobs: one as director of food development at Royal Caribbean cruises and another as a mother and gardener at her home in nearby Plantations, Florida. Each summer, she visits her native France and returns with seeds to plant in her huge garden. This dish is a family favorite, which she makes with light green zucchini grown from some of those seeds. But any summer squash will do.

YIELD: 6–8 SERVINGS

2 cups canned or homemade vegetable or chicken broth (pages 290 and 146)

1 cup long-grain rice

4 medium zucchini, grated (1½ pounds)

1 teaspoon salt, or to taste

2 large eggs

½–¾ cup grated Gruyère cheese

2 tablespoons chopped fresh basil

2 tablespoons chopped fresh parsley

½ teaspoon freshly ground pepper, or to taste

¼ cup dry bread crumbs

¼ cup (½ stick) butter, cut in little pieces

1. Preheat the oven to 350 degrees and grease a 6-cup casserole dish.

2. Pour the vegetable or chicken broth into a medium saucepan and bring to a boil. Add the rice and zucchini, cover, and reduce heat to a simmer. Cook until the liquid is absorbed and the rice cooked, about 20 minutes.

3. Beat the eggs and grated cheese in a large mixing bowl. Fold in the rice mixture, basil, and parsley. Sprinkle with about 1 teaspoon salt and ½ teaspoon pepper (or to taste), and mix well.

4. Turn the zucchini-rice mixture into the casserole dish, sprinkle the bread crumbs on top, and dot with the butter. Bake, uncovered, for 20 minutes or until the top is golden.

Vegetables and Vegetarian Dishes

In 1972, Jim Crawford walked into Catholic University in Washington, D.C., the first day of his second year of law school. Then he turned around and walked right out. "I realized I wanted to abandon law school," Jim told me one day at New Morning Farm, his vegetable truck stand that he parks near my home in Washington. "But my parents were academics, and I was supposed to become a lawyer or a professor."

Instead, he moved to West Virginia and became a farmer. He later moved to nearby Pennsylvania. "I always had this entrepreneurial streak in me," said Jim. "As a kid I would carry tomatoes from my garden around the neighborhood and sell them door-to-door." Jim met some people who were "typical dropouts who wanted to do classic communal farming." Since they had grown up on farms, they already had the skills that Jim lacked.

In 1973, Jim started taking produce from three local farms, including his own, to an organic farmers' market in a vacant lot in the Adams Morgan neighborhood of Washington—a five-hour round trip. Thirty years later, Jim is still making the same journey, twice a week, toting wares from farmers to farmers' markets and vegetable stands. With the advent of chains like Whole Foods and the interest in locally grown ingredients, Jim's business has grown. "Whole Foods has helped us indirectly," he said. "Because it has educated people about organic food."

Jim Crawford may have been one of the first people in America to see that organic produce marketed directly to consumers had the potential to make a small-scale farm viable, but he is no longer alone. According to the *Geographical Review*, the number of farmers' markets supporting local farms in the United States has grown from 342 in 1970 to nearly 3,000 in the year 2000. Seasonal, organic, and local vegetables—such as tomatoes, zucchini blossoms, eggplant, celeriac, broccoli, red and yellow beets, brussels sprouts, wild mushrooms—are on their way to becoming as common as frozen peas.

Today, avid gardeners like Mark Talisman of Chevy Chase, Maryland, surf the Internet for new varieties of vegetables and herbs, finding it an extraordinary source for seeds

Clockwise from top right: The women of the Amin house; Harvesting artichokes in Castroville, California; Daniel Boulud presents the ultimate potato pancake to the author; Washington D.C.'s Dupont Circle farmers' market; A mushroom find in the Northeast Kingdom of Vermont; Janos Wilder with an Arizona cornucopia

from all over the world and for heirloom varieties suited to a particular climate. In his home garden, Mark grows with a vengeance twenty-one varieties of tomatoes, twenty types of basil, five varieties of parsley and oregano, and ten different species of eggplant, ranging from white to purple to green and red, that literally surround his house.

In a related trend, new varieties of fruits and vegetables are turning up at supermarkets, farmers' markets, and the many organic markets around the country. For this we can thank, in large part, a mother from Los Angeles, California, named Frieda Caplan. In 1957, Frieda went to work as a cashier at her uncle's produce company, a job that allowed her to spend time with her baby daughter, Karen. She noticed that the other salespeople weren't paying attention to the mushrooms. "You have to remember that mushrooms were a specialty item, and very few people were using them in those days," she told me. "One of the few times a year they were in demand by shoppers was during Thanksgiving and Christmas." Then one chain store wanted to feature them in a holiday advertisement. "I started calling three or four mushroom growers, got in my station wagon with my baby, visited a mushroom farm in desperation, and brought back some mushrooms for the customer."

Mushrooms led to other vegetables and fruits that were still considered "exotic" in the late 1950s: shallots, Jerusalem artichokes, horseradish, limes, and papayas. By 1962 Frieda was selling these crops on consignment for local farmers in her newly opened business. One thing led to another, and today the Frieda's, Inc., purple decal can be seen on high-quality produce all over the country.

Although she is no cook herself, Frieda is a great marketer and began giving away recipes to persuade customers to try tamarillos (tree tomatoes), feijoas (an oval juicy fruit), passion fruit, and sugar snap peas.

She also changed odd names. Jerusalem artichokes—the little tubers that don't originate in Jerusalem, and are not artichokes—have become "sunchokes." One sunchoke grower in Watsonville, California, told her he was sending down an old-time vegetable that he wanted her to sell: spaghetti squash. Frieda put a label on the squash that said what it was and how to cook it.

Vegetarians, a growing demographic, have helped whet our appetite for vegetables of all descriptions. With dishes like Indian sweet potato, plantain, and zucchini mixed-vegetable stir-fry with coconut (page 257), Vietnamese stir-fried corn and chanterelles (page 228), and Brazilian *abobrinha* with zucchini, tomatoes, and lime (page 258), for example, vegetables have become much more interesting.

Sautéed Baby Artichokes with Fresh Herbs

I set out for Castroville, California, one day in mid-March, when the artichoke season was in full swing. Bright oxalis flowers carpeted the green cactus-like artichoke plants. A member of the cardoon family, each plant grows four different sizes of artichoke: jumbo, large, medium, and baby. The baby artichoke was what had brought me there.

In the fields, I watched Mexican-American workers handpick the artichokes, tossing them into *canastas*—wicker baskets—strapped to their backs. At the end of each row, a conveyor belt awaited the baskets. The artichokes were dumped into boxes, then either transferred to the cooler or loaded onto huge refrigerated trailers that came right up to the fields.

Could the Italian farmers who brought over the first root stock of red globe artichokes to San Francisco in 1921 have imagined such an industry? Three years after those farmers arrived, they migrated south to Castroville, where the temperate, foggy weather made the area more fertile for growing the tubers. In 1924, four of the original artichoke growers formed Ocean Mists, an artichoke-growing and -distributing company that now controls 90 percent of production in America and Canada, producing hundreds of millions of artichokes each year on twenty-five thousand acres of farmland.

"Baby" artichokes aren't really babies; they're fully grown. What makes them special is that the stem is an extension of the heart, the most flavorful part of the vegetable.

YIELD: 4–6 SERVINGS

8 baby artichokes
Juice of 1 lemon
1 teaspoon sea salt
2 tablespoons extra-virgin olive oil
3 cloves garlic, chopped (about 3 teaspoons)
2 tablespoons chopped fresh mint or fresh Italian parsley
Sea salt and freshly ground pepper to taste

1. Snap off the outer leaves of the artichokes, leaving only the pale inner leaves. Trim the stems and cut off the thorny tops about ¾ inch down. Cut the artichokes vertically in halves or quarters, depending on their size. Put them in a bowl and cover with cold water and the lemon juice (the juice keeps them from turning brown).

2. Bring about 2 quarts of water with 1 teaspoon of sea salt to a boil in a large pot. Add the artichokes. Turn down the heat and simmer, uncovered, until the artichokes are almost but not completely tender, about 5–8 minutes. Drain and pat them dry.

3. Heat olive oil in an 8-inch skillet over medium heat. Add the garlic and artichokes, sautéing for a few minutes, then cover and cook until tender, about 5 more minutes. Sprinkle with mint or parsley and salt and pepper. Arrange on a plate and serve immediately.

Italian Fried Artichokes

Michelle Bernstein, the talented young chef at Azul Restaurant in Miami and one of the Melting Pot chefs on the Food Network, often cooks with her Argentinean mother. Michelle, who was born in Miami, grew up with avocado, lemon, mango, and grapefruit trees in the backyard and Latin markets nearby. "At home, growing up was a beautiful combination of American and Latin," she said. "The mood was set around a table spread with food, whether we were taking care of someone who was ill, crying over a loss, or celebrating a joyous event." This recipe is one of Michelle's specialties, her interpretation of the Roman *carciofi alla Giudaia*. She serves it both at home and in her restaurant. You can get it ready ahead of time and fry just before serving. Since artichokes prepared this way are messy, you should eat them with your fingers.

YIELD: 4–6 SIDE-DISH SERVINGS

Juice of 1 lemon
2 bay leaves
1 teaspoon sea salt, or to taste
Handful of peppercorns
3 large artichokes, about 1 pound each
Grapeseed or canola oil for deep-frying

1. Bring 3 quarts of water to a boil in a large pot with the lemon juice, bay leaves, a teaspoon or so of sea salt, and the peppercorns. Drop in the artichokes. If necessary, add more water to just cover them. Cook them until they are tender but still a little firm to the touch when pierced with a fork at the stem end, about 15 minutes. Remove the artichokes from the heat with cooking tongs and let them cool slightly.

2. Remove the outer leaves from the artichokes, cut off ¼ inch from the stem and the tip ends, then cut each heart into 4 vertical pieces. Scoop out the choke and the feathery fibers embedded in the center and refrigerate the pieces.

3. Fill a wok or deep pan with about 3 inches of oil and heat to sizzling. Deep-fry 2–3 artichoke pieces at a time for a few minutes; they will puff up as they cook. Serve hot, sprinkled with additional sea salt.

Frijoles Fritos

Refried Beans El Salvadoran–Style

Refried beans are increasingly popular these days, in part because of the sharp increase in immigration from Latin America. Twice-cooked beans are eaten for breakfast with huevos rancheros (page 26), stuffed into tortillas (page 62), and served as an accompaniment to rice. You can use either black or red beans.

YIELD: 8 SIDE-DISH SERVINGS

1 pound dried red kidney beans
or black beans
¼ cup vegetable oil
½ small onion, cut in chunks
1 teaspoon salt, or to taste

1. Soak the beans overnight in cold water in a soup pot. The next day, drain the beans, return them to the pot, and cover them again with fresh water. Bring to a boil. Lower the heat and simmer the beans, uncovered, until they are soft, about 1 hour.

2. Place the beans and about 2 cups of the cooking water in a food processor with a steel blade. Purée until the beans are nearly smooth, about 1½ minutes.

3. Heat the oil in a small heavy-bottomed saucepan over medium heat, toss in the onions, and fry until brown. Add the bean purée and heat for about 7 minutes or until most of the water has evaporated, stirring occasionally. Add salt to taste and serve.

Black and White Bean Chili

"Typical chili is boring," Willee Lewis, a former teacher and past president of the PEN/ Faulkner Foundation in Washington, D.C., told me. Willee grew up with this dish in Corydon, Indiana, on a bend of the Ohio River. "What's beautiful about this recipe," she said, "is that you can always ad-lib. I like cinnamon; you can add prunes, olives, whatever you want. It's a great way to clear out your refrigerator, and it's perfect for Sunday night supper."

What I like about the recipe is the pungent addition of orange peel with the chili powder. A nice accompaniment is avocado and sour cream. You can serve it with grated sharp cheddar, but I like it without.

YIELD: 12 OR MORE MAIN-DISH SERVINGS

1 pound dried black beans, or two 15-ounce cans

1 pound dried white cannellini beans, or two 15-ounce cans

½ cup dried lentils

3 large onions, diced (about 3 cups)

2 large cloves garlic, minced (about 2 teaspoons)

1 green pepper, diced

¼ cup olive oil

One 35-ounce can tomatoes, chopped but not drained

5 overripe plum tomatoes, chopped

1 tablespoon chopped fresh oregano

4 tablespoons mild chili powder

1 teaspoon cinnamon

2 teaspoons salt

½ teaspoon black pepper

1 teaspoon ground cumin

Cayenne pepper to taste

1 tablespoon grated orange zest

1 cup corn (about 2 ears)

1. Cover the black and white beans with cold water and let them soak overnight. Drain the beans and add fresh cold water to cover them by 2 inches. Bring to a boil, then gently simmer the beans for 40 minutes, until the beans are almost soft. Add the lentils and continue cooking about 20 more minutes.

2. Sauté the onions, garlic, and green pepper in the olive oil in a stock-pot over medium heat until the onions are soft.

3. Add the beans and lentils and their cooking water, canned and fresh tomatoes, oregano, chili powder, cinnamon, salt, pepper, cumin, cayenne pepper, and orange zest. Bring to a boil, then reduce the heat and simmer for 30 minutes, adding additional water if the chili seems too thick.

4. Add the corn just before serving; stir and simmer for 5 more minutes. Serve in bowls, over spaghetti or rice, or with leftover chicken or ground beef as a topping.

> *The aroma of good chili should generate rapture akin to a lover's kiss.*
> —THE CHILI APPRECIATION
> SOCIETY INTERNATIONAL

Haitian Vegetable Stew with Chayote, Eggplant, Cabbage, and Spinach

Marcel Auguste, who came to America in 1984 from northern Haiti, lives in an area of Silver Spring, Maryland, where many other Haitians have settled. She prepares this great dish for special occasions; in fact, it was served at the Smithsonian Folklife Festival in 2004. Marcel often mixes beef and shrimp in this stew, but sometimes she prepares it with just vegetables, as I have done here.

YIELD: 8–10 SERVINGS AS A MAIN DISH WITH RICE

2 tablespoons unsalted butter

2 tablespoons extra-virgin olive oil

2½ tablespoons tomato paste

1 teaspoon salt

¼ teaspoon pepper

3 chayotes (about 3 pounds), peeled and cut in half lengthwise

1 small green cabbage (about 1 pound), cored and quartered

1 eggplant (about 1½ pounds), unpeeled, cut into 4 pieces

2 large carrots, peeled, trimmed, and left whole

16 ounces frozen or 20 ounces fresh spinach

1. Heat the butter, 1 tablespoon of olive oil, tomato paste, and salt and pepper in a large skillet over medium heat.

2. Bring a large pot filled halfway with cold water to a boil and add the chayotes, cabbage, eggplant, carrots, and some salt. When the water returns to a boil, lower the heat and simmer until the carrots are soft, about 30 minutes. Drain well.

3. Meanwhile, wash the spinach, remove the stems, and place in a pot with enough cold water to cover. Bring the water to a boil and cook until the spinach is blanched, no more than 2–3 minutes. Drain.

4. When they are cool enough to handle, return all the vegetables—except for the carrots—to the pot and gently mash them with a potato masher. Cut the carrots into ½-inch rounds and add them to the vegetables. Stirring gently, drizzle on the remaining tablespoon of olive oil. Heat for about 15 minutes or until warm and serve with rice.

Stir-Fried Collards

Greens, even the well-known ones, like spinach, that children have been turning their noses up at for years, are becoming more and more popular. Yung Chow, who lives in Columbus, Mississippi, adapted this staple of the American South when she couldn't find traditional Chinese greens like bok choy or Chinese broccoli (*gai lon*).

YIELD: 6–8 SIDE-DISH SERVINGS

3 bunches (about 1 pound each) tender collard greens

Dash salt

2 tablespoons peanut or canola oil

6 cloves garlic, chopped (about 6 teaspoons)

A few grinds of fresh pepper

2–3 tablespoons oyster sauce

½ teaspoon sugar

1. Wash and trim the collard greens, discarding any thick stems, and cut into 2-inch pieces. Bring a 4-quart pot of water to a boil and blanch the collards for 1 minute. Drain and immediately submerge the greens in a bowl of ice water. Drain again and pat them dry with a towel.

2. Heat a wok over high heat. Add the salt to the dry wok and let it brown lightly, then pour in the oil. When the oil is hot, stir-fry the chopped garlic until it is lightly browned. Toss in the collard greens and the pepper and stir constantly for a couple of minutes. Remove from the heat and stir in 2 tablespoons of the oyster sauce and the sugar, adjusting the amounts to taste. Serve immediately.

Stir-Fried Corn and Chanterelles

The corn dish came up because my mom cooked corn when we moved to the United States," Charles Phan (see box) told me. "She would shuck it and stir-fry it with pork. But at the restaurant we have so many vegetarians, so I also make it with chanterelles or shiitakes."

YIELD: 4–6 SIDE-DISH SERVINGS

¼ cup fish sauce

¼ cup sugar

¼ cup water

Juice of 1 lime

3 tablespoons vegetable oil

1. Stir together the fish sauce, sugar, water, and lime juice in a small bowl until the sugar dissolves.

2. Heat a wok over high heat with 2 tablespoons of the vegetable oil. Add the mushrooms and sear them until they're caramelized—1–2 minutes—to seal in their juices. Pour in a few tablespoons of the

1 cup fresh chanterelle or shiitake mushrooms, cut into 1-inch pieces

8 ears of corn, kernels cut off the cob to make 4 cups of kernels

¾ cup chopped scallions or green onions (about 6)

Freshly ground pepper to taste

fish sauce mixture to deglaze the pan, then remove the mushrooms and their juices to a plate. Clean the wok with a paper towel.

3. Pour the remaining tablespoon of vegetable oil into the wok. Once it's hot, sear the corn and then deglaze the wok with another tablespoon or so of the fish sauce mixture.

4. Return the mushrooms to the wok and stir with the corn over low heat. Stir in the scallions. Taste and, if needed, add a little more of the fish sauce mixture to season the dish. Sprinkle with pepper to taste and serve in a bowl.

THE SLANTED DOOR—A VERY CALIFORNIAN, VERY ASIAN, VERY FRENCH RESTAURANT

I feel like I am an Asian American," Charles Phan told me. Charles is the chef-owner of the Slanted Door in San Francisco. The Phan family fled Vietnam by boat in 1977, but not before Charles developed a taste for things French. "I grew up with all the French pastries," he said. "We had so much French food that when I was a little kid, my favorite thing was cream puffs."

Charles, who worked as a busboy in San Francisco restaurants throughout high school and college, studied architecture at the University of California at Berkeley, but he always dreamed of opening a restaurant. "I had this idea that if I ever opened a restaurant, it would have the European accoutrements of good wine, attentive service, and European desserts—but Vietnamese food," said Charles. "Asian restaurants are usually so complex that I thought I would make it like Alice Waters's, with just ten things on the menu."

In 1994 Charles decided to "do this thing I was thinking about for so long." He found a space in the Mission District of San Francisco, and with the help of his extended family opened the Slanted Door a year later. "It was an easy name to remember," Charles told me. The restaurant was an instant hit. Charles matches his foods with slightly sweet wines that don't have a strong, boozy punch: "My thinking in matching wine is to have the palate relax, to wash everything down."

As forward-thinking as Charles is, he remains rooted in tradition. "When we opened our restaurant my father set up a shrine to the ancestors," he said. As for American holidays like Christmas and Thanksgiving, the Phans celebrate them all. "Who is going to cook is the question," he told me. "Since I cook Asian all year long, I don't want to cook for the holidays. I cook Italian for my wife, and my mom cooks all Asian, so we have a little bit of everything."

Corn with Pesto Butter

Summertime means huge amounts of corn and pesto. But how many of us think about putting them together in one dish? Nicole Ciesluk, who helps run the Ciesluk (pronounced "ches-luk") farm stand in Deerfield, Massachusetts, created a pesto butter to serve with the family's Silver King and Butter and Sugar corn. I liked Nicole's idea so much, I served it at a small party I threw for Julia Child's ninetieth birthday. It was a huge success, and Julia, slathering the pesto on her corn, ate it with gusto. The pesto butter is also delicious on other vegetables, like string beans, broccoli, or roasted new potatoes.

YIELD: 12 EARS OF CORN

4 fat cloves garlic
1 cup fresh basil leaves
½ cup grated imported Parmesan cheese
½ cup (1 stick) room-temperature butter, cut into pieces
Salt to taste
12 ears corn

1. Pulse the garlic with the basil leaves in a food processor fitted with a steel blade, then add the Parmesan cheese and, last, the butter. Process just until the butter is blended.

2. Pull the husks off the corn just before cooking. Half-fill a large pot with cold water. Bring it to a boil, add salt and the corn, and simmer for no more than 5 minutes.

3. Remove the corn from the pot and immediately slather the ears with the pesto butter. Serve right away on a large platter.

Walker's Stand Corn, Red Pepper, and Zucchini Succotash

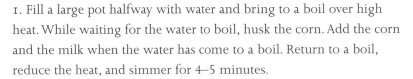

I found this modern succotash recipe at Walker's Stand, which is known in Little Compton, Rhode Island, for its corn. Made with corn, red pepper, and zucchini, this is a version of a corn and lima bean dish the Narragansett Indians ate. The recipe is very simple and a delicious change from straight corn on the cob.

YIELD: 4–6 SIDE-DISH SERVINGS

6 ears corn

2 tablespoons milk

2 tablespoons butter or extra-virgin olive oil

2 large cloves garlic, minced (about 2 teaspoons)

1 red pepper, diced

1 medium onion, diced

1 medium zucchini, diced

Salt and freshly ground pepper to taste

2 tablespoons chopped fresh parsley

1. Fill a large pot halfway with water and bring to a boil over high heat. While waiting for the water to boil, husk the corn. Add the corn and the milk when the water has come to a boil. Return to a boil, reduce the heat, and simmer for 4–5 minutes.

2. While the corn is cooking, heat the butter or oil in a large frying pan and sauté the garlic, red pepper, and onion until the onion is translucent, just a few minutes.

3. Add the zucchini to the pepper and onion and sauté for a few more minutes, until the zucchini is soft but not mushy. Remove from the heat.

4. Using tongs, remove the corn from the water and cool slightly. Scrape the kernels off the cobs (you will have about 3 cups of kernels) and toss into the other vegetables. Reheat the vegetables in the frying pan for a few minutes. Season with salt and freshly ground black pepper, then sprinkle with the fresh parsley and serve.

Corn Tamale Pie

W hile I traveled with Janos (see box), we ate a fabulous tamale pie with corn and Monterey Jack cheese at Café Poca Cosa. The café's chef, Susan Davilla, wouldn't share her recipe with us, so this is Janos's educated guess. The chipotle, a smoked jalapeño, adds a fiery touch.

YIELD: 8 OR MORE SERVINGS

3 red bell peppers, cut in half lengthwise

4 large ears sweet corn, husked and kernels removed (about 3 cups corn)

2 tablespoons extra-virgin olive oil

4 Anaheim chilies, cut in half lengthwise, seeded, and pith removed

6 cloves garlic, minced (about 6 teaspoons)

1 teaspoon salt, or to taste

¼ teaspoon freshly ground pepper, or to taste

2 tablespoons seeded and minced canned chipotle peppers in adobo sauce*

1 cup seeded, diced tomatoes

2 cups grated cheddar cheese

1 cup masa harina (instant corn masa mix)

2 large eggs

1 cup half-and-half

*The chipotles in adobo sauce, a typical Mexican marinade, are available canned in Hispanic stores and many mainstream supermarkets.

1. Preheat the broiler and set a broiling rack 2 inches from the heat. Line a cookie sheet with aluminum foil and place the red bell peppers on it skin side up. Broil until the skins are black and blistered and charred, about 7–12 minutes. Remove from the oven and put the peppers in a plastic or paper bag to steam and cool, about 10–15 minutes. Peel the charred skin, chop the peppers into ½-inch pieces, and place in a large bowl.

2. Preheat the oven to 350 degrees, move the rack to the middle of the oven, and grease a 10-inch or equivalent baking dish.

3. Toss half the corn kernels in with the red peppers. Coarsely chop the remaining kernels in a food processor fitted with a steel blade. Scrape the chopped corn and any juices into another bowl and set aside.

4. Heat the olive oil in a large frying pan and toss in the corn kernels, red peppers, Anaheim chilies, garlic, salt, and a generous grating of black pepper (don't wash out the large bowl yet). Cook over medium heat until the vegetables soften, about 10 minutes.

5. Return the sautéed corn and pepper mixture to the bowl, and stir in the chipotle peppers, tomatoes, corn chopped with its juices, cheddar cheese, and masa harina.

6. Whisk together the eggs and the half-and-half in a medium bowl, then stir into the corn mixture.

7. Pour everything into the baking dish and cover with parchment paper or aluminum foil, folding over the sides.

8. Place the baking dish in the oven and bake for 45 minutes. Remove the foil or parchment and continue baking until the pie has set, about 15 minutes more. Serve as a side dish or as a main dish for a vegetarian meal.

HOW A BOY FROM PALO ALTO BECAME A PROPONENT OF SOUTHWESTERN FOOD

After spending a few days with Janos Wilder in Tucson, Arizona, I began to understand how chefs today, coming as they do from different parts of the country, integrate their new surroundings into the food they cook, combining local ingredients with techniques they have learned along the way. One of the practitioners of so-called southwestern cuisine, Janos, who is from California, told me, "We chefs have created southwestern cuisine. Until we came along there was no such thing as southwestern food. It was Tex-Mex and Mexican."

The first thing Janos did before hiring any staff was to find gardeners who were willing to grow herbs and vegetables for him. "You should use things that are close to you, like beans, chili, and squash," he said. Today Janos is a board member of Native Seeds/SEARCH, a Tucson-based nonprofit organization whose mission is to preserve seed strains native to the Southwest. "By using local and Mexican produce, I wanted to inform my French-based food with ingredients from the region."

So I could learn more about the sources of his inspiration, I met Janos and his wife, Rebecca, in Nogales, a town on the Mexican border. Crossing the border, we had dinner at the Wilders' favorite Mexican restaurant, La Roca, located literally in the cliffs. Listening to mariachis, we ate the food that Janos selected: crisp *mochombos* (a crunchy brisket), *cabrilla* (sea bass from the Baja Peninsula), and a rich mole. The next day, we visited some of Janos's Tucson "finds" for a very long lunch. Like other regional chefs, Janos talks with native restaurateurs and incorporates their ideas into his food. That evening, we dined on Janos's food in his upscale southwestern restaurant: the *mochombos* that we had tasted in Nogales were sprinkled this time on top of ravioli filled with *oaxacan barbacoa*—braised beef. There were also smoked poblano chilies, and an edible tower of corn, mushrooms, and beans, all of which had been cultivated from a two-thousand-year-old seed source. It might not have been traditional regional food, but today it is the vibrant food of a particular region in the Southwest.

Fethe

Eggplant with Yogurt, Tahini, Chickpeas, Pomegranates, and Toasted Pita

Ramzi Osseiran, a native of Sidon, Lebanon, taught me how to make this extraordinary eggplant dish. The tahini-yogurt sauce with garlic goes back thousands of years in the Middle East. You can cook the eggplant ahead, make the tahini-yogurt sauce, refrigerate the eggplant in the sauce, and assemble the dish just before serving. Pita chips and pomegranate seeds are strewn on top of the eggplant, hence the name *fethe,* which means "little bits" in Arabic. You can substitute dried cherries or cranberries for the pomegranate if it's not in season.

YIELD: 6—8 SIDE-DISH SERVINGS

Two 1-pound eggplants
1 tablespoon salt
¼ cup balsamic vinegar
¼ cup extra-virgin olive oil
1 teaspoon minced garlic (about 1 clove)
Vegetable oil for frying
1 pita bread
½ cup pine nuts
1 cup drained canned chickpeas
Freshly ground pepper to taste
½ cup fresh pomegranate seeds, dried cherries, or dried cranberries (see page 16 for directions to open pomegranates)

TAHINI-YOGURT SAUCE
3 cups plain yogurt
⅓ cup tahini
½ teaspoon ground cumin
1 clove garlic, minced (about 1 teaspoon)

1. Preheat the oven to 400 degrees and grease 2 cookie sheets.

2. Slice the eggplants into ¼-inch-thick rounds. Sprinkle the eggplant with the salt and set it in a colander in the sink or over a bowl for 20 minutes. Towel off any liquid that accumulates.

3. Mix together the vinegar, olive oil, and garlic in a wide bowl. Coat the eggplant pieces with the dressing and place them on a baking sheet. Bake until soft, about 20 minutes.

4. While the eggplant is cooking, heat 1 inch of vegetable oil in a small skillet over medium heat. Roll up the pita bread and cut it in ½-inch strips, 2 inches in length. Fry the bread until crisp and brown, remove with tongs, and drain on paper towels.

5. Drain the skillet, reserving only a film of oil. Fry the pine nuts until golden brown.

6. Season the chickpeas with salt and pepper.

7. To make the tahini-yogurt sauce, stir together the yogurt, tahini, cumin, garlic, and salt to taste in a medium bowl.

8. When the eggplant is cooked, put a thin layer of the tahini-yogurt sauce in a 10-inch round or oval serving dish. Cover with a layer of

Salt to taste
½ teaspoon paprika

eggplant slices. Continue alternating sauce and eggplant, ending with the sauce. Sprinkle with the paprika.

9. Scatter the chickpeas, pine nuts, pomegranate seeds (or dried cranberries or cherries), and pita strips over the eggplant and serve.

Bengum Bhurta

Baked Eggplant Curry

This is a classic dish served throughout India and in most Indian restaurants in the United States. I particularly like this version with peas and cream.

YIELD: 6–8 SERVINGS AS ONE OF A FEW MAIN COURSES

3 medium eggplants (about 1 pound each)
8–9 tablespoons vegetable oil
1 large onion, diced (about 1 cup)
1 teaspoon cumin seeds
½ teaspoon cayenne pepper, or to taste
½ teaspoon turmeric
½ teaspoon ground coriander
½ teaspoon ground cumin
½ teaspoon garam masala*
1 teaspoon dried fenugreek leaves
1½ teaspoons salt, or to taste
1½ medium tomatoes, chopped
½ cup canned tomato purée
¼ cup heavy cream
3 tablespoons chopped fresh cilantro
⅓ cup green peas

1. Preheat the oven to 350 degrees and cut the eggplants in half lengthwise. Place them cut side up on a foil-lined baking sheet and drizzle with 3 tablespoons of the oil. Bake for about 30 minutes or until soft. Cool the eggplants, remove as many seeds as you can, and scoop the pulp from the skin, squeezing out the excess liquid. Chop the eggplant into 1-inch pieces.

2. Heat the remaining 5–6 tablespoons of oil in a small skillet over medium-high heat and sauté the onion and cumin seeds until the onion is translucent and soft, just a few minutes.

3. Add the chili powder, turmeric, coriander, ground cumin, and garam masala to the skillet and stir quickly to blend everything. Then add the chopped eggplant, fenugreek leaves, and salt. Stir in the chopped tomatoes and tomato purée. Bring to a simmer and cook gently, uncovered, for about 10 minutes.

4. Just before serving, add the cream and heat, then stir in 2 tablespoons of the cilantro and the green peas. Sprinkle with the remaining tablespoon of cilantro and serve over rice.

*This combination of spices includes some or all of the following: black pepper, cumin, coriander, cardamom, cloves, nutmeg, mace, cassia, caraway, cinnamon, and dried ginger. It is available in Indian markets or online.

A young Indian man walks by the freezer case, holding his cell phone with one hand while he maneuvers his shopping cart with the other. Guided by his wife, who was on the other end of the phone, he selects frozen Indian entrees before continuing down the aisle.

"He's the new kind of consumer," Indian cookbook author Julie Sahni said, pointing the man out to me during a walk through the Patel Brothers grocery store in Jackson Heights, Queens. "When I first came here in 1968, we were lucky if we got canned goods from India. Today there are Indian frozen dishes, prepared snacks, ice cream, fresh fruits and vegetables, all produced in the United States for young professional couples."

Driven by an increasing number of Indian immigrants, the market for Indian foods, like the market for Thai, Chinese, and Persian cuisine, has expanded greatly over the past thirty or so years. The Amin family, owner of Deep Foods, the leading Indian food manufacturer in the United States, has been a barometer of this change since the beginning. To learn their story, I had dinner with the family.

Before dinner, Arvind Amin offered us a glass of zinfandel and a bowl of his first product: a spicy Indian trail mix of fried noodles, cashews, and pistachios. The company now makes sixty-five different snacks as well as ice cream and frozen entrees. Arvind laughingly calls Deep Foods "the Frito-Lay, Häagen-Dazs, and Stouffer's" of Indian food.

Deep Foods' story began in the early 1970s when the Amins came to America. At the time, there were about ninety thousand East Indians in the United States, but few Indian stores, and getting Indian food was difficult. So Bhagwati, Arvind's wife, started deep-frying thin noodles made of chickpea flour in the family's garage.

"Hot Mix," the snack I tried at their house, was an instant hit. Bhagwati stuffed it into plastic bags and, as word spread, shipped it around the country via UPS. Arvind went the extra mile—literally. On weekends, he traveled to the twenty-six or so Indian stores throughout the United States to introduce the product in person.

The Indian community wanted more, so Bhagwati made different snack mixes, and added imported items like chutney, basmati rice, and chapati flour. As the business grew, more family members came from India to help. In 1977 the Amins incorporated the business and named it Deep Foods, after their younger son, Deepak. In 1985 they bought a small ice cream company and a freezer truck for deliveries. Now Deep Foods sells fourteen flavors of ice cream, including fig, pistachio, mango, and cashew raisin. Ice cream led to frozen entrees, coinciding perfectly with a high-tech boom that welcomed Indians into the workforce but gave them no time to cook.

For our meal, the Amin family served *aloo tiki* (page 248), a stuffed potato patty with a tamarind-date paste and cilantro, followed by a *bengum bhurta* (page 235), a vegetarian eggplant curry, and an Indian fusion salad of greens with *paneer* (cheese).

These days Bhagwati appears to be taking a backseat while her sons and daughters-in-law usher the company into its fourth decade. As she watched her daughters-in-law cook and clean up after the meal, I asked her the secret of living, cooking, and working with them. "Treat them like your own daughters, and leave everything to them. We always ask, 'What do you want to do?' 'Okay, whatever you want.' I never force them."

HOME IN NEW ORLEANS

We sat on wooden chairs around a glass table, holding hands as Auntie Carol Elie Gray said a blessing before the meal began. I was having dinner at the home of Gerri Moore Elie, the mother of Lolis Eric Elie, a columnist for the *New Orleans Times-Picayune* and author of *Smokestack Lightning,* a book on barbecue.

"Our deal growing up was if Lolis cooked, he could get out of washing dishes," said Gerri. "On the phone from my job I talked him through the recipes. He would ask me how to cook pork chops; he learned how to cook beans or rice or doctor pork and beans from the can, adding bacon and onion."

At many tables in New Orleans, the talk centers mainly around food. Gerri's table is no exception. As we dipped into her gumbo, the discussion turned to roux, the mixture of cooked flour and fat used in Creole cooking to thicken sauces. "I don't like my gumbo too 'rouxy,'" said Auntie Carol. Gerri's gumbo was just right, not too thin and not too thick, filled with fresh oysters, smoked andouille sausage, and crabmeat. Gumbo, often thickened with okra, is served at this home on Thanksgiving and Christmas. As the guests ate, they discussed the soup, which Lolis likes to vary by adding West Indian hot sauce and Scotch bonnet peppers.

Eggplant Casserole with Shrimp

At our dinner (see page 237), Auntie Carol gave us this eggplant and shrimp dish, traditionally served stuffed into eggplant skins. "My mother would make this dish for us growing up," she said. "We were nine children, so she put in what she could . . . dried or canned shrimp or ham . . . I put in fresh shrimp." You can substitute ham, crabmeat, or crawfish for the shrimp, or prepare it with eggplants alone. You can also put it all together ahead of time and reheat it in a 350-degree oven, sprinkled with another tablespoon or so of bread crumbs.

YIELD: 8 SERVINGS

2 teaspoons salt, or to taste

3 eggplants (1½ pounds each), peeled and chopped into 2-inch pieces

¼ teaspoon pepper, or to taste

¼–½ cup (½–1 stick) unsalted butter

1 large onion, diced

½ green pepper, diced

6 cloves garlic, minced (about 6 teaspoons)

1 pound medium shrimp, cleaned, peeled, and deveined

½ cup seasoned dry bread crumbs

1. Fill a large pot with water and bring to a boil over high heat. Add a teaspoon of the salt to the water and the eggplant pieces. Simmer for about 15 minutes or until soft. Drain the eggplant, spoon it into a large bowl, and mash with a fork, sprinkling in the remaining teaspoon of salt and the pepper.

2. Heat half of the butter in a large sauté pan over medium heat; add the onion, green pepper, and garlic and sauté until the onion is translucent. Toss in the shrimp and continue cooking, stirring occasionally, until the shrimp turns pink, about 2–3 minutes.

3. Add the mashed eggplant and cook until it has given up any remaining water, just a few minutes. Stir in the bread crumbs and taste, adjusting the seasonings. Turn out into a serving bowl and serve over rice.

Lolis Elie and his mother, Gerri Moore Elie, before sitting down to eat

Stir-Fried Turnip and Mustard Greens with Kale

You figure one bunch of greens per person," said Lolis (see page 237). "In the old days there was so much sand in the greens that I remember putting them in the sink with a lot of salt to kill the bugs. Then you soaked them and swooshed them out and repeated that several times. Today at the farmers' market I buy them already washed." (I've heard stories of putting greens in the washing machine to rid them of grit.) Lolis's preference is for flat rather than curly mustard greens. He cuts his onions in half horizontally so that guests can unravel the onion rings and mix them with the greens.

YIELD: 8 SIDE-DISH SERVINGS

4 medium onions, halved
1 cup water
4 bunches (4 pounds) mixed kale, turnip, and mustard greens
½ cup (1 stick) salted butter
Salt and freshly ground pepper to taste
Hot sauce (like Tabasco) to taste

1. Put the onions in a large Dutch oven or a heavy saucepan. Pour water over them and set over low heat. When the water starts to simmer, cover the onions with the greens (if all the greens don't fit, add only half at first). Cover the pot and simmer for 10 minutes, then add any remaining greens.

2. Drop in the stick of butter, cover the pot, and continue simmering slowly, stirring the greens every 15 minutes or so, until the onions are very soft, about 1½–2 hours. Add additional water if necessary. When the onions are completely soft, add salt, pepper, and hot sauce to taste. Giving everybody a half onion and some greens, turn out into individual shallow soup bowls with some of the liquid included, or serve them on a plate with a cup of liquid on the side.

I was eager to learn about mushrooms from Nova Kim, the wild mushroom lady of the Northeast Kingdom of Vermont, who lives mostly on foods picked in the wilderness. Hunting wild mushrooms and other wild edibles is Nova's livelihood and her love. "If you want to get high on life," she told me, "come with me in the woods for a while."

Nova and her husband, Leslie Hook, have started an annual mushroom festival as well as a mushroom society. "Most of the locals say 'yuck' to mushrooms at first," laughed Nova. "The three hundred edible mushrooms in the Northeast are not all gourmet, but they're better than what you get in supermarkets." Giant puffballs and dead man's angels go onto the focaccia (page 53), and chicken of the woods go into her soup.

Before we headed out on our mushroom foray, we had to learn mushroom basics. "Unless you are very, very sure about the wild mushroom, thank it and return it," she told me. "Mushrooms, after all, can be deadly." Nova suggests taking a spore print if you are unsure, and checking a mushroom guidebook or the U.S.D.A. guidelines. If you are still unsure, return them to the wild.

While in the woods with Nova and Leslie, I learned about much more than mushrooms.

When I look at a forest, I just see trees and foliage. When Nova and Leslie look, they see an entire world from which they get their food and livelihood. "I read about the wild the way others read mystery novels," said Nova. "And I have a wild food palate so I can taste the subtle flavors of the mild and the bitter. Most people fall into a pattern of similar flavors and are resistant to any variation."

As for Nova's favorites, she said, "I like just about all of the seventy kinds of wild mushrooms that we collect, since there is such variation in texture and flavor. Pheasant back, snow shrimp, bear's head, honeys . . . It's like asking a mother which child she likes best."

Grilled Portobellos

By far the most popular mushroom today, besides the classic white button, is the meaty portobello, an overgrown cremini. One of the first to import portobellos to the United States was Maria Venuti Forrest, who had seen and tasted them when visiting Flavio Morando, an Italian exporter, in Verona, Italy, in the early 1980s. According to Maria, she began importing and then growing portobellos outside Philadelphia. "Since I had a lot of supermarket clients in my business, I sent samples to them. They asked me what they were. They all thought it was a toadstool. I explained to them it tasted fabulous, like a meaty steak, and I found myself driving to my clients all over the eastern seaboard, cooking the portobellos up for them. I had to do a lot of in-store sampling for the consumer as well."

Maria's favorite preparation for portobello mushrooms is also the simplest—grilling. The grilled mushroom can then be served on a bun as a portobello burger, or as an appetizer or a side dish.

YIELD: 4 SERVINGS

MUSHROOMS

4 portobello mushroom caps, about 4 inches in diameter

2 tablespoons pure olive oil

Salt and pepper to taste

VINAIGRETTE

6 tablespoons extra-virgin olive oil

2 tablespoons balsamic vinegar

1 teaspoon chopped fresh garlic

1 tablespoon chopped capers

6 large fresh basil leaves, coarsely chopped

1 teaspoon chopped fresh rosemary or ½ teaspoon dried

½ teaspoon salt

Freshly ground black pepper to taste

1. Light the grill and let it get very hot, approximately 7–10 minutes.*

2. Rinse the mushroom caps and pat dry. Brush with oil on both sides; season with salt and pepper.

3. When the grill is hot, reduce the fire to medium and add the mushrooms. Cook about 10 minutes on each side, until the mushrooms are soft and well done.

4. While the mushrooms are cooking, make the vinaigrette. Whisk the oil and vinegar, stirring until emulsified. Add the garlic, capers, basil, rosemary, and salt and pepper to taste, stirring to incorporate.

5. When the mushrooms are grilled, place on a serving platter and pour the vinaigrette over them. Serve at once, or for more intense flavor, allow the mushrooms to marinate for a few hours, covered but unrefrigerated. Serve at room temperature.

*You can also broil the mushrooms.

Ragout of Wild Mushrooms with Shallots and Thyme

These days you can get wild mushrooms just about anywhere. I tasted this ragout made from forty pounds of wild Oregon morels and chanterelles at a fund-raising dinner a few years ago. Ever since, whenever I see a tempting array of wild mushrooms, I can't resist buying a bunch to make this wonderful dish.

YIELD: 8 SIDE-DISH SERVINGS

2 pounds mixed wild mushrooms (oyster, cremini, shiitake, etc.)

½ stick (¼ cup) unsalted butter

¼ cup extra-virgin olive oil

6 medium shallots, diced (about 1 cup)

4 cloves garlic, minced (about 4 teaspoons)

1 tablespoon rosemary

1 tablespoon chopped fresh thyme or ½ teaspoon dried

Salt and freshly ground pepper to taste

1½ cups homemade (page 146) or canned chicken broth

1. Clean all the mushrooms with a brush and cut them, including the tender parts of the stems, into 1-inch pieces.

2. Heat the butter and olive oil in a large skillet over medium heat. Add the shallots and sauté them until translucent. Toss in the garlic, rosemary, thyme, mushrooms, and a teaspoon of salt and ¼ teaspoon of pepper, stirring and cooking until the mushrooms have released some of their liquid, about 5 minutes. Stir in the chicken broth and continue to cook, stirring occasionally, until the mushrooms are well cooked and the chicken broth is reduced by half, about 15 minutes. Add salt and pepper to taste and serve mushrooms on their own or as a side dish with roast chicken (page 306) or meat.

Mushroom-Tofu Veggie Burgers

When I think of really healthy food, I think of Akasha Richmond, caterer to Pierce Brosnan, Billy Bob Thornton, and other health-conscious Hollywood celebrities. When she mentioned her mushroom-tofu veggie burgers, I was eager to try them. According to Akasha, veggie burgers require different treatment than hamburgers, because they fall apart when grilled. You have to cook them completely before searing them on the grill. Akasha bakes her patties in advance and freezes them, so she always has some on hand.

YIELD: 8 BURGERS

1 cup (about 8) fresh or dried shiitake mushrooms

1 tablespoon extra-virgin olive oil

1 medium onion, finely chopped (about 1 cup)

2 shallots, peeled and minced

2 cups (about 4 ounces) finely diced fresh portobello, cremini, or other mushrooms

12 ounces extra-firm tofu, drained

⅛ teaspoon salt, or to taste

⅓ cup toasted wheat germ

⅓ cup dry bread crumbs

2 tablespoons soy sauce

2 tablespoons Worcestershire sauce

½ teaspoon minced garlic (about ½ clove)

¾ cup regular (not quick-cooking) oatmeal

1 tablespoon chopped fresh parsley

1 tablespoon chopped fresh thyme, savory, or rosemary, or ½ tablespoon dried

1. If using dried shiitakes, soak them for about a half hour in 2 cups warm water or to cover. Drain, dice, and set aside.

2. Heat the olive oil in a small frying pan over medium-high heat, then add the onion and shallots. Sauté until the onion is translucent. Add the diced dried and fresh mushrooms and continue cooking for a few minutes, until they are soft but still meaty. Remove to a medium bowl.

3. Mash the tofu with a potato masher or your hands and stir into the onion-mushroom mixture. Stir in the salt, wheat germ, bread crumbs, soy sauce, Worcestershire sauce, garlic, oatmeal, and herbs. Shape into 8 patties.

4. Preheat the oven to 375 degrees and grease a cookie sheet. Put the patties gently on the sheet and bake for 20 minutes, flipping after 10 minutes. When cooked, grill if you like, for a minute or two. Carefully remove to buns or plates and serve as you would a hamburger.

Grilled Vegetables

In my family, the word *grill* is synonymous with summer. And if the grill is already on for meat or fish, there is nothing easier than grilling vegetables. Almost any vegetable can be grilled, but I especially like the flavor of onions, garlic shoots, fennel, yellow squash, red peppers, and corn grilled in its husk. All can be treated the same way.

My son David, who works in the summer for a caterer, is the one who grills these vegetables for parties. In the winter, we cook them at high heat in the oven for about five to ten minutes, depending on the vegetable.

YIELD: 8 SERVINGS

2 red bell peppers
2 zucchini
2 red onions, sliced in rounds
1 large bulb fennel
A handful of garlic shoots, if available, or scallions, or 4 ears of corn in their husks
Olive oil
Sea salt or other coarse salt
Freshly ground pepper to taste

1. Heat the grill until the embers are hot.

2. Slice all the vegetables except the corn about ¼ inch thick. With a brush dipped in the olive oil, brush the vegetables, and sprinkle them all except the corn with salt and pepper. Place some of the vegetables on the grill and cook just until charred on the outside. The garlic shoots should only be cooked for a minute or two. The corn is steamed in their husks. Make sure that they do not char too quickly—2 to 3 minutes per side should do. Flip them over and continue to grill for 2 to 3 minutes, until charred on the other side. Keep a close eye on the vegetables. Taste and sprinkle with more salt and pepper if needed. Repeat with the remaining vegetables.

3. Remove to a serving platter, layer the grilled vegetables in colorful clumps, and serve.

Stuffed Peppers with Gorgonzola Cheese, Polenta, and Pesto

I n Pawtucket, where I grew up, there were blocks of Cape Verdeans, Portuguese, and Italians," said Paula Martiesian, an artist living in Providence, Rhode Island. "My Armenian mother learned to make fried squash blossoms from our Italian neighbors. There was a lot of sharing of traditions; you had to be a total hermit not to come up against the different cultures.

"We Armenians stuff food a lot—grape leaves, peppers, lettuce leaves, apples. I was trying to make a vegetarian dish and decided to stuff peppers, so I filled them with Gorgonzola, polenta, and pesto, a combination I love."

YIELD: 10 SIDE-DISH SERVINGS

5 green bell peppers
1½ cups water
1½ cups milk
1 teaspoon salt, or to taste
1 cup stone-ground cornmeal
⅓ pound Gorgonzola cheese, cut into small cubes
1 cup pesto (page 161)
4 cups tomato juice

1. Preheat the oven to 375 degrees.

2. Cut the peppers in half crosswise and place the pieces cut side up in a deep baking dish large enough to hold all of them in a single layer.

3. Bring the water and milk to a boil with the salt in a medium saucepan over medium heat. Lower the heat slightly and, stirring constantly, pour the cornmeal into the liquid in a slow, steady stream. Doing this carefully will prevent lumps. When the cornmeal has thickened, after about 5 minutes, spoon it into the prepared peppers.

4. Put 2–3 cubes of Gorgonzola into each pepper half, pushing the cheese into the polenta. Top with the pesto and smooth it over the polenta to cover entirely.

5. Pour most of the tomato juice around the peppers and a little juice over them. Don't let the juice cover the peppers.

6. Put foil over the entire pan and seal tightly. Bake until the peppers are tender, about 1 hour.

The Ultimate Potato Pancake

Latkes, popular among Jews at Hanukkah, are now part of the common American table. But every culture has its own version: Indian, with masala spices; Californian, with goat cheese; and Vermont, with maple syrup.

The best latke I ever tasted was a *crique,* a paper-thin potato pancake that I ate in the Ardèche region of France. I have asked chefs and searched cookbooks, but most have never heard of this particular version. One day I mentioned them to chef Daniel Boulud of Restaurant Daniel in New York and he said, "When I first tasted a latke, I thought it was a *crique.*" A kindred spirit, he offered to make it for me.

I couldn't wait. Carefully, he demonstrated how to grate Yukon Gold potatoes by hand on a mandoline, sprinkling them with salt to bring out the juices, and then pressing out the liquid. He added chives, eggs, and a few black olives, gently pressed the potatoes into rounds (no misshapen pancakes at Restaurant Daniel), and fried them in olive oil. "The trick is to cook the pancake gently on the outside until crispy on the edges and slightly soft in the middle."

He also suggested varying the *crique* by grating celery root, pumpkin, or acorn squash into it, and serving it warm with goat cheese or arugula and smoked salmon.

YIELD: 4 LARGE PANCAKES (SERVES 4–6)

2 pounds Yukon Gold potatoes, peeled

2 large eggs, lightly beaten

6 tablespoons chopped fresh chives

Salt and freshly ground black pepper to taste

4 tablespoons extra-virgin olive oil

Crème fraîche, smoked salmon, or sour cream for garnish

1. Grate the potatoes by hand or in a food processor using the grating blade with the smallest holes. Scoop up ¼ of them with your hands and squeeze out the excess liquid and discard. Put the handfuls of grated potatoes in a mixing bowl and add the eggs, chives, and salt and pepper. Mix well, until everything is very well blended.

2. Heat about 1 tablespoon of the olive oil in a 10-inch nonstick sauté pan over high heat. Place ¼ of the potato mixture in the middle of the pan and, with a spatula and your hands, spread the pancake out as thinly as possible until it covers the surface of the pan. Be careful not to burn yourself!

3. Reduce the heat to medium-low. Cook the pancake until the bottom browns, about 5 minutes.

4. Invert a plate that is just slightly larger than the pan over the top. Flip the pan over so that the pancake drops onto the plate, then slide the

pancake back into the pan. (The brown side is now facing up.) Cook for about 4 more minutes, until the underside is browned. Flip the pancake over and onto a plate. Keep warm in a low oven as you cook the others.

5. Repeat these steps for the remaining pancakes, starting with 1 tablespoon of oil for each one. Serve plain or garnished with smoked salmon, crème fraîche, or sour cream.

Garlic Mashed Potatoes

When your children follow your profession, as two of superstar chef Bradley Ogden's sons have, it says something about what you have accomplished. A native of Traverse City, Michigan, Brad moved to the San Francisco Bay Area in 1983 and created a restaurant empire. When I asked him what he wanted to be remembered for, his answer was simple and direct: putting mashed potatoes on the table in a gourmet restaurant. Until chefs like Brad came along, gourmet restaurants seldom served mashed potatoes. If they did, they were pretty lackluster. Now chefs have gone Brad one step further. I have been served truffled mashed potatoes, lobster mashed potatoes, and David Bouley's mashed potatoes, which have more cream than potato! Don't peel the potatoes for this recipe—the skin adds flavor and color.

YIELD: 4–6 SIDE-DISH SERVINGS

3 pounds small red new potatoes, scrubbed thoroughly

2 teaspoons kosher or sea salt, or to taste

1 whole bulb fresh garlic, cloves separated and peeled

1 cup cream or half-and-half

1 cup hot milk

½ cup (1 stick) unsalted butter

¼ teaspoon freshly cracked black pepper, or to taste

½ cup crème fraîche (optional)

2 tablespoons snipped chives for garnish

1. Preheat the oven to 350 degrees.

2. Cook the potatoes in boiling water with salt over high heat until they are tender, about 15 minutes. Drain, then place them on a cookie sheet in the oven to dry for about 10 minutes.

3. While the potatoes are cooking, put the garlic cloves in a small saucepan with the cream or half-and-half, ½ cup of the milk, and the butter. Simmer them over medium heat until the garlic is very tender, about 15 minutes, then remove from the heat.

4. With a handheld masher or in a standing mixer with a paddle, mash the potatoes with the garlic-milk mixture and a teaspoon more of salt and ¼ teaspoon of pepper.

5. If the mash is thicker than you like, thin it with the remaining ½ cup hot milk, season to taste with salt and pepper, and keep warm until serving.

6. If using crème fraîche, stir it in just before serving. Turn the potatoes into a warm serving bowl and sprinkle with the chives.

Aloo Tiki (Stuffed Potato Patties) with Tamarind-Date Sauce and Cilantro

These thick, filled potato patties from India are a marvelous version of the potato pancake.

YIELD: 16 PATTIES (8 SERVINGS)

POTATO PATTIES

4 medium potatoes
(about 2 pounds)

1 teaspoon chopped jalapeño
pepper (about 1 small)
or green chili paste*

½ teaspoon chopped peeled
fresh gingerroot

2 tablespoons chopped
fresh cilantro

4 tablespoons cornstarch

4 tablespoons bread crumbs

½ teaspoon salt, or to taste

FILLING

2 tablespoons vegetable oil, plus
more for deep-frying patties

*Available in Indian markets and
many supermarkets.

1. Put the potatoes in a large pot, cover with cold water, and boil over high heat until they are soft, about 20 minutes. Drain, and when they're cool enough to handle, peel them. While they are still warm, mash the potatoes in a medium bowl with a teaspoon of the jalapeño pepper or green chili paste, ginger, cilantro, cornstarch, bread crumbs, and salt. Let cool some more.

2. To make the filling, heat 2 tablespoons vegetable oil in a medium skillet over medium heat and add the jalapeño pepper or green chili paste and coconut. Sauté, stirring, for 1 minute. Sprinkle with the crushed peanuts and green peas and sauté for another minute. Add the salt, sugar, lemon juice, and 2 tablespoons of the cilantro and sauté for 5 more minutes. Mash the peas slightly, then remove the skillet from the heat and let cool.

3. To assemble the patties, mold about 2 tablespoons of the potato mixture into a patty 2 inches in diameter. Using your finger, poke a hole in the center of the patty and stuff it with about 2 teaspoons of the filling. Roll each patty into a ball to enclose the filling completely,

1½ teaspoons chopped jalapeño
pepper (about two small) or
green chili paste

½ cup shredded fresh coconut or
2 tablespoons dried coconut

2 tablespoons crushed peanuts

¾ cup frozen green peas

½ teaspoon salt

1½ teaspoons sugar

2 tablespoons fresh lemon juice
(about 1 medium lemon)

3 tablespoons chopped
fresh cilantro

Tamarind-date sauce or
chutney*

* Available in Indian markets and
many supermarkets.

then flatten again into a patty. Repeat with the remaining potato dough and filling until used up—you should have about 16 patties.

4. Pour about 2 inches of vegetable oil into a wok or deep pan and heat it to 375 degrees. Deep-fry the patties a few minutes on each side, turning carefully with a slotted spoon and cooking until golden. Drain the patties on paper towels.

5. Serve the patties garnished with the remaining tablespoon of chopped cilantro and a tamarind-date sauce or sweet chutney.

Sugar Snap Peas with Red Peppers

Restaurants are clamoring for it. Brokers are bootlegging it," wrote Marian Burros, a food writer at the time for the *Washington Post,* heralding the 1979 arrival of the sugar snap pea. "People are calling it the greatest new vegetable in fifty years."

She was right. Today the sugar snap pea, a favorite of consumers and gardeners alike, outsells the snow pea in American supermarkets. This edible peapod was developed in the 1970s by Calvin Lamborn, a University of Idaho botanist with the Gallatin Seed Company. Lamborn had sent a few pods to food people like James Beard, who loved them, but it was Marian Burros who received them from Idaho friends and really spread the word.

In her enthusiasm, Marian called Frieda Caplan (page 222) of Frieda's, Inc., in Los Angeles to see if she had sugar snap peas. "I can't write about something unless the consumers can find it in our stores," she told Frieda. Frieda immediately called a few supermarket chains whose produce trucks were just about to depart for Washington, D.C. Somehow, Frieda was able to get sugar snap peas on store shelves by the day the article appeared. When Marian's story broke, people lined up at the supermarkets hoping to get their hands on what the headline said would "revolutionize the vegetable world."

YIELD: 4–6 SIDE-DISH SERVINGS

Salt to taste

1 pound sugar snap peas, rinsed

2 cloves garlic

6 tablespoons extra-virgin olive oil

2 tablespoons balsamic vinegar

2 red bell peppers, cut into long strips

Freshly ground pepper to taste

1. Fill a medium saucepan with water and bring it to a boil over high heat. Add salt to taste, then blanch the sugar snap peas for 1–2 minutes. Drain and plunge immediately into ice water for a few minutes so they retain their bright green color. Drain the peas and dry them with a towel.

2. Place the garlic, 4 tablespoons of the olive oil, salt, and the balsamic vinegar in a food processor and pulse until roughly chopped and well blended. Remove the paste and toss it with the sugar snap peas.

3. Heat the remaining 2 tablespoons of olive oil in a medium skillet over medium heat and sauté the red peppers, just until soft. Toss in the sugar snap peas and heat through. Season with salt and pepper. Serve in a shallow bowl.

Chef Morou Ouattara sprints swiftly around the kitchen of Signatures, his Washington, D.C., restaurant, assistants following in his wake. He is clearly in charge. But when Morou's mother visits from Côte d'Ivoire, his frenzied activity comes to a halt, at least at home, and he becomes a little boy again. She will not let him cook, at least not in her presence. "It is a question of tradition," said his mother, Constance Hallange. "If a man knows how to cook, it is a sign that a woman is not doing her job. There is no respect."

One evening Morou watched his mother and his sister Kady cook several dishes from Côte d'Ivoire in my kitchen. "My mom's food is what I grew up with, and I love these sauces and stews," said Morou.

Constance is proud of her son's accomplishments, and she has the quiet confidence of someone who has passed down her traditions. "I am happy that he can cook," she said. "Now when he feels like eating something, he can make it himself."

The Ouattara family comes from Bondoukou, a city of about thirty thousand near the border with Ghana. In this center of Islamic culture and commerce, Morou's late father was a coffee and cocoa wholesaler. As Morou and his family surveyed my kitchen, he commented, "The first thing that is different is the rhythm of cooking." Although his family lives comfortably in a two-story clay-brick house with a refrigerator and a propane gas cookstove, his mother cooks outside in the yard. "My mother sits on a *tabouret* [a little chair] and uses a pot set on a low fire," he said. Daily life surrounds the slow-cooking stews and the gruels that, once put into the pots, need to be stirred and tended. "It is like making polenta," said Morou. "But here you can control the fire, there you can't. Every meal becomes a feat, with my mother cooking for ten or eleven people." Morou and his ten brothers and sisters learned to cook by watching—much as his nephew, Nasser, tied to his sister's back with a colorful sling, will do in a few years.

Morou stood by his mother as she cooked, telling me, "You see how she is taking a pinch of this and a pinch of that. You can't translate that into numbers and cups. In Africa, when we watch our mother cooking, we don't have to do anything else but listen to stories. Time is different there. It is slower, like being in Miami. When an older person dies in Africa, we say that a whole library has gone up in flames."

Spinach Stew with Peanuts and Pumpkin Seeds

This ground-peanut stew is made either with chicken or with *boroboroba* (wild spinach), a vegetable available from local African farmers in some areas around America. If you can't get it, spinach is fine. Morou's family (see page 251) uses ground raw peanuts, but I find chunky peanut butter is a good alternative.

YIELD: 4–6 SERVINGS AS A VEGETABLE STEW WITH RICE

½ cup white melon seeds or pumpkin seeds

10 ounces boroboroba or 16 ounces spinach, washed

2 tablespoons vegetable oil

1 medium onion, diced (about 1 cup)

1 medium tomato, diced

1 tablespoon tomato paste

1 cup canned or homemade chicken or vegetable stock (page 146 or page 290)

1 cup chunky peanut butter

Salt and pepper to taste

Cooked rice

1. Preheat the oven to 350 degrees. Place the melon or pumpkin seeds on a cookie sheet and toast them until they start to pop, about 5 minutes. Grind the seeds in a small food grinder and set aside in a small bowl.

2. Bring 3 cups of water to a boil in a large saucepan over high heat. Blanch the *boroboroba* or spinach until it is soft, 1–2 minutes. Drain well and chop it fine or pulse it 2 or 3 times in a food processor fitted with a steel blade, being careful not to purée it.

3. Return the saucepan to the stove, pour in the oil, and heat over medium heat. Add the onion and cook until it is translucent. Stir in the tomato and tomato paste and cook for 2 minutes. Stir in the chicken or vegetable stock, peanut butter, and salt and pepper. Bring everything to a boil, then reduce the heat and cook for a few minutes, uncovered, until thickened.

4. Add the seeds to the stew and simmer for a few minutes, then stir in the spinach. Simmer slowly, uncovered, until very thick, about 25 minutes. Remove the pan from the heat, taste and adjust the seasonings, and turn into a serving bowl. Serve alone or with rice.

Palak Paneer

Indian Spinach with Fried Cheese

This absolutely delicious spinach dish, reserved for special occasions in India, has become a staple at Indian restaurants in America. The ingredients vary: some cooks use vegetable oil, others clarified butter; some use cream, others tomatoes; some use ginger, others garlic. Ramesh Kaundal, the chef at the Bombay Club in Washington, D.C., has varied the recipe since he came to this country. While he would have used clarified butter in India, here he uses vegetable oil and chopped fresh ginger.

Although Ramesh makes his own *paneer,* you can buy it in Indian grocery stores. I tried making his cheese, and it really takes no time at all. (You can also use fried extra-firm tofu if you are a strict vegan, although it won't have the same texture.)

Ramesh thinks that the secret to a good *palak paneer* is the fenugreek leaves, which are slightly bitter but flavorful. I think it's also his fresh garam masala, the Indian spice combination. He puts whole spices, like black and green cardamom, cinnamon sticks, cloves, peppercorns, coriander seeds, nutmeg, mace, and cumin seeds, in a warm oven overnight and grinds them the following day.

YIELD: 4–6 SERVINGS

Two 10-ounce bags spinach

Vegetable oil for deep-frying

1½ cups homemade (recipe follows) or store-bought paneer

1 teaspoon salt

One 2-inch piece gingerroot, peeled and diced (about 3 tablespoons)

¼ teaspoon hot chili powder or cayenne pepper

1 teaspoon fenugreek leaves

¼ cup chopped tomato, fresh or canned

1. Wash the spinach, dry it well, then chop it finely in a food processor fitted with a steel blade.

2. Heat 2 inches of oil in a large, deep frying pan over medium heat to 340 degrees. Cut the *paneer* into ½-inch cubes and deep-fry them until golden brown and crisp on the outside, about 4–5 minutes. You should be able to fit all in the pan at once. (If not, do it in batches.) Drain on paper towels and sprinkle with salt.

3. Drain the frying pan, leaving only a slight film of oil. Heat the pan over medium heat and add the ginger. Stir-fry for a few minutes, then add the spinach, fried cheese, salt, chili powder, fenugreek leaves, and tomato, stirring until the spinach is cooked. Sprinkle the spinach

4 tablespoons chopped
fresh cilantro
Pinch garam masala
¼ cup heavy cream (optional)
¼ cup water (if needed)

with the cilantro and garam masala. Finally, stir in the heavy cream, if you are using it, and, if the mixture seems too thick, add a little water. Adjust the seasonings and serve in a bowl as a side dish.

Paneer

YIELD: ABOUT 1½ CUPS PANEER

½ gallon whole milk
½ cup white vinegar
Vegetable oil for frying

1. Bring the milk to a boil in a medium pot over high heat. As soon as the milk is foamy and has risen a few inches, remove the pot from the heat and stir in the vinegar. Let sit for 5 minutes, while the curds form.

2. Using a slotted spoon, scoop the curds into a 12-by-12-inch piece of cheesecloth, then fold and tie the ends to enclose them. Place the wrapped curds in a colander over a pot or bowl in the sink, weight them down with a plate, and let them drain until they form a dry cheese, about 30 minutes. Refrigerate, wrapped, until ready to use.

Fricassee Giraumon

Braised Butternut Squash with Mustard Seeds, Chili, Curry Leaves, and Ginger

Marla Gooriah, who was born on the island of Mauritius, off the coast of Africa, came to the United States in 1979. Like most immigrants, she has learned to add American ingredients to her native food. For Thanksgiving, for example, she always makes this dish, typical of her African, Indian, and Irish heritage. The slight sweetness of the butternut squash marries well with the mustard seeds, ginger, and curry leaves, grown today in California and Florida. I serve it as a side dish with grilled meat or fish. Leftovers go nicely on garlic bread or bruschetta. Adjust the amount of hot pepper to your taste—and remember, it's easier to add hot pepper than to remove it. When I visited Marla at her home in Virginia she showed me a time-saving technique. She mashes fresh garlic and ginger together in the food processor, then keeps the mixture in a jar in her refrigerator.

1 butternut squash
(about 3 pounds)

¼ cup extra-virgin olive oil

½ large Vidalia or other sweet
onion, diced (about ¾ cup)

3 cloves garlic, chopped

1 inch fresh gingerroot, peeled
and grated (about 1 tablespoon)

6 curry leaves
(available in Indian stores)

2 teaspoons black mustard seeds

1–3 teaspoons hot pepper flakes
or pequin chilies, to taste

1 medium tomato, diced

Salt and freshly ground
pepper to taste

1 cup water

3 tablespoons sugar

½ cup chopped fresh cilantro

1. Slice the butternut squash in half lengthwise. Scoop out the seeds and the pulp with a spoon and discard them. Peel the squash and cut into 1-inch cubes. Heat the olive oil in a heavy Dutch oven or casserole over medium heat and sauté the onion, garlic, ginger, curry leaves, and mustard seeds until the seeds start to pop, about 3 minutes. Add the pepper flakes or chilies and continue cooking until the onion is translucent, about 3 more minutes.

2. Add the squash, tomato, salt, pepper, and water to the onion in the pot. Bring to a boil, then reduce the heat and simmer, covered, for 15 minutes. Uncover, stir, and mash the squash with a potato masher. Add the sugar and cook until the water has evaporated and the squash is cooked through, about 5 to 10 minutes. Adjust the seasonings, sprinkle the cilantro over the squash, and serve in a large bowl.

Sweet Potato Casserole with Pecans

Although I have always served sweet potatoes with marshmallows, Lorene Burrough, of Oil Trough, Arkansas, convinced me to try pecans instead.

Lorene cooks once a month for church potlucks. "A lot of people buy the food prepared and then they eat it," she said as she plied me with homemade bread, put-up pickles, and the best sweet potato casserole I have ever tasted. Her favorite recipes, she said, come from the homemakers' club she attends once a month.

YIELD: 6–8 SIDE-DISH SERVINGS

6 cups sweet potatoes (about 3½ pounds), peeled and cut into large chunks

Salt to taste

½ cup (1 stick) unsalted butter

1¼ cups brown sugar

⅓ cup milk

1 teaspoon vanilla extract

2 large eggs

¼ cup all-purpose flour

½ cup chopped pecans

1. Preheat the oven to 350 degrees and grease a 9-by-13-inch ovenproof casserole.

2. Bring about 3 quarts of water to a boil in a stew pot over high heat and add about a teaspoon of salt and the sweet potatoes. Boil until the potatoes are very soft, about 30 minutes. Drain them, then mash them in a large mixing bowl.

3. While the potatoes are still warm, stir in 4 tablespoons of the butter, cut into small pieces, which will melt into the potatoes. Then add ¼ cup of the brown sugar, the milk, vanilla, salt to taste, and eggs, mixing well after each addition. Transfer the mixture to the baking dish.

4. To make the topping, dice the remaining 4 tablespoons of butter into a small bowl. Add the remaining cup of brown sugar, the flour, and the chopped pecans. Blend well with your fingers, then sprinkle over the potatoes.

5. Bake until the topping is golden brown, about 30 minutes. Serve from the baking dish.

Indian Sweet Potato, Plantain, and Zucchini Mixed-Vegetable Stir-Fry With Coconut

Raghavan Iyer, an Indian Brahmin who knew nothing about cooking when he was growing up, came to the United States as a student. He met a Swedish-American man from Minnesota, they became partners and settled in Minneapolis, and Raghavan began cooking. Although a vegetarian, he has "tasters" for the nonvegetarian food he prepares. One day he met some people at Betty Crocker and so dazzled them with an Indian menu that they asked him to write *Betty Crocker's Indian Home Cooking.* Now working on his third book (not for Betty Crocker), Raghavan still makes the meal that clinched the first book contract, including this absolutely delicious mixed-vegetable stew.

YIELD: 6 SERVINGS

1 medium white potato, peeled

1 medium sweet potato, peeled

1 medium carrot, peeled

1 small green plantain, peeled

1 medium yellow summer squash

1 medium zucchini

½ cup green beans

2 tablespoons vegetable or coconut oil

½ teaspoon ground turmeric

1 cup shredded fresh coconut or ½ cup dried, unsweetened, shredded coconut

1 teaspoon cumin seed

*2–4 fresh Thai, serrano, or other small hot chilies**

1–2 tablespoons water

8–10 fresh curry leaves or 2 tablespoons chopped fresh cilantro†

1 teaspoon salt

1. Cut the potatoes, carrot, plantain, yellow summer squash, zucchini, and green beans into julienne strips, each about 2 inches by ¼ inch thick, and put them in a large bowl. You should have about 5 cups of vegetables.

2. Heat 2 tablespoons of oil in a large skillet over medium heat. Sprinkle with the turmeric, then add the vegetables, stir-frying until they are tender, about 5 minutes.

3. While the vegetables are cooking, put the coconut, cumin seed, and chilies in a blender. Cover and blend on medium speed until a smooth paste forms, stopping occasionally and scraping down the sides. Add a tablespoon or so of water if necessary.

4. Stir the coconut mixture, curry leaves or cilantro, and salt into the vegetables. Cook over low heat, covered, until warmed through, 2–3 minutes. Serve on a large platter with mango chutney (page 65) on the side.

*These chilies are very spicy, so use as many as you want for desired heat.

†Curry leaves are available at Indian markets. Although cilantro does not taste the same, I have used it instead of curry leaves, and the dish is delicious.

Abobrinha

Brazilian Sautéed Zucchini with Tomato, Peppers, and Fresh Lime

One of the truly exciting accomplishments of the last few years has been persuading farmers to grow what once were considered to be "exotic" vegetables and fruits. Up until now, they have been hard to find and their cost has been astronomical, because they were flown in from other countries.

On a hot day in August I went to the Allandale Farm in Brookline, Massachusetts, which dates back to the colonial era. Expecting to see ordinary Yankee fruits and vegetables, I was surprised to find that David Dewitt, the farmer who greeted me, was most excited about jilo, a tiny plump Brazilian green eggplant about the size of a fist. At first Dewitt was skeptical about whether there would be a market for unusual produce like jilo, *abobora,* a winter squash, and *abobrinha,* similar to but lighter than our zucchini and used in Brazil and the Middle East. Well, there was.

Dewitt's farm was growing the Brazilian vegetables in cooperation with the University of Massachusetts Extension Service, which advertised them in local Brazilian newspapers. "We had guys coming from central Maine to New York City for this stuff," said John Lee, the owner of the farm. The Extension Service also took Allandale Farm's Brazilian produce to the nearby Somerville Farmers' Market, where cooks demonstrated recipes for *abobrinha* and *pamonha,* a typical corn dish, almost like a flan. In Brazil, tiny slices of hot dogs or sausages are stir-fried with the vegetables, which are then served with rice.

1 tablespoon extra-virgin olive oil

1 medium onion,
very thinly sliced

2 cloves garlic, chopped
(about 2 teaspoons)

1 green or red pepper,
sliced into matchsticks

1 large tomato, peeled and cut
into vertical slices

1 medium zucchini,
cut into matchsticks

Salt and freshly ground
pepper to taste

Juice of ½ lime
(about 2 teaspoons)

2 tablespoons chopped fresh
parsley or cilantro

1. Heat the olive oil in a large pan over medium heat and sauté the onion and garlic until the onion is wilted, about 5 minutes.

2. Add the green or red pepper and the tomato and continue to cook for another 5 minutes.

3. Add the zucchini, cover, and cook until the zucchini is soft, about 5 minutes.

4. Season with salt and pepper to taste and squeeze the lime juice over the vegetables. Sprinkle with the parsley or cilantro. Serve at once as a side dish.

Fish and Shellfish

Clockwise from top right: "That catfish place" outside Oxford, Mississippi; Gorgeous grouper; Oyster mavens in West Virginia; The Chow clan in Clarksdale, Mississippi; Josephine Vizueta and her casuela; Shelling shrimp in New Orleans

Over the past thirty years, our appetite for fish has become insatiable, as has our willingness to try more exotic varieties. Even what used to be known as "trash fish," like mussels and monkfish, have become downright chic.

In 1965, when the Second Vatican Council lifted the Catholic Church's long-standing prohibition against meat on Fridays, George Berkowitz feared his fish market in Cambridge, Massachusetts, would go out of business. "Eighty percent of our fish was bought by Catholics and Jews on Fridays," he told me. To George's surprise, the Vatican's decree had the opposite effect. And a couple of years later, George opened a small fish and chowder restaurant next to his market. These inauspicious beginnings spawned the Legal Sea Foods chain, which now has more than twenty-eight restaurants coast to coast.

At the same time Legal Sea Foods was growing, so was immigration. "There was a tremendous influx of Asians to Boston," said George. "I remember as a kid behind the fish counter: they would pay for the fish, and we would wrap it up. Then they would unwrap it and eat the fish raw right in front of me. This was before sashimi and sushi became so popular."

What was happening in Cambridge was also happening in other coastal cities around the country. Moreover, the popularity of fish increased as Americans began to learn about the health benefits of fish, an excellent source of high-quality protein and vitamins as well as omega-3 fatty acids, particularly in dark-fleshed fish. Studies that were released in the mid-1970s indicated that Asians appeared to live longer and have lower rates of heart disease and cancer than Americans. Could fish be the reason?

While the market for fish has grown, neighborhood fresh fish markets, alas, have largely disappeared, and now supermarkets stock fresh fish all week, filleted and pre-marinated to make cooking more convenient. Rarely do we see whole fish, gutted to order, anymore.

Chefs have played a tremendous role in getting us to like fish, introducing us to new varieties and ways of cooking. Paul Prudhomme started the blackened fish trend (page 269); Nobu Matsuhisa began making miso-marinated cod at Nobu, his first restaurant in Manhattan; and some restaurants, catering to the nationwide sushi craze, now packaged their sushi for sale in local grocery stores. Moreover, chefs have been highly effective in campaigns to replenish our diminishing stocks of fish, such as Chilean sea bass; meanwhile, fish farmers have been repopularizing once-reviled fish, like catfish, while raising ever more salmon.

It is now the trend, particularly in Korean and other Asian supermarkets, to stock live carp, eel, and shrimp floating in tanks. One is reminded of New York City's Lower East Side at the turn of the twentieth century, when fish peddlers would bring carp from the Hudson River to their pushcarts and immigrant women would let the live fish swim in their bathtubs until they were ready to cook them. Now, new immigrant home cooks are showing us different ways to treat fish, like the delicious *casuela*, an Ecuadorean fish casserole (page 265), Tunisian fish couscous with striped bass (page 290), or Asian simmered halibut with rice wine (page 278). They are also fusing traditions in such dishes as Cambodian tuna and avocado salad with lemongrass and mint (page 294) and Paraguayan swordfish with avocado and mango salsa (page 293), two recipes that have become new palate pleasers at my home.

Fishmongering during Lent in the Portuguese section of Newark, New Jersey

Bluefish with Ginger, Garlic, and Basil

I am constantly amazed at how creative cooks can transform even the most ordinary ingredients. Priscilla Wamba and her husband, Elias Mofor, came to this country in the late 1990s as political refugees from Cameroon. To supplement their income, they grow native African vegetables and plants on a plot of land in Jessup, Maryland, between Baltimore and Washington, and were among the first to be part of the new farmers' initiative.

At a cooking session in Priscilla and Elias's home, a basement apartment in suburban Maryland that they share with Priscilla's sister and mother and their five children, Priscilla cooked bluefish for me, seasoning it with ginger, garlic, and the herbs from her plot. In contrast to the romantic notion that many Americans have of open-air markets, Priscilla considers herself lucky to have supermarkets. "When it rains in our country, you can't go to the market," she said. "As I am used to doing all of the cooking [in Cameroon, men don't cook at all], my children like homemade food, and now I can get the ingredients whenever I need them."

YIELD: 6–8 SERVINGS

4 tablespoons extra-virgin olive oil

1 stalk celery, halved crosswise

2 inches fresh gingerroot, peeled

7 cloves garlic

2 handfuls fresh parsley

1 handful fresh mint

1 handful fresh basil

Salt and freshly ground pepper to taste

White pepper to taste

1 whole bluefish, 4–5 pounds, gutted and cleaned

2 lemons

1. Preheat the oven to 350 degrees and brush a baking dish large enough to hold the fish with 1 tablespoon of the olive oil.

2. Put the celery, ginger, garlic, parsley, mint, basil, salt and freshly ground pepper, and white pepper in a blender or food processor and purée.

3. Rub the fish inside and out with the remaining 3 tablespoons of oil, the juice of 1 of the lemons, then the garlic-herb mixture. Place the fish in the baking dish and bake for 30 minutes. Lower the oven heat to 250 degrees and continue baking until the fish flakes, about 30 minutes more. Thinly slice the second lemon into rounds and use them to garnish the fish before serving.

Casuela

Fish Casserole with Green Plantains, Peanut Butter, and Cilantro

Casuela is an Ecuadorean coastal dish, usually made with a Latin American variety of striped bass called corvine or corbena. Baked in a casserole with a paste of plantains, pounded peanuts, and lots of garlic, then served in a sauce of peppers, garlic, onions, tomatoes, and cilantro, *casuela* has all the elements of traditional Ecuadorean food. As in the Middle East and Hungary, Ecuadorean cooks like to accent their foods with bright colors, using achiote, a seasoning made from annatto seeds, to color oil a brilliant red.

To learn how to make this dish, I visited Josephine Vizueta, an Ecuadorean cook living in New Jersey (page 102). She pounded the peanuts with her mortar and pestle and showed me how to score the skin of the plantain and lift the pulp out before grating it. The *casuela* tasted extraordinary, but it took a long time to prepare. In my own kitchen, I made a few shortcuts: I substituted paprika for achiote and chunky peanut butter for raw peanuts. And I reduced the quantities she called for. Josephine makes a large batch of *casuela* so she can send some home with her daughters and granddaughters, who live nearby. "Instead of going to Chinese restaurants and pizza places," says her elder daughter, Dolores, "my children have my mother's food . . . and my roots."

YIELD: 6–8 SERVINGS

GARLIC PASTE
2 whole heads garlic, cloves separated and peeled
1 tablespoon red wine
2 tablespoons salt, or to taste
2 teaspoons ground cumin, or to taste
1 tablespoon extra-virgin olive oil

FISH
4 pounds fillets of corvina, sea trout, striped bass, or wahoo
4 cups fish stock, fresh or frozen

1. Preheat the oven to 350 degrees and brush a 9-by-13-inch ovenproof casserole with a tablespoon of olive oil.

2. To make the garlic paste, put the garlic cloves, red wine, salt, cumin, and the tablespoon of extra-virgin olive oil in a food processor equipped with a steel blade. Process, then scrape the paste into a small bowl. Reserving a teaspoon or so, coat the fish fillets on all sides with the garlic paste, patting it down so it adheres to the skin.

3. Put the fish stock and the reserved teaspoon of garlic paste in a saucepan. Bring to a boil, lower the heat, and simmer, covered, while cooking the onions.

4. Heat 2 tablespoons of the oil and the paprika in a medium frying pan over medium heat and sauté the onion, pepper, and scallions. When the onions have begun to soften, add the tomato. Sauté for a few

3 tablespoons extra-virgin
olive oil

1 teaspoon hot paprika

1 medium onion, diced
(about 1 cup)

1 green pepper, diced
(about 1 cup)

3 scallions, sliced in
½-inch rounds

1 large tomato, diced
(about 1¼ cups)

1 cup crunchy peanut butter

3 green plantains

1 bunch fresh parsley, chopped
(about 2 cups)

1 bunch fresh cilantro, chopped
(about 2 cups)

minutes, until the tomato is soft, then stir in the peanut butter. Turn the contents of the pan into the fish stock and mix. Taste and add more salt if needed.

5. Cut the tops and the bottoms off the plantains. To peel them, make a lengthwise incision with a sharp knife, cutting completely through the outer skin, then peel the skin off a section at a time. When you feel the skin snap away from the fruit, insert your fingers and pull it off. (Be careful to use your fingers, rather than your fingernails, to rip the peel away, so you don't tear off your nails.)

6. Rub the plantains with the remaining tablespoon olive oil to moisten, cut them into 3-inch pieces, and grate them in a food processor. Add the grated plantains to the fish stock, pressing down to submerge them completely, and bring the stock to a simmer over medium heat, stirring constantly, until it reaches a pasty consistency, about 10 minutes. Add more water if the mixture gets too thick.

7. Stir the chopped herbs into the thickened sauce.

8. Spread half of the plantain sauce on the bottom of the greased casserole. Layer the fish on top, then cover with the remaining plantain sauce. Bake in the oven until the fish has browned on top, about 20 minutes.

FISH STOCK

Today, in many supermarkets you can buy frozen fish stock or fish fumet. But it's easy to make your own: Collect fish bones and/or lobster shells, add an onion or two, a leek, and a celery stalk, and sauté in a little butter. Then cover with water, add a bay leaf, salt, and a few peppercorns and simmer for about 20 minutes, uncovered, skimming off any scum that might collect. Strain the bones and vegetables and use the resulting stock as needed, freezing the rest. I sometimes freeze the stock in ice-cube trays so that I can easily extract a few cubes at a time.

Until recently, cotton was the undisputed king of the Mississippi Delta. Now, catfish, swimming in the mirror-like man-made ponds that dot the Delta, is making a play for that title. This once-reviled fish is an enormous part of Mississippi's economy and one of the most popular fish in America.

After hearing snippets about Edward Scott, the first black entrepreneur to open a catfish farm in Sunflower County, Mississippi, I wanted to meet him. Although Ed's business was prosperous, the Delta is not. But by employing (and feeding) almost one hundred people, he has helped to alleviate some of the county's economic hardship.

I visited Ed at his home in Drew, Mississippi, situated on eighty acres that include his family's cemetery. "Let me tell you about the catfish industry," he began. "They don't let no black people in there." In 1982, he went looking for a loan to start a catfish pond. Local banks refused him. Their money, Ed said, was for white farmers. But he got a partial loan from the state, dug his own pond and stocked it with fingerlings. Once they'd grown into mature catfish, Ed sold them to processors. But the more publicity Ed got, the more he was denied access to and membership in the local catfish industry. Eventually they would no longer sell him fingerlings or purchase his mature fish.

"They wouldn't let me, a black man, have fingerlings or stock in their processing plant. I was the only black man. It was a conspiracy," he told me. So, just as he dug his own pond, Ed built his own processing plant; it brought him less profit, but he could stay independent.

As Ed surveyed his land, he mused, "I didn't think that I would live to see so many changes. If you drove down to Drew on top of a bale of cotton in a wagon or a car, you couldn't honk to the white people to let you by. On the way to Drew one evening, there was an iron bridge on the way across, and a white man was coming. We had to back the mules off and let him by."

As I listened to Ed, his wife, Edna, made us Sunday lunch: biscuits, collards, macaroni and cheese, and fried catfish, which she coated in a mix of yellow cornmeal, onion salt, lemon pepper, seasoned salt, and garlic powder. Ed sat back in his easy chair and said, "You don't solve a problem by running away from it. A lot of people who left the South might have been better off if they had stayed here and fought for it. You have the same people in every race that don't care. It is much better now than it used to be. I am more hopeful for my grandchildren . . . that they will see people, not blacks and whites."

Edna Scott's Fried Catfish

While Ed Scott was raising the catfish, Edna was raising six children, teaching school, and cooking for the seventy or so employees. She showed me the now-empty commissary that she ran, cooking for the help twice a day: vegetables, meat, biscuits, sausages, coffee, and, of course, her fried catfish that she has been making since she married her husband in 1944 and now markets to friends. Edna gave me these tips (but not the recipe for her secret coating) for frying fish: coat the fish when it is at room temperature; don't salt it too much, and keep it damp; don't fry too fast, and remove the fish when it's done—it usually floats to the top of the hot oil.

YIELD: 4–6 SERVINGS

1 cup stone-ground yellow cornmeal

½ cup flour

2 teaspoons seasoning salt

2 teaspoons onion salt

1 tablespoon lemon pepper

2 teaspoons garlic powder

2 pounds catfish fillets, at room temperature

Crisco or vegetable oil for deep-frying

1. Put the cornmeal, flour, seasoning salt, onion salt, lemon pepper, and garlic powder in a small wide bowl, stirring the spices together.

2. Wash the fish fillets and shake off any extra water. Dip into the cornmeal mixture and shake off any extra. Place on a plate.

3. Heat the Crisco or vegetable oil in an electric wok or deep frying pan to a depth of at least 4 inches. When the oil reaches about 375 degrees, gently add a few of the fish fillets. The fish will naturally fall to the bottom of the pan and then come up to the top, and should turn themselves. If they don't turn, help them along, using tongs. Cook for about 3 minutes; then, using the tongs, gently remove to a paper towel and drain. Serve with tartar sauce or mayonnaise and chili sauce.

Blackened Redfish

L ouisiana food is part of my culture, blackened fish is not," Paul Prudhomme, who put his version of Cajun cooking on the culinary map, told me. But more than any other dish, it was Paul's blackened redfish that awakened our taste buds in the late 1970s. "I first discovered blackening when I was executive chef at Commander's Palace and experimented with high temperatures and cooking over an open fire," he said. "The heat went to six hundred degrees, and although the outside of the fish was black, the inside was juicy and the flavor explosive. My instinct was, Let's put it on the menu. But the management was not convinced that the customers would accept it."

Paul abandoned the idea until he opened his own K-Paul's in 1979, calling the dish simply "blackened redfish." It became so popular that the restaurant had to limit the number of orders it took each night. "We couldn't make enough of it," said Paul. "We made people order it as an appetizer and then only one person in a party could order it for the main course. In this business, when you have something new, everybody goes for it."

After Paul's cookbook *Chef Prudhomme's Louisiana Kitchen* first appeared, in 1984, people all over the country were coating redfish with hot spices and frying it in a cast-iron skillet. "When I first started using it, redfish was eighty cents a pound," he said. "A couple of years later it was nine dollars a pound. With such great popularity, the availability of redfish began to decline." Just in time, the U.S. Department of Agriculture put restrictions on catching redfish—as it has on swordfish, striped bass, and others—so the species could regenerate.

Twenty years after he introduced the dish, Paul uses a less intense heat to blacken redfish, coating it with his own Magic Seasonings spice blends. You can use a nonstick frying pan for this and, if you want, cooking spray instead of butter.

YIELD: 6 SERVINGS

1 tablespoon sweet paprika
2 teaspoons salt
1 teaspoon onion powder
1 teaspoon garlic powder
1 teaspoon cayenne pepper
¾ teaspoon white pepper
¾ teaspoon black pepper
1 teaspoon dried thyme

1. Heat a large cast-iron or nonstick skillet over medium-high heat until very hot, about 7 minutes.

2. Meanwhile, mix the seasonings thoroughly in a small bowl.

3. As soon as the skillet is hot enough to sizzle, lightly coat 1 side of each fillet with butter or cooking spray, then dredge it in the seasoning mix. Place the fish in the skillet and sprinkle the tops of all the fillets evenly with the remaining seasoning.

1 teaspoon dried oregano

Six 8-ounce redfish fillets, cut about ½ inch thick, or any other firm-fleshed fish such as snapper, salmon, pompano, or tuna

¼ cup (½ stick) unsalted butter, melted, or enough cooking spray to coat the fish

4. Cook until the undersides of the fillets are bronze, almost black, in color, approximately 2½ minutes. Then turn the fish and cook approximately 2½ minutes longer. To test for doneness, simply touch the fish in the center; properly cooked fish will have a firmer texture than partially cooked fish. You can also use a fork to flake the fish at its thickest part. If it flakes easily, it's done—or overdone! Be careful not to overcook the fish in the pan, because it will continue to cook after you remove it from the heat. Serve immediately.

MISSISSIPPI MOO SHOO

In Clarksdale, Mississippi, the birthplace of the blues, you would hardly expect to find Chinese families speaking with a southern drawl. But Gilroy and Sally Chow sounded like true southerners as they chatted with me while they stir-fried collards and crayfish for supper. In the backyard, an eight-pound catfish that had been swimming in the Mississippi River that morning was steaming in the biggest wok I've ever seen.

Chinese immigrants, mostly Cantonese, first came to the Delta soon after the Civil War, enticed by plantation owners eager to replace the newly freed African-American slaves. The Chow family, one of the hundred or so Chinese-American families living in Clarksdale, arrived later. "My father came to Mississippi in 1912 and eventually opened a grocery store," Gilroy told me as he stirred the crawfish. Until this generation moved to Clarksdale, the Chows lived behind their grocery store in Marks, a nearby town, growing Chinese vegetables in their backyard.

Too big for the fish poacher, the catfish simmered in the Chows' giant wok, a family heirloom brought from China. The recipe, also an heirloom, now has, like the Chows, a southern accent. Once cooked, the catfish is seasoned with soy sauce and garnished with garlic, ginger, scallions, and crisp bacon bits. "The bacon is something that we have incorporated," said Sally. "It's the same with our fried rice. I don't think many Chinese would make fried rice with bacon the way we do."

"What we eat connects us so that we know we are both Chinese and Mississippi Delta folks," Gilroy told me as I was leaving. Walking me to the door, he and Sally saw me off with a wave, saying, "You hurry back. Next time we'll cook y'all some turnip greens, corn bread, moo shoo, and barbecue."

Crayfish Cantonese

Crayfish, so popular in the bayou cooking of Louisiana, were considered useless in other parts of the country. Today, with the interest in Cajun and Creole cuisine, crayfish, which taste quite similar to lobster, are very popular. You can substitute shrimp or frozen crayfish, called crawdads, which should be defrosted and drained ahead of time. If using whole crayfish or shrimp, let everybody peel their own and suck the meat out with the front of their teeth.

YIELD: 6–8 SERVINGS

1 pound crayfish
½ teaspoon kosher salt
3 tablespoons vegetable oil
4 cloves garlic, chopped (about 4 teaspoons)
2 teaspoons sherry
½ pound ground fresh pork
1 teaspoon fermented black bean paste
2 teaspoons soy sauce
Dash pepper
2 cups canned or fresh chicken broth (page 146)
1 tablespoon cornstarch
2 tablespoons water
2 eggs, lightly beaten
1 teaspoon toasted sesame oil
3 scallions, sliced in rounds

1. Rinse the crayfish in cold water and drain.

2. Heat a wok until almost smoking and sprinkle it with the salt. Brown the salt lightly, then pour in 1 tablespoon of the oil. When the oil is hot, add half of the chopped garlic and stir-fry until it has browned lightly. Toss in the crayfish and stir-fry, adding 1 teaspoon of the sherry. Stir-fry the crayfish only until hot, then remove to a plate.

3. Pour the remaining 2 tablespoons of oil into the hot wok. Let it heat, then stir in the remaining garlic and the pork. Stir-fry until the pork has cooked through, then add the remaining teaspoon of sherry, black bean paste, soy sauce, pepper, and chicken stock. Bring everything to a boil, then stir and simmer.

Gilroy Chow stir-fries in his hundred-year-old wok

4. Dissolve the cornstarch in the 2 tablespoons of water in a small bowl, and stir it into the wok to thicken the broth. Stir in the eggs and let them cook for 30 seconds, then fold gently with a spoon, until they set. Return the crayfish to the wok and give everything a quick stir. Drizzle with the sesame oil and sprinkle with the sliced scallions. Serve over steamed rice.

Nouvelle American Crab Cakes

Up and down the eastern seaboard, chefs are always trying to reinvent the crab cake. I have had crab cakes with Japanese bamboo shoots, red peppers, coleslaw, Dijon mustard, capers, and chives. But of all the crab cakes I have tried, the ones I liked best were those made by the late Patrick Clark, chef at New York's Tavern on the Green, who died—much, much too young—waiting for a healthy heart to replace his ailing one.

When Patrick was chef at the Hay-Adams Hotel in Washington, I had the honor of having him and Julia Child cook in my kitchen for the *Julia's Cooking with Master Chefs* television series. Patrick had an amazing ability to integrate ingredients like jalapeños and panko, the coarse Japanese bread crumbs so popular with chefs today. The irregular, shardlike shapes of the panko add texture to the fried crab cakes. You can buy panko at many supermarkets today or at Asian markets, but if you can't find them, pulse pita chips in the food processor or use regular bread crumbs. Although Patrick served his cakes with basil mashed potatoes and roasted tomato sauce, they can also stand alone. I sometimes serve them with ginger-wasabi mayonnaise. You can also make them smaller and serve them as starters.

YIELD: 8 CRAB CAKES

3 jalapeño peppers, halved, seeded, and minced

5 scallions, thinly sliced in rounds, including the tender green parts

Juice of 2 lemons

1 tablespoon chopped fresh parsley

¼ cup mayonnaise

1 teaspoon salt, or to taste

Freshly ground pepper to taste

1 large egg, beaten

1 pound jumbo lump crabmeat

1½ cups panko (Japanese bread crumbs), or pulsed pita chips or dry bread crumbs

¼ cup extra-virgin olive oil

1. Toss the peppers and scallions with the lemon juice in a medium bowl. Stir in the parsley, mayonnaise, salt, pepper, and beaten egg and mix well.

2. Gently fold in the crabmeat, leaving any lumps intact, and ½ cup of the panko.

3. Divide the mixture into 8 patties, each about 2 inches wide, and put the remaining panko in a wide bowl. Roll each patty in the panko, then turn it onto a piece of waxed paper. Refrigerate the patties for at least 30 minutes.

4. Heat the oil to medium in a large sauté pan and quickly fry the crab cakes until they're golden brown, about 2–3 minutes per side. Drain on a paper towel and serve with roasted tomato sauce (recipe follows) or ginger-wasabi mayonnaise (page 74).

Roasted Tomato Sauce

YIELD: ABOUT 5 CUPS

1 tablespoon extra-virgin olive oil

6 plum tomatoes

3 shallots, roughly chopped

3 cloves garlic, roughly chopped

2 jalapeño peppers, halved, seeded, and minced

2 cups homemade (page 146) or canned chicken broth

½ cup chopped fresh basil

1 cup (2 sticks) unsalted butter

Salt and freshly ground black pepper to taste

1. Preheat the oven to 350 degrees.

2. Pour the olive oil into a medium ovenproof sauté pan and toss the tomatoes, shallots, garlic, and minced peppers in it. Roast in the oven for 15 minutes, then remove the pan to a burner over medium heat.

3. Add the chicken broth, bring to a boil, and simmer, uncovered, for about 15 minutes or until reduced to about 1 cup.

4. Stir the chopped basil into the pan, then carefully pour the sauce into a blender or a food processor fitted with a steel blade and purée. With the motor running, add the butter, a little at a time, until the sauce is smooth and all of the butter is incorporated. Season to taste with salt and pepper.

5. Return the sauce to the pan and keep warm over low heat. When the crab cakes are ready, pour about ½ cup of the sauce onto each plate and place a crab cake on it.

Cioppino

Shellfish Stew with Clams, Mussels, and Shrimp

This very San Francisco Italian-American take on bouillabaisse, made with tomato sauce and fennel, is cooked all over the country today. Kris Larsen, a cook and fishmonger at Larsen's Fish Market on Martha's Vineyard in Massachusetts, makes the stew for friends. "If I have leeks and fennel, I'll put them in," Kris told me in between customers. "I find cioppino a nice kind of soup for odds and ends." Kris uses odd cuts of swordfish, cod, or monkfish for the stew as they are less expensive than other cuts. She serves it with warm bread and a nice salad. According to Kris, many cooks hesitate to cook fish because of a fear of overcooking it. Her advice is to prepare all the other ingredients in advance, so you'll only have to bring the broth to a boil and let the fish cook. That way the pressure is off and you can better watch the timing of the fish.

YIELD: ABOUT 8 SERVINGS

3 tablespoons extra-virgin
olive oil

2 large onions, diced

3 cloves garlic, minced
(about 3 teaspoons)

1 leek, cleaned and diced,
using the white and some of the
green parts

1 fennel bulb, diced

1 jalapeño pepper, stem
removed, minced (optional)

2 cups white wine

4 cups clam broth

4 cups frozen or fresh fish stock
(see page 266)

1½ cups canned or homemade
tomato sauce (see page 273)

Salt and freshly ground pepper
to taste

2 dozen clams*

2 dozen mussels*

1 pound sea or bay scallops

1 pound medium or large
shrimp, peeled

1 pound cod, swordfish, or
monkfish, cut in 2-inch chunks

4 tablespoons chopped fresh
parsley or cilantro

1. The day or a few hours before you plan to serve the cioppino, heat the olive oil in a big cooking pot. Add the onions, garlic, leek, fennel, and, if you like a bit of spice, the jalapeño, and sauté until the onions are translucent. Pour in the wine and bring to a boil, reducing the liquid by about one-half.

2. Add the clam broth, fish stock, and tomato sauce, and bring to a boil again. Simmer, uncovered, for about 15 minutes. Add salt and pepper, adjusting the flavor to taste. Remove from the heat, cool, and refrigerate until ready to prepare the stew.

3. Just before your guests arrive, remove the broth from the refrigerator and bring it to a boil. Add the clams. When the first one starts to open, add the mussels, scallops, shrimp, and fish and cook about 2 minutes or until the mussels have opened. Adjust seasonings and sprinkle with parsley or cilantro and serve immediately.

*Note: Discard any mussels and clams that don't open.

Twenty years ago, fresh fish was a rarity in some parts of the country. Except for shellfish from the Gulf of Mexico, catfish trucked in from Mississippi, and lobster packed in dry ice and shipped in a box, there was little fresh seafood between Boston and Seattle. In response to the growing awareness of and demand for fresh fish, two smart Texans came up with the idea of flying fresh fish to Dallas.

In 1978, Richard Polins and Jack Baum left Texas for Boston to learn about seafood. "We went to a bunch of wholesalers on the pier in Boston and kind of told them what we wanted to do," said Jack. "These guys didn't take us seriously but said, 'Let's help the kids.' It's amazing what people will do for you when you're young."

Nearly thirty banks refused to give them a loan before they got the starter money for their company, Landlocked Seafood. They began by driving fish to Texas, leaving Boston on Thursday to arrive in Dallas by the weekend. The fish traveled in polyurethane ice containers that Jack and Richard helped design. As business grew, so did freight costs, but the two were able to negotiate a special overnight seafood rate. "We'd go to the airport at three a.m. to pick up the fish," Jack told me. "If someone rejected some fish for some reason, we'd go to the hotels and sell it off the truck." The demand was great, and business built up very quickly. The young men worked hard to train supermarket managers to handle fresh fish correctly and display it creatively. "I believe we gave the noncoastal supermarket chains the confidence that fresh fish could be a big draw for them," said Jack.

Eating lobster in Menemsha

Steamed Mussels with Leeks and Coconut Milk

Steamed mussels, once a dish that only Italian and Portuguese communities would touch, now appear on menus all across the country. While you used to have to really clean them to remove the grit, today mussels often come pre-scrubbed in two-pound mesh bags. All you have to do is give the shells a good rinsing with cold water and pull off the beard along the side. The beauty of this steamed mussel dish is that you can sauté the leeks and prepare the mussels ahead of time. Then just put everything together in a pan with a cover and steam the mussels when you are ready to eat.

YIELD: 4–6 SERVINGS

2 tablespoons butter or olive oil

2 leeks (about 1 pound), cleaned and diced, half the green and all the white parts

2 garlic cloves, minced

1 jalapeño pepper, minced (optional)

2 tablespoons fresh Thai or regular basil

1 cup coconut milk

4 pounds cleaned mussels

Freshly ground pepper to taste

2 tablespoons chopped fresh parsley

1. Heat the butter or olive oil in a heavy pan with a cover large enough to hold the mussels. Add the leeks, garlic, jalapeño pepper if using, and 1 tablespoon of the basil. Sauté for about 10 minutes or until the leeks are limp.

2. Pour in the coconut milk, add the mussels, and bring the coconut milk to a boil. When the milk is boiling, lower the heat and simmer very slowly for about 6 to 8 minutes or until the shells open. Discard any mussels that will not open.

3. Transfer the mussels and the sautéed leeks to a deep bowl, coating the mussels with the leeks and the juice. Sprinkle with the remaining basil, black pepper, and parsley and serve in soup bowls with crusty bread.

Breaded and Fried Oysters

Driving through White Sulfur Springs, West Virginia, on our way to a food writers' seminar, we spotted a sign that read "Rotary Club Oyster and Ham Dinner this Saturday." When Saturday came, a group of us left the seminar to go and eat. The ham, baked beans, and coleslaw were, as they often are these days, straight from a food service. But Phil O'Doherty's fried Chesapeake oysters, crunchy on the outside and soft inside, were little miracles. Phil, a retired food and beverage controller for the nearby Greenbrier Resort, learned the technique for breading and frying oysters as a college student in his native Massachusetts. Later, his eyeglasses streaked with grease, a CIA baseball cap perched on his head, and "Executive Granddad" written on his greasy chef's jacket, Phil stopped by to give a lesson. "You need to select the right oyster," he said. "The trick is fresh and a good size and from the East Coast."

The trick is also in the balance of spices. I use Old Bay Seasoning, one of the first, if not *the* first, commercial spicy seasoning created in Baltimore from the spices most favored to flavor crabs. It includes, among other things, celery salt, mustard, pepper, bay leaves, cloves, pimiento, ginger, mace, cardamom, and paprika. If you don't have Old Bay Seasoning, substitute a few of the above spices instead.

YIELD: 4 SERVINGS

1 pint select oysters, shucked
1 cup pastry flour
1 teaspoon Old Bay Seasoning or other seafood seasoning
1 large egg
2 tablespoons milk
1 cup fine cracker meal or bread crumbs
Canola oil for deep-frying

1. Drain the oysters in a sieve. Do not wash—it will eliminate the flavor.

2. Put the flour and the seasoning in a small bowl, beat the egg and the milk in another bowl, and place the cracker meal or bread crumbs in a third.

3. Dredge an oyster, or 2 if they are tiny, in the flour, and shake off any excess flour. Then dip into the egg wash and, finally, the bread crumbs. Place the oysters gently on a plate. Repeat with the remaining oysters.

4. Heat about 3 inches of oil to 375 degrees in a wok or deep pot. Lower gently about 5 oysters at a time into the hot oil, and fry on both sides, then drain on paper towels. Serve at once with Asian slaw (page 173).

Asian Simmered Halibut with Rice Wine

> *I do my cooking in that mad-scientist, free-styling fashion without measurements.*
>
> —HAN FENG

Whereas superstar chef Nobu marinates cod and other fish in miso, Han Feng (page 127) has a different take. She uses herbs and Chinese rice wine to marinate her halibut. If you don't have sake or rice wine for the marinade, you can use any white wine or dry sherry. I like to serve this dish with fresh steamed asparagus and rice.

YIELD: 4–6 SERVINGS

2 pounds halibut fillets

2 tablespoons Chinese rice wine or sake

2 tablespoons snipped fresh dill

1 tablespoon chopped fresh thyme

3 scallions, sliced in thin rounds

2 teaspoons sugar

1 teaspoon sea salt, or to taste

½ cup vegetable oil

1. Place the halibut fillets in a 9-by-13-inch baking dish and sprinkle them with the rice wine or sake, dill, thyme, scallions, sugar, and sea salt. Marinate in the refrigerator for about 30 minutes.

2. Heat the vegetable oil in a frying pan large enough to hold the fillets in a single layer. Gently add the fillets, along with the marinade. Bring to a slow simmer, then cover and cook until the fish flakes, about 15 minutes. Remove the fish from the frying pan and serve on a platter with rice, sauced with the cooking juice.

Point Judith Fisherman's Seafood Chowder with Monkfish, Lobster, and Scallops

Taking a late-afternoon stroll around the picturesque Martha's Vineyard fishing village of Menemsha, I met two fishermen from Point Judith, Rhode Island. They were selling their fluke and flounder to a wholesaler, who would then ship the fish to New York City's Fulton Fish Market. When I asked where they caught the fish, the answer was short: "Out there." No fisherman wants to give away his trade secrets.

They handed me a bag of freshly caught fish from off their black dragger, the *Sister Alice.* "What I would do with this," said Todd Chappell, one of the fishermen, "I would make a fish stew out of it. You know, fishermen are good cooks. This stew should taste like the sea." With a smile, he added that many fishermen start with seawater for that real salty fish base. And they use clam juice or fish stock and, depending on their catch that day, throw in a few scallops, lobster, or even chicken sausage.

Returning to my house with the fish, I asked a local chef how he would prepare the stew. Because some of the fish was more tender than other varieties, he suggested another trick: boil the vegetables in the stock until the potatoes are almost cooked, then add the sturdier fish like monkfish. After that add the scallops, layer on the flounder and fluke, and then immediately turn off the heat. The chowder I made that evening tasted just like the sea—even without using seawater.

YIELD: 6–8 SERVINGS

3 onions, diced (about 3 cups)

6 tablespoons butter

4 slices thick-cut bacon, cooked and drained (optional)

2 cups fish stock or clam juice

2 cups water

1 cup white wine

3 carrots, peeled and diced

2 pounds small red potatoes, halved

1 teaspoon sea salt, or to taste

Freshly ground pepper, or to taste

1. Sauté the onions in 4 tablespoons of the butter in a stockpot. If using the bacon, crumble it and add to the onions. Pour in the fish stock or clam juice, 2 cups of water, and the white wine. Bring everything to a boil and add the carrots and potatoes. Season the stock with 1 teaspoon sea salt and pepper to taste.

2. After about 10 minutes, with the water at a good boil, add the monkfish and the lobster and cook a few minutes. Then add the scallops, flounder, fluke, and thyme. Cover the pot and turn the heat off, then wait a few minutes for the fish to cook.

2 pounds monkfish,
cut in 2-inch pieces

2 whole lobsters, cut up

1 pound bay or sea scallops

1 pound flounder fillet in 1 piece

1 pound fluke or other soft fish
fillet in 1 piece

1 sprig thyme

2 cups milk or half-and-half

3 tablespoons cornstarch

2 tablespoons chopped
fresh parsley

3. Just before serving, pour the milk or half-and-half and the remaining 2 tablespoons butter into a saucepan and heat to a boil. Dissolve the cornstarch in ½ cup of the fish broth in a small mixing bowl, mix well, and add to the milk. Heat and stir until slightly thickened.

4. Add the milk to the broth and reheat, bringing it to a simmer. Ladle into serving bowls and sprinkle the parsley on top.

ON MONKFISH

One day in the late 1970s a fisherman dragged a monkfish into Legal Sea Foods, a fish market in Cambridge, Massachusetts. Its prehistoric-looking head constituted about 70 percent of its body weight, leaving only the tail as edible flesh for fillets. The fisherman told George Berkowitz, the market's owner, that the French paid big money for this fish. "It was probably the homeliest fish that ever was imagined," George told me.

Just then Julia Child, a loyal customer, stepped out of her Volkswagen to buy some fish for her cooking show. George showed her the monkfish, asking if she had ever heard of it. "*Loup!*" she exclaimed in her inimitable high-pitched voice. "I'll take a few pounds of the tail." She also asked George to get a whole one for television. "It took me a couple of weeks," said George. "I had to pay a fisherman not to cut off the head." Julia dragged the monkfish onto the set, and holding the ugly twenty-five-pound creature by its tail, she introduced it to America. The monkfish, which many call poor man's lobster, was a lasting hit.

Salmon *En Croûte* with Spinach and Goat Cheese

When I was trying to think of an elegant but easy main course, a friend of mine, food consultant Ann Brody, passed along this recipe, which she developed to wow her clients at dinner parties. "It brought forth oohs and aahs," she said. "A presentation piece like this, even though it's no trouble, shows that you really care about your guests. And it is just plain fun and easy to make."

Ann uses frozen puff pastry, available in supermarkets only since 1979. Before that, Pepperidge Farm had bought the patent for it from a European baker who came to work with them, offering at that time puff pastry to consumers only in their commercially produced strudel and apple turnovers.

In this savory dish, the fish and spinach steam in the pastry and the cheese melts, creating a wonderful combination of flavors in a crunchy, flaky crust.

YIELD: 10–12 SERVINGS

1 package (2 sheets) frozen puff pastry, thawed in the refrigerator and still cold

1 salmon fillet (about 3 pounds), skinned and pin bones removed

½ teaspoon salt

½ teaspoon freshly ground pepper

10 ounces garlic-herb goat cheese, softened

4 cups chopped fresh spinach

1 large egg, beaten

2 tablespoons water

1. Heat the oven to 400 degrees and grease a cookie sheet. On a floured surface, roll out 1 sheet puff pastry to a rectangle about 20 inches by 10 inches and transfer it to the cookie sheet.

2. Sprinkle the salmon with salt and pepper and lay it on top of the puff pastry, skin side down.

3. Using a spatula, spread the cheese over the top and sides of the salmon and cover it with the raw spinach. Beat the egg with the water and brush it on the pastry bordering the salmon.

4. Roll the second pastry sheet to another 20-by-10-inch rectangle and place it on top of the salmon. Gently press the dough around the salmon, pressing the edges to seal the pastry. Trim the pastry with a pastry wheel or sharp knife so that there is a ¾-inch border around the fish. Reserve the scraps. Brush the pastry with some egg wash. If you wish, cut the scraps decoratively and arrange on top. Brush again with the egg wash. Bake until golden on top, about 30 minutes. Serve hot or at room temperature on a platter.

Grilled Salmon with Goat Cheese and Roasted Tomatoes

Bonnie Moore, who teaches at L'Academie de Cuisine, just outside Washington, D.C., uses Heidi Rucker's Tack House Kitchen goat cheese in the following salmon dish. But any creamy fresh goat cheese will do. The warm fish marries well with the goat cheese and tomatoes.

YIELD: 6–8 SERVINGS

2 tablespoons olive oil
(approximately)

2 pints (4 cups) assorted
cherry tomatoes

1 tablespoon kosher salt
(approximately)

3 pounds salmon fillets

Freshly ground black
pepper to taste

8 ounces fresh goat cheese, at
room temperature

2 tablespoons chopped
fresh basil

1. Preheat the oven to 350 degrees and lightly grease with olive oil a baking dish large enough to hold the cherry tomatoes in a single layer.

2. Arrange the cherry tomatoes in the baking dish, drizzle olive oil lightly over them, and sprinkle liberally with kosher salt. Roast the tomatoes in the oven until they become soft and their skins have burst, about 15 minutes. Set aside.

3. Heat the grill to medium and oil the grill grate.

4. Season the salmon fillets with salt and pepper and grill them until they are just cooked, about 4–6 minutes a side, depending on the thickness of the fish.

5. Transfer the fillets to a serving platter. Spread the cheese over the tops of the fillets, and spoon the roasted cherry tomatoes and their juices on top. Sprinkle with the fresh basil and serve.

Note: You can also simply bake the fish in a 375-degree oven for about 15–20 minutes and then put the fresh goat cheese on top.

These days, the American countryside abounds with artisan cheese makers. But few are as enchanting as Heidi Eastham of Rucker Farm. Entering the farm, you feel as if you have left this planet and entered Heidi the Cheese Maker's Wonderland.

Nestled in the foothills of the Blue Ridge Mountains, in Rappahannock County, Virginia, the farm is home to Heidi and her husband, Lindsay Eastham. When I visited, the first thing I noticed was the glorious profusion of color: the pink house, the yellow black-eyed Susans, and the orange daylilies. In the distance stood Heidi, dressed all in blue, feeding her goats. Heidi has known this farm, in her husband's family since 1804, all her life. "I knew I would live here one day," she told me.

After they were married, Lindsay told Heidi that he wanted to start making cheese in addition to their cattle business. "At first I was scared to death," she told me. "Then I thought, cheese is in my blood." Heidi started raising Nubian goats, whose milk she uses to make the cheese. She thinks of cheese making as a spiritual enterprise. Neighbors and friends help milk the goats throughout the year. To complete the the animals' life cycle, Heidi and Lindsay eventually eat the meat when the goats get too old for milk. In the summer, she allows neighborhood children to swim in the Jordan River, which runs through the farm, after they have helped to milk the goats.

Heidi now has twenty-six kids from her herd of thirty goats. She sells her brie and tomme de chèvre Rappahannock, an unpasteurized goat cheese, exclusively to the Inn at Little Washington, about six miles away. Other soft cheese, sometimes flavored with herbes de Provence or lavender, she sells at the farm, six days a week from four to six in the afternoon. Heidi refuses to travel more than a half hour for customers, and she has no Internet service.

As we ate her fresh chèvre with slices of watermelon, Heidi, who must have been reading my mind, turned to me and said, "It is unbelievable to me every day. We are so blessed to be here. This place is for healing people."

Orange-Marinated Sweet-and-Sour Salmon

Salmon, both farmed and wild, is one of the most beloved fish in America today. I saw this dish at a fish market in Pequot Lakes, Minnesota. It looked so fresh and appealing, with lemon and orange slices arranged on top of the pink fish, that I stopped in to ask the owner, Gene Peterson (page 100), a big burly guy with a wonderful Minnesota accent, for the recipe. It's easy to make and perfect for guests.

YIELD: 4–6 SERVINGS

1¾ cups orange juice
2 tablespoons lemon juice
½ cup dark brown sugar
1 teaspoon ground ginger
2½ pounds salmon fillets
1 orange, thinly sliced
1 lemon, thinly sliced
4 tablespoons (½ stick) salted butter, cut into ¼-inch slices

1. Preheat the oven to 350 degrees and grease a 9-by-13-inch baking dish.

2. Put the orange juice, lemon juice, brown sugar, and ginger in a small saucepan. Bring to a boil, then reduce the heat and simmer, uncovered, for about 15 minutes to reduce the juices by half. Cool slightly.

3. Place the salmon fillets in the baking dish and cover them with alternating slices of orange, then lemon, then a dab of butter. Pour the orange juice mixture over the fish.

4. Cover the pan with aluminum foil and bake for 30 minutes. Remove the foil and continue to bake until the fish flakes, about 10 more minutes. Remove the fish to a warm platter and serve with rice and a salad.

Scallops with Orange-Vanilla Sauce

Today, chefs are playing around with a variety of sauces for fish. I tasted this delicious scallop dish with orange-vanilla sauce at both Frank Ruta's Palena Restaurant in Washington, D.C., and at the late Keith Korn's Ice House Restaurant on Martha's Vineyard. It would not be worth the effort to make it without using fresh vanilla beans, which provide a deeper, lingering flavor. The sauce can be prepared ahead of time and the scallops seared just before serving.

½ vanilla bean

2 cups good orange juice, completely pulpless

½ cup (1 stick) unsalted butter

2 pounds sea scallops

1 tablespoon Wondra or cake flour

Salt and freshly ground pepper to taste

2 tablespoons vegetable oil

Salt and pepper to taste

1. Using a paring knife, split the vanilla bean lengthwise and scrape out the seeds. Put the seeds and the pod in a small saucepan with the orange juice. Heat the juice and keep at a low simmer until it has reduced by half and become almost syrupy, about 30 minutes. Stir in 6 tablespoons (¾ stick) of the butter and set aside.

2. Season the scallops with the flour and salt and pepper.

3. Heat 1 tablespoon of the vegetable oil and 1 tablespoon of the remaining butter together over medium heat in a 10-inch frying pan. Sear half the scallops on 1 side until golden brown, just a couple of minutes. Then carefully flip them over and cook until golden, another 2–3 minutes. Repeat with the remaining tablespoon of oil and of butter and the remaining scallops.

4. Pluck the vanilla pod out of the sauce and reheat. To serve, spoon the sauce liberally over the scallops, either on individual plates or on a platter.

Shrimp and Grits

The late Craig Claiborne, a native of Mississippi, turned *New York Times* readers on to grits, a stone-ground corn that is finer than hominy and thinner than polenta, and to shrimp and grits after tasting the late Bill Neal's version at Crooks Corner in Chapel Hill. Typically served as a southern breakfast accompaniment, in the past thirty years grits have slowly been introduced into restaurants, with such dishes as shrimp and grits, grits and greens, and grits with avocado and tomatoes. One restaurant in Asheville, North Carolina, lists grits on its menu as "Appalachian polenta." Claiborne and others, like Nathalie Dupree, have also made grits soufflés.

Companies like Anson Mills, in Charleston, South Carolina, are trying to revive artisanal whole-grain milling. "If you mill grits properly, you get the complexity of a good wine," Glen Roberts, owner of Anson Mills, told me rhapsodically. "It will have high floral and mineral notes, backed up by an incredible combination of robust corn aroma and flavor." If you can't get stone-ground grits at your supermarket, don't settle for the instant variety. You can mail-order grits from Glen (see Mail-Order Sources).

YIELD: 4–6 SERVINGS

GRITS

2 cups water

2 cups milk

1 teaspoon salt, or to taste

¼ teaspoon pepper, or to taste

1 cup stone-ground grits

SHRIMP

6 slices bacon or ½ pound link sausage

3 tablespoons salted butter

1 clove garlic, minced (about 1 teaspoon)

1 cup thinly sliced onions

½ green pepper, diced

A few dashes of Tabasco

1 cup heavy cream

½ cup grated Parmesan cheese

1 pound shrimp, peeled and deveined

2 tablespoons lemon juice

2 tablespoons chopped fresh parsley

2 tablespoons chopped fresh chives

1. To make the grits, pour the water and milk into a 1½-quart or larger saucepan and bring to a boil.

2. Sprinkle the salt, pepper, and dry grits into the boiling milk in a slow, steady stream, skimming off the hulls on top and stirring constantly with a whisk or wooden spoon to prevent lumps from forming. This will take about 5 minutes. Reduce the heat to low and cover the pan loosely. Stirring occasionally, cook the grits slowly until they have absorbed all the liquid and are cooked to al dente, reaching a porridge-like consistency, about 45 minutes. Depending on the quality of the grits you use, the length may be less. Add more water if the grits become too thick. Adjust seasonings to taste.

3. While the grits are cooking, fry the bacon or sausage until browned in a medium skillet. When the meat is cooked, remove it from the pan and drain it in a colander or strainer set over a bowl. Save the grease and dice the bacon or sausage.

4. Heat the reserved bacon grease and the butter in a small skillet over medium heat. Add the garlic, onions, and green pepper and cook for about 2 minutes or until the onions are translucent. Sprinkle on the Tabasco, add the cream and the Parmesan cheese, and cook to reduce the cream by half.

5. Toss in the shrimp and continue to cook until they turn pink, just a minute or two. Stir in the bacon or sausage.

6. Spoon the grits into individual serving bowls and top with the shrimp mixture. Sprinkle with the lemon juice, then scatter the chopped parsley and chives over everything.

Snapper with Shiitake Mushrooms, Ginger, and Cilantro

This delicious snapper dish comes from chef Alan Wong, one of the architects of Pacific Rim cuisine. When I met Alan, I was taken by the way he watched and listened, absorbing everything. It didn't surprise me that this very talented chef and teacher apprenticed with André Soltner (page 362), the chef-owner of the legendary restaurant Lutèce, in New York.

Since unusual types of fish are so important in Hawaii, Alan uses his kitchen to educate his staff. "The restaurant is Alan's classroom," a waiter told me. Alan also takes his staff on field trips to the Honolulu Fish Auction (see page 288). "This is an environment to get the hows and the whys into the head," Alan told me. "I use the deductive process, reading, and revisiting the cooking classics."

At his Honolulu food palace, Alan Wong's Restaurant, I dined on Hudson Valley foie gras with dried prune and apricot li *hing mui* chutney, ginger-crusted *onaga* (red snapper) with sweet corn, and coconut macadamia–crusted lamb chops with taro mashed potatoes. When I asked my waiter about the soy sauce in the lamb chops, he said, "Shoyu [soy sauce] is a part of life in Hawaii. You eat it almost by osmosis."

YIELD: 4–6 SERVINGS

3 cups shiitake mushrooms, cut in julienne strips (about 4 ounces)

1 clove garlic, minced (about 1 teaspoon)

2 scallions, cut into 2-inch julienne strips

2 inches fresh gingerroot, peeled and cut in 1-inch, paper-thin julienne strips

⅓ cup chopped fresh cilantro

⅓ cup peanut oil

2 pounds red snapper, halibut, mahimahi, or other firm fish fillets

Salt and freshly ground pepper to taste

2 tablespoons toasted sesame oil

2 tablespoons soy sauce

1. Prepare the vegetables, putting the mushrooms and garlic in one pile and the scallions, ginger, and cilantro in another.

2. Heat 2 tablespoons of the peanut oil in a medium skillet over medium heat. Add the mushrooms and garlic and sauté just a few minutes.

3. Bring 4 cups of water to a boil in a large wok. Season the fish with salt and pepper and steam in a bamboo basket set over the wok for about 7 minutes or until the fish flakes.

4. Heat the remaining peanut oil with the sesame oil in a small pot until just smoking.

5. Place the cooked fish on a warm serving platter, and scatter the mushrooms, scallions, ginger, and cilantro over it. Drizzle the soy sauce on the fillets, then pour the hot oils over them. Serve immediately with rice.

My most fascinating peek into the world of seafood was a visit to the early-morning Honolulu Fish Auction, one of four or five such auctions in the United States; the others are in Boston, Gloucester, New Bedford, and Seattle. Here, the big business of sushi, multiculturalism, and fish as the symbol of a more health-conscious public came home to me. By five-thirty a.m. the wholesalers were already at work, bidding on ahi tuna, marlin, and hapuupuu (sea bass). The fish were lined up on slabs of wood and marked with orange, blue, and red cards, indicating which fishing boats they had come off just minutes before. The wholesalers were looking for a firm outer skin without blemishes. The texture of the skin, clarity of the eyes, and gills were also checked carefully.

In the middle of the auction, Brooks Takenaka, the director of a program to spread the word about Hawaiian seafood and the broker of the auction, cut a hole in the tail of a tuna, stuck his fingers inside, and pulled out a sample. As the buyers judged the fish's fat content, firmness, and taste, they reminded me of wine connoisseurs.

Although most fish is brought in fresh from the boats, bluefin, the caviar of tuna, comes in fresh or flash-frozen from as far away as Nova Scotia, Spain, and California, depending on the season. When the Japanese market was high, one bluefin would sell for as much as $125,000 a pound. "The Hawaiian people eat more fish per capita than any other place in America," said Brooks. "I could eat fish every day and come back for more."

Red Snapper Stuffed with Braised Fennel, Leeks, Onions, and Celery

M iami is kind of a new destination," Michelle Bernstein told me over dinner in her then restaurant, Azul, in Miami's Mandarin Oriental Hotel. "It's a large melting pot of people from all over the world, one of the greatest I have seen in this country. Latins want more intense flavor and large quantities. We also have all the snowbirds from New York, who want sophistication, and tourists, who pass through on their way to cruise ships and want to try something exotic."

This whole fish stuffed with roast fennel and topped with preserved lemon is my kind of dish, full-flavored and earthy. Michelle spent some time in Israel as a dancer and learned to use *za'atar,* the popular Middle Eastern spice combination that tastes of Greek oregano, thyme, sesame seeds, sumac (available in Middle Eastern markets), and lemon salt.

YIELD: 6–8 SERVINGS

5 tablespoons olive oil (approximately)

1 fennel bulb, cut in 1-inch julienne strips

2 leeks, washed well, white and light green parts cut in 1-inch julienne strips

1 yellow onion, cut in 1-inch julienne strips

4 stalks celery, cut in 1-inch julienne strips

½ cup white wine

Sea salt to taste

2–3 whole snappers, about 2¾ pounds each, gutted and left whole

2 tablespoons lemon juice

A few black peppercorns, ground

1 teaspoon za'atar

1 teaspoon ground sumac

1 diced preserved lemon (page 171)

1. Preheat the oven to 425 degrees.

2. Heat 2 tablespoons of the oil in a medium frying pan over medium heat and sauté the fennel, leeks, onion, and celery strips until soft. Add the wine, bring to a boil, and reduce it for a minute or two. Add the sea salt to taste.

3. Stuff the snappers with the sautéed vegetables and wrap each fish in jute or other twine. Place them side by side in a 9-by-12 inch baking pan and sprinkle with the remaining olive oil, the lemon juice, ground pepper, *za'atar,* and sumac, and toss the preserved lemon on top.

4. Bake for about 25 minutes or until done. Remove the jute or twine. Transfer the fish to a large platter and serve with rice and a vegetable like fried artichokes (page 224).

Tunisian-American Fish Couscous with Striped Bass and Flounder

E ver since Jeffrey Steingarten, food writer for *Vogue* magazine, told me about Tunisian fish couscous, I've been in search of the dish. When I was invited to attend a fundraiser in Tiburon, California, where Simone Joseph, who hails from the Tunisian port town of Sousse, told me she was going to make her family's version of the dish, I readily accepted.

Her couscous is a meal in itself: a vegetable fish soup, followed by couscous, fish balls, and poached fish. I returned home determined to translate and simplify this dish for busy Americans, who are always looking for the exotic, yet easy.

Most of this recipe can be prepped in advance and finished with a few minutes of simmering before serving. If you do steps one through four several hours or even a day ahead, the recipe is quite simple. You can use harissa or any other hot sauce to spice it up. This is not an everyday dish, but one well worth the effort. Thank you, Jeffrey Steingarten, for putting me onto this couscous.

YIELD: 8–10 SERVINGS

BROTH

2 tablespoons extra-virgin olive oil

1½ medium onions, diced (about 1½ cups)

2 celery stalks, cut in 6 pieces

3 carrots, peeled and quartered

3 medium tomatoes, peeled and quartered

4 cups water

3 tablespoons tomato paste

1 teaspoon salt, or to taste

½ teaspoon freshly ground pepper

1. To make the broth, heat the olive oil in a heavy soup pot over medium heat. Sauté the onions until they are translucent, then add the celery stalks, carrots, and tomatoes. Stir in water, tomato paste, and salt and pepper to taste. Bring everything to a boil, then reduce the heat and simmer, covered, for about 20 minutes. Remove the pot from the heat and set it aside.

2. To make the fish balls, process the soft white fish, ¾ cup of the bread crumbs, the eggs, salt, pepper, onions, parsley, 1 cup of the cilantro, 2 tablespoons of the mint, 4 cloves of the garlic, and the cinnamon in a food processor equipped with a steel blade. Pulse until all of the ingredients are thoroughly blended. The texture should be pastelike, not mushy. If it's too thin, add some more bread crumbs; if too thick, add a little water. Refrigerate the fish mixture for at least a half hour.

1½ pounds fresh soft-flesh
white fish like sole, flounder,
or whiting

¾–1 cup dry bread crumbs

2 eggs, lightly beaten

1 teaspoon salt, or to taste

¼ teaspoon pepper

1½ onions, roughly chopped
(about 1½ cups)

1 cup chopped fresh parsley

2 cups chopped fresh cilantro

6 tablespoons chopped
fresh mint

7 cloves garlic

¼ teaspoon ground cinnamon

4 tablespoons extra-virgin
olive oil

3 tablespoons tomato paste

1 cup water

2 pounds fresh fillets of striped
bass, Chilean sea bass, grouper,
or your favorite firm white fish

3 scallions, diced

½ cup snipped fresh dill

1 teaspoon–2 tablespoons
harissa (page 175) or other
hot sauce

1 pound couscous

3 zucchini or yellow squash,
quartered lengthwise

3. To form the balls, dip your hands into cold water and mold the fish mixture into balls a little larger than walnuts and place them on a large plate. You should have about 2 dozen balls.

4. Heat the olive oil in a large, heavy frying pan and sauté the remaining 3 cloves of garlic. Remove the garlic before it burns and becomes bitter. Add the fish balls and brown them on all sides. You don't want to crowd the pan, so depending on the size of your pan, you might have to do this in 2 batches.

5. Dilute the tomato paste in the cup of water and pour into the frying pan. Bring to a boil, then reduce the heat and simmer all of the fish balls, uncovered, for a few minutes, to just coat them with the sauce. Set aside.

6. Cover the fish fillets with the remaining cup of cilantro (reserving a bit for garnish), the spring onions, fresh dill, the remaining 4 tablespoons of mint, a few grinds of pepper, and 1 teaspoon of the harissa or hot sauce. Go lightly with the harissa; you can always add more later if you want to make the sauce spicier.

7. Just before serving, cook the couscous according to the package instructions.

8. Discard the celery from the vegetable broth and transfer the broth to a wide 10-quart pot, such as the base of a couscousière or a casserole large enough to hold the fish fillets in a single layer. Bring the broth to a boil and add the zucchini and the herb-covered fish fillets. Top with the fish balls, adding a cup or so of water if needed, to almost cover. Reduce the heat, cover the pot, and simmer until the fish fillets are cooked, about 10–15 minutes.

9. Pile the couscous in a pyramid on a big serving platter. Arrange the fish balls and the vegetables around the couscous. Smother with some of the broth and sprinkle on the reserved cilantro. Serve the fish fillets on a separate platter. Pour the extra harissa into a little bowl and serve the dish with cooked salads like turnip and orange salad (page 174) or a tomato salad on the side.

Grilled Sesame Swordfish with Monterey Bay Pesto Sauce

When Sally (see box) was growing up, her family grilled sardines and mackerel. This was the pesto they made then, which she and her sister, Rose Marie, use today on grilled shrimp or fresh fish. You can prepare the sauce up to a day ahead, film the surface with olive oil, and store it, covered, in the refrigerator. Just bring it back to room temperature before serving. It is also delicious on swordfish kebabs.

YIELD: 6 SERVINGS

PESTO SAUCE

½ cup chopped fresh parsley

¼ cup chopped fresh basil

3 cloves garlic

2 tablespoons fresh lemon juice

¼ cup extra-virgin olive oil

½ teaspoon salt, or to taste

⅛ teaspoon freshly ground pepper, or to taste

FISH

Six 6-ounce swordfish steaks, about 1 inch thick

1 tablespoon extra-virgin olive oil

1½ teaspoons sesame seeds

1 teaspoon coarse salt

Cooking spray

1. Preheat the grill to medium.

2. To make the sauce, process the parsley, basil, garlic, and lemon juice in the bowl of a food processor equipped with the steel blade. While the motor is running, gradually pour in the olive oil. Add the salt and pepper, adjusting to your taste.

3. While waiting for the grill to heat up, prepare the fish. Rub the swordfish steaks with the oil, then sprinkle them with the sesame seeds and the salt, rubbing both in with your fingers. Coat the grill rack with cooking spray. Grill the fish for about 4 minutes on each side or until the fish flakes easily when tested with a fork. Serve immediately with the pesto sauce poured on top or on the side.

Sally Ferrante Calabrese grew up in a tight-knit Italian family in the oceanside city of Montery, California. Her grandfather, Pietro Ferrante, pioneered the fishing industry on this peninsula by inventing the lampara net, which, scooping up mackerel, sardines, and anchovies, revolutionized the way people fished. "As a young boy my grandfather ran away from Sicily and joined an English merchant marine ship, where he traveled around the world," Sally told me as we ate lunch in her yellow kitchen. "Eventually he came here in the early 1900s."

Pietro, whose bust is in the town's main square, later opened one of the first fish canneries, just like those immortalized in John Steinbeck's classic novel *Cannery Row.* "I grew up in the heyday of the sardine industry," Sally told me. "You just got used to the 'aroma' during canning season."

The family gatherings, especially over fish barbecues, were frequent and crowded with all ages. "In the summertime, when the weather was beautiful," she recalled, "families would gather together and go down to the beach and barbecue mackerel right fresh from the sea."

After a lifetime of grilling, Sally stresses a few basics: "The grill must be nice and hot so the fish doesn't stick to it," she advises. "Watch the fish closely, so that it won't overcook. And if you use an indoor grill, spray it with vegetable oil, but as little as possible so that it doesn't smoke up the house. Keep the fish six inches from the grill and turn it twice."

Although life is more scattered for the family now, the two-hundred-strong Ferrante clan still gathers each year for a reunion, where old recipes, reinvented, constantly appear.

Swordfish Topped with Avocado and Mango

I learned how to prepare this easy, colorful, full-flavored dish from a Paraguayan woman living in Virginia. The swordfish (in Latin America, corbena or sea bass was most likely used) is marinated with garlic and lime juice, baked, and then topped with avocado and mango, which act like a chunky salsa. By chopping rather than puréeing, the flavors shine through. If you prefer, you can also grill the fish.

YIELD: 6–8 SERVINGS

3 pounds swordfish steaks, about 1½ inches thick

2 cloves garlic, minced (about 2 teaspoons)

Salt and freshly ground pepper to taste

2 tablespoons extra-virgin olive oil

Juice of 3 limes (about 6 tablespoons)

2 ripe Hass avocados

2 mangoes

½ red onion, finely chopped

1 cup chopped fresh cilantro

½ jalapeño pepper, stem and seeds removed, minced

1. Rub the fish with the garlic, then season with salt and pepper. Drizzle a little of the olive oil in a baking dish and place the fish on top. Sprinkle the fish with the juice of 1 lime and the remaining olive oil. Cover with plastic wrap and marinate in the refrigerator for at least 3 hours.

2. Preheat the oven to 425 degrees and bring the fish to room temperature.

3. Bake the fish for 20 minutes or until just cooked. It will feel firm when touched.

4. While the fish is baking, peel and cut the avocados and the mangoes into 1-inch chunks and put in a wide bowl with enough of the remaining lime juice, to taste. (See instructions for cutting a mango on page 17.) Toss with the onion, cilantro, and jalapeño pepper.

5. When the fish is done, remove to individual serving plates, spoon some of the avocado-mango salsa on top, and serve immediately.

Tuna and Avocado Salad with Lemongrass and Fresh Mint

The first upscale Cambodian restaurant in the United States was the Elephant Walk in Somerville, Massachusetts, run today by Nadsa de Monteiro and her mother. When Nadsa was a young girl, privileged and protected, she could never have predicted the journey she would take from Cambodia to Boston. But the 1975 takeover of Cambodia by the Khmer Rouge changed the life of this diplomat's daughter forever.

When the Cambodian government fell, Nadsa's family sought asylum in the south of France. There, her mother, always a wonderful cook, opened a restaurant, and the entire family helped out. Later, after reconnecting with her high school sweetheart, whom she had met when her father was stationed in Taiwan, Nadsa married and moved to Boston. Her parents joined her there a few years later. And in 1991, the family opened the Elephant Walk, housed in a renovated police station.

This Cambodian raw tuna with lemongrass, lime, and mint is a dish I particularly love.

SAUCE

2 cloves garlic, coarsely chopped (about 2 teaspoons)

2 shallots, coarsely chopped (about 2 tablespoons)

¾ tablespoon coarsely chopped gingerroot

2 tablespoons roasted peanuts

5 teaspoons fish sauce

1½ tablespoons white or rice vinegar

1 tablespoon fresh lime juice

1 tablespoon sugar

½ teaspoon salt

¼ teaspoon black pepper

¼ teaspoon dried red pepper flakes

8 ounces sushi-grade fresh tuna, preferably top-quality loin

2 semiripe avocados, firm enough to be sliced

1 tablespoon finely minced lemongrass

1 tablespoon finely minced shallot

2 teaspoons thinly sliced fresh mint leaves

2 teaspoons thinly sliced Thai basil

2 handfuls of baby greens like mâche or mesclun

2 tomatoes, cut into 12 slices for garnish

1. To make the sauce, dry-toast the garlic, shallots, and ginger in a heavy skillet over medium-high heat, stirring often, until softened and lightly browned, 3–4 minutes. Put them in a spice grinder or small food processor and process, pulsing on and off, until well chopped. Then add the peanuts and chop just until crunchy.

2. Stir the peanut mixture together with the fish sauce, white or rice vinegar, lime juice, sugar, salt, black pepper, and dried red pepper flakes in a small bowl. Mix well and set aside.

3. Just before serving, cut the tuna into ¾-inch cubes and put in a large bowl. Halve the avocados lengthwise and remove the pits. Cut into cubes the same size as the tuna. Gently toss the tuna and avocado cubes with the lemongrass, shallots, mint, basil, and ¼ cup of the sauce.

4. Spread the greens on a platter and spoon the tuna and avocado onto it. Garnish with the tomatoes and serve with the remaining sauce on the side.

Poultry

Clockwise from top right: Alan Wong and his chefs; Su-Mei Yu outside Saffron, her Thai chicken carryout restaurant in San Diego; Yama Camara preparing chicken yasa; A Hmong feast; A free-range chicken on Martha's Vineyard

B efore the seeds of the food revolution," wrote Craig Claiborne, the *New York Times'* longtime food editor, "there was one dish of foreign inspiration that reigned supreme: curry. It was the one great dish for special occasions." In recent years, we have been awakened to a brave new world of flavor. And chicken, more than any other meat, has brought these new flavors to our tables.

Our chicken dishes are now seasoned with tandoori, a spice combination from northern India; *za'atar*, a Middle Eastern spice mix; and Cajun seasonings. There are also new flavors from all over Latin America and Asia.

Americans not only want to taste new flavors; they want to learn different ways of cooking. We are embracing brining in every form, from kosher chicken brined in salt to Peruvian chicken marinated in black beer, vinegar, salt, pepper, garlic, and cumin. While new marinades keep appearing on grocery store shelves, the quest for homemade sauces continues. Immigrants have helped launch the marinade craze, with recipes such as Vietnamese barbecued Cornish hens (page 311) and Gambian chicken with onions, mustard, and Badia, a Latin American seasoning salt (page 310).

Fast-food kitchens have also started turning out some spicy chicken dishes. Pollo Campero, a Guatemalan fried chicken chain, is so popular among Latin Americans that when stores opened in Los Angeles and Washington, D.C., people lined up to buy their chicken (page 308), which is marinated with citrus, garlic, and dried oregano before being deep-fried in a tempura-like batter.

In spite of all this, it is harder and harder to find a whole chicken in the markets now. According to Jim Perdue of Perdue Farms, in 1970 most chickens were sold whole. "In those days the butcher would cut up the parts for you," he told me. "Ninety percent of the chickens were roasted. Now 10 percent are left whole for roasting." Call it the McNugget Factor. Chicken producers like Perdue are not only cutting up our chickens, they are boning and skinning them as well, a job once left to the neighborhood butcher.

The good news is that with increased concerns about health, compassionately raised chickens with minimal antibiotics as well as organic free-range chickens—so much tastier than the tired, wan-looking birds often found in supermarkets, and well worth the higher cost—are available almost everywhere. "Our chickens are not organic, nor are they free range," Scott Sechler, president and owner of Bell & Evans, one of the fastest-growing poultry companies today, told me. "But they are never given antibiotics and they live in high-tech chick condos." Understanding the reality of the fast-paced world in which we live, Bell & Evans makes chicken nuggets out of hand-cut chunks of breast meat with a very light, all-natural breading, sold frozen in a retail box in the prepared-foods departments in gourmet stores throughout the country.

Heritage varieties of turkey—the American Bronze, Bourbon Red, Jersey Buff, Narragansetts, and others—are livening up Thanksgiving and can be bought online through Heritage Breeds, Inc. And what upscale restaurant does not have American duck foie gras on the menu today?

Although dried plums are prunes, the name *prune* conjured up a medicinal image of the product for prune eaters who used to be over seventy years of age," Richard Pederson, executive director of the National Dried Plum Board, told me. "So we wanted to change the image to appeal to a younger audience." Following a successful petition to the FDA to rename prunes dried plums, the wrinkled fruit has been flying off the shelves. When a Houston television station did a taste test, 90 percent of people preferred dried plums to prunes.

Chicken Marbella

The ingredients in chicken marbella might have seemed wildly exotic to our palates in 1979. Who would think that we would eat prunes, green olives, and copious amounts of oregano and garlic? Our adventuresome palates were awakening.

—SHEILA LUKINS

More than any other recipe in Sheila Lukins's wildly successful *Silver Palate Cookbook*, which she coauthored with Julee Rosso in 1979, chicken marbella became a standard at dinner parties—bold, sweet, and savory flavor made with lots of garlic, vinegar, brown sugar, oregano, dried plums, and olives. When I make it, I use boneless chicken breasts and double the amount of olives and prunes—oops, I mean dried plums (see box).

YIELD: 10–12 SERVINGS

6 pounds boneless, skinless chicken breasts, halved

1 bulb garlic, finely puréed

¼ cup dried oregano

Coarse salt and freshly ground pepper to taste

½ cup red wine vinegar

½ cup extra-virgin olive oil

2 cups pitted dried plums

1 cup pitted green olives, or a mix of olives such as Greek, Moroccan, or French

1. Place the chicken in a large bowl. Cover it with the garlic, oregano, coarse salt and pepper, vinegar, olive oil, dried plums, olives, capers and juice, and bay leaves. Rub the chicken well with the marinade and refrigerate, covered, ideally overnight, but at least for 2 hours.

2. Preheat the oven to 350 degrees.

3. Arrange the chicken in a single layer in 1 or 2 large, shallow baking pans and spoon the marinade over it evenly. Sprinkle the chicken pieces with brown sugar and pour white wine around but not on them.

4. Bake for about 40 minutes, basting every 10 minutes with the pan juices.

½ cup capers with about a
tablespoon of their juice
6 bay leaves
1 cup brown sugar
1 cup white wine
¼ cup finely chopped fresh
Italian parsley or fresh cilantro

5. Using a slotted spoon, transfer the chicken, dried plums, olives, and capers to a serving platter. Moisten with a few spoonfuls of pan juices and sprinkle generously with the parsley or cilantro. Pass the remaining pan juices in a separate bowl.

Chicken Breasts with Spinach and Tomato

This is one of my favorite ways to cook a boneless breast of chicken. It comes from Giuliano Hazan, the son of Marcella Hazan, who brought regional Italian cooking to the American table with her *Classic Italian Cookbook*. Since Giuliano was raised in America, his recipes have a lighter touch than his mother's. But they hold true to her example. "I try to make things easy and accessible to busy home cooks," said Giuliano.

I follow Giuliano's advice and cut the chicken breasts in half horizontally, which he says makes them more tender than if they are pounded in the Italian tradition. All you need with this dish is a salad and a little pasta, and you have a meal.

YIELD: 6–8 SERVINGS

3 whole boneless,
skinless chicken breasts
(6 halves)
4 tablespoons extra-virgin
olive oil
3 cloves garlic, chopped
2 cups canned Italian plum
tomatoes, chopped
but not drained
One 20-ounce bag fresh spinach,
or two 12-ounce packages
frozen spinach
3 tablespoons butter
Salt and freshly ground
pepper to taste

1. With a large, sharp boning knife, cut each whole breast into 2 halves, lengthwise. Then carefully cut the thickness of each half horizontally so you have 12 thin pieces.

2. Heat 3 tablespoons of the oil in a medium frying pan and sauté the garlic. When it starts to sizzle, dump in the tomatoes. Simmer until the tomatoes have thickened a bit and are no longer watery, about 15 minutes.

3. Stir in the spinach and let it steam in the sauce.

4. Heat the remaining tablespoon of oil and the butter in a 12-inch skillet over medium heat. When the butter starts to foam, sauté the chicken briefly, for about 2 minutes on each side. Sprinkle with salt and pepper.

5. Place a piece of chicken on each plate, spoon on the tomato and spinach sauce, and serve.

Chicken Meat Loaf

"The fowl we use have not been abused with injections of antibiotics or hormones . . . they're just naturally fed . . . you'll taste the difference," reads the menu at Park & Orchard, a restaurant in East Rutherford, New Jersey, describing their Pennsylvania-raised chickens. Formerly a health food store, this homey family business boasts one of the best wine lists in New Jersey. "It is more important to get the food out hot than to make it look good," said Ken Gebhardt, who owns the restaurant with his brother, Buddy. The Gebhardt brothers opened the restaurant in 1978 with just a few tables in a space at the corner of Park and Orchard Streets. It was such a success that they have upgraded twice before arriving at their present location. One of their classic dishes is chicken meat loaf, a dish which can also be made with ground turkey, and which has been rapidly competing with beef meat loaf around the country.

YIELD: 6–8 SERVINGS

2 tablespoons vegetable oil
1 large onion, diced
1 medium green pepper, chopped
2 pounds coarsely ground chicken or turkey
2 large eggs
1 teaspoon salt
½ teaspoon ground black pepper
1 teaspoon poultry seasoning
4 tablespoons ketchup
2 tablespoons chopped fresh parsley
1 tablespoon soy sauce
1 cup plus 2 tablespoons chicken stock, homemade (page 146) or canned
1 cup fresh bread crumbs, made by pulverizing 2 slices of day-old bread

1. Preheat the oven to 350 degrees.

2. Heat the vegetable oil in a medium skillet and sauté the onion and pepper over medium heat until the onion is golden.

3. Place the ground chicken or turkey and the sautéed onions and pepper in a large mixing bowl. Using your hands, blend in the eggs, salt, pepper, poultry seasoning, 2 tablespoons of the ketchup, parsley, soy sauce, chicken stock, and fresh bread crumbs, mixing just enough to combine; do not overblend. The more you mix, the denser the loaf will be.

4. Mold the meat loaf into a large loaf pan, about 9 by 5 inches. Smear the top with the remaining 2 tablespoons of ketchup. Cover it with foil, place it on a cookie sheet, and bake for 45 minutes. Remove the foil and bake for an additional 45 minutes, or until an instant-read thermometer inserted in the center reads 170 degrees. Carefully remove the loaf from the pan and serve it on a platter with garlic mashed potatoes (page 247) and sugar snap peas (page 249).

Vietnamese Chicken-Stuffed Tomatoes with Sweet-and-Sour Sauce

With the fall of Saigon in 1975, hundreds of thousands of Vietnamese were forced to leave their country. Since Quynh Nguyen's father had worked for the U.S. government, the family was able to flee on a boat to the Philippines. "I was so scared, we didn't know where we were going," Quynh told me as she used chopsticks to mix her meat in her McLean, Virginia, kitchen. "Several families got together and paid for the boat." From the Philippines, Quynh's family came straight to Virginia, where they have been ever since. Quynh has always loved to be in the kitchen.

In Saigon, she told me, "we lived with my grandparents and ate most of our meals with them." But when Quynh and her parents left, her grandparents stayed behind. This dish was one that she used to cook with her grandmother. She now makes it for her husband, two sons, and parents. Her grandmother, who was from Hanoi, used ground pork, but Quynh prefers ground turkey or chicken.

YIELD: 6 SERVINGS

STUFFED TOMATOES

6 large tomatoes

1 pound ground chicken

1 medium onion, finely chopped (about 1 cup)

1 teaspoon sugar

3 tablespoons fish sauce

4 tablespoons extra-virgin olive oil

Freshly ground pepper to taste

1 bunch watercress, large stems removed

3 cups cooked white rice

1. To make the stuffed tomatoes, cut the tomatoes in half and remove the seeds, keeping the pith intact. You will create 12 nice pockets for the stuffing. Discard the tomato seeds, but save the juice and any pith that has been removed.

2. Blend the chicken, onion, sugar, and fish sauce together with chopsticks or your hands. Add 2 tablespoons of the olive oil and about 5 cranks of a pepper mill.

3. Stuff each of the tomato halves with about ¼ cup of the chicken filling, pressing the filling gently into the crevices and mounding the rest on the top. Brush with the remaining 2 tablespoons of oil. You can do this ahead of time.

4. Preheat the grill to medium heat and place the tomato halves on it, stuffed side down. Cover the grill and cook for about 10 minutes or until the chicken is charred. Then flip the tomatoes over and cook for about 10 minutes or until they are lightly charred and the chicken is cooked.

SAUCE

1 teaspoon extra-virgin olive oil

3 tablespoons chopped onion

1 tomato, chopped

3 cloves garlic, chopped

2 tablespoons cornstarch

1 teaspoon rice wine
(also called mirin)

2 teaspoons rice vinegar

1 teaspoon soy sauce

3 tablespoons water

1 tablespoon sugar

½ teaspoon hot chili sauce
(Quynh uses the Sriracha brand)

5. To make the sauce, heat the olive oil in a medium saucepan over medium heat. Chop the reserved tomato scraps and their liquid, and add to the onions along with the other chopped tomato and the garlic. Increase the heat to high and cook, stirring occasionally, for about 5 minutes.

6. Mix the cornstarch, rice wine, and rice vinegar in a small bowl, then stir in the soy sauce, water, and sugar and add, a third at a time, to the sauce, stirring constantly for about 1 minute, until the sauce thickens, pressing the large pieces of tomato on the side of the pan to smash them and smooth them out. Reduce the heat to as low as possible. Add the hot chili sauce and keep warm until ready to use.

7. When removing the stuffed tomatoes from the grill, the charred tomato peel will fall off naturally—if not, just pull it off. Serve the tomatoes on top of a small bed of watercress, with a little bit of the sauce and ½ cup of cooked rice. Of course, use chopsticks.

FOUR STORY HILL FARM—BUTCHER TO THE BEST CHEFS IN AMERICA

There are more niche farmers in Pennsylvania than in practically any other state. One of the most unusual is Sylvia Pryzant of Four Story Hill Farm, known for her milk- and corn-fed chickens as well as her fine milk-fed veal and apple- and fig-fed pigs. Sylvia has a long history with animals. Her father was a *schochet* (Jewish ritual slaughterer) in Tunisia. She met her Bronx-born husband, Stephen, in Israel, where he was milking cows and tending calves on a kibbutz. When they came to this country, their dream was to have a dairy farm. It was too expensive, so they started with veal calves, then expanded to poultry and hogs.

There was a lot of drama the day I arrived at the farm, which is located in a small town called Damascus. A sow was giving birth. Four baby piglets, their umbilical cords still attached, had already emerged. But the labor continued. A tiny, brave woman with a big heart, Sylvia grew concerned as she watched. Putting on rubber gloves, she hopped into the pen to midwife the remaining piglets. "You are doing such a good job, you are such a good mother," she encouraged the sow as she gently patted her side. As it turned out, the pig had delivered all the babies by then, and she rolled over and went to sleep.

Sylvia cares equally for her customers, some of the best chefs in America. But the Pryzants' clientele didn't just happen. When she and Steve first got into the business of raising milk-fed veal, Sylvia sent a note to Tom Colicchio, chef of New York's Gramercy Tavern, introducing herself and telling him that she used natural feed for her animals and a mom-and-pop slaughterhouse that takes pride in what they do. "I was hoping somebody would listen to us and give us a chance," she said. "After all, in the nineties, chefs couldn't get meat from small farms." To her delight, Colicchio called her and placed an order. Soon after, word began to spread, and now Sylvia sells to top restaurants around the country. "We do it the old-fashioned way," Sylvia said in her French-accented voice. "With direct contact."

Lemon-Stuffed Roast Chicken with Herbs

For me, no other comfort food can beat roast chicken. I had never tasted a chicken like the one Sylvia sent me (see page 305). "Our chickens have enough fat from corn and milk," said Sylvia. "It adds to the taste of the bird."

Roast chicken is an easy one-pot meal if you surround the chicken with vegetables and use lots of garlic and herbs for flavor. Just put it in the oven and take it out when it's done. Every culture in America has its own variation, often jealously guarded, with different flavorings and different timing.

YIELD: 4—6 SERVINGS

1 lemon, fresh or preserved (page 171)

One 3–4-pound good-quality roasting chicken

4 tablespoons extra-virgin olive oil

Sea salt or kosher salt and freshly ground pepper to taste

6 cloves garlic

1 handful of fresh herbs, such as rosemary, sage, and thyme, plus extra mixed herbs for garnish

1 onion, unpeeled, cut in 4 pieces

2 potatoes or sweet potatoes, cut in 4 pieces

2 carrots, peeled and cut in 4 pieces

1 zucchini, quartered

1. Preheat the oven to 425 degrees. Lightly butter the bottom of a roasting pan or line it with parchment paper.

2. Cut the lemon in half and rub the chicken with the juice and then with a tablespoon or so of the olive oil. Sprinkle with salt and pepper, less salt if using a preserved lemon.

3. Stuff the chicken with the two lemon halves, a few cloves of the garlic, and the herbs. Place the chicken breast up in the roasting pan. Strew the remaining garlic, the onion, potatoes, carrots, and zucchini around the chicken. Rub with the remaining olive oil. Roast the chicken for 60 minutes, basting occasionally.

4. Reduce the heat to 375 degrees and roast until the juices run clear when you pierce the thigh, about 15 minutes or until the internal temperature reaches 170. Take the chicken out of the oven and let rest for about 10 minutes, if you want, putting a saucer under the legs to raise them up a bit and allow the juices to flow down to the breast.

5. To make a gravy, remove the chicken to a serving platter, surround it with the vegetables, and place the roasting pan with everything that's left in it over a moderately high heat. Pour about ½ cup water into the pan to deglaze it, scraping up and incorporating into the gravy any bits and pieces that are stuck to the pan. Let it simmer for a few minutes, skim off the fat, and then pour into a bowl to be passed at the table.

6. Sprinkle fresh herbs over the chicken and vegetables to garnish, and serve with the gravy.

Hoisin Roasted Chicken

Because Chinese ingredients like hoisin sauce are readily available nowadays, it is much easier for us to make chicken the way Alice Chow, from Clarksdale, Mississippi, does. She likes to serve the roasted chicken cut up in pieces, but I like to bring in the almost mahogany-colored roast and carve it at the table. Serve it with rice and collards (see page 228).

(see page 228).

YIELD: 4–6 SERVINGS

One 4½-pound chicken

1 teaspoon kosher salt, or to taste

¼ teaspoon freshly ground pepper, or to taste

2 teaspoons mashed garlic (about 2 cloves)

2 tablespoons chopped fresh cilantro

3–4 tablespoons hoisin sauce

Vegetable oil spray

1. Preheat the oven to 350 degrees.

2. Season the chicken well with salt and pepper. Then, using your fingertips, rub the chicken well inside and out with some of the mashed garlic and place the remaining garlic and the cilantro in the cavity of the chicken.

3. Smear the hoisin sauce over the entire chicken as well as in the cavity. Put the chicken on the rack of a roasting pan.

4. Roast the chicken breast side up for 45 minutes. Turn it over and roast it for another 45 minutes or until brown and done, spraying it with vegetable oil spray every 20 minutes throughout the cooking.

5. Let the chicken sit for about 10 minutes before carving. Cut into pieces and serve on a large platter, or carve the bird at the table.

Guatemala-Inspired Fried Chicken

A Guatemalan fried chicken company called Pollo Campero (Country Chicken) has created a sensation within the Latin American communities in the United States. Pollo Campero is so popular in Guatemala and El Salvador that people were bringing doggy bags of it to the United States. "It is like Coors beer," said Jim Perdue, who provides the chickens for their East Coast operation. "When it was something only available on the West Coast, people were bringing it with them to the East." After being marinated in lemon, garlic, oregano, and other strong seasonings, the chicken is then dipped in flour and fried. With the help of a few chicken investigators like *LA Weekly* and *Gourmet* magazine's Jonathan Gold, I arrived at a home version. Here is my rendition of Pollo Campero's wonderful chicken.

YIELD: 6–8 SERVINGS

One 3-pound chicken, cut into 8 pieces
Juice of 1 lemon
3 cloves garlic, pulverized
1 teaspoon ground cumin
2 tablespoons dried oregano
2 tablespoons kosher salt
½ teaspoon ground black pepper
Vegetable oil for deep-frying
1 cup cake flour

1. Sprinkle the chicken with the lemon juice, then rub in the garlic and sprinkle on the cumin, oregano, salt, and pepper. Place in a bowl and refrigerate, covered, overnight.

2. When ready to cook the chicken, heat about 5 inches of oil to 340 degrees in a wok or a deep pot.

3. While the oil is heating, dip the chicken in the flour briefly, shaking off any excess flour.

4. Fry, turning once, until golden brown, about 6 minutes per side. Remove the chicken pieces from the oil with tongs and drain them on paper towels. Eat immediately.

Chicken with Barbecue Sauce

My sister-in-law Ginny Nathan is probably the most reliable cook I know. She has been following recipes since before I met her thirty-some years ago and always tries new dishes on company. Like many of us, she started exclusively with *Gourmet* (she keeps all the back issues in her basement) and then branched off to *Bon Appétit* and occasionally *Eating Well*. She will frequently change ingredients, as in this dish, made at Ginny's home once a week. This recipe came from her mother, who was also a great cook, but Ginny has added some cayenne pepper and chili powder to it. Her daughter-in-law Jessica added even more heat to the recipe. This is one of those recipes we all need because it is so quick and delicious.

YIELD: 4 SERVINGS

2 whole chicken breasts, halved, or 4 drumsticks and 4 thighs

Salt and pepper to taste

SAUCE

1 teaspoon extra-virgin olive oil

¼ medium onion, diced (about 3 tablespoons)

1 tablespoon cider vinegar

2 tablespoons lemon juice

1 tablespoon brown sugar

½ cup ketchup

2 teaspoons Worcestershire sauce

1 teaspoon Dijon mustard

½ teaspoon chili powder

¼ teaspoon cayenne pepper

¼ cup water

Hot sauce to taste

1. Preheat the oven to 350 degrees. Season the chicken well with salt and pepper and arrange in a baking pan with a little space in between. Cook for about an hour or until the chicken is crisp and any water that may accumulate on the bottom has evaporated.

2. While the chicken is cooking, heat the olive oil in a small saucepan and sprinkle on the diced onion. Stir-fry until the onion is golden. Add the cider vinegar, lemon juice, brown sugar, ketchup, Worcestershire sauce, Dijon mustard, chili powder, cayenne pepper, water, and hot sauce to taste. Bring to a boil and then simmer, uncovered, for a few minutes, until slightly thickened.

3. When the chicken is cooked, drain any fat. Spoon the barbecue sauce on the chicken. Either finish the chicken under the broiler or finish on the grill until the sauce has slightly blackened and becomes caramelized on the chicken. Serve any extra sauce on the side.

Chicken *Yasa*

Grilled Chicken Gambian-Style

Yama Camara is a natural cook. The designated person to cook for weddings, baby showers, and other events in the Gambian community of Montgomery County, Maryland, Yama immigrated to the United States in 1996. In this country a friend from Latin America introduced her to Badia, the Cuban spice combination with a cumin and turmeric base. She also uses Maggi, popular throughout Africa. "Every little kid knows Maggi in Gambia because it is everywhere," she told me.

"At home my mother cooked chicken in a frying pan over a charcoal fire outside," said Yama. "We ate it for lunch or dinner. I am so surprised Americans like it so much."

YIELD: 6 SERVINGS

CHICKEN

12 chicken legs

5 tablespoons white vinegar

2 tablespoons Dijon mustard

1 teaspoon dried oregano*

1½ teaspoons ground cumin

1½ teaspoons salt

1 teaspoon black pepper

2 cloves garlic, minced

ONION SAUCE

4 large onions, sliced in rounds

3 heaping tablespoons Dijon mustard

2 teaspoons ground cumin

2 teaspoons dried oregano

1 teaspoon salt

1 teaspoon black pepper

2 orange or red habanero peppers, chopped†

½–¾ cup vegetable oil

1. Wash the chicken legs in white vinegar. Then score them with a knife, making three 2-inch slashes in each.

2. Rub the mustard into the chicken with your hands. Sprinkle the oregano, cumin, salt, and pepper all over and rub the garlic into the chicken. Place the legs in a bowl and refrigerate, covered, for a few hours or overnight.

3. To make the onion sauce, using your hands, toss together in a bowl the onions with the mustard, cumin, oregano, salt, and black pepper. If you are using the peppers, cut them with a fork and knife, wearing rubber gloves to protect your hands (and your eyes, in case you rub them), then add the pieces to the sauce.

4. Heat the vegetable oil in a 12-inch frying pan and sauté the mixture over medium heat until the onions are soft and brown.

5. Preheat the oven to 450 degrees. Spread the sautéed onions in a baking dish and lay the chicken on top. Roast for 1 hour, basting and turning every 10 minutes. Serve with rice or couscous.

* If using Maggi and Badia, use 6 teaspoons of the Maggi and 2–3 of the Badia seasoning rather than oregano and cumin.

† Be careful of these peppers—they are very hot. Handle with caution. Use seeds or not, as you wish.

I have noticed that many immigrants use Swiss-made Maggi or other seasonings to intensify the flavor of their dishes, especially those with chicken in them. Maggi, one of the first cubed bouillons, was created in part to add flavor to watered-down soups when meat was scarce—during wartime, for example—or unaffordable. Made with monosodium glutamate (MSG), a flavor enhancer, lovage-based Maggi and similar seasonings are frequently used in countries where cooks cannot get fresh herbs and spices.

Today, new seasoning salts and flavor intensifiers are coming on the market. Joseph Badia, an immigrant from Cuba living in Miami, started making his own spice combinations using cumin and other flavors in the 1970s. They are now sweeping the Caribbean. In countries where salt is not used the way it is here, fish sauce and Worcestershire sauce, both made with a base of fermented anchovies, give dishes the salty flavor our palates crave.

Vietnamese Grilled Cornish Hens with Sake Marinade

When I visited Quynh Nguyen (see page 303) at her home in suburban McLean, Virginia, the phone was ringing and her two young sons were running around. A first-generation American who fled Vietnam on a boat, Quynh cooks both American and Vietnamese. She and her husband like to barbecue for their friends and family, adapting her homeland's dishes to her adopted country's tastes. She prepared for me these absolutely delicious grilled Cornish hens, marinated in sake, star anise, cinnamon, ginger, garlic, and other spices. "The sake alone doesn't have the spice taste to it," said Quynh. "So I took garlic, ginger, star anise, cumin seeds, and cinnamon from a pho recipe and put it into the rice-flavored sake." Quynh uses the same marinade, sometimes made from vodka, for cut-up chicken and short ribs as well. Instead of grilling, I sometimes bake the marinated chicken for an hour at 375 degrees and then run it under the broiler until brown, but it doesn't have the same charcoal flavor. Serve it with vermicelli noodles or rice and an Asian coleslaw (page 173).

Sake Marinade

Quynh makes this fragrant rice-flavored marinade from big bottles of inexpensive sake that she buys at the liquor store. You can make it from vodka as well. I mix up a batch of the marinade and keep it on hand in the refrigerator for months.

YIELD: 4 CUPS MARINADE

10 cloves garlic, unpeeled
2 shallots
4 cups sake or vodka
2 cinnamon sticks
4 inches gingerroot
2 whole nutmegs
3 whole cloves
2 tablespoons fennel seeds
4 star anise

1. Place the garlic and the shallots on a grill or under a broiler for a few minutes, until they are slightly charred and the juices are flowing from them. Remove from the grill with tongs and set aside on a plate.

2. Pour the sake into a wide-mouthed bottle. Add the grilled garlic and shallots as well as the cinnamon sticks, ginger, nutmegs, cloves, fennel seeds, and star anise. Let sit, covered and refrigerated, for at least a week.

Grilled Cornish Hens

YIELD: 4 SERVINGS

2 Cornish hens, split in half
4 tablespoons chopped garlic
7–8 tablespoons Thai fish sauce, preferably Squid brand
1 teaspoon salt or 5 tablespoons Maggi liquid*
5 tablespoons honey
¼ teaspoon pepper, or to taste
1 medium onion, diced (about 1 cup)
1¼ cups olive oil
½ cup sake marinade (recipe above)

1. Put the Cornish hens in a bowl and cover with the garlic, fish sauce, salt or Maggi, honey, pepper, onion, olive oil, and sake marinade. Cover with plastic wrap and marinate for a few hours in the refrigerator.

2. Preheat the grill to medium. Place the hens on the hot grill, skin side down, and cook for 10 minutes. Turn and cook again, until done.

* Instead of using Maggi liquid, I use salt. Maggi just intensifies the flavor, and it has MSG in it.

Grilled Thai Chicken With Lemongrass

Su-Mei Yu was born and raised in Thailand, went to college in Kentucky, and settled in California. Always fascinated by food, she often visited flea markets in Thailand, and loved finding memoir-like funeral books, which described what had mattered most to the deceased. Often it was food, and recipes would be found in the book's pages. Little by little, Su-Mei was able to put together old Thai recipes and trace the evolution of the cuisine over two centuries. She learned, for example, that Thai cuisine was less sweet and spicy before Portuguese missionaries brought hot peppers to the country.

Su-Mei herself became a bit of a culinary missionary. When she settled in San Diego, she opened Saffron, a Thai chicken carryout. She had wanted to offer a healthy alternative to batter-coated fried chicken. She did a little more than that.

"Today her restaurant is one of the icons of San Diego," said Sam Popkin, a professor at the University of California at San Diego. "She is well into her millionth chicken. If you went on a picnic and you had her chicken, you would be in heaven."

Although this is one of Su-Mei's recipes for barbecuing chicken, you can also cook it for forty minutes in a 350-degree oven and then broil it for a final five minutes.

YIELD: 4 SERVINGS

One 3-pound chicken, halved lengthwise, rinsed thoroughly, and patted dry

1 teaspoon sea salt

1 large bulb garlic, separated and peeled

1 stalk lemongrass, outer hard part removed, minced

1 tablespoon white peppercorns, dry-roasted and ground

⅓ cup fish sauce

Juice of 1 lemon

Vegetable or olive oil spray

1. Place the chicken half, skin side down, on a chopping board. Pound with a mallet or heavy frying pan to crack the bones and flatten slightly. Flip the chicken over and repeat the process. Do the same with the other chicken half and set aside.

2. Place the sea salt, garlic, lemongrass, white peppercorns, fish sauce, and lemon juice in a food processor, and purée. Transfer the mixture to a large resealable plastic bag, put the chicken in, and seal. Toss the chicken in the bag to coat with the marinade. Let sit in the bag at room temperature for at least 30 minutes or up to 1 hour. (You can also let the chicken marinate in the refrigerator, for no more than 3 hours.)

3. Light the grill. When the charcoals are white hot, rake the hot coals to 1 side of the grill, leaving the other side empty. (For a gas grill, set to medium-high heat.)

4. Remove the chicken from the plastic bag and spray the grill and the chicken generously with the vegetable oil spray. Place the chicken on

the side of the grill directly over the hot coals, and grill until the skin is slightly charred, about 1–2 minutes. Flip the chicken over and sear the other side.

5. Slide the chicken to the other side of the grill, away from the hot coals. Cover and grill-smoke the chicken for 50 minutes to an hour. Be sure to leave vent holes on the top of the grill cover open. (For a gas grill, reduce the heat to medium-low.) Occasionally turn the chicken to prevent burning.

6. To check for doneness, pierce the chicken in the fold between the breast and thigh. The juices should run clear and not pink. Remove the chicken from the grill when thoroughly cooked, and cover with a tent of aluminum foil to keep warm. Let the chicken rest for 10 minutes, then cut into 4 pieces and serve.

VANNS SPICES

In the early 1960s, a friend from Bombay introduced Ann Wilder to the explosive flavors of India. To Ann, a home cook living in Riverton, New Jersey, it was a revelation. "I just loved the boldness of those spices. I had never tasted coriander, turmeric, fenugreek, or even cumin before," she told me. "This was before Madhur Jaffrey and other Indian cookbook writers began to open our palates."

After moving to Baltimore with her husband, Richard, she discovered a shop in nearby Washington, D.C., that sold Indian saris and spices. "Finally I could duplicate our friend's tandoori spice mix," she said. When the sari shop closed, she looked everywhere before deciding to try making her own. By trial and error, she developed a mixture that worked. "I learned so much and then started putting together other seasoning blends like curry, another blend which is similar to tandoori but has turmeric in it," she said. Her neighborhood grocer urged her to label and package her blends, which he then sold.

Soon, a small Baltimore spice shop called the Harbor Place agreed to carry her blends—and, to Ann's surprise, they sold. So she began spice foraging all over the world, seeking the best hand-harvested oregano from Turkey, basil from Italy, and Tellicherry black pepper from India.

In 1981, two years before Paul Prudhomme made Cajun seasonings popular, Ann wrote the business plan for her new company. Today, Vanns Spices offers more than three hundred spices. Now when she cooks tandoori chicken, she uses Vanns tandoori rub.

Indian Tandoori Chicken

andoori refers to the outdoor clay oven (*tandoor*) used in northern India to cook almost everything. Today, tandoori chicken has become an American favorite. The marinating spices that give this chicken dish its distinctive color and flavor are easy to find in specialty food stores across the country, as well as on the Internet. Most Indian cooks skin the chicken and then rub the spices into the flesh. If you don't have access to a *tandoor* (most people don't), you can just use a home oven or outdoor grill.

YIELD: 6 SERVINGS

1 tablespoon kosher salt

1 tablespoon ground coriander

1 teaspoon cayenne pepper

6 cloves garlic, peeled

2 tablespoons fresh ginger, peeled and minced

1 teaspoon ground cinnamon

2 teaspoons Spanish paprika

1 teaspoon ground fenugreek

1 teaspoon cardamom seeds, from peeled pods

2 tablespoons fresh lemon juice

2 tablespoons ketchup or tomato paste

2 tablespoons heavy cream

1 cup plain yogurt

3 pounds chicken drumsticks or thighs, skin removed

1. Using a spice grinder or mortar and pestle, make a paste of all the spices. Stir the lemon juice, ketchup, cream, and spice paste into the yogurt.

2. Using a paring knife, make several small gashes on each chicken piece and then rub them with the spicy yogurt marinade. Refrigerate for 24 hours, turning occasionally.

3. Preheat the oven to 375 degrees and place the chicken pieces in a roasting pan. Roast for 45 minutes, turning the pieces over after 20 minutes, then put them under the broiler just to darken slightly. Better still, grill the chicken outdoors. Serve with chutney, salad, and Indian bread.

Khoreshteh Fesenjan

Sweet-and-Sour Chicken, Pomegranate, and Walnut Stew

Like many immigrants to America, Nahid Mohamadi, who came from Iran in the early 1970s, had to learn to cook through letters and phone calls. "It became a routine for my mother to send me a new recipe in our weekly letters," Nahid told me. "In the meantime I made a habit of eavesdropping on the cooking conversations I heard among a few Iranian wives I had come to know through my husband's job. I would have asked for their recipes, but I was just too embarrassed to admit that I was not a cook."

Eventually, Nahid learned, and she learned well. She prepared for me this rich Iranian stew, the jewel of Persian cooking. Beloved by anyone who comes across it, it is surprisingly simple to prepare. The tartness of the pomegranates marries well with the walnuts. In the north of Iran, *fesenjan* traditionally included walnuts, apricots, and prunes, and in the south, walnuts and pomegranates.

Serve this stew with Iranian rice (see page 211).

YIELD: 6–8 SERVINGS

1 medium onion, chopped

¼ cup extra-virgin olive oil

1 pound walnuts, finely chopped in a food processor

10 chicken thighs, with the bones, skin, and fat removed

1 teaspoon salt

1 tablespoon fresh lemon juice

½ cup sugar

2 tablespoons ketchup

⅓ cup pomegranate juice concentrate or syrup

Small pinch of saffron

4 cups water

1. Sauté the onion in the olive oil in a medium pot until light golden brown.

2. Pulse, don't purée, the walnuts in a food processor, using a steel blade. You want the walnuts to have some crunch.

3. Add the chicken, walnuts, salt, lemon juice, sugar, ketchup, pomegranate concentrate, saffron, and water to the onion. The chicken pieces do not have to be in 1 layer as long as they are covered with sauce.

4. Bring everything to a boil, then reduce the heat and cover the pot loosely. Cook for an hour at a slow and constant simmer, stirring occasionally. Serve over Iranian rice.

Tallarin con Pollo

Ecuadorean Chicken with Spaghetti

Josephine Vizueta, an Ecuadorean American and a versatile cook (see page 102), gave in to her young daughters' pleas for spaghetti with tomato sauce. But instead of serving them Ragú she concocted her own version, using chicken rubbed with a whole bulb of garlic, cilantro, green peppers, spaghetti, and Parmesan cheese. "This was one of the first dishes that my mother-in-law made for me," said Lewis Rothenberg, Mrs. Vizueta's son-in-law. "It is basically spaghetti and chicken, but it had a flavor different from anything I had ever tasted."

YIELD: 6 SERVINGS

One 3–4-pound chicken, cut into 8 pieces

1 whole bulb of garlic, cloves peeled and minced

1 teaspoon salt, or to taste

1 cup dry red wine

3 tablespoons extra-virgin olive oil

1 large onion, diced

1 green pepper, diced

2–3 tomatoes, diced

3 tablespoons Parmesan cheese

12 ounces spaghetti, broken into 4-inch pieces

1. Wash and dry the chicken and put it in a large bowl. Rub the chicken all over with half of the garlic. Sprinkle it with the teaspoon of salt and toss lightly with the wine. Let the chicken sit in the bowl while you prepare the vegetables.

2. Heat a Dutch oven or frying pan with a cover over medium-high heat and pour in the olive oil. When the oil is hot, stir in the onion and the remaining garlic. Sauté for a few minutes, stirring occasionally, and then add the pepper. When the onion is translucent, stir in the tomatoes. Cover and simmer slowly for about 10 minutes.

3. Add the chicken to the sauce and simmer, uncovered, for about 20 minutes, stirring occasionally, until the chicken is cooked. Stir in 2 tablespoons of the Parmesan cheese.

4. Cook the spaghetti according to the instructions on the box, then drain it and stir it in with the chicken. Sprinkle with the remaining cheese and serve.

When I arrived at Xa and Xia Vang's house in St. Paul, vans outside were being filled with vegetables for the next day's farmers' markets. Inside, women were cooking in the kitchen, toddlers were running around, men were sitting, and telephones were ringing. A symbol both of his prominence in the Hmong community and of his faith in America, Xa shares his house with four generations of his family. "Every weekend we have sixty people," said Xia, who is a nutritionist. "We are used to this. We are always happiest in a group."

The Hmong, an ethnically Chinese uprooted mountain people living in Laos, assisted U.S. forces during the Vietnam War. After the Com-

munist takeover, they came to this country in great numbers, largely through the sponsorship of the Lutheran Church. They settled in California, Wisconsin, North Carolina, Michigan, and particularly in Minnesota.

In 1983, the Vangs went into the farmers' market business with the help of Steve Young, a local lawyer. "I knew that the Hmong, as an agrarian community, grew vegetables well," said Mr. Young. "They understand soil." With aid from the Agricultural Extension program at the University of Minnesota, the Hmong Farming Cooperative was formed. But they found they had difficulty competing with wholesalers who imported vegetables cheaply from Mexico.

"People couldn't count on our irregularity," said Xa. So they began selling at farmers' markets, where the shoppers understood and welcomed locally grown produce. Soon the farmers were learning to present their food attractively and hand out recipes. Today names like Yang and Vang are replacing Ericson and Jenkins at market stalls.

In Xia's kitchen, the women were cooking a cucumber soup served cold with sugar; chicken soup with oyster mushrooms; stir-fried chayote tops with summer spinach and salty pork; stir-fried fatback with the leaves of pepper bushes; bitter melon; and a lovely Southeast Asian chicken curry with galanga (see page 153) and lemongrass.

Xia Vang prepares a stir-fry in her St. Paul kitchen

Hmong Chicken Curry with Coconut Milk, Lime Leaves, and Hot Pepper

I have tasted variations of this curry, which is a stew with savory flavorings, in many Southeast Asian homes in the United States. You can play with this recipe as the Hmong do, substituting snow peas, broccoli, or whatever is in season. You can also replace the chicken with shrimp or scallops.

YIELD: 8 SERVINGS

2 stalks lemongrass

3 whole star anise

3 slices galanga or gingerroot, peeled

1 teaspoon turmeric

1–2 hot small red chili peppers

5 cloves garlic

2 tablespoons vegetable oil

1½ cups coconut milk

4–5 Kaffir lime leaves

3 scallions cut in 1-inch pieces

1½ pounds boneless chicken breasts, cut in 2-inch strips

1 large onion, diced

3 carrots, peeled and cut into 2-inch diagonal pieces

One 8-ounce can bamboo shoots, drained

1 pound string beans or asparagus, cut in 1-inch pieces

1–2 tablespoons fish sauce

2 tablespoons chopped fresh Thai basil (optional)

Salt to taste

Juice of 2–3 limes

1. Remove the outer stalks of the lemongrass; you need only the fragrant inner ones. Using a mortar and pestle or a clean coffee grinder, grind the lemongrass with the star anise, galanga or ginger, turmeric, chili peppers, and garlic until smooth. Heat the vegetable oil in a small sauté pan and stir-fry the freshly ground mix for a few minutes.

2. Pour the coconut milk into a large casserole and bring to a boil. Stir in the lime leaves, reduce the heat, and simmer, uncovered, for 10 minutes. Add the ground spices and simmer for 5 minutes more.

3. Add the scallions, chicken, onion, and about 1½ cups of water or just enough to nearly cover. Bring everything to a boil, reduce the heat, and simmer for 15 minutes, uncovered.

4. If needed, add 1 more cup of water and return everything to a boil. Add the carrots and bamboo shoots and, 5 minutes later, the string beans or asparagus. Cook until the vegetables are done. Add the fish sauce, Thai basil (if using), salt, and lime juice to taste. Adjust the seasonings and serve with noodles or rice.

Jamaican Jerk Chicken

W hen I was growing up in Jamaica, jerk chicken was something that you ate only in one part of the island," Dr. Neville Gibbs, a neurologist who moved to the United States in 1977, told me. Now, with the influx of Jamaican immigrants to America and Americans' love affair with hot food, jerk chicken has spread everywhere. Whenever Neville's son, Nigel, announces that his friends want to come over on the weekend, Neville starts marinating jerk chicken. His son's friends (including my son) love it.

Neville cooks his chicken outdoors on a grill, but it can be done in the oven as well. First he cleans the chicken with lime, because it "takes away any raw smells." He uses habanero peppers (also known as Scotch bonnet peppers), which he brings back with him whenever he travels to Jamaica. He handles the peppers with caution. And you should too. Cut them with a fork and knife, and wear rubber gloves. The resin on the peppers can make your hands feel like they're on fire, and should you rub your eyes, you can burn them badly. Although Neville uses only allspice, jerk chicken recipes vary. You can also include cinnamon, thyme, and nutmeg, all of which are native to Jamaica. The only thing missing is the local wood that is used to produce the smoke.

YIELD: 8 SERVINGS

Two 3½–4-pound chickens

Juice of 2 limes

2 tablespoons salt, or to taste

1 bunch scallions, both white and green parts

2 whole bulbs plus 3 cloves garlic, cloves peeled but left whole

¼ cup whole allspice

⅔ cup soy sauce

4 habanero (Scotch bonnet) peppers, seeds removed (or use milder peppers, if desired)

9 tablespoons olive oil

1. Split the chickens down the center, cutting the backbone almost but not quite through so the 2 halves open up in a butterfly or angel shape. Put the chicken pieces in a large bowl and rub them with the lime juice and salt.

2. To make the marinade, purée the scallions, the 2 bulbs of garlic, allspice, soy sauce, 3 of the peppers, and 6 tablespoons of the olive oil in a blender or food processor. Pour over the chicken and toss with your hands to fully coat it. Remember to immediately wash your hands (or wear rubber gloves)! Cover the bowl and place it in the refrigerator overnight. You can also put each chicken in a resealable bag with the marinade.

3. The next day, about an hour before cooking, remove the chicken from the refrigerator and dice the remaining pepper and the 3 remaining cloves of garlic.

4. Heat the remaining 3 tablespoons of olive oil in a heavy frying pan,

over medium heat. Add the pepper and garlic and sauté until the garlic is golden. Reserving the marinade, brown the chickens separately in the hot oil, about 4 minutes on each side. Remove the chicken to a plate and set it aside. Pour the remainder of the marinade into the frying pan; cover and cook slowly for about 10 minutes.

5. Put the chicken on a slow grill. Basting with the reduced marinade once or twice and turning, grill the chicken pieces until they are cooked through, about an hour. If you prefer, you can cook them in a 375-degree oven for 60 minutes.

6. Cut each half of the chickens into 4 pieces and serve them alone or with corn with pesto butter (page 230) and rice.

Arroz con Pollo

Chicken with Rice

On the fourth Friday of every month there is a fiesta on the streets of Miami's Little Havana, the neighborhood around Calle Ocho (Eighth Street) where the first Cuban immigrants rolled cigars at the turn of the twentieth century. As they became more successful, Cuban Americans gradually moved out of the neighborhood. But near the old cigar factories, people still sit around playing cards and bocci. Today, some of those who left are returning to Little Havana. A new generation of cooks are drawn there as well.

Caprice Tassinari, whose mother is Cuban and father is Italian, recently opened Tete, a Mediterranean-Asian-Italian-Cuban restaurant with "a pinch of salt and a pinch of love." "All Cuban food goes back to the Mediterranean," Caprice told me one evening in her kitchen. "We take the basics and put it together. Then we top it with the fruits and spices of the Caribbean."

In Miami, the classic Cuban *arroz con pollo* is becoming more and more like Spanish paella, with mussels, olives, and peas added to the dish. Cuban cooks are passionately partisan on the subject: some like wet rice, some like it dry; some cook their chicken until it falls off the bone, and some cook it just until done; some use green peppers, some use red peppers, and some use both. Although Caprice uses only chicken legs in her rendition, I include a whole chicken cut in pieces so my family can have their pick of the parts they like. If you marinate the chicken ahead of time, this dish is a snap to prepare.

YIELD: 6–8 SERVINGS

4 cloves garlic, mashed

1 tablespoon kosher salt

1 teaspoon black pepper

1 teaspoon ground cumin

1 teaspoon dried oregano

½ cup dry sherry

4 whole chicken legs, cut in half, or one 3½–4-pound chicken, cut in 8 parts

¼ cup olive oil, preferably Spanish

2 large onions, roughly chopped

1 green bell pepper, cut in 1-inch pieces

1 red bell pepper, cut in 1-inch pieces

1 bay leaf

½ teaspoon hot paprika, or to taste

½ teaspoon saffron strands, crumbled

One 12-ounce bottle beer

1–2 cups chicken broth

2 cups Valencia or other short-grain rice

10 mussels in their shells (optional)

One 10-ounce package frozen peas

¼ cup green olives

Pimiento strips for garnish

1. Mix together the garlic, salt, pepper, cumin, oregano, and sherry in a small bowl. Rub the marinade over the chicken and refrigerate, covered, for at least an hour.

2. Remove the chicken from the marinade. Heat the olive oil in a wide pan—a paella pan is good—and brown the chicken on all sides. Remove the chicken to a plate, then sauté the onions and peppers until the onions are translucent, adding more olive oil if needed. Return the chicken to the pan and add the bay leaf, paprika, saffron, 1 cup of the beer, and 1 cup of the chicken broth.

3. Return to a simmer and cook for 5 minutes. Gently stir in the rice. Add the remaining beer and chicken broth and about a cup of water to cover the rice and simmer, uncovered, until the rice is cooked, about 30 minutes. Taste it and adjust the seasonings if necessary.

4. Just before serving, add the mussels (if you like), peas, and green olives. Cook for a few minutes, covered, until the mussel shells open and the peas are cooked, discarding any mussels that don't open. Garnish with pimiento strips and serve out of the pan.

Bread Crumb Baked Chicken

Fried chicken is an American classic. But today we want the taste of fried chicken without the fat. This dish accomplishes that. Sally Calabrese of Monterey, California (see page 293), used to watch her grandmother prepare chicken this way. She always used yesterday's homemade Italian bread to make the crumbs, but Sally is happy with store-bought bread (challah and Italian are her favorites). The topping is delicious on chicken, lamb chops, or fish such as halibut, swordfish, or mahimahi. The chicken is best right out of the oven, but it also tastes good reheated or at room temperature. Serve this chicken with the Haitian vegetable dish on page 227.

YIELD: 6–8 SERVINGS

½ loaf day-old bread, such as challah or other egg bread, enough to make 2 cups bread crumbs

¼ cup chopped fresh parsley, washed and well dried

3 cloves garlic, minced

1 teaspoon salt

½ teaspoon pepper

1 tablespoon sugar

2 tablespoons grated Parmesan cheese

¼ cup extra-virgin olive oil

¾ cup all-purpose flour

2 large eggs, beaten

8–10 pieces chicken—thighs, drumsticks, breasts, or boneless breast, as you prefer

1. Preheat the oven to 350 degrees.

2. To make the bread crumbs, slice off the bread crusts and then cut the bread into cubes. Toast the cubes in the oven until golden, about 5 minutes. Put the toasted cubes in a food processor and pulse until you have coarse crumbs. Toss the crumbs in a bowl with the parsley, garlic, salt, pepper, sugar, and Parmesan cheese.

3. Drizzle half of the olive oil on the bottom of a 9-by-13-inch glass baking dish.

4. Place the flour in 1 shallow bowl, the beaten eggs in another, and the bread crumbs in a third. Dip each piece of chicken in the flour, then the egg, and then the crumbs. Be sure each piece is fully covered with crumbs and arrange them in the baking dish. Drizzle the rest of the olive oil over the chicken to keep it moist. Bake, uncovered, for about 40–50 minutes (less for boneless breasts), until golden and done. Serve on a platter.

Pollo alla Cacciatora

Chicken Cacciatore

This recipe, from Roberto Donna of Restaurant Galileo in Washington, D.C., is better than any chicken cacciatore I have ever tasted. It has the woodsy flavor of mushrooms, the depth of wine, and the slight hint of tomatoes that Americans associate with the dish. For Roberto, this is comfort food that his mother used to make in San Raffaele Cimena, the little town outside Turino where he grew up. Serve this with pasta or potatoes.

YIELD: 4–6 SERVINGS

1 ounce dried porcini mushrooms, coarsely chopped

½ cup warm water

3 tablespoons butter

3 tablespoons extra-virgin olive oil

1 whole chicken (about 3–3½ pounds), cut into 8 pieces

½ cup flour

1 red onion, diced

1 small carrot, diced

1 clove garlic, minced

1 bay leaf

½ cup white wine

1 cup chicken broth

1 cup chopped tomato, fresh or canned, with the juice

Salt and pepper to taste

2 tablespoons chopped fresh parsley

1. Put the dried mushrooms in a bowl, cover them with the water, and let them soak while you prepare the chicken. When they are soft, strain them over a bowl and reserve the liquid.

2. Set a large sauté pan with a cover over medium heat and melt the butter and warm the olive oil in it. Dredge the chicken pieces in the flour, shaking off any excess. Brown the chicken on all sides in the butter and olive oil, about 8–10 minutes.

3. Either remove the chicken or push it to one side of the pan, then add the onion and carrot and sauté for about 3 minutes. Add the garlic and bay leaf and sauté for another minute. If you have removed the chicken from the pan, return it to the pan now.

4. Pour in the wine, bring it to a boil, and cook for 1 minute. Add the chicken broth, tomato, mushrooms, salt and pepper to taste, and the liquid from the mushrooms. Bring everything to a boil, reduce the heat, and simmer, covered, for 30 minutes. This is best made in the morning or the day before you want to serve it. Simply reheat in the pan. Turn onto a platter and spoon the sauce over. Sprinkle with parsley just before serving.

In December 1983, Marian Burros ran a story in the *New York Times* entitled "Foie Gras Goes American," showing how the fattened goose or duck liver is made and quoting French chefs, such as André Soltner of Lutèce, who pronounced American foie gras "fantastic." Others, like the late Jean-Louis Palladin—a foie gras lover who used to joke that he grew up in the belly of a duck—helped spread the gospel, generously sharing their sources and showing other chefs how to cook the product.

It seems hard to imagine, but before 1982 you could buy only foie gras preserved in cans or jars from France. Then Ariane Daguin, who comes from a French foie gras–producing family and had come to New York to work at Trois Cochons, met two Israeli kibbutzniks holding some duck livers (wrapped in newspaper) that they had grown in the Hudson Valley of New York. "It was the real foie gras," Ariane, who is now the presi-dent of D'Artagnan, purveyors of foie gras and other meats, told me. "It looked fresh and raw and nice. These two guys knew how to raise the ducks. But they didn't know how to sell foie gras. We thought we could help them do that." Ariane and a coworker, George Faisan, eventually left their jobs and turned her kitchen over to foie gras production.

About the same time, Michael Ginor, an American student studying abroad in Israel, tasted foie gras that had been cut in chunks and briefly pan-grilled. He was hooked. When Michael came back to the United States he joined the two Israelis in raising and processing more ducks, and then started Hudson Valley Foie Gras, working closely with Ariane. Today, Hudson Valley is supplying their livers to restaurants all around the country. High-end chefs are serving sautéed foie gras in every conceivable manner: with plums, pickled white anchovies, and even mole sauce.

Grilled Foie Gras Salad with Summer Fruit and Fig Glaze

When I visited Michael Ginor at his farm in the Hudson Valley, he grilled foie gras for me, a recipe made here more simply. If you have trouble locating fresh or frozen foie gras, consult Mail-Order Sources.

YIELD: 4–6 MAIN-COURSE SERVINGS OR 8–10 APPETIZER SERVINGS

FIG SYRUP

8 fresh Calabrian or Black Mission figs, quartered

1 pound dried figs, coarsely chopped

1 cup sugar

2 cups water

FOIE GRAS

8 wooden or metal skewers, about 12 inches long

2 peaches or nectarines, quartered

4 apricots, halved

2 plums, quartered

1 fresh foie gras (about 1½ pounds), lobes separated and cut into eight 1-inch cubes*

Coarse salt to taste

Freshy ground pepper to taste

2 tablespoons chicken fat or vegetable oil

2 small pita breads, quartered

1 bunch frisée salad greens, cleaned and torn

Juice of 1 lemon

*You could also make this dish with about 2 pounds of chicken livers instead of the foie gras.

1. To make the syrup, place the fresh and dried figs, sugar, and water in a large pot. Bring to a simmer and cook until the dried figs turn mushy, about 30 minutes. Strain the mixture through a food mill, or if you prefer a chunkier texture, merely pulse in a food processor. (This syrup can be made ahead of time, and stored in the refrigerator.)

2. If you are using wooden skewers, soak them in water for about 10 minutes while you preheat the grill to high and prepare the fruit and duck.

3. Thread pieces of peach or nectarine, apricot, and plum on 4 of the skewers. Then thread the foie gras cubes on the remaining 4 skewers. Season the foie gras generously with coarse salt and pepper. Brush all the skewers with chicken fat or vegetable oil and set them aside.

4. Once the grill is hot, grill the fruit, turning once, until slightly tender, about 3 minutes. When cool enough to handle, remove the fruit from the skewers and set aside.

5. Then put the foie gras skewers on the grill and cook on all sides until caramelized, about 2 minutes. Remove from the grill. When cool enough to handle, carefully remove from the skewers and set aside with the fruit.

6. Place the pita quarters on the grill and cook on both sides, until golden brown.

7. Toss the frisée salad greens with salt, pepper, lemon juice, and the remaining chicken fat or vegetable oil. Arrange attractively in the center of a large platter or on individual plates. Place the foie gras and fruit on top. Drizzle with a little of the fig syrup. Arrange the pita wedges around the edge of the platter and serve immediately.

Pacific Rim Roast Turkey with Oyster Sauce, Cilantro, and Ginger

After he graduated from the Culinary Institute of America, Dennis Friedman worked at Alan Wong's restaurant (see page 287) in distant Honolulu. Once a month, all the chefs would split up into teams of two or three and cook for about fifty senior citizens. "This was a way of giving back to the community in the Asian culture," said Dennis. "Alan was honoring his elders by cooking dinner for them." Each team had to create a unique dish from Hawaiian ingredients selected by the chef. "Alan used this as a way to see how creative we could be," Dennis told me. "He challenged us to think."

As an incentive to his young chefs, Alan turned the monthly meal into a contest. Near Thanksgiving one year, turkey was the theme. One team fried drumsticks; another crafted turkey roulade. Dennis's team flavored their turkey with cilantro and ginger as well as both hoisin and oyster, two dark, thick sauces with similar flavors. "Adding the two just gives more bite and body to the glaze," says Dennis. "The oyster sauce has that added flavor derived from shrimp and oyster shells."

YIELD: 12–15 SERVINGS

MARINADE

2 inches gingerroot, peeled and grated

3 cloves garlic, minced, plus 5 whole cloves

½ cup hoisin sauce

¼ cup oyster sauce

1 bunch cilantro, stems left whole and leaves chopped, with 1 tablespoon set aside (about 2 cups)

1 bunch scallions, chopped, with 1 tablespoon set aside

½ cup (1 stick) unsalted butter, at room temperature

Salt and freshly ground pepper

One 12–15-pound turkey

1 lemon, halved

1. Preheat the oven to 425 degrees and put a rack in a roasting pan.

2. Mash and mix the ginger, minced garlic, ¼ cup of the hoisin sauce, the oyster sauce, cilantro leaves, the white part of the scallions, and butter in a medium mixing bowl.

3. Season the turkey both inside and out with salt and pepper.

4. Stuff the cilantro stems and the scallion greens, the 5 cloves of garlic, and the lemon halves into the cavity of the turkey.

5. Spread the ginger paste over the turkey and then rub the top with the remaining ¼ cup hoisin sauce.

6. Roast the turkey for 20 minutes, then reduce the heat to 350 degrees and cook, basting every 20 minutes or so, for another 2 hours, or until the bird reaches an internal temperature of 160 degrees. If the top gets too dark, cover the turkey with aluminum foil. Let rest before carving. Sprinkle the remaining cilantro and scallions over the bird. Serve with sweet potatoes.

Meat

Clockwise from top right: Nancy Kohlberg at her Cabbage Hill Farm; Mel Coleman—a master at the grill; Planting at the Mount Kisco Day Care Center; Eliza MacLean and some of her heritage pigs on her farm outside Chapel Hill, North Carolina; Brisket with apples and apricots; Bill and Nicoletta Niman

In 2001, Eric Schlosser caused a sensation with *Fast Food Nation*, an exposé of what goes into the foods we eat. Americans started questioning how cows, lambs, and pigs are raised, fed, and slaughtered; if they are not taken care of properly, how does this affect the consumer? Restaurants like the Zuni Café in San Francisco, aware of the fact that we are increasingly concerned, often write on the menu the provenance of their meat. The description "Paul Willis–raised pork" tells the customer that the chef knows the quality of the pork, which came from pigs raised on Willis's family ranch in Iowa.

More and more, small producers of meat improve the quality, affecting the choices that Americans make. A good example is Bill Niman, who has established a confederation of about five hundred ranches around the country where good husbandry is practiced. On his two-thousand-acre ranch in Bolinas, California, outside of San Francisco, Bill and his wife Nicoletta Hahn's Black Angus and Black Baldy—a cross between Hereford and Angus—cattle graze on open grass fields. I visited during calving week and noticed that one pasture housed females either about to give birth or having given birth. I was told that for the first year of the calves' lives they will stay here, close to their mothers. When the calves have grown enough, the mothers become pregnant again and the calves are taken to a nearby pasture, where the grass is at its most nutritious, just about to go to seed. Then both mother and calf eat the seed from the grass, which is wheat, barley, and oats. They remain in adjacent pastures until the following spring, when they will be trucked to Iowa and fed on grain for five months until they are slaughtered.

Bill started out his career as a homesteader here in the 1960s, teaching at a local school to avoid the draft for the war in Vietnam. After school and on weekends he tended his horses, goats, chickens, and pigs with his late first wife and Orville Schell, the writer. "In those days everyone was bartering," Bill told me over a cup of tea in his kitchen. The Nimans live in a home that Bill built himself. "Between 1975 and 1980 we were selling directly to the consumer. Then Chris Kumpf at Café Beaujolais and Judy Rodgers at Zuni Café read about us and made contact. From there our business took on a life of its own." By the early 1980s, Orville Schell's writing career was launched and Bill continued on his own. "I learned so much about cattle and pigs from neighbors," he said. "We did our very best to get conventional wisdom from people who are working directly with animals. We learned that pigs need corn and soybeans and that cattle need lots of grass and water. Through photosynthesis and God's work it is converted to good meat." He continued, "I am driven by a sense of saving farms and I want to influence rural landscapes." His own land has been sold to the National Park Service with the proviso that he and Orville Schell can live there the rest of their lives.

Like Bill Niman, country music star Teddy Gentry has become a proponent of grass-fed beef. When he received his first paycheck from RCA Records in 1980, he bought his grandfather's farm in Fort Payne, Alabama. Unlike his grandfather, who struggled, unsuccessfully, to grow cotton, Teddy decided to sow grass, build fences, and buy a few cows. "God meant for a cow to eat grass," Teddy said. "Corn-feeding animals is detrimental to your health, so none of our cattle is raised in confined lots. We follow organic practices but are not organic." Now, twenty-five years later, his starter cows have multiplied into thousands, and Teddy is selling his beef throughout the South.

On a farm near Chapel Hill, North Carolina, Eliza MacLean raises a breed of heritage pork called long-nosed Ossabaw hogs, originally dropped off by the Spanish on Ossabaw Island, Georgia, five hundred years ago and sustained there through the years. "We can tell by their DNA that they were brought over by the early Spanish settlers," she told me. With the help of family farm–oriented companies, Eliza, as well as other farmers across the nation allied with Niman Farms and Heritage Breeds (an online mail-order house), are trying to revive these hard-to-find heritage breeds of pigs with the eating quality of a century ago. "With the hurricane and environmental changes in the 1980s, big hog farmers took over from the little people," she said. Eliza is slowly raising her herd size to sell to consumers who are willing to pay the extra money for quality animals that are raised humanely.

On her farm in Mount Kisco, New York, Nancy Kohlberg is emblematic of a growing number of hobbyist farmers concerned with the environment. With the blessing and encouragement of such organizations as the Sierra Club, American Livestock Breed Conservancy, and the Animal Welfare Institute, she has successfully raised rare breeds like black pigs and Shetland sheep. Now their meat is served at her nearby restaurant, the Flying Pig.

Many factors have contributed to these changes. Until the 1970s, Chicago was the nation's hub for beef and pork—or as Carl Sandberg called it, the "hog butcher to the world." From the vast Chicago stockyards, "dressed beef" was hand-selected by meat packers to accommodate the demands of butchers all over the country.

Today, slaughtering and processing is done closer to the farms and feedlots where the majority of the animals are raised, and the meat is often flash-frozen or aged nearby. The precut vacuum-packed meat is then sold to supermarket chains and discounters like Costco. The result is that independent butchers can no longer compete and have been forced out of business around the country. Cuts are now limited in quality and variety. And, as the meat companies and distributors get larger and larger, most meat seems to have a concomitant decline in flavor.

Commercial meat is being produced with less fat content, as well. To make pork, for example, billed as "the other white meat," pigs are raised inside for their entire lives to achieve that profile. If new varieties of lean meat are the good news, the bad news is that in the process the meat has lost a lot in texture and flavor. The same is true for the new, less naturally fatty meats, such as bison and beefalo (a cross between beef and buffalo), which are being raised for the market. "The effort to make us health-conscious has taken the flavor out of the meat, by eliminating all the fat," said Jim Tabb (page 334), a barbecue buff from North Carolina who prefers beef well marbled with fat. "What we want to do is to raise pork that is like that other *red* meat," said Eliza MacLean. "We want to bring back marbling like an Angus steak, to have intramuscular fat, which makes for a healthier outdoor-suited animal and thus a better-tasting meat."

Fortunately, the fad for nonfat white meat, stripped of flavor, has been augmented by the influx of new Americans, who accent their dishes with special flavors so the quality of the meat is less important. And the demand for types of meat such as goat has increased dramatically. New immigrant groups will combine meats and grains in interesting new ways, such as in *bulgogi*, a Korean barbecue (page 343), fajitas (page 342), or couscous with dates and lamb or beef from Mali (page 346). We now season our ground beef for unusual meatballs like those from Tabriz, Afghanistan (page 349), or Armenian rack of lamb with pomegranate sauce (page 351).

Red meat consumption may have decreased from seventy-nine pounds per person in 1970 to sixty-four pounds in 1995, but Americans still love their meat. And we are more discriminating about our choices.

Look at the labels when buying meat. Ask questions. Don't forget: the direct line to good flavor is how the animals are raised.

CONVENTIONAL OR FACTORY-FARMED AND MASS-PRODUCED: Animals are raised on large farms. They are housed on concrete slabs with no bedding, and they never go outdoors. Antibiotics and synthetic growth hormones are used, and the animals' feed often includes animal by-products. Animals are artificially inseminated, and weaned at a very early age.

GRASS-FED: Animals have access to outdoor pasture and bedded pens for 80 percent of their lives. When grass is not available, they live on a corn and soy diet. They are weaned at five to six weeks and no antibiotics or growth hormones are used, but the animals are vaccinated to immunize them against disease when appropriate, and vitamins and minerals are added to the feed.

CERTIFIED ORGANIC: Organic agriculture is USDA accredited and certified, but that does not necessarily ensure free range. The animals are not immunized, never receive antibiotics or added growth hormones, and are fed only certified organic feed.

KOSHER AND HALLAL: Only animals that have split hooves and chew their cud (this eliminates hogs) are used. The important point of both *hallal* and kosher is how the meat is slaughtered. Laws that date back three thousand years to the Bible and later to the Koran dictate that the killing of all animals and birds requires a sage instructed in the ritual of slaughter so that the animal is killed instantly. After their swift slaughter, the sage rejects cattle with certain types of adhesions, cuts, and bruises. For *hallal* meat, the person who applies the cut should say a prayer for each individual animal, dedicating it to Allah, and the action of killing should take place in the direction of Mecca. Kosher slaughtering is done by a ritual slaughterer. Since the Bible declares an absolute prohibition against the consumption of blood, after the animal is killed the meat goes through a salting process, which consists of first soaking the meat in cold water, then covering it with coarse salt as a brine to draw out the blood. The salt is then shaken off, and the meat is washed three times so that no blood remains.

Flying over the Aegean Sea late one afternoon in 1961, navy pilot Jim "Trim" Tabb saw smoke rising from a ship below. He headed down, hoping to determine what the trouble was. But there was no trouble. The crew were standing calmly on deck grilling steaks on half-gallon drums, unaware that they were sending smoke signals into the sky. When he realized what was going on, Jim took off his oxygen mask and flew over the fantail of the destroyer at about ten to twenty feet, filling his nostrils with the aroma. When he returned to his aircraft carrier, his commander asked him what on earth he'd been doing. A Missouri native, Jim didn't hesitate to tell the truth: "I miss barbecue so much that I just had to smell that smoke after having been at sea for five months." His commanding officer simply rolled his eyes and walked away.

Jim Tabb loves barbecue. He loves to eat it, he loves to cook it, and he loves to judge it. His business card reads "Captain, TWA, retired, barbecue judge, aficionado, writer, consultant, philanthropist, and cook."

After the navy, Jim flew for Trans World Airlines for thirty years. "In every city, I would ask for barbecue," he told me. But his search often came up empty. "I didn't find it in Tel Aviv or Cairo. Well, I found shrimp barbecue in Cairo, but where do you find Egyptian shrimp? Bombay's not a great barbecue city either." Through the years he has eaten every kind of barbecue imaginable and has liked almost all of them. "I'm not too big on souse," he confessed. "I made souse—pig's feet, ears, and snout—only once."

Jim Tabb and his daughter get ready to barbecue

Because of fire and air-quality laws in many cities, real, long-cooked, smoked barbecue is hard to find in the States. "Once I called Calvin Trillin of *The New Yorker* when I was barbecuing a whole hog at the Brooklyn Brewery," Jim recalls. Calvin, a barbecue maven himself, didn't believe him: "Get out of here. They won't allow barbecue in Brooklyn," he said. Jim insisted that they did. All the police wanted to know was if they were cooking with hickory and when it would be ready.

Now that he's retired, Jim spends his time hopping between barbecue events. His favorite is ribs. "First, you take off the rib membrane and put a dry rub on and let the meat sit overnight in the refrigerator," he said. Not any old dry rub— Jim has his own special mix of thirteen different spices. He's used this mix for more than thirty years, and the formula for it is in a sealed envelope not to be opened until his death. "I caught my daughter sneaking around trying to figure it out," he said. "I told her that she might have all the ingredients but not the proportions.

So she gave up." He signed a confidentiality agreement with Vanns Spices in Baltimore (see page 314) to mix and produce his rub mix, which they bottle as Trim Tabb's Pig Powder. He would only tell me that sugar and salt are two of the ingredients.

Although Jim would not reveal his dry rub or sauce recipes, both of which have been winning awards for years, he did suggest how to doctor some of the best store-bought sauces—KC Masterpiece, which was sold by a dentist in Kansas City to Kraft Foods, and Gates Sauce, also from Kansas City: "If you want it sweeter, add some honey, molasses, or Karo syrup," he suggests. "If you want it more vinegary, add white vinegar, and if you want it hotter, add cayenne. It's all just a little food chemistry." That's easy for him to say. For the rest of us, here is his daughter's recipe and a couple of barbecue techniques—but with a Jim Tabb reminder. "We're moving so fast in this computer age," he said. "Everything is hurry up. Barbecuing hasn't changed since its beginnings. It's the last thing left that you have to do slow and long."

Barbecued Beef Brisket

L ee Ann Whippen is a Chesapeake, Virginia, caterer and barbecue buff who makes brisket so tender it tastes like butter. Although she uses her dad's spice rub (see box), you can season your brisket with his Trim Tabb's Pig Powder or, as Lee Ann also recommends, Bad Byron's Butt Rub. She cooks it in a wonderful beer-based mop sauce and serves it with a knockout barbecue sauce on the side.

Many busy cooks do what I often do: they cook the brisket a day ahead and refrigerate it, allowing the flavor to deepen. When ready to serve, simply remove the fat, slice the brisket against the grain, and reheat. Start this dish two days ahead. It's very easy and well worth the time.

YIELD: 10–12 SERVINGS

BRISKET

One 8–9-pound "choice" beef brisket, trimmed of fat to a thickness of ¼ inch

½ cup dry barbecue rub of your choice (see above)

1. Sprinkle the brisket generously with the dry rub and rub it in. Wrap the meat in plastic and refrigerate it overnight.

2. The next day, remove the brisket from the refrigerator and leave it out for about 1 hour to come to room temperature.

Barbecued Beef Brisket (continued)

BEER-BASED MOP SAUCE
OR MARINADE

¾ cup cider vinegar

1½ cups beer

¼ cup water

¼ cup vegetable oil

1 tablespoon dry barbecue rub

2 tablespoons
Worcestershire sauce

1 teaspoon coarsely ground
black pepper

1 teaspoon liquid smoke

BARBECUE SAUCE

½ medium onion, finely chopped

5 tablespoons butter

1 cup canned tomato sauce

1 cup ketchup

⅓ cup chili sauce*

¾ cup dark brown sugar

½ cup honey

1 cup white vinegar

1 teaspoon ground allspice

1 tablespoon dry mustard

2 teaspoons freshly ground
black pepper

2 teaspoons chili powder

3 tablespoons
Worcestershire sauce

2 fat cloves garlic, smashed

1 tablespoon paprika

3 tablespoons fresh lemon juice
(about 1½ lemons)

3 tablespoons maple syrup

* You can find the sweet chili sauce
near the ketchup in your supermarket.

3. Preheat the oven to 200–225 degrees. Unwrap the meat and place it in a heavy roasting pan with a cover.

4. While the oven is preheating, make the beer mop sauce by stirring in a small saucepan the cider vinegar, beer, water, vegetable oil, dry rub, Worcestershire sauce, black pepper, and liquid smoke. Bring the mixture to a boil, reduce the heat, and simmer, uncovered, for about 10 minutes.

5. Baste brisket with the mop sauce. Cook in the oven for 6 hours, basting again with the mop sauce every hour and turning occasionally. Keep the brisket covered while cooking.

6. Remove the cover and continue to cook until the internal temperature of the brisket reaches 185 degrees, about another 1 hour.

7. During the last hour of cooking, make the barbecue sauce. In a small frying pan set over medium heat, sauté the onion in the butter until soft. Add all the remaining ingredients for the sauce; bring to a boil, then reduce the heat to low and simmer, uncovered, for 20 minutes.

8. Shortly before serving, remove the brisket from the oven and let it stand for 15 minutes. Slice the meat crosswise, against the grain, into ⅛–¼-inch slices. Arrange the slices on a serving platter and cover them with the barbecue sauce. You can also make this a day ahead, refrigerate, skim off the fat, and cut and reheat the brisket.

Note: If you are using a gas grill, preheat it to 200–225 degrees. Soak some hickory chips in water for ½ hour, then drain. Turn off 1 burner and place the meat on that side. Wrap the soaked hickory chips in foil, poke holes in the top of the foil for the smoke to escape, and place the chips directly on the heated side. After 3 hours of cooking, place the brisket on 2 pieces of heavy-duty aluminum foil, pour ¼ cup of the mop sauce on top of the brisket, and seal tightly. Place in a 350-degree oven for the additional 1–2 hours, until the internal temperature reaches 185 degrees.

Brisket with Apricots and Apples

Almost everybody likes brisket, that fragrant, flavorful, and—if you cook it right—fork-tender cut of breast meat. There are two rules for cooking brisket: cook it long, and cook it with the fat. Since it comes from the grainier forequarters of the steer, slow cooking is required to tenderize the meat, even more so these days with pretrimmed, young, or "select" meat.

For the cholesterol conscious, the thick layer of fat on "choice" meat can seem alarming. But Sanford Herskovitz, aka Mr. Brisket, a meat purveyor in Cleveland, Ohio, is outspoken on the subject: "When there is no fat you absolutely kill the taste," he says. "If you cut the fat off beforehand, your brisket is 'ferfallen.' You have defeated your purpose. The first cut or flat portion of the brisket is available, oven ready, at virtually all supermarkets around the country."

Brisket is the Zelig of the kitchen—it takes on the character of whoever cooks it. In the early part of the twentieth century, recipes for brisket with sauerkraut, cabbage, or lima beans were the norm. As American tastes became more exotic, cranberry sauce, chili, onion soup mix, root beer, lemonade, and now even sake have all worked their way into recipes. I tried this fruited brisket at my sister-in-law Shelley Nathans's house in Berkeley, California. Shelley adds more fruit, and I add more onion, but either way, it's a winner.

YIELD: 8–10 SERVINGS

2 onions, chopped

4 cloves garlic

1 tablespoon ground ginger

2 tablespoons vegetable oil

One 5–6-pound brisket

Salt and pepper to taste

2 apples, chopped (about 2 cups)

1 cup dried apricots, halved

½ cup dried cranberries

1 cup dried plums, pitted

1–2 cups apple juice

1–2 cups canned beef or chicken broth

1. Preheat the oven to 350 degrees.

2. Brown the onions, garlic, and ginger in the oil until the onions are golden. Then scatter the mixture in a roasting pan.

3. Season the brisket with salt and pepper and gently lay it on top of the onions. Add the apples, apricots, dried cranberries, dried plums, and enough apple juice and beef or chicken broth to almost cover the brisket. Cover the roasting pan with a lid or aluminum foil and cook for 3 hours, basting occasionally.

4. Remove the brisket, cool, and refrigerate overnight.

5. Just before serving, reheat the oven to 350 degrees. While the brisket is still cold, skim off any fat that has accumulated on top of the juices,

and slice off the excess fat from the meat. Slice the meat against the grain, place in a baking dish with the reserved juices, cover, and reheat for about a half hour. Remove brisket to a platter, surrounded by the fruits and the sauce. Serve with potato pancakes (page 246) or noodles.

Miss Mamie's Short Ribs of Beef

Although Norma Jean (see box) uses short ribs for this recipe, you could use beef cheeks—just braise them 1½ hours longer, or until tender. Make the dish a day in advance, and it will taste better the next day. You should figure about three ribs for each person.

YIELD: 6–8 SERVINGS

5 pounds beef short ribs (about 20 pieces), each 3½ inches long

1–1½ teaspoons sea salt, or to taste

¼ teaspoon black pepper, or to taste

2 onions, chopped

2 celery stalks, chopped

2 medium turnips, chopped

3 whole carrots, peeled and sliced in rounds

½ bulb garlic, minced

1 bay leaf

5 sprigs fresh or ½ teaspoon dried thyme

1 cup red wine

¼ cup commercial or homemade barbecue sauce (page 336)

3 cups canned or fresh beef broth

1. Season the ribs heavily with salt and pepper to taste. Heat a large heavy frying pan with a cover and sear the meat on two sides. You may have to do this in two batches. Remove the meat to a plate.

2. Add the onions, celery, turnips, carrots, and garlic to the frying pan. Sauté for a few minutes in the fat from the beef. Return the ribs to the pan, and add the bay leaf, thyme, wine, barbecue sauce, and enough beef broth to almost cover the ribs. Bring to a boil, cover, and simmer for 1½ hours or until tender, checking periodically and moving the ribs around with tongs. Cool the ribs in the pan and refrigerate overnight.

3. The next morning, skim off the fat that has accumulated. Reheat for about 15 minutes and serve with garlic mashed potatoes (page 247) or good Bukharan bread (page 66).

On New York's Upper West Side, near the Cathedral of St. John the Divine, is a cozy restaurant called Miss Mamie's Spoonbread Too. Yellow Formica tables, a red checkerboard floor, and two trompe l'oeil curtains decorated with strawberries invite the diner inside for down-home southern cooking. Miss Mamie was the mother of the owners, Norma Jean Darden and Carole Darden. When I arrived, Norma Jean greeted me in a stunning Halston polka-dot velveteen coat, given to her by the fashion designer himself. With a raspy voice and an extraordinary smile, she told me that she started out as a model for *Vogue* and later became an actor.

Born in Newark, New Jersey, she spent summers at her grandparents' home in Wilson, North Carolina, until she was thirteen years old. "I loved Wilson. There was freedom there," she said. "June bugs, mud pies. We had older relatives with wonderful food and great memories of eating with them on important occasions." Together with her sister Carole, she crafted a cookbook with photos and memories that they called *Spoonbread and Strawberry Wine.* "*Roots* came out when our book came out," she continued. "They called us the 'baby *Roots.*'" If not the first cookbook to combine recipes with personal reflections and photos, it was certainly one of the first.

After Norma Jean's acting teacher, Wynn Handman, read the cookbook, he suggested that she write a play about her life. She did, calling it *Spoonbread and Strawberry Wine* as well. The play led to a catering business, then restaurants, and now a jazz club in the new Time-Warner Building in midtown Manhattan.

Although basic North Carolina "soul food" has remained the same over the years, Norma Jean has made a few adjustments to accommodate modern trends. Having a father with diabetes also inspired her to make their dishes a little healthier. The candied yams are cooked with orange juice and a little sugar; there is no pork in the collards; she uses less butter in the corn bread; and her chicken is either roasted or fried in oil, rather than lard—but her short ribs recipe, which has come back into style, has stayed exactly the same.

Norma Jean Darden at Miss Mamie's

A number of barbecue buffs had told me about this Memphis barbecue mecca. When I got there I was surprised to see the restaurant is located in a strip mall; the place has a bare, warehouse look, with a few Formica tables, a plant or two, and pictures of famous clientele on the wall. But in spite of the decor, a steady stream of the faithful were lined up for barbecued beef, pork, bologna, and Cornish hens, cooked on a Rube Goldberg–type smoker right in the front of the store. "We call it a Chicago-style pit," Desiree Robinson, the owner, told me, "because it's cooked in front of the customers, not out back."

Desiree Robinson (left) and her children

Desiree and her late husband, Raymond, started Cozy Corner in 1977, after returning from living in Denver, where they had opened their first Memphis barbecue restaurant. "We were both only children," explained Desiree. "Going to Denver was the best thing. Raymond said if he hadn't taken me away, I would never have left my mama." But the two, who met in high school in Memphis, knew they would return there to care for their parents. When they opened the restaurant it was a family affair, and it has continued to be one, with Desiree's three grandchildren helping when they are on school breaks.

From the spices in their secret rub to the barbecue sauce to the beans, ingredients come first. Raymond junior stokes the fire all day, and Desiree's daughter, Val, runs the register. "Our secret barbecue ingredient used to be instant coffee," Desiree told me. "We didn't like Cajun spice in our deep-fried turkey, so we got rid of it." When her husband was alive, the two would drive three hundred miles to find barbecue they liked; the best they found was at Dreamland in Tuscaloosa, Alabama.

Coffee-Laced Barbecue Sauce

Desiree (see box) makes this all-purpose coffee-laced barbecue sauce at home. She puts it on lamb, beef, pork, chicken, and baked beans.

1 cup ketchup

⅓ cup hot sauce

⅓ cup Worcestershire sauce

⅓ cup brown sugar, honey, or molasses

2 tablespoons (¼ stick) butter

2 tablespoons lemon juice

1 teaspoon instant powdered coffee or Sanka

1 tablespoon cider vinegar

Put all the ingredients in a medium saucepan, and simmer, uncovered, stirring occasionally, for 30–40 minutes. Use some and save the rest in a covered jar in the refrigerator.

FAJITAS
Tacos al Carbon

When Homero Recio, a lecturer at Texas A&M's Department of Animal Science, was growing up in the lower Rio Grande Valley of South Texas, he ate tough, flavorful cuts of meat, cooked over mesquite, a local hardwood. The name *fajitas* (*faja* in Spanish means "belt" or "girdle") refers to the diaphragm muscle of a steer, what we call skirt steak, not a cut Americans typically ate. "When the cattle were freshly slaughtered, some of the cuts were not as desirable as the back strip and the tenderloin," Homero told me. "But the 'hanging pieces,' like the heart, livers, and skirt steak, were flavorful."

Homero researched the history of fajitas by interviewing elderly cowboys from the King Ranch in the Rio Grande Valley. They told him that the first fajitas were made by ranch hands, whose pay restricted them to scrap meat like the head, intestines, and skirt steak. They would flavor it with salt and garlic salt, grill it right on the coals, and eat it in flour tortillas with hot peppers.

Fajitas didn't make it beyond the area until restaurateurs like Ninfa Rodriguez Laurenzo, also from South Texas, put them on the culinary map. Ninfa moved to Houston with her husband in the late 1960s, and together they opened a tortilla factory. With a family to support, Ninfa decided to add a tiny ten-table restaurant to her tortilla factory, located in a working-class neighborhood of Houston. Word soon spread about her tacos al carbon, fajita meat wrapped in a soft flour tortilla and served with onions and pico de gallo, a spicy combination of onions, green chilies, tomatoes, and cilantro. Ninfa sold 250 on her first day of business. People came from all over to taste the dish, locally known as "tacos ala Ninfa." And later, fajitas spread all over the country.

Grilled Fajitas

Far too many people know Mexican food as a "mixed plate"—a crisp taco filled with ground meat heavily flavored with an all-purpose chili powder; a soggy tamal covered with a sauce that turns up on everything—too sweet and too overpoweringly onioned—a few fried beans and something else that looks and tastes like all the rest.

—DIANA KENNEDY, *THE CUISINES OF MEXICO*

A favorite dish of Tex-Mex food, which Diana Kennedy refers to above, is fajitas: charcoal-grilled skirt steak folded into a fresh, warm flour tortilla and served with fresh chilies, onions, and tomatoes. This is Ninfa's fajitas recipe (see page 341), given to me by Ann Criswell, longtime food editor of the *Houston Chronicle*.

YIELD: 8–10 SERVINGS

1 large orange
2 lemons or 3 limes
¼ cup pineapple juice
¼ cup white wine
¼ cup water
¼ cup soy sauce
1 garlic clove, minced (about 1 teaspoon)
1 tablespoon freshly ground black pepper
3 dried whole arbol chilies, crushed
3 tablespoons melted butter
2 pounds skirt steak, less than ¾ inch thick, from the outside cut (flank steak may be substituted)
16–20 fajita-size flour tortillas
Grilled onions (page 244)
2 tomatoes, sliced into rings
2 green peppers, sliced into rings

1. Two hours before serving, grate the orange and the lime or lemon zest into a large glass bowl. Then squeeze the juice (you should have about ¼ cup each of orange and lemon or lime) into the same bowl and add the pineapple juice. Stir in the wine, water, soy sauce, garlic, black pepper, chilies, and melted butter.

2. Trim the excess fat from the steak and peel off any membranes. If the meat is thicker than ¾ inch at its thickest part, cut in half horizontally so the meat will cook evenly and quickly.

3. Put the steak into the marinade, turn to coat it completely, cover the dish with plastic wrap, and marinate at room temperature for no longer than 2 hours.

4. Preheat the oven to 350 degrees and prepare a charcoal grill or preheat the broiler.

5. Grill the steak 3 inches above very hot coals (or about 4 inches below the broiler), for 5–6 minutes a side. Let rest a few minutes. Cut crosswise against the grain into very thin, finger-length strips.

6. Meanwhile, warm the tortillas in the oven 5 minutes, then remove them to a basket and cover with a towel to keep warm.

7. Arrange the steak on a hot platter, along with the grilled onions, tomato slices, and green pepper rings. Serve with the warm tortillas and let your guests assemble the fajitas as they wish.

8. You can serve this dish alone or with guacamole (page 98), refried beans (page 225), and sour cream.

Bulgogi

Korean Barbecued Beef

At a dinner party in Sturgeon Bay, Wisconsin, we ate Sheboygan bratwurst, rutabaga pasties, and aged cheddar cheese—all good Wisconsin fare. But my dinner partner, Jim Brogan, who hails from Green Bay, kept talking to me about his recipe for *bulgogi,* a luscious Korean barbecue beef, now a staple at his annual Fourth of July party.

While Jim was studying at the University of Wisconsin in the mid-1960s, he and his roommate did a favor for a Korean graduate student. The fellow wanted to repay them, so he showed them how to make his favorite dish, *bulgogi.*

Jim, who took a lasting fancy to this steak dish, described *bulgogi* as peppery and caramelized. The trick to making it is in slicing the meat. If you do it yourself, put the meat in the freezer for an hour to make it easier to cut. Cut against the grain, making it a bit thicker than carpaccio (paper-thin air-dried beef). "Most butchers will want to give you minute steak, but ask for sirloin," Jim told me. Meat for *bulgogi* is available precut in many Asian markets. (While traveling the country, I noticed that you can buy brisket of beef sliced paper-thin for *bulgogi* at many markets, like the De Kalb in Atlanta.) Traditionally, this dish is served wrapped in romaine lettuce or with rice and kimchee, a pickled cabbage dish, but any tart, cold salad (Vietnamese slaw, page 173) will go well with it. I have added some ginger to Jim's rendition. If you want it more fiery, you can add more cayenne and black pepper, but this mild version is hot enough for me.

YIELD: 8–10 SERVINGS

½–¾ cup sugar

2 teaspoons freshly ground black pepper, or to taste

2 teaspoons cayenne pepper, or to taste

½ cup vegetable oil

1 cup good-quality soy sauce

3 pounds sirloin tip, sliced paper-thin against the grain in 4- to 5-inch slices*

3 bunches scallions, trimmed and finely chopped, including the green portion

2 tablespoons grated fresh ginger (optional)

* If the butcher freezes the sirloin roast and slices it on a machine while the meat is still somewhat firm, you will get the required thinness.

1. Make the marinade by stirring together ½ cup of the sugar, 2 teaspoons black pepper, 2 teaspoons cayenne pepper, vegetable oil, and soy sauce in a medium bowl. Taste, and if it isn't hot enough for you, add more pepper and cayenne pepper, and then more sugar to balance the flavor.

2. Put the sliced meat, scallions, and ginger in a gallon-size resealable plastic bag.

3. Pour the marinade into the bag, making sure the meat is well covered. If you need more marinade, pour in a little additional oil. Let the meat marinate on the counter for no longer than 2 hours or in the refrigerator overnight, occasionally pressing and gently shaking the bag to mix the marinade.

4. Heat a grill or a hibachi. Drain the marinade from the meat and grill the slices for about 2 minutes total, turning once. Remove with tongs and arrange on a serving platter with rice or romaine lettuce.

Asparagus Stir-Fry with Steak and Tofu

For the Chinese of the Mississippi Delta, this asparagus stir-fry with tofu, thinly sliced beef, and oyster sauce conjures up memories of China. One time Sally and Gilroy Chow, of Clarksdale, Mississippi (page 270), bought oyster sauce at Kroger's. "It tasted like cough syrup," Sally told me. "It wasn't anything like what we get in the Chinese stores." When Sally and Gilroy got married thirty some years ago, Chinese staples were brought in from California or New York. "Twenty years ago we had to go to Dallas or Houston for Chinese groceries," Gilroy said. "Now we can go to Memphis, where you can find lots of Chinese grocery stores. We can find baby bok choy, tofu, *heung fun* (five-spice powder), hoisin, chicken fat, *hog ma* (tripe)—things you wouldn't find at Kroger's." This dish, with its meat and asparagus, blends the best of America with the Chows' traditional Chinese cooking.

½ pound sirloin, flank, or strip
steak or any tender beef, sliced
into 2-inch-long thin, but not
paper-thin, strips

1 tablespoon soy sauce

6 cloves garlic, minced
(about 6 teaspoons)

One 14-ounce container firm tofu

1½ pounds fresh asparagus

¼ teaspoon salt

3 tablespoons canola oil

1 tablespoon dry sherry

1 small onion, thinly sliced

4 ounces mushrooms,
cut into small chunks
(about 1¼ cups)

2½ tablespoons cornstarch

1 cup chicken stock or canned
chicken broth

3 tablespoons oyster sauce

½ teaspoon toasted sesame oil

1. Marinate the beef in a bowl with the soy sauce and ⅓ of the chopped garlic for 30 minutes in the refrigerator.

2. Rinse the tofu in cold water and drain. Slice in 1-by-2-inch strips and set aside near the stove.

3. Bring a pot of water to a boil. Break off the tough ends of the asparagus and cut the spears into 2-inch pieces. Parboil for a minute, drain, and immerse in cold water to chill. Drain again and dry.

4. Heat a wok, sprinkle salt into it, and brown salt for a minute or two to season the wok, then add 2 tablespoons of the canola oil. When the oil is hot, add another third of the garlic and the asparagus and stir-fry for 2 minutes. Remove to a large serving bowl.

5. Pour the remaining tablespoon of canola oil into the wok. When hot, add the remaining garlic. Stir in the marinated beef and the sherry, then toss in the onion and mushrooms and stir-fry for 2 more minutes. Remove to the bowl with the asparagus.

6. Dissolve the cornstarch in 2 tablespoons of cold water in a small bowl, then whisk the chicken stock into it. Pour the mixture into the wok and bring to a boil to thicken. Return the asparagus and beef to the wok to heat through, thinning the gravy, if needed, with a little water or stock.

7. Add the tofu, stirring gently. Sprinkle on the oyster sauce and sesame oil, stir again, taste, and adjust seasonings.

8. When everything is hot, turn onto a platter and serve with steamed rice.

Couscous de Timbuktu

Lamb Stew with Dates and Couscous

At the 2003 Smithsonian Festival of American Folklife in Washington, D.C., Amatha Sangho Diabate, a professor at Spellman College in Atlanta, demonstrated several dishes from her native Mali, including a lamb stew with twelve different flavors from spices and vegetables. This *couscous de Timbuktu,* a grand feast dish in her country, is usually cooked in a clay pot on the ground over coals. Amatha often makes it in her kitchen in Atlanta, bringing the stew to potluck dinner parties. Here she uses beef, though she learned to make the dish with lamb. You can use either.

YIELD: 8–10 SERVINGS

4 pounds stewing beef or lamb, cut in 2-inch chunks

3 teaspoons salt, or to taste

Freshly ground black pepper to taste

⅓ cup vegetable oil

4 cloves garlic, thinly sliced

1 tablespoon ground cumin

1 teaspoon fennel seeds

½ tablespoon ground cardamom

2 tablespoons ground ginger

½ tablespoon finely ground black pepper

1–2 tablespoons cayenne pepper

1 teaspoon grated nutmeg

One 28-ounce can whole tomatoes

2 cups water

3 medium onions, diced

1½ teaspoons ground cinnamon

1 cup dates, pitted and puréed in a food processor (about 6 dates)

2 tablespoons chopped fresh parsley for garnish

1. Season the meat with salt and pepper. Heat the oil in a large Dutch oven or deep heavy pan over high heat and sear the meat, along with the garlic, in the hot oil (you may have to do this in 2 batches). Add the cumin, fennel seeds, cardamom, ginger, black pepper, cayenne pepper, and nutmeg and stir-fry for a few minutes.

2. Place the meat and the spices in a large pot. Add the tomatoes and enough water to cover and bring to a boil. Lower the heat and simmer, covered, for about 1 hour.

3. Add the onions, cinnamon, and dates and simmer, uncovered, until the beef is tender and the sauce has reduced and thickened, about 40 minutes. Taste and adjust the seasonings, sprinkle with the chopped parsley, and serve with couscous.

Grilled Steak

W hen I met Mel Coleman of Coleman Natural Meats at a Washington restaurant, I couldn't miss him, with his Stetson and cowboy boots. Having ordered a rib-eye steak, his favorite, he showed me the marbling in it. "Every steak needs some marbling for flavor," he said. This proponent of grain-fed beef told me how his father had been in the cattle business in Colorado and that he had wanted to go into it too, but prices for cattle were very low. So in partnership with his father he changed direction, forming Coleman Natural Meats with USDA natural beef certification. "The need and opportunity to increase the flavor of beef opened doors for us," he said. Even with hundreds of thousands of heads of cattle in Colorado, he recalls the best steak of his life. "It was in Japan," he told me. "A simple steak made from Kobe beef. It was perfect, grilled with nothing on it, then dotted with wasabi, and sprinkled with coarse salt." His advice to the would-be steak griller: "patience, patience, and more patience"—as you will see. Steak is always better over a hot charcoal grill.

YIELD: 4 SERVINGS

Four 1-inch boneless rib-eye steaks (about 12 ounces each)

Coarse salt and freshly ground pepper to taste

1. Prepare a charcoal fire or turn a gas grill to high. Bring the steak to room temperature. The grill is hot enough when you can hold your hand 6 inches away from the grate for only a few seconds.

2. Just before placing the steak on the grill, season it with salt and pepper on both sides. Don't salt ahead of time, as the salt will "cure" the steak and toughen it.

3. For each inch of thickness of the steak, grill it 4 minutes per side for medium-rare, a bit less for rare or very rare, and a bit more for medium or well done.

4. Place the steaks on the grill and leave them alone for at least 4 minutes, or until you first see juices well up on the outer rim of the surface of the steak, like little beads. For a very rare steak, flip it over immediately. For medium-rare, flip the steak over when you see little beads appear in the center of the steak. Remember—this is the only time you flip it.

5. Once the steak is flipped, do nothing until you see beads of juices

well up in the center of the cut or have reached 4 minutes for a 1-inch-thick cut. If the steak is 1½ inches thick, you may want to grill it 6 minutes per side.

6. When the steak is done, the rule is, again, patience! Let your steak rest on the cutting board for a minimum of 5 minutes. Don't rush it to the plate, no matter how good it looks. While the steak is resting, the juices are naturally welling throughout the flesh, making for a very flavorful, moist-tasting cut of meat. Don't even slice into it to check the temperature! After 5 minutes of rest, dig in and enjoy.

Plantains with Picadillo

Nancy Joseph demonstrated this recipe at a cooking program called "Sharing Memories Through Our Cooking and Conversation," in Kendall, Florida. She explained to the audience that her Polish grandparents, en route to the United States in the early twentieth century, got off the boat in Havana, Cuba. There, Nancy's parents—and a generation later, Nancy herself—were born. When Nancy was four, the family moved to Miami, then to Puerto Rico. As a result, her early life was a tour of different Latin cuisines. After Nancy finished speaking, she offered the women at the program a taste of this delicious layered plantain dish with picadillo (sautéed ground beef with raisins, onions, and green peppers). For Nancy, it evokes the memories and flavors of her Latin childhood.

YIELD: 10–12 SERVINGS

Vegetable oil for frying

6 large ripe plantains, peeled and each cut into 5 lengthwise slices

2 medium onions, chopped

1 large green pepper, chopped in 1-inch pieces

3 cloves garlic, minced (about 3 teaspoons)

2 pounds lean ground beef

1. Pour about ¼ inch of vegetable oil into a heavy frying pan and set over medium heat. When the oil is hot, fry the plantain strips in batches (you don't want to crowd the pan) until golden, about 2 minutes on each side. Remove the plantains with tongs and drain them on paper towels, blotting any remaining oil. Repeat until all the slices have been fried.

2. Preheat the oven to 350 degrees.

3. Heat about 3 tablespoons of the vegetable oil from the plantains in

⅓ cup pitted green olives
¼ cup raisins
1½ cups canned tomato sauce
1 cup white wine
Salt and freshly ground pepper to taste
3 large eggs, well beaten

the frying pan and sauté the onions and pepper until they are tender. Add the garlic and stir-fry for 1 minute. Add the ground beef and cook over medium-high heat until it loses its red color, breaking it up and mashing it with a potato masher until the mix is as fine as possible.

4. Reduce the heat to low and add the olives, raisins, tomato sauce, white wine, and salt and pepper to taste. Cook, stirring occasionally, for 10–15 minutes.

5. Layer half the plantain slices in a shallow 13-by-9-inch glass baking dish and cover them with the meat mixture. Top with the remaining plantain slices; the slices should touch each other but not overlap. Pour the beaten eggs on top and spread over the plantains.

6. Bake in the oven until the top is golden brown, about 30 minutes.

Tabriz-Style *Kofta* (Meatballs)

A woman I know whose husband was a foreign correspondent used to hand-roll hundreds of meatballs when her husband was in a war zone; this simple, repetitive act was both comforting and calming.

Today, we have so many types of meatballs: Italian, with Parmesan cheese and tomato sauce; Moroccan, with cinnamon and olives; Lebanese, with cracked wheat; and Swedish, with cream. We even have vegetarian meatballs, made with tofu. Perhaps the most unusual of all are these Iranian meatballs from Tabriz. Literally a meal within a meatball, they are filled with barberries, dried plums, split peas, and walnuts. Formerly one of the great culinary centers of Iran, Tabriz was known for its giant meatballs. "In the olden days, these meatballs were the size of a basketball, with a boned, cooked chicken and hard-boiled eggs right in the center," said Nahid Javadi, who came to this country from Tabriz with her husband almost thirty years ago. "They were cooked outside in a large kettle over a wood fire."

Nahid's meatballs are much smaller. Often she substitutes less-expensive ground beef for the lamb, and she has eliminated the whole chicken and hard-boiled eggs. But she always includes walnuts, dried plums, and the tart dried barberries, a fruit that grows wild in the United States and is found commercially today through Iranian suppliers, at many U.S. health food stores, and over the Internet.

YIELD: 8 SERVINGS

MEATBALLS

2 tablespoons olive oil

3 medium onions, diced

3½ cups water

½ cup uncooked short-grain rice

½ teaspoon turmeric

1½ teaspoons salt, or to taste

½ cup yellow split peas

2 large eggs, lightly beaten

1 medium onion, quartered

¼ teaspoon black pepper

1 teaspoon ground cumin

1 pound ground lamb or beef

2 cups mixed fresh herbs
(summer savory, chives,
scallions, and dill)

½ cup dried barberries, cleaned,
washed, and drained well

¼ cup roughly chopped walnuts

4 pitted dried plums,
roughly chopped

MEAT SAUCE

⅔ of the cooked onions from
the meatballs

3 cups canned beef broth

1 tablespoon tomato paste

1 cup canned tomatoes, or
1 large tomato, chopped

3 tablespoons vegetable oil

2 teaspoons salt

Black pepper to taste

1 teaspoon ground cumin

Juice of 1 lemon

½ teaspoon saffron dissolved in
2 tablespoons hot water

1. To make the meatballs, heat the olive oil in a medium frying pan over medium heat. Add the onions and sauté them until they are golden brown, about 15 minutes. You will need ⅓ of the onions for the meatballs; save the rest for the sauce.

2. Pour 1½ cups of the water into 1 saucepan and 2 cups water into another. Bring both to a boil. Pour the rice, ¼ teaspoon of the turmeric, and ½ teaspoon of the salt into the first saucepan, and the split peas, remaining turmeric, and another ½ teaspoon of salt into the second. Return both to a boil, cover the pan with the rice, and half-cover the pan with the split peas. Simmer until they are both mushy and soft, about 20 minutes for the rice and 25 for the peas. Set aside the rice and drain the peas.

3. Put the rice and drained split peas, eggs, onion, ½ teaspoon salt, the pepper, cumin, ground meat, and herbs in a food processor equipped with a steel blade. Pulse until smooth with flecks of the green herbs still intact. Remove the bowl of the processor to the refrigerator and chill the contents for an hour or so.

4. When the meat is cold, remove from the refrigerator. Mix the barberries, walnuts, and dried plums together.

5. To shape the meatballs, dip your hands into a bowl of ice water. Shape the meat into 8 tennis ball–size pieces. Poke a hole in the center of each ball with your thumb and fill it with a heaping tablespoon of the fruit and nut mixture. Reshape into a ball to fully enclose the fruit and set on a plate. Continue with the remaining meat and filling.

6. Preheat the oven to 350 degrees.

7. To make the sauce, put the fried onions you set aside earlier, along with the beef broth, tomato paste, tomatoes, oil, salt, pepper, cumin, lemon juice, and saffron in a Dutch oven or large ovenproof pot and stir. Bring to a boil and simmer for a few minutes.

8. Add the meatballs to the sauce and put the pot in the oven, cover, and cook for about 1 hour, basting with the sauce 3 times.

Oven-Roasted Rack of Lamb with Pomegranate Sauce

After giving a cooking class at Zov Karamardian's Bistro in Tustin, California, I stayed at her home. Late at night, she brought out wonderfully fresh fruit and Armenian string cheese, which we nibbled while she told me about her family's journey from Syria and Turkey to Jaffa to San Francisco, and finally to Tustin, in Orange County.

When Zov was a child, her parents would take her to Fresno to watch women making pomegranate leathers from the ripe, late October fruit. Then she would eat at Bali's, an Armenian restaurant in San Francisco, where the lamb was glazed with a honey-thick pomegranate syrup. Today, in her upscale Orange County restaurant, Zov uses pomegranate syrup in her own interpretation of the lamb dish.

YIELD: 4–6 SERVINGS

2 racks of lamb, 1½ pounds each (7–8 ribs each), excess fat removed

4 tablespoons olive oil

1 tablespoon freshly ground pepper

Kosher salt to taste

LAMB MARINADE

4 tablespoons Dijon mustard

3–4 cloves garlic, minced (about 3–4 teaspoons)

1 tablespoon chopped fresh or 1 teaspoon dried rosemary

1 tablespoon chopped fresh or 1 teaspoon dried thyme

POMEGRANATE SAUCE

1½ tablespoons olive oil

2 shallots, peeled and minced (about 2–3 tablespoons)

3 cloves garlic, minced (about 1 tablespoon)

1. Rub the lamb with 2 tablespoons of the olive oil and sprinkle with the pepper and salt.

2. To make the marinade, stir the mustard, garlic, rosemary, and thyme together in a small bowl, then rub over the meat. Let sit in the refrigerator an hour or so or overnight.

3. Preheat the oven to 350 degrees.

4. Place an ovenproof skillet, large enough to hold both racks of lamb, over medium-high heat. Add the remaining 2 tablespoons of olive oil and heat until it's almost smoking. Brown the lamb on both sides, then put the pan in the hot oven.

5. Roast the lamb until a meat thermometer inserted in the center of the meat reads 130–135 degrees (the meat will be medium-rare), about 15–20 minutes. Carefully transfer the meat to a cutting board and let it rest, uncovered, for 10 minutes.

6. Meanwhile, make the pomegranate sauce: Drain any fat remaining in the skillet, pour in the olive oil, and heat on medium-high. Add the shallots and garlic and sauté for 1 minute, stirring occasionally. Pour in the broth and pomegranate molasses. Increase the heat to high and boil until the liquid has reduced by half, about 10 minutes. Remove the pan

½ cup canned beef broth, or homemade lamb stock

*2 tablespoons pomegranate molasses**

3 tablespoons butter, cut into 3 pieces and softened

Salt to taste

from the heat and whisk in the butter 1 tablespoon at a time. Sprinkle with salt to taste, if needed.

7. Cut the lamb between the rib bones and divide among 4–6 plates. Spoon the sauce on top and serve immediately.

*You can find pomegranate molasses, often labeled concentrated pomegranate juice, in Middle Eastern markets and most specialty food stores.

GRASS-FED LAMB AT JAMISON FARM

Like many farmers, Sukey and John Jamison wake up to the sound of lambs bleating and birds chirping. But unlike most farmers, they don't have to get up and feed their animals—the animals feed themselves.

On the Jamisons' 210-acre farm in Latrobe, Pennsylvania, the lambs' menu changes frequently. Raised naturally, they wander freely from paddock to paddock, grazing on grassy meadows. They dine on bluegrass, white clover, wildflowers, wild onion, garlic, and ramp—whatever is in season—picking up different flavors as the seasons change. "Our lamb tastes like what it eats," John told me as we walked through his meadows. "Depending on the season it might taste like wild garlic and wild onion. It doesn't taste like lamb in stores."

We passed one meadow where about a hundred lambs had munched down the grass. John and his sheepdogs led them to another pasture where there was more shade and grass. The Jamisons use a rotational system developed by French biochemist André Voisin—a time-consuming process that requires them to adapt grazing schedules to the availability of grass on the farm. But they feel strongly that other, more streamlined methods would compromise the quality of their lamb.

Sukey and John became farmers after returning to Latrobe, where John worked in his family's coal business. Sukey convinced him to move the family to a farm where they could raise their three children. "I didn't like cows. They seemed so big and dumb, and if one stepped on my foot, I knew it would be all over," Sukey told me in her cozy kitchen. "So I began raising lambs."

Eventually the Jamisons bought more lambs, some ewes, and a ram. The first ad for their lamb, in *Smithsonian Magazine,* evoked little response, so they sold their meat to friends and family. Then, in 1985, they advertised in *The New Yorker*. Soon the calls began to come in, and they started a mail-order business that focused on home cooks.

In 1987, after donating lamb to a high-profile benefit dinner for Children's Hospital in

Pittsburgh, John wrote a letter to each of the seven chefs who had cooked for the benefit. Only one responded, but that one phone call transformed the Jamisons' business.

The late Jean-Louis Palladin (page 141) told John he needed three twenty-two-pound milk lambs for that Saturday. The Jamisons took three lambs away from their mothers (lambs stop nursing full-time at about three months, but they can continue for months after that), slaughtered them, wrapped them in gel ice packs, and drove them to Washington.

Carrying the lambs over their backs, the Jamisons entered the restaurant at about eleven o'clock at night. A waiter threw the carcasses on a stainless-steel work table. Then Jean-Louis entered and immediately started to pull apart the meat, feeling the back to see if it was finished correctly and touching the pink flesh. He started speaking rapidly in French to the other chefs, and then, in very Frenchified English, said, "I didn't mean to be so emotional. When I get to this country the lamb was '*sheet*.'" Then he compared the Jamison lamb to Sisteron, one of the finest varieties of lamb in France.

After our stroll through the meadows, the Jamisons and I went back to the kitchen via the side garden, where fresh asparagus was coming up. John picked a few spears to go along with our dinner—lamb, of course.

Jamison Farm Lamb Stew

Americans are familiar with leg of lamb, but we don't often cook lamb in a stew. The Jamisons learned this recipe from Jean-Louis Palladin, who made it using one of his signature secret ingredients—V8 vegetable juice.

YIELD: 8 SERVINGS

9 sprigs fresh parsley
4 sprigs fresh sage or
½ teaspoon ground sage
5 small sprigs fresh rosemary or
½ teaspoon dried rosemary
9 small sprigs fresh thyme or
1 teaspoon dried thyme
9 large fresh basil leaves or
1 teaspoon dried basil
2 tablespoons extra-virgin olive oil

1. Put the parsley, sage, rosemary, thyme, and basil in the center of a piece of cheesecloth and tie into a sack with a string. Set aside.

2. Heat the olive oil in a large heavy stockpot over high heat for 2 minutes. Scatter the lamb cubes in the hot oil and sauté them for about 2 minutes, stirring constantly. You need to do this in 2 batches. Add the onion, garlic, and shallots and cook for about 5 minutes. Add the wine, V8 juice, tomato paste, and broth or water, stirring to blend in the paste. Season with salt and pepper, and drop in the prepared herb sack. Bring everything to a boil, then reduce the heat and simmer, uncovered, for 30–45 minutes.

2½ pounds stewing lamb (shoulder), cut into 1-inch pieces

1 medium onion, chopped

2 garlic cloves, minced (about 2 teaspoons)

2 tablespoons chopped shallots (about 2 shallots)

½ cup white wine

3 cups V8 vegetable juice

One 6-ounce can tomato paste

3 cups lamb (made from shoulder bones), veal, or chicken stock, or water

1 tablespoon sea salt

1 teaspoon coarsely ground black pepper

2 stalks celery, coarsely chopped (about 1 cup)

1 white turnip, peeled and coarsely chopped (about 1 cup)

1 cup chopped leeks (about 1 leek), both white and green parts

2 cups (about 8 ounces) white or cremini mushrooms

Juice of 1 lemon (about 2 tablespoons)

3 carrots, peeled and diced (about 1½ cups)

3. Add the celery, turnip, and leeks and simmer for 25 more minutes or until almost cooked.

4. Wash the mushrooms in the lemon juice, cut them in half if large, and add them to the stew, along with the carrots. Simmer for another 15 minutes, remove the herb sack, and serve the stew by itself or with rice or pasta.

Sukey and John Jamison on their farm

Firehouse Sausages, Onions, and Peppers

It's no secret that New York firehouses are known for their good cooks. So I was eager to visit one at mealtime. I went to Ladder Company 3 on East Thirteenth Street, one of the firehouses hardest hit by 9/11. As I walked in, I was struck by the wall covered with memorials to valiant firefighters.

Asking me to join them for lunch, Jimmy Andruzzi said, "We consider ourselves the brotherhood. It's like one big family." As we ate the brisket that Jimmy had prepared, someone commented that it didn't quite taste like the brisket made by a fireman who lost his life on 9/11. While we ate quietly, the man put his arm around Jimmy, telling him, "It's still okay."

Jimmy comes from a family of cooks. His mother taught him and his three brothers how to prepare food, and they all still do. (Two of the brothers are also firemen. The third, Joe, is an offensive guard with the New England Patriots.) "My dad would tell us to help my mom since there were no girls in the family," said Jimmy. "She gave us the basics; we watched because we wanted to help and we wanted to learn."

When it's Jimmy's turn to cook at the station, he has to take into consideration that an alarm might suddenly pull him away from his frying pans. "We jump up and leave, and we never know if we'll come back or not," he told me. At one meal he prepared this sausage dish, browning the meat on top of the stove and then transferring the frying pan to the oven. When I asked him why the two steps, he said that it is easier just to turn off the oven—the residual heat keeps the sausages warm until the firefighters return; otherwise the dish would be cold. In my own kitchen I just use one step. Serve this dish with a green salad and pasta.

YIELD: 6–8 SERVINGS

⅓ cup extra-virgin olive oil

2½–3 pounds sausages, half hot and half sweet, whole or cut up

1 large Spanish onion, quartered

½ bulb of garlic cloves, chopped

2 red peppers, cut in strips

2 green peppers, cut in strips

½ cup chopped fresh or 2 tablespoons dried basil

1. Pour 3 tablespoons of the olive oil into a large heavy frying pan set over medium-high heat. Brown the sausage for just a few minutes on both sides. Remove the meat to a plate.

2. Heat the remaining olive oil in the pan, then add the onions, garlic, and peppers and sauté, shaking the pan occasionally, until the onions start to release their juices and soften. This should take no more than 5 minutes.

3. Add the basil, salt and pepper, crushed tomatoes, crushed red pep-

Salt and freshly ground pepper to taste

3 cups crushed tomatoes

½ tablespoon crushed red pepper

Dash oregano

1 cup red wine

per, oregano, and red wine. Simmer, uncovered, for about 30 minutes. Return the sausage to the sauce for the last few minutes of cooking and simmer until it is cooked through. Turn onto a platter and serve alone or with pasta.

CABBAGE HILL FARM AND MOUNT KISCO DAY CARE CENTER

"The healthiest foods are closest to home" is the motto of the edible education program at the Mount Kisco Day Care Center's intergenerational program in Westchester County, New York. Nancy and Jerry Kohlberg, two local philanthropists, enthusiastically support the project and believe it brings together local children and the elderly in a common goal of learning about food and about the land that produces it.

Mrs. K., as Nancy is known at Cabbage Hill Farm, has long grown organic produce, raised grass-fed meat with the help of neighboring farms, and nurtured farm animals, many of them rare species, such as Highland and Devon cattle, Shetland sheep, and large black pigs. In the day care center, young and old gather to sow seeds in raised beds, harvest the vegetables, and prepare them for lunch and dinner, after which they always scrape their plates into the compost pile to keep the cycle going.

While the elders sit with little children, shelling peas or peeling carrots, a nutritionist talks to them about the health-giving properties of different foods and how enjoyable they can be. A grandmother rocks a baby, another shares stories with the toddlers, and they all grow closer through their appreciation of the foods they have produced together.

Sweet and Sour Stuffed Cabbage with Beef

This stuffed cabbage recipe, handed down to Nancy Kohlberg from her late mother, is prepared at the Mount Kisco Day Care Center and at Nancy's restaurant, the Flying Pig (located in the railroad station), with grass-fed beef. Nancy's mother's recipe appeared in the early 1940s in *Fox Meadow Favorites* in Scarsdale, where Nancy lived as a child. Except for the kind of meat used, the recipe has stayed the same.

Use a trick I learned years ago: After picking or buying the cabbage, place it in a gallon bag and freeze it. A day before cooking, defrost it at room temperature in a bowl to catch all the liquid. The leaves will be soft enough that you don't have to boil the cabbage to separate them. I find that this dish is one that tastes better the next day. For those of you under thirty, this chili sauce is the sweet kind found next to ketchup in the supermarket.

YIELD: ABOUT 24 ROLLS

1 head of cabbage, frozen (2 pounds)
2 pounds ground beef
1 medium onion, grated
1 clove garlic, minced (about 1 teaspoon)
Salt and freshly ground pepper
2 tablespoons chicken fat or vegetable oil
1 whole medium onion, chopped
⅓ cup brown sugar
Juice of 1 lemon
⅓ cup raisins
⅓ cup chili sauce
Salt and pinch of freshly ground black pepper

1. Defrost the cabbage the night before cooking. When it is completely defrosted, separate the leaves.

2. Preheat the oven to 350 degrees.

3. Mix the ground beef, the grated onion, and the garlic with the salt and pepper in a large bowl. Place 1 heaping tablespoon of the filling on each cabbage leaf. Tuck the ends in and roll up. Arrange the cabbage rolls seam side down in a 6-quart ovenproof casserole.

4. Heat the chicken fat or oil in a small frying pan and sauté the chopped onion for about 5 minutes. Stir in the brown sugar, lemon juice, raisins, and chili sauce and simmer for a few more minutes. Spoon the sauce over the cabbage leaves. Cover and bake in the oven for about 2 hours.

5. Turn the stuffed cabbage rolls onto a serving platter, spoon the sauce over, and serve.

Pork *Adovada*

The pork *adovada* at the M & J Sanitary Tortilla Factory in Albuquerque, served tucked into tortillas, is well worth the trip. As you enter this down-home restaurant you are greeted by candles surrounding an open Bible. Strands of garlic and chilies—to ward off evil spirits—adorn the white stucco walls. And there are paintings everywhere, many donated by artists who bartered their art for meals.

Bea and Jake Montoya's tortillas, made in the back on a tortilla machine that friends helped to assemble, accompany every dish. The most popular is the pork *adovada,* a traditional recipe that uses pork cushion—part of the pork butt—and was developed first by Jake. Then Pete Juarez, a friend from Mexico, added more seasonings, and Bea kept experimenting, cooking the stew until they arrived at the best formula. When we were leaving, Bea said to me, "I pray to God to bless all my food. The homeless are my guardian angels."

Bea Montoya at her restaurant in Albuquerque

YIELD: ABOUT 6–8 SERVINGS

1½ tablespoons salt

9 cloves garlic, chopped (about 3 tablespoons)

¼ teaspoon cumin seeds

½ teaspoon dried oregano

2 whole pork cushions or shoulder, about 2½–3 pounds in total, cut in 2-by-½-inch strips*

6 cups water

4 dried red chili pods (7–8 inches long; Colorado, Hatch, Chimayó, California, or Big Jim)

1 pequin or other hot pepper (optional)

1. Blend together the salt, garlic, cumin seeds, and oregano in a spice grinder or small food processor. Rub into the pork, cover with plastic wrap, and marinate 5 hours or overnight in the refrigerator.

2. When ready to cook the meat, place in a pot with 4 cups of the water. Bring to a boil, then simmer slowly, covered, over low heat for 40–45 minutes, skimming off the scum that accumulates.

3. While the meat is cooking, soak the dried chilies in the remaining 2 cups warm water for about 15 minutes, or until they are soft. Purée in a food processor along with a little of the soaking water. Add to the pot and continue simmering slowly, covered, for another 45 minutes, stirring occasionally. Adjust the seasonings. Remove the pork from the pot and shred. Return to the pot and reheat. If you like it hotter, add a little pequin, then serve tucked into tortillas.

* I have also made this dish with turkey and chicken; just halve the cooking time.

Sausage with Cabbage and Caraway Seeds

Bruce Aidells, the founder and creative personality behind Aidells Sausage Company, got started in the sausage business by accident. At the time, he was working at the Poulet restaurant and charcuterie in Berkeley, where he combined his love of chemistry with his love of food learning to make French and Italian sausages when Americans were still looking toward Europe. "Suddenly I got fired from Poulet," Bruce told me. "It was the best thing that happened to me." The year was 1983, and Bruce, a new homeowner, wanted to figure a way to both cover his mortgage and be his own boss. After spending twenty-five dollars to build a butcher's block table—he already had a refrigerator and a grinder—Bruce developed a relationship with a local sausage company and started producing the kind of sausage that Americans would soon love—andouille, then Italian sausage and chorizo. Within six months, he was making four hundred pounds of sausage a week. Today, his thirty different kinds of sausage, including the most popular—chicken-apple, sun-dried tomato, and habanero—are sold coast-to-coast.

Taking his lead, I now mix red cabbage with different types of sausage, simmering them with onions and apple. Sometimes I serve this dish alone, or for a complete meal I toss them with cooked bow-tie noodles. Easy to prepare, this is a great crowd pleaser, and I often bring it to potluck dinners.

YIELD: 6–8 SERVINGS

4 tablespoons vegetable oil

2 pounds (about 10 links) sausage, like kielbasa or chicken-apple

1 onion, diced

One 2-pound head of red cabbage, quartered, cored, and shredded

2 tart green apples, cored and cut into 1-inch cubes

1. Heat the oil in a Dutch oven or heavy skillet with a top and brown the sausage for about 5 minutes, turning occasionally. Remove from the pan.

2. Add the onion to the pan and sauté until translucent, about 5 minutes. Then add the cabbage and apples and continue to cook, stirring occasionally, about 5 more minutes. Pour on the cider vinegar and beef or chicken stock, and sprinkle with the caraway seeds, marjoram, bay leaves, and salt and pepper to taste. Bring to a boil, cover, and simmer

¼ cup cider vinegar

1 cup canned beef or chicken stock

1 teaspoon caraway seeds

½ teaspoon dried marjoram

2 bay leaves

1 teaspoon salt, or to taste

¼ teaspoon pepper, or to taste

slowly for another 25 minutes, stirring occasionally. Adjust the seasonings and return the sausage—whole or, if you would prefer, sliced in 1-inch rounds—to the pot. Cover and simmer a few more minutes or until the cabbage is soft. Turn onto a plate and serve as is or tossed with bow-tie pasta.

Jambalaya with Sausage and Shrimp

I have eaten many meals at the home of Paul Osterman, the academic dean at MIT's Sloan School of Management. Paul and his wife, Susan Eckstein, are both professors and view housekeeping and child rearing as a dual responsibility—and Paul chose to be the cook in the family, as he does not like to wash dishes. His food tastes great, although he has that guy way of putting the food on the table without ceremony. But it doesn't matter. This jambalaya, a dish he prepares for company, was superb. He believes spicy food makes his guests happy. And his family can eat the leftovers throughout the week. Although he has been preparing this recipe for years, he can't resist changing it a little every time.

YIELD: 6–8 SERVINGS

1 pound shrimp, peeled, with shells reserved

1 cup clam juice

2 cups canned chicken broth

1 cup water

3 tablespoons extra-virgin olive oil

1. To make the stock, rinse the shrimp shells in a colander, then put them in a large pot with the clam juice, chicken broth, and the water. Simmer over low heat, partially covered, for about 1 hour. Strain the stock to remove the shells and reserve. You should have 2 cups of stock. Add water to make 2½ cups.

2. While the shrimp stock is simmering, mix the ingredients for the seasoning mix for the sausage in a small bowl.

1 pound link sausage, sweet or spicy Italian sausage, or turkey kielbasa, cut in bite-size pieces

3 medium onions, chopped (about 3 cups)

6 cloves garlic, chopped (about 2 tablespoons)

1 green bell pepper, chopped

1 red bell pepper, chopped

2 medium tomatoes, chopped

2 cups uncooked long-grain rice

2 teaspoons salt, or to taste

1 cup canned or homemade tomato sauce

¼ cup chopped fresh parsley

SEASONING MIX FOR THE SAUSAGE

1 teaspoon ground cumin

1 tablespoon paprika

1 tablespoon minced garlic

2 teaspoons freshly ground black pepper

Cayenne pepper to taste

3 teaspoons cinnamon

SEASONING MIX FOR THE JAMBALAYA

3 bay leaves

Cayenne pepper to taste

1 teaspoon paprika

1 tablespoon fresh oregano or 1 teaspoon dried

1 teaspoon dried thyme

1 teaspoon dried basil

2 teaspoons freshly ground black pepper

3. Heat a tablespoon or so of the olive oil in a small frying pan and add the sausage pieces, sprinkling them with the sausage seasoning mix. Brown until almost blackened and the sausage is cooked through. Set aside.

4. Mix the seasoning mix for the jambalaya in another bowl.

5. To make the jambalaya, pour the remaining olive oil into a large frying pan. Over medium heat sauté the onions, garlic, and green and red peppers, together with half the jambalaya spice mixture. Continue until the onions are translucent, then add the chopped tomatoes, the rice, and the salt and sauté for another 3 minutes. Stir in the tomato sauce, the stock, the remainder of the seasoning mix, and the sausage pieces. Bring to a boil, cover, and turn the heat to very low. Cook for about 20 minutes or until the rice is done but still moist. Remove the cover, stir in the peeled shrimp, and cook until pink. Discard the bay leaves. Remove to a serving platter, add salt to taste, and sprinkle with parsley. Serve immediately.

Choucroute Garni

Braised Sauerkraut with Sausages and Meat

When I asked André Soltner, former chef at New York's Lutèce, what he thought about all these superstar chefs today, he had a lot to say. "We chefs are not movie stars but craftsmen," he told me. "Chefs are going overboard. There are a few guys who create, but all the others copy. Chefs are here to cook good food so that the customers feel good after the meal. If I want to change ingredients with the Japanese or Chinese, I go to a Chinese restaurant."

André worked the stove in his restaurant throughout his entire career. Even when he served haute cuisine, he also offered the everyday food of his native Alsace. "It's crazy," he added. "The real food, it is not all this blah blah and fireworks and stuff. I make real French food."

One of his Alsatian recipes is *choucroute garni,* which today, with all the good sausages available, can be a very exciting dish. It is often served at Super Bowl parties with smoked pork, corned beef, duck breast, or just a variety of sausages. I like to make it using corned beef and an array of horseradish sauces, mustards, and relishes.

YIELD: 8–10 SERVINGS

4 pounds sauerkraut

3 tablespoons chicken or duck fat or vegetable oil

¼ pound smoked goose breast or smoked pork, diced

1 medium onion, thinly sliced, plus 1 whole medium onion, peeled

2 cups (approximately) dry white Alsatian wine

2 cups (approximately) water

2 bay leaves

1 tablespoon juniper berries

1 tablespoon caraway seeds

2 garlic cloves, smashed

1. Preheat the oven to 325 degrees.

2. Wash the sauerkraut in cold water, then drain it. Wash it again, this time in very hot water. Drain it and squeeze out the water by forming the sauerkraut into balls and pressing them between your hands.

3. Melt the chicken or duck fat or warm the vegetable oil over medium heat in a large, heavy-bottomed, ovenproof pot. Stir in the goose breast or smoked pork and the sliced onion. Sauté for a few minutes, but don't let the onions brown. Pour in the wine and 1 cup of the water and add 1 bay leaf.

4. Wrap the remaining bay leaf, the juniper berries, the caraway seeds, and the garlic cloves in a piece of cheesecloth. Tie with a string and drop into the pot.

4 whole cloves

Freshly ground black pepper to taste

6 medium baking potatoes, peeled, washed, and quartered (about 2 pounds)

3 pounds cured and cooked corned beef or roast pork

8 cooked sausages such as bratwurst or apple

5. Insert the 4 cloves into the whole onion and add it to the pot, followed by the sauerkraut, pepper, and potatoes. If necessary, add enough more wine or water so that the liquid half covers the vegetables. Bring to a boil.

6. As soon as the liquid reaches a boil, cover the pot, slide it into the preheated oven, and cook for 1 hour.

7. Add the corned beef or roast pork to the pot, return to the oven, and cook for another 15 minutes.

8. Remove the pot from the oven and add the sausages. Bring everything to a simmer over medium heat for about 5 minutes or until the sausage heats through. Remove the spice bag and whole onion.

9. To serve, spoon the sauerkraut onto the center of a serving platter. Slice the corned beef or pork against the grain and arrange the slices on top of the sauerkraut. Surround the sauerkraut with the sausage and the potatoes. Accompany *choucroute garni* with bottles of mustard, horseradish sauce, and relishes—and, of course, a dry Alsatian wine.

Rum Ribs

John Phillips, a food hobbyist (page 210) who lives in Manhattan, has been fiddling with this rib recipe for years. One day, he was watching Alton Brown making ribs on the Food Network, using dry rub and then braising in the sauce. John tried to duplicate Brown's technique, using his own ingredients. The succulent ribs he now makes prove how successful he was. Since his family roots are in Nevis and St. Kitts, John likes to cook with a Caribbean accent, adding flavors like dark rum, ginger, and lime. This slow-cooked dish is definitely for weekends or parties—it takes time. But you can do the braising a day ahead and refrigerate the ribs. Before serving, let them come to room temperature, then brush them with the reduced glaze and finish them off under the broiler.

Rum Ribs (continued)

DRY RUB

1 teaspoon salt

1½ teaspoons ground cloves

5 cloves garlic, minced
(about 5 teaspoons)

1 teaspoon finely ground
black pepper

2 teaspoons ground ginger

2 bay leaves, crushed

2 whole racks of baby-back pork
ribs (about 2 pounds each)

BRAISING LIQUID

1 cup dark rum

½ cup firmly packed
brown sugar

Juice of 3–4 limes (⅓ cup freshly
squeezed lime juice)

Grated zest of 2 limes

1. Preheat the oven to 250 degrees.

2. To make the dry rub, stir together the salt, cloves, garlic, pepper, ginger, and crushed bay leaves in a small bowl. Place each slab of baby-back ribs on a piece of heavy-duty aluminum foil, shiny side down. Sprinkle each side of the ribs generously with the rub, patting the spices gently into the meat. Wrap the foil around the ribs, fold to seal, and refrigerate for at least 1 hour or overnight.

3. To prepare the braising liquid, stir together the rum, brown sugar, lime juice, and zest in a small bowl.

4. Arrange the ribs on a baking sheet. Open 1 end of each foil-wrapped packet, pour in half of the braising liquid, and reseal. Tilt the baking sheet to distribute the braising liquid equally in each packet. Braise the ribs in the oven for 2½ hours.

5. Remove the ribs from the oven; open 1 end of the foil and pour the braising liquid into a cup. Skim the fat off the top of the braising liquid or refrigerate until the fat separates, then remove the fat. Bring the remaining liquid to a simmer in a small saucepan and cook until it is reduced by half or it reaches a thick, syrupy consistency.

6. Open each packet completely and brush some of the glaze over the ribs. Broil the ribs resting on the foil until the glaze caramelizes lightly. Be vigilant—the glaze will burn if left under the broiler a few moments too long. Remove from the broiler, slice each rack into rib portions, and serve the remaining glaze on the side. This is delicious served with coconut rice (page 210).

Desserts

When I first moved to Washington, D.C., more than twenty-seven years ago, I discovered the most delicious lemon tart at a local restaurant. I recently made the recipe for the first time in ages and was surprised to find that it didn't taste nearly as good as I remembered so I worked on the recipe and improved it. It was then that I realized how much baking, more than any other cooking art, has changed over the past few decades. In the beginning, cookbook authors like Julia Child tantalized us with French desserts like *tarte tatin* and *tarte aux citrons* that Child, in her seminal works, demystified. Later, cookbook writers like Alice Medrich, Rose Levy Berenbaum, and Lisa Yockelson, as well as magazines like *Cook's Illustrated*, deconstructed these classic recipes to come up with so-called perfect renditions. As a result, we are today much more informed cooks.

Our ingredients are better than ever too, in part, thanks to people like John Scharffenberger, a self-proclaimed member of the upper-middle-class diaspora. "My original plan was to grow marijuana, raise goats, and plant grapes," John told me in his Berkeley, California, office. John did try growing strawberries and making champagne before he found himself in the chocolate trade.

One day, standing around in his friend Robert Steinberg's kitchen, John tasted some chocolate Robert had just brought back with him from France. Robert, a dilettante foodie, was trying to reproduce the French chocolate in his home kitchen, using a coffee roaster to roast the cocoa beans from which chocolate is made. John was beguiled by the chocolate and became obsessed with the idea of making good chocolate in America.

"We spent about a year talking about the chocolate business," John told me. "We looked at the structure of the flavor of the beans we found in the world of cacao. We found that some were fruity with no finish, some had incredible depth with no high

Clockwise from top right: Red velvet cake; Ann Amernick taking chocolate chip cookies from the oven; Anne Luzzatto's apple-apricot crostata; Putting up applesauce on an Amish farm; Elizabeth Ryan and a basket of her Hudson Valley apples; Famous Amos at his home in Hawaii

note, some had a wonderful fruitiness that showed itself in the middle palate, some were smoky and smelled like ham."

John stuck with chocolate, and today Scharffen Berger, an American chocolate company headquartered in Berkeley, is changing the way Americans taste chocolate. "We want consumers to really look at the cacao percentage in milk and dark chocolate. That is where the flavor comes from," John told me. "We're not a fancy brand. Our chocolate is for everybody who likes to cook and eat."

There are other ingredients that we are being urged to reconsider, too. Today, many of us use fresh Mexican (or Bourbon or Tahitian) vanilla beans; top-quality French, Belgian, and now American chocolate; gourmet butters; and stone-ground organic flour.

Beautifully presented desserts at restaurants are trickling down to the home cook. Just as chefs have tantalized our appetites with little tastes at the beginning of the meal, they are now giving us a big bang at the end with beautifully presented desserts. They have given us chocolate-almond cake with chocolate mousse filling (page 373), homey desserts like pineapple upside-down cake (page 388), and molten chocolate cake (page 371), mango cheesecake (page 387), Thai sticky rice with mango (page 414), and even a delicious rum cake from Jamaica (page 384).

One summer my daughters and I took a trip to the Big Island of Hawaii. Trekking across an active volcano, we thought its black lava, still smoldering, resembled swirls of chocolate sauce. That quickly put us all in the mood to taste some real chocolate. The next day, the three of us visited the Original Hawaiian Chocolate Factory, located in Kahalu'u on a cocoa plantation nourished by the rich volcanic soil. The factory, outside of Kailua Kona, is owned and run by Bob and Pam Cooper, who hail from North Carolina. "Ours is the only chocolate in the United States that is grown, hand-picked, and processed in one place," Bob told us the moment we entered his office. "Usually the beans are a blend from different geographical regions around the world, all fifteen to twenty degrees north or south of the equator. Our challenge is to produce chocolate that tastes good using only 100 percent Hawaii-grown cocoa beans." And that is what they are doing. Their first bittersweet chocolate appeared in 2000.

As we walked outside, Bob plucked a twig with tiny white and pink flowers for my daughters and said, "This is how chocolate starts." Those flowers grow into an oblong pod that is about eight

inches long and resembles a football. Handing us one, he told us that inside the pods are cocoa beans. The pods are split open with a machete, and the cocoa beans, about twenty-five to forty per pod, are scooped out and put in untreated wood boxes to ferment for about a week, after which they are left to dry in the sun for a month. Once dried, the beans are roasted and their shells broken open by machine. The nib inside is the meat of the cocoa bean.

The nib is then put into a conch shell, aerating the chocolate, to develop the flavor and smoothness. "This refiner is a pivotal piece of chocolate-making equipment," Bob explained, as he showed us one of his machines. "It grinds and presses the nib into a chocolate liqueur." Cocoa butter, sugar, and vanilla are added next, the amounts of each determining how bitter and how sweet the chocolate will be. Finally, the chocolate is heated to a very precise temperature—a process called tempering—and poured into molds. "The tempering process gives chocolate its true essence of flavor, smooth finish, and snap, the sign of good-quality chocolate," Bob told us as he gave us a taste of that true essence. "This is the truest in Mother Nature's flavor, the Hawaiian way."

Chocolate Red Velvet Cake with Chocolate Icing

When I was growing up, I always wanted a simple chocolate cake for my birthday. I still do. This velvety chocolate cake gets its name from its smooth texture and reddish hue. The original recipe called for red beet juice—in some parts of the country it is called beet cake—but was altered by manufacturers who added red food coloring to the cake. "Red coloring is evil and dangerous for children and other living things," Carole Greenwood, a chef in Washington, D.C., told me. She refuses to use food coloring but loves this buttermilk-based velvety chocolate cake, and uses red wine vinegar or beet juice for the color. She also makes her version less sweet, using both good-quality cocoa powder and bittersweet chocolate.

YIELD: 1 CAKE SERVING 8 PEOPLE

1 cup (2 sticks) unsalted butter

½ cup water

½ cup good-quality cocoa powder

2 extra-large eggs

1 tablespoon vanilla extract

1 cup buttermilk

1½ teaspoons baking soda

2 tablespoons pickled beet juice or red wine vinegar

1½ cups bleached all-purpose flour

½ cup cake flour

½ cup cornstarch

1 teaspoon salt

1½ cups granulated sugar

1. Preheat the oven to 375 degrees and grease two 9-inch round cake pans.

2. Melt the butter in a small saucepan over low heat. Remove the pan from the heat, stir in the water and cocoa powder, and allow the mixture to cool.

3. Beat the eggs in the bowl of an electric mixer, then add the vanilla, buttermilk, baking soda, and beet juice or red wine vinegar and stir well.

4. Sift together the all-purpose flour, cake flour, cornstarch, salt, and sugar into the bowl. Pour in the butter and then the egg mixture and blend thoroughly on low.

5. Pour the batter into the prepared cake pans. Bake for about 20–25 minutes or until the cake pulls away from the sides of the pan and a toothpick inserted into the center comes out clean.

6. Cool the cakes for a few minutes, then turn them out onto wire racks, and frost and fill the center with the chocolate icing.

Chocolate Icing

YIELD: ENOUGH FROSTING FOR 1 CAKE SERVING 8 PEOPLE

1 cup heavy cream
½ tablespoon unsalted butter
2 tablespoons sugar
8 ounces bittersweet chocolate, finely chopped
2 teaspoons vanilla extract
⅛ teaspoon salt

1. Place the cream, butter, and sugar in a small saucepan and stir over medium heat until hot and bubbly.

2. Remove the pan from the heat and add the chocolate, stirring slowly until smooth and silky. Add the vanilla and the salt. Taste and adjust the sweetness to your taste. Cool for about 15 minutes before frosting the cake.

Molten Chocolate Cake

The most popular dessert I've ever created started as a mistake," wrote Jean-Georges Vongerichten, one of the most creative chefs working today. Like many chefs, Jean-Georges served a tiny, rich, simple chocolate cupcake, like French grandmothers used to make, as part of his petits fours platter. "One day, I overcompensated and removed the cakes from the oven far too early. I would have realized that in a second but got distracted before I had a chance to check them. By the time I turned around, somebody else had cut into one, and the hot undercooked interior had spilled out onto the plate. After I was done screaming, I realized that the effect was beautiful."

Thus, an instant American classic was born: molten chocolate cake, aka fallen soufflé cake, a dessert now found just about everywhere. For convenience, you can mix ahead and place the batter in muffin tins and refrigerate. Be sure your oven temperature is accurate because timing is key to this recipe.

YIELD: 8 SERVINGS

1 cup (2 sticks) unsalted butter, plus some for buttering the muffin tins
1–2 tablespoons cocoa for dusting the molds
8 ounces good bittersweet chocolate, such as Scharffen Berger or Ghirardelli

1. Preheat the oven to 450 degrees. Butter 8 muffin tins and lightly dust them with cocoa powder. Tap out the excess cocoa.

2. Using a double boiler, gently heat the butter and chocolate together until the chocolate is melted, then remove the pan from the heat and let cool slightly.

4 large eggs

4 large egg yolks

½ cup sugar

⅓ cup unbleached all-purpose flour

Vanilla ice cream

Fresh berries

3. Beat the eggs, yolks, and sugar together with a whisk or electric beater in a medium bowl until pale and thick.

4. While the chocolate is still warm, give it a quick stir and fold into the beaten eggs. Add the flour and whisk just enough to blend everything together.

5. Spoon the batter into the 8 tins. (At this point, you can cover and refrigerate the desserts for several hours or overnight; just make sure to leave time to bring them to room temperature before baking.)

6. Bake for 10 minutes, at which point the center will still be quite soft but the sides will be set.

7. Remove from the oven. Run a knife around each tin and invert the cakes onto a cookie sheet and let sit for about 10 seconds. Carefully transfer each cake to individual serving plates and serve immediately with vanilla ice cream and fresh berries.

A CHOCOHOLIC'S DREAM

Picture this: chocolate fudge, chocolate walnut cheesecake, chocolate marquise cake with pistachio sauce, chocolate mousse almond cake, truffles, chocolate pie, and more than a dozen other luscious chocolate desserts, all under one roof.

For the past twenty or so years, Joel and Lynda Mulhauser have held a chocolate dessert party for thirty guests at their home in Washington, D.C. The rules are simple: the Mulhausers offer their home—decorated with posters, cards, mugs, and other homages to chocolate—and prepare a buffet dinner, and the guests bring chocolate desserts, each numbered so that their creators are anonymous.

During the dessert tasting, chocolate lovers divide into two categories: those who favor sweeter milk chocolate versus bittersweet chocolate purists. Each person rates the desserts, giving five points for the first prize selection, three for second, and one for third.

First prize takes home a piece of the Mulhausers' chocolate memorabilia: chocolate cookbooks, chocolate champagne corks, or cookie jars with chocolate in them. One year, the prize was a subscription to *Chocolatier* magazine in a box filled with chocolate kisses. Consolation prizes—large chocolate bars or something else, anything else, chocolate—go to every guest. And the next day, the Mulhausers, with a refrigerator full of desserts, enjoy the leftovers.

Chocolate-Almond Cake with Chocolate Mousse Filling

This chocolate cake, described by the winning cook (see box) as a "puzzle with a surprising inside almond touch," was created by Jimmy Schmidt, chef of Detroit's Rattlesnake Club, and appeared in *Bon Appétit* magazine.

"I use all organic ingredients to marry the texture of a very rich chocolate cake with an intense chocolate mousse," Jimmy told me. "The bittersweet chocolate is melted and no other sugar is added so you have a deep chocolate flavor."

CAKE

Butter for greasing the pan

2 tablespoons confectioners' sugar

9 large eggs, separated, at room temperature

¾ cup sugar

1 tablespoon vanilla extract

Pinch of salt

¾ cup unsweetened Dutch-process cocoa powder

¼ teaspoon cream of tartar

14 ounces almond paste* (not marzipan)

1–2 tablespoons plus ¾ cup amaretto liqueur

MOUSSE

27 ounces bittersweet chocolate, chopped

3 tablespoons unsalted butter

4 cups heavy cream, at room temperature

Whipped cream (optional)

* Available at most supermarkets or from baking suppliers.

1. Preheat the oven to 350 degrees. Butter a jelly-roll pan and line it with parchment paper. Butter the paper and dust a clean kitchen towel with the confectioners' sugar.

2. Beat the egg yolks, sugar, vanilla, and salt in a large bowl until pale yellow and thick. Sift the cocoa powder onto the yolks and whisk it in.

3. In a standing mixer with the whisk attachment, whip the egg whites with the cream of tartar until soft peaks form. Stir about ⅓ of the egg whites into the egg yolk mixture. Gently fold in the remaining egg whites, just until combined.

4. Quickly but carefully spread the batter evenly in the prepared pan. Slide the pan into the oven and bake until the cake is springy to the touch, about 25 minutes.

5. Pulse the almond paste with 1 tablespoon amaretto liqueur in a food processor until the paste is soft enough to roll out, adding a little more amaretto if necessary to get the right consistency.

6. Scrape the almond paste onto a sheet of wax paper, cover it with another sheet, pat it flat, then, with a rolling pin, roll it into a rectangle approximately 9 by 14 inches. Refrigerate it, encased in the wax paper, until needed.

7. Remove the cake from the oven and turn it out onto the sugar-dusted towel. Peel off the parchment paper. Trim ½ inch off the edges of the cake.

8. Peel 1 piece of the wax paper off the chilled almond paste. Turn the almond paste over, lay it on top of the still-hot cake, and peel off the remaining wax paper. Roll the cake up jelly-roll fashion. Let it cool completely.

9. Pour the ¾ cup amaretto into a shallow bowl or pie plate. Cut the jelly roll into ⅓-inch-thick slices. Briefly dip 1 side of each slice into the amaretto. Cover the bottom of a 10-inch springform pan with the slices, dipped side down, working from the edge to the center, arranging the seam ends of the slices so they face the same direction. Press them firmly to fit snugly into the pan. Refrigerate while preparing the mousse.

10. For the mousse, melt the chocolate and butter together in a double boiler over barely simmering water, stirring until smooth. Pour it into a large bowl and immediately begin gently stirring in—in 3 batches—the heavy cream. When all the cream has been thoroughly blended in, pour everything onto the amaretto cake slices in the springform pan. Cover the cake and refrigerate it overnight.

11. Invert the cake onto a serving plate. If you want, decorate with whipped cream.

Citron-Scented Sponge Cake with a Splash of Berries and Candied Lemon Zest

Ellyn Goodrich, the former pastry chef at the Homestead Restaurant in Homer, Alaska, has had to learn to make do with what is available. Married to a commercial fisherman, she has no problems when her ingredients come from the sea, but she often does when they are from the land. When making this sponge cake, she candies lemon zest and uses the huge salmonberries that grow in Homer, fresh in summer and frozen in winter.

Candied Zest

YIELD: I CUP ZEST

2 lemons
4 cups water
2½ cups sugar

1. Peel the outer skin of the lemons—you don't want any of the bitter white pith—and cut it into thin strips. Bring 2 cups of the water to a boil, add the strips of zest, and boil them for 2 minutes to remove any bitterness. Drain.

2. Stir 2 cups of the sugar into the remaining 2 cups of water and bring to a boil. Stir until the sugar is fully dissolved. Add the zest, lower the heat to medium, and cover. Simmer for 10 minutes.

3. Drain the zest in a colander and then spread it in a single layer on a piece of wax or parchment paper to cool. Rinse and dry the colander. Toss the zest with the remaining sugar. Put the sugared zest back in the colander and shake off the excess sugar. Store the candied zest in an airtight container.

Sponge Cake

YIELD: 12 SERVINGS

9 large eggs, separated
1¾ cups sugar
Grated zest and juice of
2 lemons, plus 1 tablespoon
lemon juice
Grated zest of 1 orange
¾ cup all-purpose flour
2 teaspoons salt
3 pints mixed raspberries,
blueberries, blackberries,
and diced strawberries

1. Preheat the oven to 325 degrees and grease a 10-inch Bundt pan.

2. Beat the egg yolks in a large mixing bowl until pale and thick, then pour in 1½ cups of the sugar in a slow and steady stream. Stir in the zest and the juice of the 2 lemons and the orange zest.

3. Sift together the flour and salt and fold it into the yolks.

4. Whip the egg whites until stiff but not dry. Stir about a third of them into the yolks, and then quickly, yet gently, fold in the rest. Pour the batter into the Bundt pan.

5. Bake in the preheated oven until the cake pulls away from the sides of the pan, about 50 minutes. Take it out and let it cool for a few minutes, then turn it out onto a plate to cool completely.

6. An hour before serving, mix the berries with the remaining ¼ cup sugar and the tablespoon lemon juice.

7. Take a sharp knife and cut out a few inches from the center of the top of the cake. Fill the hole with the berries, reserving some to scatter around the sides of the cake. Garnish the cake with the candied zest (preceding recipe) and bring it to the table.

Apple Strudel

Jim Kantzios's wife, Maria (see page 378), perfected the art of making flaky apple strudel using the Athens brand of phyllo dough years ago. Contrary to popular wisdom, Maria recommends removing phyllo from the freezer the night before baking. "The dough has to be relaxed when you use it," she said. "If it is humid in the kitchen, the only thing is to sprinkle a little cornstarch between the layers. If the phyllo dries out or you are too slow at working with the phyllo, put a wet towel over it." This recipe calls for eight sheets of phyllo dough, but you may need a few more in case it tears. Carefully cover any dough you do not use and refrigerate; do not refreeze.

YIELD: 6–8 SERVINGS

Juice of 1 lemon
6 Granny Smith apples
¾ cup (1½ sticks) unsalted butter, plus 2 tablespoons butter
½ cup brown sugar
¼ cup plus 2 tablespoons granulated sugar
¼ cup cognac, brandy, orange liqueur, or sherry
2 tablespoons raisins (optional)
¾ teaspoon ground cinnamon
Pinch ground cloves

1. Half-fill a large bowl with cold water and the lemon juice. Peel and core the apples. Cut them in half from top to bottom, and then thinly slice each half crosswise. Put the apple slices in the bowl of cold lemon water as you work to keep them from discoloring.

2. In a medium frying pan, melt 4 tablespoons of the butter with the brown sugar and ¼ cup of the granulated sugar. Drain the apple slices and toss them in the pan along with the liqueur and the raisins. Simmer slowly for about 25 minutes, stirring occasionally, until the apples are soft and the juices have reduced by half. Take the pan off the heat and add ½ teaspoon of the cinnamon and the cloves. Let cool.

¼ cup walnuts
8 sheets phyllo dough, defrosted
1 large egg
1 tablespoon milk
Confectioners' sugar for dusting
Vanilla ice cream

3. Prepare the nut mixture by pulsing the nuts, the remaining 2 tablespoons of sugar, and the remaining ¼ teaspoon cinnamon in a food processor equipped with a steel blade until almost crumblike but still crunchy.

4. Preheat the oven to 375 degrees and grease a jelly-roll pan.

5. Remove the phyllo dough from the package and cover it with a damp cloth. (You should always keep the sheets of phyllo you are not working with covered; otherwise they will dry out.) Melt the remaining 8 tablespoons of butter.

6. Brush the tops of 2 sheets of phyllo dough with butter and place one on top of the other. Sprinkle some of the nut mixture on top. Cover this layer of nuts with 2 more sheets of phyllo, each brushed with butter. Sprinkle the top layer with more nuts and cover it with half the apples, leaving a 1-inch border on the short side of the phyllo nearest you. Carefully fold the border in and roll up the dough and filling as you would a jelly roll, brushing with butter as you go. When you have finished rolling, carefully lift the roll and place it in the prepared pan. Repeat with the remaining phyllo dough and filling to make 2 rolls.

7. Mix the egg and the milk to make a wash. Brush the wash over the dough. Using a serrated knife, score the tops of the dough in 4–6 evenly spaced places, depending on how big you want your slices. Brush again with the wash and bake until golden, about 30 minutes. This can be done several hours before you want to serve it. When cool, slice through the phyllo. Just reheat it for 5 minutes in a 375-degree oven and sprinkle with the confectioners' sugar. Serve with ice cream if you wish.

Thanks to the ingenuity of two hardworking Greek Americans, it is rare that Greeks or Greek Americans—or anyone else, for that matter—make phyllo dough (pronounced "*fee-lo*") from scratch anymore.

Jim Kantzios and his wife, Maria, came to the United States from their native Macedonia in 1951. They settled in Cleveland and opened Athens Import and Bakery, selling Greek foods to the growing Greek population. At the time, most Greek Americans made phyllo dough at home or bought it at their neighborhood bakery. Jim himself toiled in his basement, making phyllo dough mostly for Greek holiday dishes.

After mixing high-gluten flour with water, salt, and a bit of oil, Jim would roll out the dough on a round table, walking around and gently stretching it until it was so thin it was translucent. "Just before Easter, we had to make so much phyllo for our clientele. We thought we could make it easier."

In 1953, when Jim was augmenting his salary by working on an assembly line at the Ford Motor Company, he had a dream that he could develop a machine that would roll out phyllo dough the way a pasta machine rolls out pasta. After sixteen years of experimenting, he joined forces with his nephew, George Pappas, and together they perfected a machine that makes a very thin dough.

Phyllo is now sold in supermarkets everywhere, even in their native Greece. And it is all produced by the same machine that Jim and George developed.

What makes this story even more amazing is that phyllo dough is now used in place of strudel and flaky Indian doughs, as well as many other kinds of pastry dough. Today, New York's Poseidon Bakery, on Ninth Avenue, is probably the only place that still makes phyllo by hand daily. And their clientele is no longer predominantly Greek. They sell to Indian, Hungarian, Czech buyers—you name it.

Greek Americans are also finding new uses for phyllo. At Greek Orthodox church fairs in Jacksonville and Orlando, "Never on Sundae" is a popular dessert: vanilla ice cream, leftover crushed phyllo dough, and nuts, drizzled with honey.

Baklava Ice Cream Cake with Grand Marnier Sauce

I first tasted this amazing cake at Ziziki's Restaurant in Dallas. Its creator, chef-owner Costa Arabatzis, grew up in Redlands, California, on his Greek grandmother's spanakopita and pastitsio. After graduating from Cornell's hotel and restaurant management school, Costa moved to Dallas. There, in 1994, he opened Ziziki's, an upscale contemporary restaurant with a menu based on his grandmother's Greek and his mother's Italian recipes. His love of ice cream led him to invent this baklava ice cream cake, alternating layers of his grandmother's baklava with rich vanilla bean ice cream and a honey-cinnamon syrup drizzled over the cake, capped with orange slices and a dash of Grand Marnier. What I like is that the ice cream tempers the sweetness of the baklava.

YIELD: ABOUT 12 SERVINGS

CAKE

1 cup (2 sticks) unsalted butter
1 pound shelled walnuts
½ cup sugar
1 teaspoon ground cinnamon
½ teaspoon grated nutmeg
2 pounds (about 20 sheets) phyllo dough

1. Melt the butter in a small saucepan over low heat. Remove the pan from the heat and cool for 2–3 minutes.

2. Preheat the oven to 325 degrees and lightly brush a jelly-roll pan with a bit of the butter.

3. Scatter the walnuts on a cookie sheet and bake until fragrant and toasted, about 10 minutes. Let cool slightly, then coarsely grind or chop them with the sugar, cinnamon, and nutmeg in a food processor fitted with a steel blade. Add 3 tablespoons of the butter and pulse just enough to moisten it.

4. To assemble the baklava, lay a sheet of phyllo on the bottom of the jelly-roll pan, brush it with some of the butter, cover it with another sheet of phyllo, and brush that sheet as well. Repeat this process until you have used 10 sheets. (As you work, keep a moist cloth over the unused sheets of phyllo to keep them from drying out.)

5. Set aside 1 cup of the nut mixture for later use on the ice cream. Sprinkle the remaining walnuts evenly on top of the assembled phyllo layers. Cover them with 10 more sheets of phyllo, brushing each sheet with butter as before.

6. With a very sharp knife, score 2-inch squares, slicing through only the top phyllo sheets. (This is done to help bake the phyllo more

SYRUP

1¼ cups honey

1¼ cups water

1¼ cups sugar

1 cinnamon stick

Juice and zest of ½ orange

½ teaspoon grated lemon zest

½ teaspoon vanilla extract

¼ cup Grand Marnier or other
orange-flavored liqueur

½ gallon vanilla ice cream with
vanilla bean

Orange slices

Fresh mint for garnish (optional)

evenly; it is also easier to slice after baking if the cuts are already there.) Bake until the top of the baklava is evenly golden, about 35–40 minutes.

7. Prepare the syrup while the baklava is baking. Bring the honey, water, sugar, cinnamon stick, orange juice and zest, and lemon zest to a boil in a medium saucepan. Reduce the heat and simmer gently, uncovered, until the sauce has thickened to a syrup, about 30 minutes. Remove the pot from the heat and immediately stir in the vanilla extract and the Grand Marnier. Set the sauce aside and let it cool.

8. Remove the baklava from the oven and evenly pour about 1 cup of the cooled syrup over it. Let cool for several hours.

9. Use the bottom of a 10-inch springform pan to guide you as you cut 2 circles from the baked dough. You may have to patch together the second circle. Gently, using 2 spatulas, transfer 1 circle to the bottom of the pan. Press down.

10. Remove the ice cream from the freezer to slightly soften it. Work quickly so that the ice cream doesn't melt, or it won't freeze properly. Spoon on half of the vanilla ice cream. Cover with the remaining baklava circle. Spoon and spread the remaining ice cream on top and sprinkle with the reserved walnuts, gently patting them down into the ice cream. Place in the freezer uncovered for 1 hour to harden, then cover with aluminum foil and freeze several hours or overnight.

11. To serve, slice in wedges. Splash each piece with a little of the remaining syrup or serve the syrup on the side. Garnish with orange slices and fresh mint.

In 1973, in a converted dry cleaning joint not far from Harvard Square, Steve Herrell made ice cream history. The shop, called Steve's, with its mismatched chairs and wild-colored tables, looked like so many other college hangouts. It wasn't. One look at the wall, where ice cream flavors were written colorfully on little slats of wood, made that clear. Malted vanilla, cookie dough peanut butter swirl, and triple chocolate pudding: who'd ever tasted—or, for that matter, imagined—such flavors thirty years ago?

Long lines formed every night for Steve's ice cream; he was clearly onto something. Not content just to scoop his handmade ice cream into a cone, Steve had come up with "mix-ins," thereby cementing his place in ice cream history.

When Steve's opened, mainstream ice cream flavors included vanilla, chocolate, strawberry, coffee, peach, maple walnut, and lemon. The only premium ice cream was Häagen-Dazs, started by a Polish immigrant named Reuben Mattus. (Mattus gave his ice cream a Danish-sounding name because the Danes had been good to the Jews during World War II.) Even Häagen-Dazs's most exotic flavors at the time were rum raisin and boysenberry. Steve Herrell decided the time was right to mix things up a bit.

"Steve Herrell was a legend. He pioneered the rejuvenation of homemade ice cream and mix-ins," said Jerry Greenfield, cofounder of Ben & Jerry's ice cream. One day in the mid-1970s, Ben Cohen and Jerry Greenfield came to watch Steve, the first to chop up Heath bars and Oreo cookies and mix them into ice cream. "At first we incorporated mix-ins," said Jerry Greenfield of the early days of Ben & Jerry's. "Then we realized that we weren't very good at it." These days, Ben & Jerry's Chocolate Chip Cookie Dough is equally as popular as vanilla and chocolate, their Vanilla Heath Bar Crunch ice cream has given new life to the Heath bar, and ice cream chains throughout the country use spades and scoopers to incorporate candy and cookie mix-ins.

Now in his late fifties, Steve reigns at Herrell's, the ice cream parlor he opened in 1980 on a side street in Northampton, Massachusetts, after he sold the Steve's company in 1977. "I missed ice cream and I missed the action," said Steve as he looked out over his shop, brightly painted in what he calls "Caribbean colors." These days, he sits high up in a glass office, built so he can watch his customers enjoying his ice cream.

Sitting across from Steve in one of his wooden booths, I asked him how he felt thirty years after his idea had spread throughout the country with little financial benefit to him. "Good," he said. "I feel it is very rewarding that people love so much what I have done. I can barely handle this small business with bookkeeping, personnel, and a landlord. Fortunately, it is balanced by seeing and talking to happy customers, seeing people enjoying their sundaes and shakes. My success is still word of mouth." Thanks, Steve, for all the smiles.

Mango Ice Cream Cake

I learned the technique of making pure ice cream cake from Steve Herrell (see page 381), but this cake is inspired by my daughter Daniela, who likes mango and vanilla ice cream. The intensity of the dried mango slices and preserved ginger only enhances the flavor. This also works well with ginger ice cream. Whichever ice cream you try, work as quickly as possible when making this cake. Once the ice cream melts, it doesn't refreeze properly.

YIELD: 10–12 SLICES

3 pints mango ice cream

1 cup crystallized ginger, chopped small

1 cup dried mango slices, chopped small

3 pints vanilla ice cream

1 cup mango purée* or preserves

1 fresh mango, thinly sliced

1. Take the mango ice cream out of the freezer to soften slightly. Put a 9-inch springform pan in the freezer to chill.

2. When the ice cream can be scooped, take the cake pan out of the freezer. Working quickly, scoop up all the mango ice cream into the cake pan and flatten it, pressing down on a small spatula. Don't leave any gaps on the side. Sprinkle the dried ginger and mango over the ice cream and press each piece in firmly so you won't have trouble with the next layer of ice cream. Return the cake pan to the freezer to harden, for least 20 minutes.

3. When the mango ice cream is stiff again, take out the vanilla ice cream and let it soften slightly. Take the cake pan out of the freezer, scoop the vanilla ice cream into it, and smooth the top. This will be the bottom layer (the cake is inverted), so its top doesn't have to be perfectly smooth. Return the cake to the freezer for a couple of hours to harden before serving.

4. Fill a bowl wide enough to fit the cake pan with very hot water. Take the cake out of the freezer and carefully dip the sides of the pan in the hot water, almost to the top. Hold it there for about 15 seconds, then remove the pan, dry the pan off, run a knife around the inside, and invert the cake onto a serving plate. If you are not serving the cake right away, return it to the freezer.

5. When you are ready to serve the cake, spoon the mango purée or preserves over the top, starting in the center and moving in concentric circles out to the edge. Let the purée or preserves spill over and down the sides of the cake. Top the cake with the thinly sliced fresh mango.

* Mango purée is available at Indian and Latin American food stores.

Gary Danko's Gingerbread with Roasted Caramel Pears

This is a perfect fall dessert, one I first ate at the home of Celia Tejada, a designer for Pottery Barn in San Francisco. Chef Gary Danko, who was cooking that night for some friends, calls this gingerbread cake "an essay in simplicity." He was sitting at Celia's counter, calmly making this homey dessert as the guests milled around.

Gary serves his homemade gingerbread with roasted caramel pears and nutmeg ice cream.

YIELD: 8 SERVINGS

ROASTED CARAMEL PEARS
¾ cup dark brown sugar
8 Bartlett pears, perfectly ripe
½ cup apple cider, as needed

GINGERBREAD
2 cups all-purpose flour
2 teaspoons baking soda
1 teaspoon ground cloves
1 teaspoon ground ginger
½ teaspoon grated nutmeg
¾ teaspoon salt
3 large eggs
1 cup sugar
1 cup molasses
½ cup corn oil
1 cup boiling water

Ice cream or whipped cream

1. Preheat the oven to 350 degrees. Grease a 9-inch cake pan and line the sides and bottom with parchment paper.

2. To roast the pears, spread the brown sugar over a 12½-by-16½-inch sturdy aluminum sheet pan with sloping sides. Peel and halve the pears. Using a melon baller, scoop out the cores and lay the pears cut side down on the brown sugar. They should fit snugly into the pan.

3. Bake until the pears are tender and their juices have thickened to a light caramel syrup, about 30 minutes. Check after 15 minutes. If the pan is dry, add a little apple cider to help dissolve the sugar. After 30 minutes turn the pears over and bake 5–10 more minutes. The result should be golden pears with a nice caramel syrup. Cool in the pan until serving time.

4. While the pears are baking, make the gingerbread. Sift the flour, baking soda, cloves, ginger, nutmeg, and salt into a large bowl.

5. In a separate bowl, stir together the eggs, sugar, molasses, and oil. Stirring constantly, slowly pour in the boiling water. Pour the liquid ingredients onto the dry and stir to blend.

6. Pour the batter into the prepared cake pan. Bake in the middle of the oven until a skewer comes out clean, about 35–45 minutes. Cool and remove from the pan.

7. Place the cake on a serving platter and strew the pears over. Serve with the warm caramel syrup and a scoop of vanilla ice cream or a dollop of whipped cream.

Mo-Bay's Jamaican Rummy Rum Cake

W̲hen Annette Hew came to New York from Jamaica more than thirty years ago, she lived in an apartment building in Brooklyn. One Christmas, deciding to bake some cakes for extra money, she posted a flyer in her building and bought fifteen baking pans. "That Christmas I made a hundred cakes all by myself in my home," Annette told me. Soon word spread. Restaurants and supermarkets wanted this rummy, moist cake.

Her daughter Sheron, who has a background in marketing, had an idea to start a Caribbean restaurant and bakery. "There was so much demand for my mom's cake that the restaurant evolved from the rum cake," said Sheron. "I felt here was an opportunity to grow, to advance. Everything is possible in America if you are willing to roll up your sleeves."

Now Mo-Bay, short for Montego Bay, a down-home restaurant in Brooklyn's Fort Greene neighborhood, serves Caribbean soul food fused with Asian flair. "Jamaican food is a culinary mix-up," said Annette, who is herself Jamaican and Chinese.

The cake is literally soaked in rum and given a butter bath with crushed walnuts. Serve it warm with vanilla or rum raisin ice cream.

YIELD: 12 SERVINGS

CAKE
1 cup (2 sticks) unsalted butter
2 cups sugar
4 large eggs
3 cups all-purpose flour
2 teaspoons baking powder
1 teaspoon salt
½ cup dark rum, such as Myers's
6 tablespoons crushed walnuts

RUM SYRUP
1 cup (2 sticks) unsalted butter
1 cup sugar
1½ cups dark rum, such as Myers's
3 tablespoons crushed walnuts

1. Preheat the oven to 325 degrees and grease and flour a 10-inch springform pan.

2. In the bowl of an electric mixer, cream the butter and sugar until they are fluffy. Add the eggs 1 at a time, blending until smooth. Then, with the mixer still running, add the flour, baking powder, salt, rum, and nuts, blending until smooth. Pour into the prepared pan.

3. Bake in the oven for 1 hour and 10 minutes or until a knife comes out clean when inserted in the center.

4. Just before removing the cake from the oven, prepare the syrup. Melt the butter in a saucepan. Add the sugar and stir until the butter is melted. Add the rum and bring to a boil for a few minutes. Poke the cake with toothpicks. Pour half the hot rum syrup over the hot cake and sprinkle the walnuts on top. Let cool before removing from the pan. Heat the remaining syrup and serve on the side. You may want to heat each piece in the microwave just before serving.

Orange, Date, and Nut Cake—
A Wandering Cake from Turkey to Cuba to Miami

One afternoon, Cuban-born Rebeca Esquenazi was talking in Spanish while cooking with two of her friends at her apartment in Miami. A bean soup bubbled on the stove as she fried plantains for that evening's dinner. Palm trees laid a blanket of shade over her second-floor balcony, cooling the hundred or so perfectly crafted *burekas* and *bulemas*—Turkish flaky pastries filled with feta cheese, spinach, and potatoes—that she had set out there in disposable pans, along with several of her orange date nut cakes.

Rebeca came to the United States from Cuba in 1966, seven years after Castro's revolution. Throughout the 1970s, she watched as more and more Cubans made Miami their home. "These days Miami is becoming even more Latin," she told me. "People are coming now from Argentina, Peru, Colombia, Venezuela, and Brazil." With many women working, Rebeca worries that recipes like hers are endangered. "The old traditions will get lost," she said. "Women don't have the time for cooking because they are not attached to this kind of work. Many people order food out. If I did that my husband would kill me."

This delicious, centuries-old Turkish *tishpishti* cake, enriched with oranges, dates, nuts, and bread crumbs, is very easy to make. In Turkish, *tez* means "quick," and *pisht* means "done." Usually made with semolina, Rebeca's version calls for bread crumbs.

YIELD: AT LEAST 12 SERVINGS

3 cups sugar
1½ cups water
4 whole oranges
½–1 cup orange juice
6 large eggs
1 cup vegetable oil
¼ teaspoon salt
2 cups fine dried bread crumbs or matzo meal
2 cups coarsely ground walnuts
1 cup tightly packed chopped dates
2–3 tablespoons orange liqueur, such as Grand Marnier or triple sec, or to taste

1. Make a sugar syrup by stirring 1½ cups of the sugar into the water in a heavy saucepan. Bring to a boil, stir until all the sugar is dissolved, then lower the heat and simmer, uncovered, until the syrup is reduced to a third of its original volume, about 40 minutes.

2. While the syrup is simmering, preheat the oven to 350 degrees and grease a 9-by-13-inch baking pan.

3. Zest the oranges, being careful to avoid the bitter white pith. Then juice the oranges. Add enough additional juice to what you have just squeezed to make 2 cups.

4. Break the eggs into a large bowl and beat them well with the remaining 1½ cups sugar. Pour in both the orange juice and the oil and continue mixing.

5. Stir in the salt, bread crumbs, walnuts, dates, and orange zest. Turn into the greased pan and bake in the oven until golden, about 45 minutes. With the cake still hot and in the pan, cut it into 2-inch diamond-shaped pieces.

6. Stir the orange liqueur into the sugar syrup and pour it over the hot cake. Let the cake sit a few hours before serving.

Mango Cheesecake

One day in San Francisco, I had dinner at Bacar, where I ordered a smooth yet tart mango cheesecake for dessert. A marriage of rich New York cheesecake and the tropical freshness of mangoes, it was one of the best cheesecakes I had ever tasted.

I was unable to track down Christine Strickland, the pastry chef, so I tried to re-create her recipe and adapt it for home cooks. I checked the Internet and asked friends, playing around with variations, until I came up with this version.

YIELD: 10–12 SERVINGS

CRUST

2½ cups graham crackers (about 25 squares or 8 ounces)

½ cup shredded sweetened coconut

4 tablespoons sugar

¾ cup (1½ sticks) unsalted butter, melted

MASCARPONE FILLING

Two 8-ounce packages cream cheese, at room temperature

8 ounces (1 cup) mascarpone cheese, at room temperature

2 large eggs

¾ cup sugar

1 teaspoon vanilla extract

MANGO TOPPING

2 mangoes (about 2½–3 cups chopped ripe mango plus some diced for garnish)

3–4 tablespoons sugar

Juice of 2 limes (3 tablespoons)

3 tablespoons water or liqueur of your choice

Pinch of salt

1 tablespoon cornstarch

1. Preheat the oven to 350 degrees.

2. Using a food processor, pulse the graham crackers and coconut into coarse crumbs. Add the sugar and melted butter and stir until all of the crumbs are moist. Using your fingers, evenly spread the crumbs into the bottom and an inch up the sides of a 10-inch springform pan. Refrigerate for 10 minutes, then bake the crust in the middle of the oven for 10–12 minutes. Remove and let it cool completely.

3. Using a standing mixer with a paddle attachment, beat the cream cheese, mascarpone cheese, eggs, sugar, and vanilla until smooth. Pour the batter into the springform pan on top of the crust and bake until a knife comes out clean when inserted in the center, about 1 hour and 10 minutes. Cool completely.

4. Purée 2 cups of the mango with 3 tablespoons of the sugar, lime juice, 2 tablespoons of the water or liqueur, and salt. Pour into a saucepan and simmer, stirring occasionally, for a few minutes, adding another tablespoon of sugar if needed.

5. Dissolve the cornstarch in the remaining tablespoon of water or liqueur and pour it into the mango mixture, heating for a few more minutes or until thick.

6. Spoon the topping over the cheesecake and scatter the remaining diced mangoes over the top.

Pineapple Upside-Down Cake

Although the syrupy golden rings sat in their exotic cans on our shelves year round, we only tasted them during Christmas. Momma used the juice to make almost-black fruit cakes. Then she lined heavy soot-encrusted iron skillets with the pineapple rings for rich upside-down cakes. Bailey and I received one slice each, and I carried mine around for hours, shredding off the fruit until nothing was left except the perfume on my fingers. I'd like to think that my desire for pineapples was so sacred that I wouldn't allow myself to steal a can (which was possible) and eat it alone out in the garden, but I'm certain that I must have weighed the possibility of the scent exposing me and didn't have the nerve to attempt it.

—MAYA ANGELOU, *I KNOW WHY THE CAGED BIRD SINGS*

Pineapple upside-down cake, a delicious twentieth-century concoction that evolved when canned pineapple rings from Hawaii hit the grocery shelves, has been given a facelift by American chefs and recent immigrants from Latin America. Skillet cakes were popular in the nineteenth century because they could be baked on top of the stove and were made with whatever was in season—cherries, peaches, apples, and later pineapples.

On a trip to Hawaii, I asked some members of the Dole Pineapple family about the upside-down cake. Elizabeth Porteus, a very sharp ninety-two-year-old and the daughter of the founder, James Dole, found a recipe for pineapple pudding, also known as pineapple upside-down cake, in her great-aunt Helen Alexander's *Hawaiian Cook Book* from 1935.

Three pineapple princesses: DeLacy Ganley, Elizabeth Dole Porteus, and Barbara Dole Porteus

I have taken suggestions from this recipe and come up with a new yet traditional interpretation of my own. Instead of using canned pineapples, I use the extraordinarily sweet fresh pineapples coming from Costa Rica. Don't worry that the recipe skimps on batter, which barely covers the pineapples. One pineapple upside-down cake enthusiast told me that the best part of this cake is that you don't have to make an icing! Just flip the baked cake over, drizzle a little rum on top, and serve.

¾ cup (1½ sticks) unsalted butter, at room temperature

1 cup dark brown sugar

1 ripe pineapple, peeled, cored, and cut in ¾–1-inch-thick rounds

1 cup granulated sugar

1 large egg

1 teaspoon vanilla extract

½ cup milk

2 cups bleached all-purpose flour

¼ teaspoon salt

2 teaspoons baking powder

2 tablespoons rum

Whipped cream or ice cream

1. Preheat the oven to 350 degrees.

2. Melt half a stick of the butter, pour it into a 9-by-13-inch baking pan, and spread with your fingers to cover the bottom completely. Sprinkle on the brown sugar.

3. Arrange the pineapple rings on top of the brown sugar. If there is leftover pineapple, just fit it in between the rings.

4. Put the rest of the butter and the sugar in the bowl of a standing mixer and beat until creamy and pale.

5. Add the egg, vanilla, and milk, fully incorporating each before adding the next.

6. Sift the flour, salt, and baking powder and add to the bowl. Mix only long enough to blend thoroughly.

7. Spoon the cake batter onto the pineapple rings and bake until golden on top, about 45 minutes. Remove from the oven, wait a few minutes, then turn the cake out onto a platter and sprinkle on the rum. Serve hot with whipped cream or ice cream.

COOKIES

". . . as an adult, if I want a cookie, I have a cookie, okay? I have three cookies or four cookies or eleven cookies if I want. Many times I will intentionally ruin my entire appetite. Just ruin it. And then I call my mother right after to tell her that I did it. 'Hello, Mom, yeah, I just ruined my entire appetite . . . cookies.' "

"Oh look, Elaine, the black-and-white cookie. I love the black and white. Two races of flavor living side by side. It's a wonderful thing, isn't it?"

—JERRY SEINFELD, SEINFELD,
"THE HEART ATTACK EPISODE,"
WRITTEN BY LARRY CHARLES AND JERRY SEINFELD

Ann Amernick's Melt-in-Your-Mouth Chocolate Chip Cookies

"All chocolate chip cookie recipes come from Ruth Wakefield's 1930s Toll House cookie recipe," Wally Amos, aka Famous Amos, told me as he was making—what else?—chocolate chip cookies at his beach house in Nanikai, Hawaii. With so many variations on that simple recipe, it's hard to imagine that all chocolate chip cookies share a common lineage. As Wally admits, "The only thing that is a constant is that you pay attention to your cookies."

But today, thanks to better ingredients, chocolate chip cookies can taste even better. Pastry chef Ann Amernick's chocolate chip cookies literally melt in your mouth. "You have to use butter with the highest fat content you can find," Ann told me, pausing in her work at Palena, the restaurant she owns with chef Frank Ruta (see page 40) in northwest Washington, D.C. "The higher the fat in the butter, the less water there is and that means a more tender cookie." Ann, a baking purist, also suggests using the best chocolate you can buy and chopping it into little pieces with a big chef's knife.

Once an assistant pastry chef at the White House, Ann learned from former White House pastry chef Roland Mesnier to mix all cookies at the lowest speed of the mixer and finish them off by hand. Another of Ann's tricks is to put the baked chocolate chip cookies in the microwave for five seconds before serving to warm them up and slightly melt the chocolate. Instead of parchment paper, you can use another fabulous new invention, the Silpat baking mat, which is so easy to clean. I keep at least two in my kitchen, one for savories and another for desserts.

YIELD: 24 COOKIES

1 cup (2 sticks) unsalted butter, softened
¾ cup light brown sugar
¾ cup granulated sugar
2 large eggs
1 teaspoon vanilla extract
2½ cups all-purpose flour
½ teaspoon salt
¾ teaspoon baking soda
12 ounces bittersweet chocolate, chopped, or chocolate chunks

1. Preheat the oven to 350 degrees. Grease 2 cookie sheets and cover with parchment paper or Silpat baking mats.

2. Beat the butter and sugars until creamy and pale in the bowl of a standing mixer set on the lowest speed, about 3–4 minutes.

3. Still at the slowest speed, add the eggs, 1 at a time, waiting until the first is fully incorporated before adding the second; then add the vanilla.

4. Add the flour, salt, and baking soda to the standing mixer and stir until incorporated.

5. Fold in the chopped chocolate or chocolate chunks. Using an ice cream scoop or scooping about ¼ cup of the dough into plump rounds, arrange the dough on 2 cookie sheets, leaving about 2 inches between cookies. Bake for 5 minutes, then rotate the trays and bake for another 5 minutes.

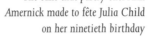

The cake that pastry chef Ann Amernick made to fête Julia Child on her ninetieth birthday

Cocadas

Brazilian Coconut Cookies with Chocolate Chips

The Brazilian population of Martha's Vineyard has made its presence felt, especially in the kitchen. A Brazilian who works at Humphrey's Bakery started making these chewy coconut cookies, with chocolate chips for the American palate. After I tasted them for the first time, I went right home, figured out the recipe, and made them for my family, who loved them. Here they are.

YIELD: ABOUT 20 *COCADAS*

3½ cups unsweetened shredded coconut
¼ cup all-purpose flour
1 cup sugar
1 cup semisweet chocolate chips
2 extra-large eggs, plus 1 egg white

1. Preheat the oven to 325 degrees. Grease 2 baking sheets and cover them with parchment paper.

2. Mix the coconut, flour, sugar, and chocolate chips in a bowl. Add the eggs and extra egg white and mix with your fingers until well blended.

3. Gently shape dough into patties of about 2 tablespoons each and set them on the baking sheets, leaving about 2 inches in between the cookies. Bake for about 20–25 minutes or until golden on top. Cool completely.

Oatmeal Dried-Cherry Cookies

In Door County, Wisconsin, oatmeal dried-cherry cookies are easily as popular as oatmeal raisin cookies. And it's due in large part to farmers like Mike and Kathy Johnson. In the 1980s the Johnsons, facing high interest rates and shrinking crop prices, began looking for additional income during the winter.

Although Door County is known for its tart, fleshy Montmorency cherries, few people were drying them commercially. So Mike and Kathy and their four children started doing it, with a home dehydrator and a supply of frozen cherries, which are processed and sprinkled with sugar to preserve their color. It worked. A year later they established Country Ovens, which now uses about a million pounds of dried cherries per year from Door County only. From eight pounds of fresh cherries, the Johnsons produce one pound of dried cherries. They also handle dried cranberries and blueberries, which they sell at their store and on their website (see Mail-Order Sources).

YIELD: APPROXIMATELY 4 DOZEN

1 cup (2 sticks) unsalted butter, softened
1 cup firmly packed brown sugar
½ cup granulated sugar
2 large eggs
1 teaspoon vanilla extract
1½ cups all-purpose flour
1 teaspoon baking soda
1 teaspoon cinnamon
½ teaspoon salt
3 cups uncooked old-fashioned oats
2 cups dried cherries

1. Preheat the oven to 350 degrees.

2. Put the butter and sugars in the bowl of a standing mixer and beat until creamy and pale. Add the eggs, 1 at a time, waiting until the first is fully incorporated before adding the second; then add the vanilla. Sift together the flour, baking soda, cinnamon, and salt and gradually pour into the bowl.

3. Stir in the oats and dried cherries, mixing well. Drop by rounded tablespoonfuls onto 2 cookie sheets, leaving about 2 inches between cookies. Bake until golden brown, about 10–12 minutes. Cool before removing them from the cookie sheets. Repeat with the remaining batter.

Ginger Cookies

Every Christmas, Lynne and Alan Greenwald send me a batch of perfectly made ginger cookies in an inviting paper bag. It seems that the cookie originated in a long-forgotten New England inn. This may be true—I grew up with a similar cookie in Rhode Island—but whatever its origins, the cookie worked its way to California, where Lynne's mother baked them in the mid-1970s and kept them in a tin in the freezer. "When we arrived at Christmas, we would start eating them out of the tin, frozen," Lynne told me. Since the Greenwalds use only organic ingredients, they make them slightly different than we New Englanders did. They urge you to use a heavy standing mixer and unsulfured molasses, because blackstrap and extra-dark molasses are too bitter.

YIELD: ABOUT 4 DOZEN COOKIES

1 cup (2 sticks) unsalted butter, at room temperature
2 cups sugar
½ cup unsulfured molasses
2 large eggs
1 teaspoon salt
2 teaspoons baking soda
2 teaspoons ground ginger
1½ teaspoons ground cloves
2 teaspoons ground cinnamon
4 cups sifted bleached all-purpose flour

1. Preheat the oven to 350 degrees and place the racks near the center of the oven.

2. Put the butter with 1½ cups of the sugar in the bowl of an electric mixer and beat until creamy and pale, then add the molasses and the eggs, continuing to beat.

3. Sift together the salt, baking soda, ginger, cloves, cinnamon, and flour, then, with the mixer set to its lowest speed, add this mixture 1 cup at a time. The last cup may be difficult, as the dough becomes very, very stiff.

4. Place the remaining ½ cup sugar in a bowl. Coat your hands with some of the sugar and roll the dough into balls roughly 1 inch in diameter, then roll each ball in the sugar to coat it.

5. Place the balls 2–3 inches apart on ungreased cookie sheets. Bake for 12–13 minutes, switching racks halfway through. Repeat with the remaining cookie dough. If you want, sprinkle any remaining sugar over the finished cookies.

When Laurence Gottlieb and his two brothers opened Gottlieb's Restaurant and Dessert Bar in Savannah, Georgia, they revived the family's baking tradition. Their great-grandparents, Russian immigrants, had peddled their rye bread and other baked goods on the streets of Savannah in the years after the Civil War. Shortly thereafter, Gottlieb's Bakery became a Savannah institution, baking breads and cookies like benne wafers and chocolate chewies for one hundred years.

Laurence Gottlieb when he was sous chef at the Inn at Little Washington

Isser Gottlieb, Laurence's father, closed the bakery in 1994, partly because of competition from in-store bakeries in supermarkets. Although the family loved baking, the last thing they wanted for their sons was to get into this precarious business. To their chagrin, all three sons went for it. "When I heard Laurence wanted to be a chef, my heart sank down to my toes," said his mother, Ava. "I knew what a grueling business it was. He had such wonderful thin fingers. I thought he would be an oral surgeon. Those hands would fit into someone's mouth."

Although Laurence is now a chef of his own restaurant, he still remains under his mother's watchful eye. "Momma always asks if I need anything," says Laurence. "They have had a hard time letting go. My mother's on a mission to give me food and to get me married."

Chocolate Chewies

Chocolate chewies, which were a crispy, chewy favorite from Gottlieb's Bakery in Savannah, are now being made at the Gottlieb Restaurant and Dessert Bar. But there is a difference. Laurence uses very fine-quality Valrhona cocoa for his bite-size version.

YIELD: APPROXIMATELY 2 DOZEN

2 cups chopped pecans
2½ cups confectioners' sugar
½ cup Valrhona or other good-quality cocoa
2 tablespoons flour
Generous pinch of salt
3 large egg whites
1 teaspoon vanilla extract

1. Preheat the oven to 350 degrees and line 2 greased cookie sheets with parchment paper, or use Silpat baking mats.

2. Scatter the pecans on 1 cookie sheet and toast in the oven, stirring occasionally, until fragrant and slightly brown, about 5–10 minutes. Remove from oven and let cool.

3. Put the sugar, cocoa, flour, and salt in the bowl of an electric mixer equipped with a whisk and beat until well blended. Beat in the egg whites 1 at a time, scraping down the sides of the bowl as necessary. Add the vanilla and beat at high speed for 1 more minute.

4. Fold in the pecans with a spoon, mixing until blended. Drop by mini scoopfuls or tablespoons onto the cookie sheets, leaving 2 inches between cookies for spreading. Bake for 15 minutes, turning the sheet around halfway through baking time, until dry on the surface but soft in the centers. Remove from the oven. Cool on the parchment paper or Silpat. Then peel off the cookies. Store in an airtight container for 2 days or in the freezer for 1 month.

Maida Heatter's Chocolate Cheesecake Brownies

One of the people that the late *New York Times* food columnist Craig Claiborne discovered was a home baker named Maida Heatter, who later became the author of *Maida Heatter's Book of Great Desserts* and several other books. Maida, who lives in Miami, is still using her kitchen as a laboratory. An absolutely gracious woman who lives on an inland waterway overlooking the Atlantic Ocean, Maida always offers her guests some of her famous biscotti or other cookies. As we chatted, she told me that one of the most exciting events in her life was the Economic Summit Meeting in Williamsburg in 1983, when Craig invited a few American chefs like Paul Prudhomme, Alice Waters, Wolfgang Puck, and Maida to showcase American food. Maida created these chocolate cheesecake brownies for the event.

YIELD: 16 BROWNIES

½ cup (1 stick) unsalted butter, plus butter for greasing the pan
1 cup chopped pecans
4 ounces unsweetened chocolate
Pinch of salt, if desired
1½ cups sugar
1 teaspoon pure vanilla extract
4 large eggs
½ cup plus 1 tablespoon all-purpose flour
½ cup packed shredded unsweetened coconut
8 ounces cream cheese, at room temperature
2 tablespoons unsweetened cocoa

1. Preheat the oven to 350 degrees and set a rack in the bottom third. Line the bottom and sides of a 9-by-9-inch pan with a 12-inch square of aluminum foil, gently pressing the foil into place and then greasing it.

2. Toast the pecans in a pan in the oven until fragrant, about 7–10 minutes.

3. To prepare the brownie layer, place the butter and chocolate in a heavy 2-quart saucepan over low heat and stir occasionally until melted. Remove from the heat and stir in the salt, 1 cup of the sugar, and ½ teaspoon of the vanilla. Stir in 2 of the eggs, 1 at a time. Add the ½ cup flour and mix well, then stir in the pecans and coconut. Turn the batter into the prepared pan and smooth the top.

4. To prepare the cheesecake layer, beat the cream cheese in the bowl of an electric mixer until it is soft. Blending in each ingredient before adding the next, add the cocoa and the remaining sugar, vanilla, eggs, and flour. The batter will be very loose.

5. Pour the cheesecake batter in a ribbon over the brownie layer. With an icing spatula or the flat side of a teaspoon handle, gently marbleize the batter by swirling it in a wide zigzag pattern. Smooth the top.

6. Bake for about 30 minutes or until a toothpick gently inserted in the middle comes out clean.

7. Cool to room temperature, then place in the freezer until firm, about 1 hour.

8. Cover the brownie pan with a piece of wax paper and on top of that, a cookie sheet. Turn the pan and cookie sheet upside down, remove the pan and peel the foil off the brownie cake. Cover with a cutting board or another cookie sheet and then turn upside down again, so that the cake is now right side up.

9. Cut into 16 large squares, wiping your knife with a damp cloth between cuttings.

Aunt Vicky's Oatmeal Date Bars

Every Christmas as far back as I can remember, my aunt Vicky would send us a box of these date nut bars, which were only wrapped in wax paper," said Margaret Hensler, a good home cook of Lebanese background. "We would immediately place them in the refrigerator, and they would last through the holidays." Oatmeal date bar recipes appear in cookbooks at least as far back as Fannie Farmer's original cookbook. The difference in this Lebanese-American version is the addition of walnuts, a perfect match for dates.

YIELD: ABOUT 2 DOZEN COOKIES

1¾ cups oatmeal
1¾ cups all-purpose flour
Dash of salt
1 cup dark brown sugar
1 cup (2 sticks) unsalted butter
1 teaspoon baking soda
2 cups chopped dates
1 cup chopped walnuts
1 cup granulated sugar
½ cup water
½ cup confectioners' sugar

1. Preheat the oven to 350 degrees and grease a 9-by-13-inch baking pan.

2. Put the oatmeal, flour, salt, brown sugar, butter, and baking soda in a bowl and, using your fingers, mix until you have a crumbly dough. Spread half of the dough in the baking pan and set aside the other half.

3. Place the dates, walnuts, granulated sugar, and water in a pan and boil a minute or two, until slightly thickened. Let cool to room temperature. Spread this over half of the oatmeal dough, then pat the other half of the dough on top. Bake for 30 minutes.

4. When cool, cut into small pieces, ¾ inches by 1½ inches, and roll in the confectioners' sugar.

Nectarine Cobbler

As I travel the country, I taste cobblers and crisps everywhere I go—those familiar fresh fruit desserts topped with a crust and baked. A cobbler may have a crust or a biscuit topping, the dough making a cobbled effect on top of the baked fruit. A crisp, on the other hand, has a crumbled topping made of flour, butter, sugar, and, sometimes, oatmeal or nuts. Both are delicious and can be made with whatever fruits are in season. During the summer I freeze ripe fruit cobblers and crisps unbaked.

In some parts of the country it is customary to bring cobblers and crisps to both happy and sad occasions. Tom Head, food editor of *Washingtonian* magazine, likes to bring this nectarine cobbler to family gatherings in West Monroe, Louisiana, along with his mother's sour cream pound cake.

YIELD: ABOUT 6–8 SERVINGS

FRUIT
7–8 nectarines
(about 2½ pounds), peeled
Juice of 1 lemon
¼ cup dark brown sugar
¼ cup granulated sugar
¼ teaspoon cinnamon

COBBLER
1½ cups all-purpose flour
⅓ cup plus 2 tablespoons sugar
1 teaspoon baking powder
½ teaspoon baking soda
½ teaspoon salt
¼ cup (½ stick) cold unsalted butter
½ teaspoon vanilla extract
⅔ cup buttermilk

Heavy cream or ice cream

1. Preheat the oven to 400 degrees.

2. Bring a large pot of water to a boil. Drop the nectarines in and blanch them for 1–2 minutes. Using tongs or a slotted spoon, remove them from the water and cool slightly. When cool enough to handle, peel the nectarines, cut them into thin crescent-shaped slices, and place in a 9-by-13-inch glass baking dish.

3. Sprinkle with the lemon juice, both sugars, and cinnamon.

4. To prepare the cobbler topping, combine the flour, ⅓ cup sugar, baking powder, baking soda, salt, and butter in the bowl of a food processor equipped with the steel blade, or mix by hand. Process or mix until crumbly, then add the vanilla and enough of the buttermilk that the dough just holds together but remains very sticky.

5. Gather the dough together and pat it out on a floured board or a floured piece of wax paper to ¾ inch thick. Cut into 3-inch rounds with a biscuit cutter or a glass dipped in flour. Arrange the biscuits over the fruit and sprinkle lightly with the remaining 2 tablespoons of sugar. Bake it for 30–35 minutes or until the top is golden and the fruit is bubbling. Serve from the baking dish with heavy cream or ice cream.

Potluck Berry Cobbler

In the Ozarks, entertaining means potluck: after church and before music. "When we started doing our shows at the dinner theater, we would offer cobbler with ice cream," said Jean Jennings, a dulcimer player and singer in Mountain View, Arkansas. Jean is known for her cobblers, which she makes with blackberries, peaches, raspberries, and strawberries and rhubarb. The secret, Jean told me, is not too much sugar. Since Jean makes her cobblers throughout the year, she often uses frozen berries that she picks in the summer. "Just let them thaw before starting the cobbler," she told me. "Use any fresh, juicy fruit, but taste for the right amount of sugar."

YIELD: 8 SERVINGS

8 cups of berries or diced fruit: blackberries, peaches, apricots, raspberries, or strawberries and rhubarb

½ teaspoon cinnamon

1 cup sugar, plus 2 tablespoons for sprinkling

2⅓ sticks unsalted butter

2 cups all-purpose flour

¾ teaspoon salt

1. Preheat the oven to 400 degrees.

2. Put the fruit, cinnamon, sugar, and 1 stick of the butter in a large saucepan over medium heat and cook until the butter has melted and some of the liquid of the fruit has evaporated. Stir occasionally. Transfer the fruit to a 9-by-13-inch baking pan.

3. Mix the flour, salt, and remaining butter in a medium bowl, using your fingers to work the dough until it is crumbly. Gradually add 2–3 tablespoons of ice water to the dough, using just enough water that the dough holds its shape when you form it into a ball. Roll the dough out to a 9-by-13-inch rectangle about an eighth of an inch thick. Gently spread the dough over the berries. Make several slits in the dough so that steam can escape as the cobbler bakes. Sprinkle the top with a little sugar.

4. Place in the oven and bake for 15 minutes, then reduce the heat to 350 and bake until golden brown, about another 20 minutes.

One of the best things that have happened in America is the way we have rediscovered heirloom varieties of fruit. And what varieties we are finding in areas like the Hudson Valley in New York. "The Hudson Valley is one of America's oldest and most important fruit-growing regions," Elizabeth Ryan, the owner of Breezy Hill Orchards, a sixty-acre farm in upstate New York, told me, her long blond hair swinging as she chattered away with enthusiasm. "The apples have power, they have punch, it is what gets me going," this walking, talking apple encyclopedia told me over a glass of her own cold apple cider.

Elizabeth came to the Hudson Valley in 1982 with a degree in pomology from Cornell University. "I spent a lot of time with growers," she told me. "I became obsessed with the study of fruit production. It was still a traditionally male field then. . . . In those days there were few women chefs and few women winemakers. For a few years I managed some fields and then I came here to a rundown little farm. We had Gravensteins, Winesaps, and Northern Spies, all heirloom varieties of nineteenth-century apples. I am very interested in flavor."

For crisps and pies, Elizabeth favors October-harvested apples like Jonathan and Jonathan crosses such as Jonagold, Melrose, and Monroe. "I like Winesaps, especially the old strains. They originated in New Jersey three hundred years ago. I have one that has wonderful red streaks through the flesh. It makes a gorgeous crisp or pie. I sometimes add a little quince for flavor or add plums to apple pie. The important thing to look for in a cooking apple is flavor and texture. Try blending the apples."

Whenever Elizabeth travels, she stops at "the least commercial-looking" fruit stands and asks the oldest person there what she should get. "Lots of the old-timers wax euphoric over old-fashioned early-season apples like Yellow Transparents and Red Astrakhans that are pretty hard to come by." In California she favors Pippins and Gravensteins, in the Midwest and Mid-Atlantic Jonathans, in New England Northern Spies, Baldwins, Rhode Island Greenings, and once in a while Porters and Blue Pearmains. In Pennsylvania and the Appalachian Mountains, she says, there are still a lot of Yorks and York crosses like Nittany Tec that, if properly grown, can be very good.

Elizabeth, a founding member of five New York farmers' markets, also suggests Stayman, Granny Smith, Braeburn, Pink Lady, Macoun, Honey Crisp, and McIntosh. As important as the flavor of an apple is, proper storage is also essential: if apples are stored right, in a plastic bag with some moisture in the refrigerator, they will stay crisp.

After her litany of apple varieties finally petered out, Elizabeth paused a moment before saying, "Almost all apples are great for eating."

Apple Cranberry Crisp

I love apple crisps. For me, they are one of the first signs of fall. When I was a child, my mother used the apple crisp recipe in Craig Claiborne's first cookbook, and I have been playing around with that basic recipe ever since. Cranberries add color, and preserved ginger, one of my favorite flavors, gives this recipe a zing. Today we can find all sorts of unusual seasonal apples at farmers' markets (see box). In the late spring and early summer I substitute three pounds of rhubarb and two pints of strawberries for the apples and cranberries and omit the ginger. Peaches mixed with raspberries and blueberries make a great combination in the summer. Easy to make, a crisp is best served with a splash of good heavy cream or ice cream.

YIELD: AT LEAST 8 SERVINGS

FRUIT FILLING

8 apples, such as Jonathan or Stayman, peeled, halved, cored, then sliced in 6 pieces, and halved (about 9 cups, or 3 pounds)

1 cup cranberries (optional) or 2–3 diced plums

½ cup granulated sugar

2 tablespoons all-purpose flour

1 teaspoon cinnamon

Juice and grated zest of 1 lemon

2 tablespoons chopped preserved ginger (optional)

TOPPING

¾ cup flour

½ cup chopped walnuts

⅔ cup dark brown sugar

¼ teaspoon salt

½ cup (1 stick) unsalted butter

Heavy cream or ice cream

1. Preheat the oven to 375 degrees and grease a 9-by-13-inch baking pan, or equivalent baking pan.

2. Mix the apples and the cranberries and scatter them in the pan. Sprinkle the fruit with the sugar, flour, cinnamon, lemon juice and zest, and preserved ginger, if using. Let sit for a few minutes.

3. Mix the flour, walnuts, brown sugar, and salt together in a bowl. Using your fingers, work the butter into the dry ingredients until you have a coarse, crumbly dough. Sprinkle over the fruit.

4. Bake in the oven until the fruit is soft and bubbly and the top golden and crisp, about 40 minutes. Serve warm with heavy cream or vanilla ice cream.

Note: You can substitute old-fashioned oats for the walnuts, but it won't make as crisp a crisp.

Going through my files, I found letters from an Amish family my children and I befriended seventeen years ago. On a lark, one Saturday morning last October, using MapQuest as my guide, I drove to their address in Bird-in-Hand, Pennsylvania. Finding the country road, we came upon two Amish women dressed in hand-made nineteenth-century long dresses and suits. When we mentioned the name Lizzie Stolzfus, one said, "Oh, she lives up the road now. They moved to a farmette." Arriving at the house, it seemed that no one was home. There was no car outside, no light in the windows. I knocked on the door, and a lady dressed in purple with a black apron and her hair pulled back under a white cap came out. "Are you Lizzie Stolzfus?" I asked. When she said yes, I told her that I had met her seventeen years ago. Recognizing me from the cookbook I had given her, she invited us in.

When we arrived, Lizzie had been in her basement putting up sauce from Ginger Gold apples, a new variety that she likes. Jars filled with grape juice, pears, peaches, cantaloupe balls, meatballs, pizza sauce, ketchup, and tomato sauce lined the walls. Because the Amish have no electricity, they rent freezer lockers nearby where they keep frozen meat and soup, which they had preserved on my first visit.

When Lizzie invited us to lunch, we readily accepted. The kitchen has a gas stove run by propane and a refrigerator run by a generator. I remembered the natural gas lamp above the table where the children used to study. All eleven of them are married now and live the same simple life as their parents.

Within minutes Lizzie had dinner, the main meal of the day, on the table. The children, who go to Amish school until the age of fifteen, come home for a hot lunch in the middle of the day. We started our meal with a moment of silence and then dug in: boiled potatoes straight from the garden; corn, cut from the cob and mixed with fresh lima beans; green salad with grated carrots; and a hard-boiled egg. For dessert we ate fresh peaches and homemade shoofly pie.

After visiting the garden, filled with aging green beans, beets, asparagus, strawberries, grapes, carrots, cabbage, lettuce, lima beans, rhubarb, and celery, we left, realizing that Lizzie had to finish canning her apples. We promised that we would return again—sooner than seventeen years.

Applesauce

YIELD: 4 CUPS

4 pounds apples, quartered
2 cinnamon sticks
½ cup apple juice
Honey, brown sugar, or maple syrup to taste

1. Place the apples and the cinnamon sticks in a pot with the apple juice. Bring to a boil, cover, and simmer over low heat, stirring occasionally to turn the apples and making sure they do not stick. You may want to add some more liquid. Cook about 20 minutes or until the apples are soft. Remove the cinnamon sticks.

2. Put the apples and their juice through a food mill. Taste and adjust seasoning by adding honey, brown sugar, or maple syrup to your liking.

THE KIWI QUEEN

In 1962, a buyer for Safeway Supermarkets contacted Frieda Caplan, the founder of Frieda's Finest in Anaheim, California. He was looking for Chinese gooseberries, a fruit that a customer had tasted while visiting New Zealand. Since Mrs. Caplan was in the business of importing exotic vegetables and fruits, she obliged the buyer and ordered 240 flats (about 2,400 pounds) of gooseberries. When the oval fruits arrived, the customs agent suggested a catchier name, like kiwi, a bird that he knew came from New Zealand. When Frieda heard the story, she contacted the people in New Zealand and introduced the Chinese gooseberry as the kiwi. Already known as the mushroom queen (see page 222), Frieda became the kiwi queen as well.

Although it seems like an overnight success story, it took about eighteen years for the kiwi to work its way into the market. "We began marketing kiwifruit in 1962," Frieda told me at her home in Anaheim. "But it wasn't until around 1980, when innovative chefs in fancy restaurants from New York to California, like Jeremiah Tower and Wolfgang Puck, began featuring it on their menus that the kiwi really started to gain its current popularity, first with the food media and then with the general public. That's why we fondly call kiwifruit our 'eighteen-year overnight success story.'"

Wolfgang Puck's Kiwi *Clafouti*

Here is a delicious and colorful kiwi *clafouti* developed by Wolfgang Puck.

YIELD: 8 SERVINGS

1 prepared pie crust (page 415)
4 large eggs
1 cup heavy cream
¾ cup sugar
4 teaspoons pear, blueberry, or other fruit brandy
8 kiwis
Confectioners' sugar

1. Preheat the oven to 350 degrees.

2. Roll out the pastry dough and fit it into a 10-inch quiche pan 1½ inches deep. Crimp the edges, then remove the excess dough. Line the pan with parchment paper or aluminum foil, fill with dried beans or rice, and bake the crust for 10 minutes, then remove the weights. Bake for 5–10 minutes, until the crust is brown. Remove the pan and reduce the oven temperature to 325 degrees.

3. Break the eggs into a small bowl and stir in the cream, sugar, and brandy, mixing well until blended.

4. Peel and cut each kiwi into 4 sections and place in the pastry shell. Pour the egg batter over and bake for 45–50 minutes, until the *clafouti* has puffed up and browned.

5. Remove the tart from the oven and turn on the broiler. Dust the top with confectioners' sugar and set it under the broiler for about 1 minute to caramelize the sugar. Be careful not to let the sugar burn. Cool on a rack and serve at room temperature.

Rhubarb Tart with Fresh Strawberries and a Currant Glaze

R hubarb, gooseberries, and sorrel are the lemons of the North," Judith Jones, my editor, told me in her kitchen. For years, Judith has summered in the Northeast Kingdom of Vermont, living in a house of hemlock wood on a hilltop. Like most New England cooks, she used to make rhubarb pie the old-fashioned way, with a double crust, cooking the rhubarb and strawberries in the pie. But something always seemed off to her. "I never like the taste of cooked strawberries," she told me. "And the rhubarb always makes the pie crust a little soggy." So she showed me how to make this favorite rhubarb recipe she had developed: an open-faced pie filled with cooked rhubarb and topped with strawberries glazed with currant jelly or gooseberry jam.

The beauty of this recipe (besides its amazing flavor) is that its separate parts can be made in advance and assembled just before guests arrive for dinner. Try to make this tart when tiny fresh strawberries are available locally in your part of the country. Their flavor shines through. When using a food processor to make the pie dough, pulse as long as it takes to say the word "alligator" very quickly. Do this ten times and you will have a very light dough. Judith learned this trick from cookbook author Lydie Marshall.

YIELD: SERVES 6

FRUIT
1 pound fresh rhubarb
½ cup sugar
½ cup currant jelly or gooseberry jam
1 pint fresh strawberries

CRUST
1 cup all-purpose flour
¼ teaspoon salt
2 tablespoons sugar
½ cup (1 stick) unsalted butter
1½ tablespoons ice water

Vanilla ice cream or whipped cream

1. Starting a day or a few hours in advance, cut the rhubarb into 2-inch pieces, discarding any leaves, and toss in a bowl with the sugar. Cover the bowl, let the rhubarb release its juice, and put it in the refrigerator for a few hours or overnight.

2. Transfer the rhubarb and any juices from the bowl to a medium saucepan and cook it down, slowly, uncovered, until the rhubarb pieces have fallen apart, about 25 minutes. Remove the cooked rhubarb with a slotted spoon and reserve any remaining liquid in the saucepan for the currant or gooseberry glaze.

3. To make the glaze, cook down the rhubarb juices in the saucepan just a bit, then stir in 6 tablespoons of the jelly or jam. Cook briefly to liquefy the jelly or jam, then remove from the heat, but keep in a warm place.

4. To make the dough, mix the flour, salt, and sugar together in the bowl of the food processor. Then cut the butter in small pieces, drop

them through the tube of the food processor, and pulse long enough to say "alligator" 10 times. Pour in the ice water and pulse again, saying "alligator" 8 times. Transfer the dough to a marble countertop or work surface and smear it out with the heel of your hand in small increments, then gather the dough together into a round. You can also use your fingertips to mix the flour, salt, sugar, and butter by hand to the consistency of cornmeal. Then drizzle on the water and work it into the dough before smearing it out with the heel of your hand. Cover with plastic wrap and refrigerate at least 15 minutes or until ready to use.

5. Preheat the oven to 425 degrees.

6. Sprinkle some flour on the marble or a countertop and on a rolling pin. Roll out the dough to an approximately 11-inch circle, then press it into an 8-inch tart pan with a removable bottom. Do not worry if the dough cracks a bit—just press it together.

7. Line the crust with aluminum foil and fill with small weights, such as dried beans, rice, or pebbles. Bake for 15 minutes, then remove the foil and weights, reduce the oven to 350 degrees, and bake for another 10 minutes. Remove the crust from the oven and let it cool slightly.

8. Smear the still-warm crust with the remaining jelly, then spoon on the rhubarb. Hull the strawberries, split them in half if they are quite large, and place them in concentric circles on top of the rhubarb. Spoon a bit of the glaze over each strawberry. Serve as is or with vanilla ice cream or whipped cream.

Judith Jones working in her garden

Apple-Apricot *Crostata*

In the early 1980s, when Anne Luzzatto's children were little, she summered in Venice, Italy, at her in-laws' ancestral home. Like many Italian mothers-in-law, Anne's taught her how to make a favorite familial dessert: a *crostata* made out of a butter crust called a *friolla*. "She brought me into her kitchen in Venice with its wonderful Italian marble table," Anne told me. And ever since, she has been making this marvelous tart with a delicious butter crust, a classy final act for dinner parties in New York, where she lives.

YIELD: 1 TART, SERVING 10–12 PEOPLE

3 Granny Smith or other good cooking apples (about 1½ pounds)
½ cup sugar
1 cup (2 sticks) unsalted butter
2 large egg yolks
1½ cups unbleached all-purpose flour
Pinch of salt
½ cup apricot preserves

1. Preheat the oven to 425 degrees and grease a 10-inch fluted tart pan with a removable bottom.

2. Peel, core, and slice the apples into crescents about ¼–⅛ inch thick. You should have about 24 pieces.

3. Put the sugar, butter, egg yolks, flour, and salt in a large bowl and rub everything together with your fingers or combine the ingredients in a food processor fitted with a steel blade and process in quick pulses until the dough forms a ball. Either way, do not overwork the dough.

4. Flouring your hands, shape the ball of dough into a round and pat into the tart pan. Working with your fingers and a cake knife or wide spatula, spread the dough evenly around the pan and up the sides. The dough should be about ½ inch thick up the sides and spread evenly across the bottom of the pan, then trim and flatten the edges with a knife. Starting on the outside and working toward the center, lay the apple slices in an overlapping, concentric circle.

5. Heat the apricot preserves in a saucepan over low heat until it has liquefied. Using a pastry brush, paint the apples and the visible crust with the apricot glaze.

6. Place the tart pan on a cookie sheet and bake in the middle of the oven for 15 minutes. Reduce the heat to 350 degrees and continue cooking until the crust is deep golden brown, about 45 minutes. Bring to room temperature, unmold, and put on a platter or serving dish.

Grape Crostata

Noel Bleier is an avid, energetic, and inventive baker who often volunteers to make dessert for parties in Lexington, Massachusetts, where she lives. When the request came in to make a dessert for a dinner where I tasted this *crostata*, grapes were the only fruit she had in her kitchen. This is her delicious, off-the-cuff creation with grapes, which I later learned is a Kentucky specialty.

YIELD: 6 SERVINGS

PASTRY
1½ cups all-purpose flour
1 tablespoon sugar
¼ teaspoon salt
10 tablespoons (1¼ sticks) very cold unsalted butter, cut in 8 pieces
¼ cup ice water

GRAPE FILLING
3 ounces cream cheese, softened
¼ cup sugar
1 egg yolk
3 tablespoons chopped walnuts
2 cups black or red seedless grapes, halved
2 tablespoons sugar mixed with ½ teaspoon cinnamon

Vanilla ice cream or crème fraîche

1. Put the flour, sugar, and salt in the bowl of a food processor equipped with the steel blade. Pulse to mix, then add the butter, pulsing until the dough resembles coarse meal. With the motor running, pour the ice water through the feed tube all at once. Continue pulsing until the dough comes together.

2. Remove the dough from the food processor and shape it into a log about 6 inches long. Wrap with plastic and refrigerate until well chilled, about an hour, or overnight.

3. Preheat the oven to 400 degrees.

4. To make the filling, blend the cream cheese, sugar, and the egg yolk until smooth in the food processor.

5. Cut the dough into 6 equal pieces. Sprinkle a little flour on a countertop and roll out each disk to a 5- to 6-inch circle. Lay them on 2 large baking pans lined with parchment paper.

6. Spread about 1 tablespoon of the cream cheese filling into a 2-inch circle in the center of each piece of pastry. Sprinkle 1½ teaspoons of walnuts and a heaping ⅓ cup of grapes on top.

7. Gently fold the pastry border up over the edges of the fruit, leaving most of the fruit exposed in the center, and pleat the edges.

8. Sprinkle each tart with a little of the cinnamon-sugar mixture.

9. Bake until brown and bubbly, about 12–15 minutes. Serve immediately with ice cream or crème fraîche.

Lemon Tart

I remember the first time I tasted a lemon tart. It was in Paris during my junior year abroad. My friends and I would go from pastry shop to pastry shop, sampling so many wonderful sweets. But the *tartes au citron*! I had never tasted anything so delicious. I thought I was alone in my passion, but now they are more popular at pastry shops and upscale American restaurants than lemon meringue pie (which I also love). When I moved to Washington in the late 1970s, Suzanne's Restaurant, a small restaurant in Dupont Circle, was famous for her lemon tart. This is a variation of her original recipe, one I love to serve at my home.

YIELD: 1 PIE, SERVING 8 PEOPLE

2 cups water
2 cups sugar
4 lemons
3 whole eggs
4 tablespoons (½ stick) unsalted butter
1 prebaked sweet butter pie crust (see page 415)

1. Pour the water into a heavy saucepan. Add 1 cup of the sugar and bring to a boil.

2. Slice 1 of the lemons into thin circles, drop them into the water and sugar, lower the heat, and simmer for about 30 minutes, uncovered. Drain.

3. Preheat the oven to 375 degrees.

4. Grate the zest of the remaining 3 lemons to get 2 tablespoons of zest, then squeeze the lemons to get about ¾ cup of juice.

5. Whip the eggs and remaining sugar in the bowl of a heavy-duty mixer at medium speed. Gradually add the lemon juice and zest.

6. Pour into a medium saucepan, add the butter, and cook over medium heat, stirring constantly, being careful not to boil, until the lemon thickens into a curdlike custard, about 5 minutes.

7. Pour into the prebaked crust and bake for about 20–25 minutes or until firm. Garnish with the slices of lemon.

Chocolate Bread Pudding with Dried Cherries and Brandied Cream Sauce

It started out as a plain old-fashioned bread pudding on the Sunday brunch menu at a hotel in Washington, D.C. The chef at the time, Greggory Hill, decided to use, instead of the traditional bread, the day-old croissants left over from the previous breakfast. Then, tasting Venezuelan chocolate for the first time, he somehow thought the chocolate would go well with the flavor of dried cherries. The dark rich chocolate, buttery croissants, and tart cherries all combined to make one of the best bread puddings I have ever tasted. Greggory still serves this dish at his current restaurant, David Greggory, in Washington. This is a surprisingly easy recipe and a highlight of Sunday brunch.

YIELD: 6–8 SERVINGS

¼ cup dried cherries

½ cup brandy (or enough to soak the dried cherries)

1 vanilla bean

6 cups heavy cream

12 egg yolks

1½ cups sugar

¾ teaspoon salt

6 day-old or frozen croissants (2½ ounces each)

4 tablespoons coarsely grated bittersweet chocolate

1. Six hours before starting this recipe, put the dried cherries in a small bowl and cover with the brandy.

2. Preheat the oven to 350 degrees and oil an 8-by-8 or comparable baking pan.

3. Split and scrape the seeds out of the vanilla bean and put both pods and seeds in a saucepan with the heavy cream. Let them steep over a very low heat for about 10 minutes, then remove the vanilla bean.

4. Place the egg yolks, sugar, and salt in a bowl and mix well. Whisking constantly, slowly pour in the hot cream, then strain into a large bowl. Pour about a third into the top of a double boiler.

5. Break the croissants into 4 pieces each and submerge them in the remaining cream and egg sauce in the mixing bowl. Let soak for about 10 minutes so that the croissants can absorb the liquid.

6. Transfer the contents of the bowl to the baking pan. Reserving the brandy, drain the cherries and dot the bread pudding with them.

7. Sprinkle the chocolate on top and bake in the oven for about 25 minutes or until set.

8. Meanwhile, add the reserved brandy to the remaining cream sauce in the double boiler and cook over low heat, stirring occasionally. Cook until the sauce coats the back of a spoon, about 10 minutes. Serve the warmed custard in a serving bowl and spoon over the bread pudding.

Tosca's Tiramisu

"What is 'tiramisu'?"
"You'll find out."
"Well, what is it?"
"You'll see!"
"Some woman is gonna want me to do it to her and I'm not gonna know what it is!"

—SLEEPLESS IN SEATTLE

Tiramisu, Italian for "carry me" or "pick me up," has taken America by storm. An Italian trifle layered with mascarpone cheese and either sponge cake or ladyfingers, it is flavored with a coffee-almond liqueur called Tiramisu. At first it was served only at very elegant Italian restaurants, but today one finds it in bastardized (but not necessarily less tasty) versions all over the country. This recipe was developed from an ongoing tiramisu-making contest chef Cesare Lanfranconi of Tosca Restaurant in Washington, D.C., had with his mother, who still lives in

Chef Lanfranconi takes time off to cook with kids

a small village in Italy, near Lake Como. The first few years his mother won. Then, after Cesare returned from cooking school in Lombardy, the birthplace of mascarpone, a sweet creamy cheese that is often mixed as a dessert with liqueurs, chocolate, and sugar, he won.

YIELD: 8 SERVINGS

3 large eggs, separated

½ cup sugar

1 pound mascarpone cheese

1 cup espresso coffee

½ cup Marsala wine or dark rum

12 ladyfingers or two 10-inch squares of sponge cake

1 tablespoon Dutch-process cocoa powder for dusting

1 teaspoon espresso grounds

1. Put the egg whites and half the sugar in the bowl of an electric mixer and whip until stiff.

2. Whip the egg yolks in a separate bowl with the remaining sugar until pale, then fold in the mascarpone cheese. Gently fold in the egg whites. Cover and refrigerate.

3. Mix the coffee and liqueur together in a small shallow bowl. Dip the ladyfingers or sponge cake in the coffee and liqueur mix.

4. Layer some of the egg yolks and mascarpone on the bottom of a 10-inch round mold and cover with a layer of the soaked ladyfingers or sponge cake. Continue layering, ending with the mascarpone. You will have 3 layers. Cover and refrigerate for at least 2 hours. Just before serving, sprinkle with cocoa and the espresso grounds.

Let them eat cake at Kyle and Meta Valentic's wedding

Mulled Pears with Star Anise, Cinnamon, and Vanilla

One day, thinking about poached pears, I wandered over to the residence of the French ambassador to see the chef, Francis Layrle. In his refrigerator he happened to have rosy Bosc pears sitting in an amazing poaching liquid. He had mixed Bordeaux wine with Ceylon cinnamon, several kinds of black pepper from Malabar, star anise from China, Tahitian vanilla beans, and Turkish cardamom. When Francis first came to the United States, he was less adventuresome with his poaching liquid, using the classic vanilla, cloves, and pepper. Now his poached pears explode with spices from all over the world. As do mine. Don't throw away the poaching liquid—you can use it again and again.

YIELD: 12 SERVINGS

2 bottles inexpensive red Bordeaux wine

1⅔ cups sugar

4 pieces whole cardamom

1 vanilla bean, split and seeds removed

10 peppercorns

6 cloves

4 star anise

12 Bosc pears, peeled and left whole

½ cup roasted pecans or pine nuts

Ice cream or whipped cream

1. Bring the wine to a boil in a saucepan large enough to hold the pears standing up in a single layer. Add the sugar, cardamom, vanilla pod and seeds, peppercorns, cloves, and the star anise. Simmer uncovered for 10 minutes.

2. Submerge the pears in the liquid and simmer for 25 minutes or until they are tender when pierced with a fork.

3. Remove from the heat and leave the pears in the pot until ready to serve. When ready, remove and cut them in half. Serve 1 upside down and the other right side up, with a sprinkle of roasted pecans or pine nuts and some whipped cream or ice cream. Some rustic cookies like the ginger ones on page 393 would go well alongside.

Khao Nieu Mamuang

Sticky Rice with Mangoes

I got this recipe from Nangkran Daks, who owns the Thai Basil Restaurant in Chantilly, Virginia. Born in Thailand, she married an American Peace Corps volunteer and the two returned to the United States together. "In 1964 when I came here," she told me. "I was so homesick for Thailand. I was walking my first child, born a year later, toward the Thai embassy and saw Thai chili peppers growing. I stole them because I was so hungry for them." That's what got her into the restaurant business. She wanted to introduce Americans to the dishes she had loved at home. "In those days you had to go to Chinatown to get anything Asian. Now Thai ingredients are everywhere." And so are mangoes! Sticky rice is essential to this dish, which is eaten as a snack in the afternoon in Thailand. Americans love it as a dessert.

YIELD: 6–8 SERVINGS

3 cups white Thai sticky rice
1 cup sugar
1 teaspoon salt
1½ cups coconut milk
3–4 tablespoons toasted sesame seeds
4 ripe mangoes, peeled and sliced

1. Soak the rice in cold water to cover for 4 hours. Drain well in a sieve.

2. Bring an inch or so of water to a boil in a wok or the bottom of a steamer. Then line a steamer basket with cheesecloth and transfer the rice to that. Steam, covered, on high heat for about 15 minutes or until the rice is cooked and soft. During this time the rice should not touch the water.

3. Meanwhile, gently stir the sugar, salt, and coconut milk in a medium saucepan over medium-low heat until the sugar is dissolved. Reserve ½ cup of this for the topping.

4. Stir in the rice, mix well, and cover. Let sit for about 15 minutes. Do not peek.

5. Peel the mangoes and slice them from the stem end down over the pit. (See page 17 for instructions.) Cut halves lengthwise, then crosswise into 10 or 12 bite-size pieces.

6. Divide the sticky rice among 6–8 plates. Spoon a little of the reserved coconut milk over the top, sprinkle with the sesame seeds, and surround with the mango.

Vermont Apple Pie

Perhaps the perfect accompaniment to Amy Huyffer's wonderfully rich vanilla ice cream is her apple pie. "For me, I would never make an apple pie with anything other than a McIntosh apple," Amy told me. "My decision to move back East after years of living in Wyoming and Oregon was based in no small part on the unavailability of a good Mac west of the Mississippi River."

YIELD: 8 SERVINGS

CRUST
1 cup (1 stick) unsalted butter
2 cups all-purpose flour
¼ cup sugar
Dash salt
¼ cup cold milk (approximately)

FILLING
2 pounds (about 3–7 medium apples depending on the size) good McIntosh apples, peeled, cored, and sliced into about 16 slivers (about 8 cups). Also use Rhode Island Greening, Jonathan, or Granny Smith apples
⅓ cup dark brown sugar
2 tablespoons maple syrup
Grated zest of 1 orange or lemon
2 tablespoons orange juice
2 tablespoons flour
1 teaspoon cinnamon
¼ teaspoon grated nutmeg
¼ teaspoon ground cloves

Vanilla or maple ice cream

1. To make the crust, cut the butter into small pieces and toss into a food processor along with the flour, sugar, and salt. Pulse until the texture is like very coarse meal. Pour on the milk a tablespoon at a time, pulsing until the dough comes together in a ball. Be careful not to add too much milk or the dough will be impossible to roll out. Shape the dough into a disk, cover with plastic wrap, and refrigerate for at least 45 minutes.

2. Preheat the oven to 450 degrees.

3. Toss apple slices in a large bowl, along with the brown sugar, maple syrup, orange zest, orange juice, flour, cinnamon, nutmeg, and cloves.

4. Roll a little more than half the dough on a floured board into an 11-inch round. Carefully fold it in half and then in half again. Place the dough in a 9-inch Pyrex pie plate, unfold, and press in all around, scraping off any odd ends. Spoon the apples into the pie plate. Incorporate the dough scraps in the remaining dough and roll out into another round as thin as the first, fold in half and then half again, and carefully lay it on the apples. Unfold and crimp the edges to seal by pinching with your thumb and second finger. Make a few half-inch slits with a knife on top of the pie to let steam escape.

5. Place the pie on a foil-lined baking sheet, slide it into the oven, and bake for 15 minutes. Reduce the heat to 350 degrees and bake until the crust is well browned and the filling is bubbling, about another 40 minutes or more. Remove from the oven and cool slightly. Serve with vanilla or maple ice cream.

Acknowledgments

Working with my extraordinary editor, Judith Jones, has been a privilege. She guided, scolded, and supported me every step of the way throughout the writing of this book, including hosting me in her magical mountain home in Vermont. Supporting her at Alfred A. Knopf were Sonny Mehta, Paul Bogaards, Ken Schneider, Carol Devine Carson, Sheila O'Shea, Maria Massey, and so many more who believe in the importance of the written word and the look of a book. I am indebted to them all.

I want above all to thank each of the individuals, some who must remain anonymous, who graciously gave of their time and hospitality in allowing me to portray them and their food. They are of course the keynote of the book. Secondly, I want to thank those who facilitated my travel through the United States by giving me the opportunity to speak to so many groups. Through them I obtained many ideas that led me to the stories that fill this saga. I thank Richard Kurin, Diana Parker, Steve Kidd, and the staff of the Smithsonian's Festival of American Folklife, Antonia Allegra and her Symposium for Professional Food Writers at the Greenbrier, members of the International Association of Culinary Professionals, John T. Edge and his Southern Foodways Alliance, and Charlie Pinsky of Frappe, Inc., and John Potthast of WETA.

As I have in my other books, I want to thank Peggy Pearlstein of the Library of Congress, who always finds any facts I am seeking. And I thank Amy Bartscherer, Bronwyn Dunne, Carol Brown Goldberg, and Cathy Sulzberger, who have been great listeners, tasters, and, above all, friends. Nick Fox, Kathleen McElroy, and Sam Sifton, my editors at the *New York Times*, as well as Barbara Fairchild of *Bon Appétit* and Krista Ackerbloom Montgomery of *Cooking Light*, have all encouraged me to write articles about authentic home cooks, some of whom appear in this book. Gail Ross, my agent, was always at my side when I needed her. Both David Gerson and Linda Spillers were extremely generous with their photographic skills.

As I traveled around the country, the following people were willing to share their expertise with me and led me to others they felt I should interview: Ariane and Michael Batterberry, Michael Bauer, Mitch Berliner, Daniel Biever, Stan Bromley, Marialisa Calta, Ann Criswell, Dale Curry, Didi Emmons, Judith Evans, Marcie and Bill Ferris, Brent Frei, Eugene Giannini, Jonathan Gold, Alexandra Greeley, Wynn Handman, Sharon Himmell, Jeremy Iggers, Pableaux Johnson, Barbara Kafka, Marty Katz, Steve and Leslie Katz, Aviva Kempner, Judy Klinkhammer of the Ozarks Folklife Center, George Lang, Benjamin Levy, Kathy Martin, Michael McCarthy, Frances Moore Lappé, Joan Namkoang, Drew Nieporent, Wayne Nish, Sam Popkin, Pamela Reeves, Phyllis Richman, Sarah Rohan, Terry and Wayne Rusch, Lydia Shire, Art Siemering, Shedric Wallace, Marsha Wiener, Barry Wine, Ann Yonkers, and Steve Young.

I want to thank my traveling companions: my mother, Pearl Nathan; Colleen Fain; and Debbie Lesser, who navigated and humored me. And I thank Nadine and Bill Bloch, John and Gisella Brogan, Marilyn and Hugh Nissenson, and Susie and Peter Thistle, who hosted me. Jean Bernhard, Jamie Daggon, Ann Hennings, Susie Kramer, Dalya Luttwak, Michael Lukas, Amanda Pike, Jessica Wurwaug, and my interns from the Sidwell Friends School assisted me in testing, fact-checking, and editing. Matt McMillen helped me to tweak this manuscript. I want to also thank the Politics and Prose Coffee Shop for providing me a relatively quiet place in which to work.

I have spent the past thirty years or so writing cookbooks. This project was my hardest, because of the sheer breadth of the subject matter. Inevitably, my obsession took at times a toll on my family. So I especially thank Allan, Daniela, Merissa, and David, for being such good sports in supporting and enabling me to journey through the landscape of contemporary American food.

Mail-Order Sources

Aidells (sausages)
1625 Alvarado Street
San Leandro, CA 94577
(510) 614-5450
www.aidells.com

Andrej's European Pastry
   (*potica*)
5 West Lake Street
Chisholm, MN 55719
(218) 254-2520
www.poticawalnut.com

Anson Mills
   (stone-ground cornmeal)
1922-C Gervais Street
Columbia, SC 29201
(803) 467-4122
www.ansonmills.com

Badia Spices
P.O. Box 226497
Miami, FL 33172
(305) 629-8000
www.badia-spices.com

Breezy Hill Orchards
828 Centre Road
Staatsburg, NY 12580
(845) 266-3979

Chef Paul Prudhomme
Magic Seasoning Blends
P.O. Box 23342
New Orleans, LA 70183
(800) 457-2857
www.chefpaul.com

Chef's Garden
9009 Huron-Avery Road
Huron, OH 44839
(800) 289-4644
www.chefs-garden.com

Coleman Natural Meats
5140 Race Court
Denver, CO 80216
(800) 442-8666
www.colemannatural.com

Coteau Connoisseur Wild Rice
218 West Warren
Luverne, MN 56156
(507) 283-2338

Country Ovens, Ltd.
   (dried cherries)
229 East Main Street
Forestville, WI 54213
(800) 544-1003
www.countryovens.com

D'Artagnan
   (foie gras, pâtés, sausages,
   smoked delicacies, organic
   game and poultry)
280 Wilson Avenue
Newark, NJ 07105
(800) 327-8246
www.dartagnan.com

Deep Foods
1090 Springfield Road
Union, NJ 07083
(908) 810-7502
www.deepfoods.com

Earthbound Farms
1721 San Juan Highway
San Juan Bautista, CA 95045
(800) 690-3200
www.nsfoods.com

Fairchild Tropical Botanic Garden
10901 Old Cutler Road
Coral Gables, FL 33156
(305) 667-1651
www.fairchildgarden.org

Four Story Hill Farm
21 Four Story Lane
Honesdale, PA 18431
(570) 224-4137

**Frieda's Inc. (unusual fruits
  and vegetables)**
4465 Corporate Center Drive
Los Alamos, CA 90720
(714) 826-6100
www.friedas.com

**Harry Here Farm
  (jonnycake meal)**
410 Ten Road
Exeter, RI 02822
(401) 294-3106

Herrell's Ice Cream
8 Old South Street
Northampton, MA 01060
(413) 586-9700
www.herrells.com

**Hudson Valley Foie Gras
  (foie gras and duck)**
80 Brooks Road
Ferndale, NY 12734
(845) 292-2500
www.hudsonvalleyfoiegras.com

Jamison Farms (lamb)
171 Jamison Lane
Latrobe, PA 15650
(800) 237-5262
www.jamisonfarm.com

**Jasper Hill Farm
  (cow's milk cheese)**
P.O. Box 272
884 Garvin Hill Road
Greensboro, VT 05841
(802) 533-2566
www.jasperhillfarm.com

**Jenney Grist Mill
  (organic cornmeal)**
9 Spring Lane
Plymouth, MA 02390
(508) 747-4544
www.jenneygristmill.com

**King Arthur Flour Baker's
  Catalogue**
58 Billings Farm Road
White River Junction, VT 05001
(800) 827-6836
www.bakerscatalogue.com

**Leona's Restaurante de Chimayó
  (tortillas, tamales, chilies)**
P.O. Box 280
Chimayó, NM 87522
(888) 561-5569
www.leonasrestaurante.com

**Lions' Gate Bed and Breakfast
  (macadamia nuts, Kona
  coffee)**
Lions' Gate Coffee and Macadamia
  Nut Farm
P.O. Box 761
Honaunau, HI 96726
(800) 955-2332
www.coffeeofkona.com

Martin Rice Company
22326 County Road 780
Bernie, MO 63822
(573) 293-4884
www.martinrice.com

McEvoy Ranch (olive oil)
P.O. Box 341
Petaluma, CA 94953
(866) 617-6779
www.mcevoyranch.com

Mozzarella Company
2944 Elm Street
Dallas, TX 75226
(800) 798-2954
www.mozzco.com

Native Seeds
526 North Fourth Avenue
Tucson, AZ 85705
(520) 622-5561
www.nativeseeds.org

Niman Ranch (grass-fed meat)
1025 East Twelfth Street
Oakland, CA 94606
(866) 808-0340
www.nimanranch.com

Ocean Mist Farms (artichokes)
1085 Cara Mia Parkway
Castroville, CA 95012
(831) 633-2144
www.oceanmist.com

The Original Hawaiian
Chocolate Factory
78-6772 Makenawai Street
Kailua-Kona, HI 96740
(808) 322-2626
www.originalhawaiian
chocolatefactory.com

Pacific Farms (wasabi)
P.O. Box 51505
Eugene, OR 97439
(800) 927-2248, ext. 313
www.freshwasabi.com

Phillips Mushrooms
1011 Kaolin Road
Kennett Square, PA 19348
www.phillipsmushroomfarms.com

Sahadi's
(products from Middle East)
187 Atlantic Avenue
Brooklyn, NY 11201
(718) 624-4550
www.sahadis.com

Santa Barbara Pistachios
P.O. Box 21957
Santa Barbara, CA 93121
(800) 896-1044
www.santabarbarapistachios.com

Scharffen Berger Chocolate
914 Heinz Avenue
Berkeley, CA 94710
(510) 981-4050
www.scharffenberger.com

Small World Coffee
14 Witherspoon Street
Princeton, NJ 08540
(609) 924-4377
www.smallworldcoffee.com

Smokey Hollow Fish Company
4282 Tower Square
Pequot Lakes, MN 56472
(218) 568-4244

Vanns Spices
6105 Oakleaf Avenue
Baltimore, MD 21215
(410) 358-3007
www.vannsspices.com

Vermont Butter & Cheese
Company (cheese and butter)
Websterville, VT 05678
(800) 884-6287
www.vtbutterandcheeseco.com

Winchester Cheese Company
(Gouda)
32605 Holland Road
Winchester, CA 92596
(951) 926-4239
www.winchestercheese.com

Zingerman's
(mail-order specialty foods)
422 Detroit Street
Ann Arbor, MI 48104
(888) 636-8162
www.zingermans.com

Bibliography

Batmanglij, Najmieh. *Food of Life*. Washington, D.C.: Mage Publishers, 1986.

Belasco, Warren. *Appetite for Change: How the Counter Culture Took Over the Food Industry, 1966–1988*. New York: Pantheon Books, 1989.

Brenner, Leslie. *American Appetite: The Coming of Age of a Cuisine*. New York: Avon Books, 1999.

Brown, Allison. "Counting Farmers Markets." *Geographical Review* 91, October 2001.

Bruce, Scott, and Bill Crawford. *Cerealizing America*. Boston: Faber and Faber, 1995.

Burros, Marian. "Foie Gras Goes American." *New York Times*, December 21, 1983.

Claiborne, Craig. *A Feast Made for Laughter*. New York: Doubleday, 1982.

———. "20 Years of American Gastronomy: The Revolution." *New York Times*, April 18, 1979.

Fitch, Noel Riley. *Appetite for Life*. New York: Doubleday, 1997.

Franey, Pierre. *A Chef's Tale*. New York: Alfred A. Knopf, 1994.

Gabaccia, Donna R. *We Are What We Eat*. Cambridge: Harvard University Press, 1998.

Gitlin, Todd. *The Sixties: Years of Hope, Days of Rage*. New York: Bantam, 1987.

Glezer, Maggie. *Artisan Baking*. New York: Artisan, 2000.

Halweil, Brian. *Eat Here*. New York: Norton, 2004.

Herbst, Susan Tyler. *Food Lover's Companion*. New York: Barron's Educational Series, 2001.

Hess, John L., and Karen Hess. *The Taste of America*. New York: Grossman Publishers, 1977.

Jones, Evan. *Epicurean Delight: The Life and Times of James Beard*. New York: Alfred A. Knopf, 1981.

Kuh, Patric. *The Last Days of Haute Cuisine*. New York: Penguin Books, 2001.

Kutler, Stanley. "Immigration Act of 1965." *Dictionary of American History*, 3rd ed. New York: Charles Scribner's Sons, 2003.

Lappé, Frances Moore. *Diet for a Small Planet*. New York: Ballantine Books, 1971.

Oldenburg, Ray. *The Great Good Place*. New York: Paragon House, 1989.

Pollan, Michael. *The Botany of Desire*. New York: Random House, 2001.

———. "The Future of Food." *New York Times Magazine*, May 4, 2003.

Reardon, Joan. *M.F.K. Fisher, Julia Child, and Alice Waters: Celebrating the Pleasures of the Table*. New York: Harmony Books, 1994.

Rice, William. "The Heat Is on the Great Chefs of Tomorrow." *Washington Post*, April 29, 1979.

Schettler, Renee. "Miso Goes Mainstream." *Washington Post*, April 28, 2004.

Schlosser, Eric. *Fast Food Nation*. New York: Houghton Mifflin, 2001.

———. "Order the Fish." *Vanity Fair*, November 2004.

Schneider, Elizabeth. *Uncommon Fruits & Vegetables: A Commonsense Guide*. New York: William Morrow, 1998.

———. *Vegetables from Amaranth to Zucchini: The Essential Reference*. New York: Morrow Cookbooks, 2001.

Sheraton, Mimi. "Eat American Food!" *Time*, August 26, 1985.

Stephen, Beverly. "American Chefs Are the New Rising Stars." *New York Daily News*, July 5, 1979.

Trager, James. *The Food Chronology*. New York: Henry Holt, 1995.

Trang, Corinne. *Essentials of Asian Cuisine*. New York: Simon & Schuster, 2003.

Trillin, Calvin. "Bowlful of Dreams." *The New Yorker*, January 28, 2002.

Index

(Page numbers in **bold** refer to illustrations.)

Illustration Credits

The illustrations reproduced in this book were provided with the permission and courtesy of the following individuals and organizations:

Al Forno Restaurant: 46 (lower right)

Susie Almendarez: 96

Reenie Barrow: 60

Susan Belsinger: 21

Laura Bogaards: 147

Paul Bovert: 24

David Burack: 406

Ronny Buxbaum: 144, 145

Gilroy Chow: 260 (lower left)

Mel Coleman: 328 (center right)

Len De Pas: 7

Michael Dirchenall: 411

Susan Eckstein: 361

Marci Cohen Ferris: 275, 328, 394

Kathy FitzGerald: 95, 124 (lower left), 156 (lower left), 169, 220 (lower left), 259

Tim Fuller: 220 (upper left)

Allan Gerson: 339

David Gerson: 10 (center right), 22, 42, 173, 175, 186 (center left), 255, 296 (lower right), 328 (center left), 366 (upper and lower right), 409

Maria Gudiel: 90 (center right)

Thomas Heinser: 124 (upper right)

Frances Janesch: 128, 278

Bridget Kennedy: 224

Nova Kim: 220 (center left)

Maryland Public Television: 220 (lower right)

Mount Kisco Day Care Center: 328 (lower right)

© The New Yorker Collection 2003 Donald Reilly from cartoonbank.com. All Rights Reserved: 75

© The New Yorker Collection 2004 William Hamilton from cartoonbank.com. All Rights Reserved: 91

© The New Yorker Collection 2004 Bruce Eric Kaplan from cartoonbank.com. All Rights Reserved: 162

© The New Yorker Collection 2003 Roz Chast from cartoonbank.com. All Rights Reserved: 299

Bruce Newman: 35

Nora Restaurant: 151

Ocean Mist: 220 (center right)

Rancho La Puerta: 99

Pamela Reeves: 296 (lower right)

Lou Rothenberg: 90 (upper right), 260

Eero Ruuttila: 112, 113

James Scherer: 280

Cynthia Smith: 46 (upper left)

Smithsonian Folklife Festival: 346

Linda Spillers: 72, 168, 251

Stone Barns: 103

Ten Penh Restaurant: 124 (lower right)

Tree of Life Rejuvenation Center: 156, 163

Joe Tropiano: 189

Washington Youth Garden: 14, 15

All other illustrations are by the author.

Jacket photo credits:
  Front of jacket: (Top row, left to right) Joan
  Nathan, David Gerson, Joan Nathan;
  (Middle row, left to right) Tim Fuller, Joan
  Nathan, Maryland Public Television;
  (Bottom row, left to right) Linda Spillers,
  Linda Spillers, David Gerson
  Back of jacket: (Top to bottom) David Gerson,
  Thomas Heinser, Pamela Reeves, Kathy
  FitzGerald

Permissions Acknowledgments

A Note About the Author

Joan Nathan was born in Providence, Rhode Island. She graduated from the University of Michigan with a master's degree in French literature and earned a master's in public administration from Harvard University. For three years she lived in Israel, where she worked for Mayor Teddy Kollek of Jerusalem. In 1974, working for Mayor Abraham Beame in New York, she cofounded the Ninth Avenue International Food Festival. Ms. Nathan is a frequent contributor to the *New York Times* and other publications. In addition to her eight other books, she is the author of *Jewish Cooking in America*, which won both the James Beard Award and the IACP/Julia Child Cookbook of the Year Award. She was the host of the nationally syndicated PBS television series *Jewish Cooking in America with Joan Nathan*, based on the book. Recently, she was the guest curator of Food Culture, USA, the 2005 Smithsonian Folklife Festival, which was based on research for this book. The mother of three grown children, Ms. Nathan lives in Washington, D.C., and Martha's Vineyard with her husband, Allan Gerson.

A Note on the Type

The text of this book was set in Monotype Joanna, a typeface designed by Eric Gill, the noted English stonecutter, typographer, and illustrator. It was released by the Monotype Corporation in 1937. Reflecting Eric Gill's idiosyncratic approach to type design, Joanna has a number of playful features, chief among them the design of the italic companion as a narrow sloped roman.

Composed by North Market Street Graphics,
Lancaster, Pennsylvania

Printed and bound by Tien Wah Press, Singapore

Designed by Cassandra J. Pappas